Adlerian Lifestyle Counseling

Adlerian Lifestyle Counseling

Practice and Research

Warren R. Rule and Malachy Bishop

Routledge
Taylor & Francis Group
New York London

Published in 2006 by
Routledge
Taylor & Francis Group
711 Third Avenue
New York, NY 10017

Published in Great Britain by
Routledge
Taylor & Francis Group
2 Park Square, Milton Park
Abingdon, Oxfordshire OX14 4RN

First issued in paperback 2014
Routledge is an imprint of the Taylor & Francis Group, an informa business

Library of Congress Cataloging-in-Publication Data

Rule, Warren R.
Adlerian lifestyle counseling : practice and research / Warren R. Rule, Malachy Bishop.
p. cm.
Includes bibliographical references and index.
ISBN 978-0-415-95216-3 (hbk)
ISBN 978-0-415-86122-9 (pbk)
1. Adlerian psychology. I. Bishop, Malachy. II. Title.

BF175.5.A33R85 2005
158'.9--dc22 2005008590

informa
Taylor & Francis Group
is the Academic Division of Informa plc.

Visit the Taylor & Francis Web site at
http://www.taylorandfrancis.com

and the Routledge Web site at
http://www.routledge-ny.com

This book is dedicated

— by Warren Rule —

to these dear friends,
all Professors Emeriti,
who, for a quarter century,
were superb colleagues in
the Department of Rehabilitation Counseling
at Virginia Commonwealth University
and
whose individual and collective humanness provided
the most enriching professional environment
that one could ever hope to have had:
Dr. Richard E. Hardy, Chair
Dr. Gerald L. Gandy
Dr. George R. Jarrell
Dr. Robert A. Lassiter, Jr.
Dr. E. Davis Martin, Jr.
Mr. Rehab Keith C. Wright

and

— by Malachy Bishop —

to my love and my life, Lisa, and our dear children, Hailey, Riley, and Elliot

ABOUT THE AUTHORS

Warren R. Rule, Ph.D., is Professor Emeritus in the Department of Rehabilitation Counseling at Virginia Commonwealth University. He has worked as a rehabilitation counselor and at counseling centers in higher educational institutions. Dr. Rule received his Ph.D. from the University of South Carolina and is a licensed professional counselor. He has over 60 publications in the areas of rehabilitation, counseling, and psychology.

Malachy Bishop, Ph.D., CRC, has worked as a rehabilitation counselor and educator for over 10 years. He completed his doctoral study in rehabilitation psychology at the University of Wisconsin–Madison and completed predoctoral clinical internships in neuropsychology and rehabilitation psychology. He is currently an assistant professor in the Rehabilitation Counseling Program at the University of Kentucky.

CONTENTS

Foreword xiii

Acknowledgments xv

Preface xix

Introduction

Chapter 1 Introduction 3
WARREN R. RULE

Chapter 2 Structured Processes and Techniques of Lifestyle Counseling 15
WARREN R. RULE

Practice

I. Dealing with Resistance

Chapter 3 Lifestyle Self-Awareness and the Practitioner: Understanding and Reframing Resistance Using Angels and Devils as Metaphor 45
WARREN R. RULE

Chapter 4 Corrective Reactions to Client Negativism Using a Combined Facilitative and Adlerian-Based Approach 55
WARREN R. RULE

II. Mental Health Therapy

Chapter 5 The Earliest Recollection: A Clue to Present Behavior 65
WARREN R. RULE

Chapter 6 Life-Style Interpretation Using Imagination of the Ideal Social Self 69
WARREN R. RULE

Chapter 7 Pursuing the Horizon: Striving for Elusive Goals 75
WARREN R. RULE

Chapter 8 Lifestyle Self-Awareness and the Practitioner 83
WARREN R. RULE

III. School Counseling

Chapter 9 Adlerian Methods in School Psychology 95
WARREN R. RULE

Chapter 10 Adlerian Methods: Case Study 105
CHRISTOPHER OVIDE AND WARREN R. RULE

IV. Rehabilitation

Chapter 11 Lifestyle and Adjustment to Disability 115
WARREN R. RULE

Chapter 12 A Holistic Group Approach to Offender Rehabilitation 137
WARREN R. RULE

V. Leisure Counseling

Chapter 13 Avocational Counseling for Lifestyle Adjustment 163
WARREN R. RULE

Chapter 14 Enhancing Leisure Counseling Using an Adlerian Technique 179
WARREN R. RULE AND MORRIS W. STEWART

VI. Counseling Uses of Humor

Chapter 15 Increased Internal-Control Using Humor with Lifestyle Awareness 191
WARREN R. RULE

Chapter 16 Increasing Self-Modeled Humor 199
WARREN R. RULE

Research

I. Empirical Considerations

Chapter 17 Self-Actualization: A Person in Positive Movement or Simply an Esteemed Personality Characteristic? 209
WARREN R. RULE

II. Therapeutic Relationships

Chapter 18 Contextual Influences on Production of Early Recollections 229
JOSEPH M. BAUSERMAN AND WARREN R. RULE

Chapter 19 Associations between Personal Problems and Therapeutic Interventions as Reflected by Variables in Early Recollections and Gender 237
WARREN R. RULE

III. Career Choice

Chapter 20 Birth Order and Communication Skills of Pharmacy Students 249
MATTHEW M. MURAWSKI, PATRICK MIEDERHOFF, AND WARREN R. RULE

Chapter 21 Family Constellation and Birth Order Variables Related to Vocational Choice of Dentistry 255
WARREN R. RULE AND ANN T. COMER

IV. Parental Behavior

Chapter 22 Personal Adjustment Variables in Early Recollections and Recalled Parental Strictness-Permissiveness 267
WARREN R. RULE

Chapter 23 Birth Order and Sex as Related to Memory of Parental Strictness-Permissiveness 273
WARREN R. RULE

Chapter 24 Childhood Memory of Parental Authority as Related to Family Constellation Variables 277
WARREN R. RULE AND ANN T. COMER

Chapter 25 Parental Strictness-Permissiveness and Long-Term Memory 283
WARREN R. RULE AND ANN T. COMER

V. Personal Characteristics

Chapter 26 Intelligence and Earliest Memory 287
WARREN R. RULE AND GEORGE R. JARRELL

Chapter 27 Birth Order and Earliest Memory 293
WARREN R. RULE

Chapter 28 Early Recollections and Expected Leisure Activities 297
WARREN R. RULE AND MICHAEL D. TRAVER

VI. Group Behavior

Chapter 29 Life-Style Characteristics: Early Recollections and Observable Group Behavior 307
WARREN R. RULE AND DONALD H. MCKENZIE

Chapter 30 Early Recollections as a Variable in Group Composition and in Facilitative Group Behavior 315
WARREN R. RULE AND DONALD H. MCKENZIE

VII. Social Factors

Chapter 31 Early Recollections: Predictors of Stress in an Analogue Social Situation 323
MICHAEL D. TRAVER AND WARREN R. RULE

Chapter 32 The Relationship between Social Interest Dimensions of Early Recollections and Selected Counselor Variables 331
KATHRYN E. ALTMAN AND WARREN R. RULE

Conclusion

Chapter 33 Adler's Approach: Present Contributions and Future Implications 341
MALACHY BISHOP

Index 349

FOREWORD

What Drs. Rule and Bishop have provided is an excellent compendium of articles whose foremost contribution is the manner in which they guide the professor, the student, and the practitioner to apply the Individual Psychology of Adler to a diverse array of topics relevant to rehabilitation counseling as well as to a broad spectrum of psychological practice.

The strength of many of the following articles lies in the ability of the authors to alert the reader to clues used by experienced therapists, without which the student or novice therapist may become discouraged by his inability to be the helper he wishes to be.

The opportunity to review these samples of a lifetime of contribution by my former student and colleague has brought me many smiles. It scarcely seems possible that 35 years have passed since Warren Rule and I pioneered the introduction of Individual Psychology training institutes in the southern United States.

Events that have occurred during the passage of this period of time seem to help underscore the notion that Individual Psychology is a psychology whose time has come. For the knowledgeable Adlerian, social interest, or sense of community feeling, is not only the keystone of good mental health, but also holds the greatest promise for peaceful and cooperative relationships in the national, international, and global arenas. Dr. Bishop focuses upon this promise when he notes that social interest may have become more relevant and important than ever in the current sociopolitical climate. Evidence of the value of this theoretical construct is almost surely illustrated by the remarkable surge in Individual Psychology on the international scene and especially in former communist countries such as Lithuania, Latvia, Estonia, Bulgaria, Slovakia, the Czech Republic, Hungary, Romania, and Russia, where interest in the study and spread of Individual Psychology has manifested itself through the establishment of organizations and training institutes in the relatively short period since the end of communism in these countries.

The publication of this collection of readings is one more valuable addition to the growing body of literature that facilitates such important advancement toward universal interest in and feeling for community.

Francis X. Walton, Ph.D., Psychologist
Former President , North American Society of Adlerian Psychology
Faculty Member, International Committee for Adlerian Summer Schools and Institute

ACKNOWLEDGMENTS

Gratitude is the greatest of all the virtues—and the parent of all the rest.

— **Cicero**

FROM WARREN R. RULE

In helping to compile a book that largely represents 30 years of attempting to make a scratch on the Adlerian walls of practice and research, I am indeed gratified and humbled in considering the profound impact that Adlerian ideas and teachers have had on me professionally and personally. And, at this point, as I reflect on Adler's fundamental belief that virtually everything we have ever done occurs in an interpersonal context, I feel especially blessed by the many people who have contributed to my efforts to offer something that I hope will be useful.

Heartfelt thanks are extended to Dr. Francis X. Walton, my Adlerian mentor, who provided and nurtured the Adlerian spark and whose formative and powerful influence will be subsequently discussed in more detail. May the circle be unbroken.

I am greatly indebted to the hundreds of graduate students enrolled in my Adlerian classes over the past 33 years. Not only were these groups a great source of interactive learning, but also they gave me the marvelous gift of knowing that I was on the right road. I cherish the many beautiful friendships that evolved from these meaningful (and fun!) experiences. For three decades, the very warm bonds of friendship, formed during the early years, with Steve Aukward, Marty Barlow, Nelson Calisch, Shelly Habeck, Bob and Marty Lassiter, Sarah Liddle, Martin Maples, Pat Rogers, Kath Sadler, Jim Sproul, Mike Traver, J.I. Wainwright, and others have a nourishing spirit that seems to transcend the years.

The facilitative magic of the late Dr. Donald H. McKenzie, doctoral advisor, teacher, and friend, continues to be gentle on my mind and contributes to giving me a sense of existential grounding. Without his steadfast interest and unfaltering support, as well as without the compassionate encouragement of therapeutic wizard Dr. George Jarrell and of Jane Brady Rule, I doubt that I would have undertaken doctoral work.

Approximately a third of the following chapters, most of which are former journal articles or book chapters, were originally published with co-authors. Remembering these colleagues and the collaboration brings a keen sense of appreciation. Although each of them is subsequently receiving due credit in the appropriate chapter, I would like to acknowledge all of them here. A special thanks is due to Kitty Altman, Joe Bauserman, Ann Comer, Chris Ovide, George Jarrell, the late Don McKenzie, Pat Miederhoff, Mike Murawski, Mick Stewart, and Mike Traver.

A tip of the hat goes to Dr. Kenneth R. Thomas, who introduced me to the splendid co-author of this book, Dr. Malachy Bishop. Malachy's creative competence, perseverance, and gentle openness are all gratefully appreciated by me.

From a more personal perspective, I continue to realize that the supportive and nurturing persons who have been in one's life provide much of the motivating energy, as well as the wish and the will, to do whatever meaningful things that one does do. I cherish the unshakeable bond of love for my late father, Richard Rule, and for my dear mother, Iris Rule. Each has been, in complementary realms of life, an extraordinary teacher and role model. My brother, Dick, and my sister, Cindy, continue to bring joy and are integral parts of the invisible plane that undergirds the nuclear family.

Finally, boundless gratitude goes to my daughter, Lauren, and my son, Brian. These precious and miraculous gifts in my life are a never-ending source of pride, meaning, optimism, and unconditional love.

FROM MALACHY BISHOP

I thank those educators who introduced me to Adler and his ideas, through which my life and work have been enriched; and especially to

Dr. Ken Thomas, a fine man and teacher, who encouraged me, challenged me, and always welcomed open discussion and honest debate.

I thank my wife, Lisa, for her patience and support during this project and all the others. I realize that supporting me has indeed been a major life task. Sincere thanks also go to Emily Boag, MRC, for her hard work and commitment during the preparation of this manuscript.

Finally, my most heartfelt thanks to Warren Rule, a true Adlerian, for allowing me the opportunity to assist with this collection of his works, for his dedication throughout his career to sharing his insights and experiences, and for his kind and encouraging ways. It is through Dr. Rule that I, like so many, have discovered the many ways in which Adler's work can be applied in rehabilitation counseling to better understand our work and better serve our clients.

PREFACE

BACKGROUND: REFLECTIONS OF THE SENIOR AUTHOR

In the 35 years that have passed since the senior author first became fascinated with this approach, the contributions of Alfred Adler have been receiving much deserved, widespread attention. Increasing numbers of Adlerian practitioners, therapeutic centers, educational offerings, empirical research, and publications all reflect this rebirth and development.

In the concluding chapter of this book, the junior author expands on specific present contributions of Adlerian psychology and discusses the future implications of this very useful approach to helping others. Between this background chapter and the concluding one, 16 practitioner-oriented chapters and 16 empirically based research chapters are presented. Each of them was originally published as a refereed journal article or as a book chapter. All were written by the senior author, solely or in collaboration with others. However, in keeping with the Adlerian spirit of respecting whatever is useful from the past, a brief discussion here may be beneficial regarding the senior author's perception of the formative historical context preceding these publications that now comprise these 32 chapters.

The Formative Era

In the late 1960s and early 1970s, when the senior author was first introduced to Adlerian psychology, the broader social landscape was seething with experiment and change. The convergence of social and Vietnam-war protests, counterculture influences, and general questioning of authority provided the stimulus for an overall seeking of innovative and unheralded ways of thinking and doing.

Institutions of higher learning were often interactive producers and recipients of this "Let's try it" mentality. Many doctoral programs in counselor education and other training facilities were influenced by this highly charged atmosphere of openness to learning, which was further enhanced by their underlying emphasis on humanism. This fertile educational environment, enriched by an increasing broader societal respect for human potential, contributed to allowing Adler's ideas to blossom more fully. His pioneering perspective had been incubating and carefully tended by an ongoing special handful of dedicated visionaries for half a century, and now, it seemed, life had caught up with Adler's ideas.

The University of South Carolina

As a doctoral student in the Counselor Education Program at the University of South Carolina, I (the senior author) was indeed fortunate in being a part of a department wherein the faculty members, personally and professionally, were characterized by both a fresh openness and a student orientation. Dr. Francis X. Walton of the University Counseling Center had just returned to this fruitful academic environment, after having studied at the Alfred Adler Institute in Chicago (now called the Adler School of Professional Psychology). He radiated unabashed enthusiasm for Adler's approach to counseling and psychotherapy. This, coupled with Frank Walton's natural warmth and magnetism as well as his common-sense logic, was intriguing and inspired me to learn more about these novel ideas.

Prior to my entering the doctoral program, I had worked for several years as a rehabilitation counselor with clients diagnosed as mentally ill. I realized that as I entered this Ph.D. program, I was looking for and hoping to incorporate a counseling approach that was flexible, practical, and still had a heart. The two prevailing—and competing—therapeutic approaches at the time were client-centered therapy (later to be termed "person-centered"), developed by Carl Rogers, and behavior therapy, developed and advocated by many interested in the psychology of learning. (Behavior therapy later appropriated a defining "cognitive" component, i.e., "cognitive behavior therapy," that had an eerie and unacknowledged similarity to the long-established therapeutic approaches of Adler, Ellis, Beck, and others.) I knew myself to be too cognitive by nature to be a client-centered-therapy purist, although I had, and still have, great admiration for those few who can use this therapeutic approach exclusively. The traditional behavior-therapy approach of classical and operant conditioning techniques seemed to me to be sometimes useful, yet somewhat tediously burdened with hubris and lacking something soulfully human. After several Adlerian graduate courses with Frank Walton, encourager par excellence, and a year's internship under his supervision, as well as attending a number of Adlerian workshops, I was convinced—for reasons discussed more specifically in future chapters—that I had found a solid, yet flexible, way of helping that would be the core of my counseling approach.

Others at the University of South Carolina, as a result of Frank Walton's influence, became interested in Adler's approach and have made later contributions of their own. Dr. Daniel Eckstein, enrolled in the doctoral program in Counselor Education at that time, has written many Adlerian publications and has been very active in Adlerian professional organizations. Dr. Thomas Sweeney, then Chair of the Counselor Education Department at the University of South Carolina and later the author of a major Adlerian textbook, graciously allowed me to use the participants in one of his institutes as subjects for my Ph.D. dissertation, which was one of the first dissertations, I believe, in the country that utilized the early recollections of subjects in an experimental design.

Thus, the openness, vitality, and creativity of others encouraged me to dig deeper into Adler's ideas. Discussed below is a brief summary of my perceptions of existing Adlerian practice and research during this time.

Adlerian Practice and Research

During this formative era for me, most of the teaching of Adler's ideas was conducted by private institutes, individual practitioners, and the (North) American Society of Adlerian Psychology. The teaching of graduate Adlerian coursework at colleges and universities across the nation was very limited. The larger institutes for Adlerian training were in Chicago and New York. Dr. Rudolph Dreikurs, Adler's foremost student in this country and the founder of the Adler Institute in Chicago, had just died in 1972. Yet, Adler's work there was carried on through the teaching and consultancies of Dr. Harold Mosak, Dr. Bernard Shulman, Robert Powers, and others. Alfred Adler's son, Kurt, was active in the Adler Institute of New York. Several other training facilities were developing in, e.g., Minneapolis, Minnesota and Eugene, Oregon. The Dinkmeyers, father and son, were writing and consulting. Frank Walton was planting the seeds for the Adlerian approach in the South.

Very impressively, many prominent Adlerians lived their social lives consistent with the same generous Adlerian spirit and social interest that they promoted as concepts when teaching Adler's ideas. For instance, Harold and Birdie Mosak and Frank and Kathy Walton were especially welcoming and hospitable to students and colleagues as house guests, treating them as equals worthy of warm respect.

The professional literature, including theoretical and practitioner-oriented publications, were just beginning to expand during this era. Prior to that, in 1956, Heinz and Rowena Ansbacher had completed the remarkable job of editing many of Adler's writings and publishing them in a single volume. Their scholarship, the *Journal of Individual Psychology*, various journal articles, and the collected writings of Adlerian advocates, e.g., Dreikurs (1967), Mosak (1977), O'Connell (1975), Shulman (1973), and others, provided considerable impetus to establishing Adler's approach as one of the major ones in counseling and psychotherapy. Notably, in 1971, a special issue of *The Counseling Psychologist* was devoted to Adler's approach (Whitely, 1971). Also, in 1975, Mosak and Mosak published Volume 1 of an exhaustive bibliography of Adlerian psychology. However, only very few textbooks (e.g., Ford & Urban, 1963; Corsini, 1973) that overviewed counseling and psychotherapy had yet included an entire chapter devoted to Adler's approach. This was definitely to change in subsequent years.

People interested in Adler's approach were starting to benefit from the increasing professional involvement of other gurus in the counseling field who held beliefs similar to some of Adler's concepts. For instance, Dr. Albert Ellis, founder of (then called) Rational Emotive Therapy, and Dr. Murray Bowen, founder of Family Systems Theory, were distinguished participants in panel discussions at Adlerian conferences.

Despite the growing practitioner awareness of Adler's approach, respect from the empirical researchers and devoted numbers-crunchers was, it seemed, more elusive. Although many of the thorny problems of empirical research in the behavioral sciences are discussed more fully in Chapter 17 on Self-Actualization, the criticism seemed to me to have some merit. For instance, as Ford and Urban (1963) noted, Adler discussed some of his concepts in very molar, or even simplistic terms, and he sometimes referred more to consequences to be obtained in the therapeutic process rather than detailing procedures to be used in achieving them. However, many Adlerians believed (and still believe) that dividing a whole into parts in order to study the whole can somehow ruin the essence of what is being studied. As an example, even a seemingly precise topic for study such as the Adlerian approach to family constellation, commonly referred to as birth order, is fraught with tricky difficulties (discussed more fully in Chapter 2).

Possibly quantification and reductionism would have ruined the honesty, as well as the holistic, nature of Adler's concepts. Adler's concepts, indeed, seemed to have a common-sense honesty about them. Perhaps the achievement of reductionistic specificity then (and now) would have violated the intent of Adler's respect for the integrity and resourcefulness of the individual. In discussing Adler's conceptual honesty, Manaster (1982) noted that:

> Adlerian psychology has been too honest. The two most successful schools of psychology in this century have either damned man, and thereby provided an almost universal cop-out for people, or belittled man while holding out the promise that mechanical adjustments could improve his lot. Adlerian psychology has put the burden of proof, of success, of progress and fulfillment on the individual. It has said, in effect, life is not a bowl of cherries; you are not and won't be perfect but might be better—it is up to you. (p. 259)

I think that I realized it is tempting and easy to delude ourselves in our clinical expectations and therapeutic generalizations. Yet, I wondered how counseling practitioners would be able to function if they waited for the empirical researchers to provide the answers. It seemed like a balance must be achieved between the counseling-as-art practitioners and the counseling-as-science advocates.

In the years following this era to the present, I attempted to achieve a balance in my publications between practice and research. Accordingly, and as previously noted, 16 practitioner and 16 empirical articles/chapters have been selected for inclusion in this book. The wish is that the reader will be provided with some ideas that may generate other ideas. Also, the hope is that these contributions, built on Adler's wonderfully unique, yet eclectic, approach, will add to the practitioner's sense of resourcefulness and stretch the imagination of the researcher.

Warren R. Rule

Richmond, VA

REFERENCES

Ansbacher, H. L., & Ansbacher, R. R. (Eds.). (1956). *The Individual Psychology of Alfred Adler.* New York: Basic Books.
Corsini, R. J. (Ed.). (1973). *Current psychotherapies.* Itasca, IL: Peacock.
Dreikurs, R. (1967). *Psychodynamics, psychotherapy, and counseling.* Chicago: Alfred Adler Institute.
Ford, D. H., & Urban, H. B. (1963). *Systems of psychotherapy.* New York: Wiley.
Manaster, G. J. (1982). Our personal views, In G. J. Manaster & R. J. Corsini (Eds.). *Individual psychology: Theory and practice* (pp. 257–259). Itasca, IL: Peacock.
Mosak, H. H. (1977). *On purpose: Collected papers.* Chicago: Alfred Adler Institute.
Mosak, H. H., & Mosak, B. (1975) *A bibliography for Adlerian psychology.* Washington, D.C.: Hemisphere.
O' Connell, W. E. (1975). *Action therapy and Adlerian theory.* Chicago: Alfred Adler Institute.
Shulman, B.H. (1973). *Contributions to individual psychology.* Chicago: Alfred Adler Institute.
Whitely, T. (Ed.) (1971). Special Issue: Alfred Adler. *The Counseling Psychologist* 1(1).

Introduction

1

INTRODUCTION

Warren R. Rule

In contemporary living, the term "lifestyle" has a broad range of meanings to different individuals and is used in an expanding variety of contexts:

> The television advertisement shows an attractive young woman, her long, blond hair flowing with the wind as she rides along the sunlit beach in her convertible sportscar. The TV announcer pleads with the viewers to use Goldendust Shampoo "so your lifestyle, too, will be golden and glamorous!"
>
> The middle-aged banker sits behind a neatly organized desk. He is alone and in a wistful mood. This melancholy person reflects on the past, assesses the present, projects into the future, and hears himself declare aloud, "I need a change in lifestyles."
>
> The panting jogger runs up the hill and, despite his physical discomfort, creates in his mind the shopping list of items he will

This chapter, "Introduction," from Warren R. Rule (Ed.), *Lifestyle counseling for adjustment to disability*, 1984. Rockville, MD: Aspen Systems Corporation.

use this evening: various vitamins, selected vegetables, juices, etc. He then prides himself for making the right decision "to live a healthy lifestyle."

The couple, while dining in an exclusive restaurant, raise glasses of wine in a toast to each other. One glowingly says, "Our lifestyle is really filled with fun, isn't it?"

The teenager gazes in despair out of her hospital window. Recently she has been told that she will never walk again. She quietly cries and thinks over and over, "My lifestyle is ruined forever."

These examples reflect an array of meanings attributed to the term "lifestyle." The connotations suggest that one's lifestyle is basically one's appearance, which can be embellished by discreet selection of consumer products; that one's lifestyle can be readily and radically changed by doing something different in one's life, such as switching jobs; that one's lifestyle is essentially one's commitment to managing a healthy body; that lifestyle is a joint enterprise that also can be measured by the number of fun activities it entails; and that one's lifestyle can be ruined by a major occurrence such as a severe injury. Many other examples abound in the spoken and written language.

However, the term "lifestyle," coined by Alfred Adler more than 50 years ago, meant something considerably more fundamental than is reflected in the above contemporary examples. Adler, a pioneer in the helping professions, conceptualized the lifestyle as being more basic and unique to the individual as a person and, as such, would be the mental pattern itself that influenced the individual choices made in each of the above examples. This concept would seem to be a much more useful approach to understanding the individual than the various implications of the term currently in vogue. Adler's view of lifestyle—one that can be very valuable to the helping practitioner—constitutes one of the broad underpinnings of this book.

LIFESTYLE

Adler believed that each individual develops a "lifestyle" during his early years that exerts a major influence on one's thoughts, feelings, and behavior throughout life. These childhood years certainly do not totally determine how an individual will develop in later life; however, they probably have a large bearing on the thought patterns on which the person will take a sensitive position. Adler's definition of lifestyle focuses heavily on the core of personality, especially on the individual's unique mental map. Lifestyle is seen as the pattern of dimly conscious beliefs and goals that the person uses for interacting with others and for measuring self-worth. Expressed another way, the emphasis is on the individual's long-standing holistic pattern of dimly conscious expectations.

In general, we are not aware of how pervasively the lifestyle pattern is at work in our daily lives: the way we relate to others, our choice of clothes, our choice of mate, our successes, our failures, the situations we avoid, the viewpoint we take toward the limitations of a disability, etc. Each individual lifestyle has a bearing on the choices already made and on the ones to be made.

The overriding mental pattern is regarded as the bottom line: this subjective pattern reflects those key cognitive dimensions on which a person takes a sensitive position. This mental pattern, in turn, influences the individual's feelings and behaviors in response to life's circumstances. Therefore, as the person moves through life, this overriding pattern is usually more difficult to alter than are feelings and behaviors.

Because of the consistency of the cognitive nature of the lifestyle, it is often very useful to the individual to have an awareness of his unique lifestyle pattern when he is facing problems or making decisions. This is particularly so because the lifestyle—the time-tested pattern of fundamental expectations—becomes most apparent (especially to the skilled observer) when the individual is experiencing stress.

The lifestyle concept and methods of lifestyle assessment will be discussed extensively in the next two chapters. Now let us direct our attention to an overview of important historical considerations.

BACKGROUND

"It is the personal meaning of the disability to the individual that is crucial in rehabilitation counseling practice" (Wright, 1980, p. 73). This perspective is certainly in keeping with the lifestyle counseling approach illustrated in this book. However, traditionally the personal meaning of disability was not always accepted by helping practitioners as the most beneficial consideration in adjustment to disability. Even today, acceptance of this concept is not universal, although it may be seen as a professional milestone, which values the dignity of the individual as ultimately significant.

Historical Perspective

According to Shontz's (1975) historical review, contemporary health practices evolved from two contrasting traditions: animism and mechanism. Animism assumes that "a special substance or force gives life or magic powers to otherwise non-living objects. The substance or force is usually called soul or spirit, and it usually has mental powers" (p. 4). Animistic thinking has expressed itself, especially in the early stages of health care, in practices to release evil influences (e.g., skull boring, torture, purgatives, bleeding), as well as in the more humane practices of prayer, incantation, rest, and recreation. Mechanism focuses on the orderly materialism that served as the foundation for early science and technology. The ancient Greeks (e.g., Democritus, Hippocrates) provided the intellectual orientation for the mechanistic approach. This method of thinking received a rebirth after the thirteenth century, particularly in the form of naturalistic observation, as demonstrated by the anatomist Vesalius and the biologist Harvey.

Centuries later, much controversy stemmed from variations and refinements of the viewpoints of animism and mechanism. Some further developed their ideas in accordance with one or the other framework, particularly the mechanistic, e.g., Darwin, Freud, Skinner; some attempted resolution, e.g., Descartes for religion and science, Kant for mind and body, and Smuts for unity of mind and body, which launched the holistic perspective (Shontz, 1975).

The holistic viewpoint, a very significant concept in lifestyle understanding, was developed, as Shontz explains,

> to decompartmentalize the study and treatment of the human being. According to this view, the person is an indivisible totality and must be understood as such. Holism is responsible for the team approach to patient care, and it has provoked a return to concern for all aspects of the patient's condition. Because of its influence, medical specialists have become more willing to respect the opinions of nurses, social workers, vocational counselors, psychologists, and others whose professional concern is with less obviously somatic aspects of patients' problems. (p. 26)

Shontz further concluded that while holism is not yet a science, its doctrines have evolved in several directions. One direction is the variations of humanistic psychology that recognize the limitations of the mechanistic view of human nature and focus on the uniqueness of each person. Such concepts as identity, way of life, integrity, and self-direction have been developed by Maslow, Rogers, some existentialists, and gestaltists. Another direction of holism is general systems theory, as developed by von Bertalanffy, which asserts that "systems exhibit lawful uniformities and must be studied intact if these uniformities are to appear; at present, however, systems theorists admit that their ability to deal with structures as complex as living organisms is limited" (Shontz, 1975, p. 27).

Adler, along with his lifestyle approach, would primarily be aligned with the humanistic psychology movement (Ansbacher & Ansbacher, 1956), although he has, as well, been described as being "[t]he psychological theorist who most closely approximated an application of systems concepts to the individual level" (Amerikaner, 1981, p. 33). We need to know a bit more about this creative and most influential man.

Adler and His Influence

Alfred Adler was born in Vienna in 1870. As a child he suffered from rickets and his decision to pursue a medical career resulted in part from a near-fatal bout with pneumonia at age five. After several years as a general medical practitioner, Adler became associated with Sigmund Freud and turned his attention to psycho-analytic explorations. However, Adler's developing concepts were at odds with Freud's (Adler was especially dissatisfied with Freud's view of the sexual instinct as omnipotent) and they parted ways. Thereafter he continued to develop his own approach, being influenced as well by other viewpoints (e.g., Vaihinger's philosophy of "As If," Smut's approach to holism and evolution) and by his experiences as a physician in World War I. Before coming to the United States he established a network of child guidance clinics and societies. He continued to have an impact in this country through his teaching, lecturing, and writing. While on a lecture tour in Scotland in 1937, he died at the age of 67.

For many years, Adler's thinking was overshadowed by that of Freud. Some have even naively regarded the two as similar. However, as Ford and Urban (1963) noted in their comparative review of systems of psychotherapy:

> In contrast to Sigmund Freud, Adler developed a point of view that sought to study behavior from the vantage point of the subjective rather than the objective observer; emphasized the goal-directed rather than the drive-impelled causation of behavior; stressed the unity and integration of behavior rather than the

> conflict of disparate elements; proposed the use of molar and holistic concepts rather than restricted units of analysis; held an idiographic rather than a nomothetic purpose in studying behavior; and in short, differed from Freud in the most fundamental and basic fashions possible. (p. 303)

Adler's ideas are receiving increasing attention, as evidenced by increasing Adlerian practitioners, research, writings, educational opportunities, and societies (Allen, 1971; Ansbacher & Ansbacher, 1970). In addition, many theorists who studied under Adler have developed eminence in their own right (e.g., Eric Berne, Rollo May, Victor Frankl). Adler's approach, which he termed "Individual Psychology" to stress the indivisible nature of the individual, has achieved widespread influence. Sometimes only the barest acknowledgment is given by others, as discussed in O'Connell's "The 'Friends of Adler' Phenomenon" (1976), and sometimes forthright declarations are rendered, such as Albert Ellis' conclusion (1973) regarding Adler's contribution: "It is highly probable that without his pioneering work, the main elements of rational-emotive therapy might never have been developed" (p. 112). Ellenberger (1970), in his comprehensive review of the history and evolution of psychiatry, observed that:

> Any attempt to assess the influences of Adler's work brings about a paradox. The impact of Individual Psychology stands beyond any doubt.... It would not be easy to find another author from which so much has been borrowed from all sides without acknowledgment than Alfred Adler. (p 645)

Thus, Adler's influence has been receiving justified recognition; however, misunderstandings regarding many of Adler's concepts continue to persist.

Misunderstandings of Adler

Unfortunately, a number of writers in the field of rehabilitation and adjustment to disability have contributed to a misrepresentation or an oversimplification of some of Adler's ideas. This seems to be the result of either a superficial understanding of Adler's concepts or an overemphasis on his earlier writings.

Early in his career (1907) Adler developed a theory of behavior based upon organ inferiority. This concept, as well as related ones, such as compensation and inferiority, have received particular attention in the field of rehabilitation. Often overlooked is the fact, however, that in the subsequent quarter century, Adler continued to develop and to refine his approach, especially the central concept, the lifestyle. A number of those attempting to apply Adler's ideas to the field of rehabilitation have focused on the original, less-developed concepts, which seem, because of their labels at the time, to be the most related to rehabilitation. In so doing, unfortunately, some critics have been tempted to generalize from the shortcomings of this limited perspective to the overall worth of the Adlerian approach to rehabilitation.

Adler's refined concept of the lifestyle is a more complete approach to understanding human nature. His later thinking reflects a shift from an organic to a sociopsychological explanation of behavior, a refinement of inferiority and compensation, an increased emphasis on the creativity of the individual, and an even sharper focus on the personal attitude toward disability and the goals to which a disability can be directed. Indeed, as we shall note frequently, the lifestyle approach developed by Adler is essentially educational in nature.

DISABILITY

The concept of disability used in this book is intentionally broad. The description by Goldenson (1978) is generally appropriate:

> As used today, it denotes any relatively severe chronic impairment of function resulting from disease, accident or congenital defect. The impairment, or limitation, may be in one or more of the following spheres: (a) physical, affecting ambulation, coordination, speech production, vision, etc.; (b) mental, affecting ability to think, remember, and comprehend, or general learning ability; (c) social, affecting ability to communicate and establish relationships with other people; (d) emotional, affecting self-image, self-acceptance, mental health; (e) occupational, affecting vocational or homemaking ability. (p. 7)

Concepts related to disability, such as handicap and limitation, are frequently used interchangeably. In fact, Wright (1980), in referring to the terms "disability," "limitation," and "handicap," concluded that "no other area of the rehabilitation nomenclature produces such semantic confusion as these three words" (p. 67). As an example, he noted that "It is particularly confusing that the words disability and handicap in rehabilitation are comparable to impairment and disability, respectively in American medicine" (p. 69). Various distinctions regarding the difference between "disability" and "handicap" (e.g., Bitter, 1979; Dunham & Dunham, 1978; Wright, 1980) suggest that "disability" is essentially the physical, mental, or emotional impairment that becomes a "handicap" if the condition contributes to lowered self-assessment, reduced function, or limited opportunities. Thus, in this sense, a disability may not be a handicap. However, Dunham and Dunham (1978) note that "Differentiating between 'disability' and 'handicap' becomes more controversial with the mentally ill.... The concept gets even more blurred when applied to the criminal, the obese, the drug addict, or the alcoholic" (p. 13).

Another relevant issue is the role that others' attitudes and actions have in contributing to an individual handicap. This influence will be discussed in this book only to the extent that such discrimination becomes a part of the individual's awareness; exploration of the broad societal implications of discrimination against the disabled is outside the scope of this book.

In order to avoid semantic dilemmas, the term "disability" will be consistently used throughout this book. This use of "disability" is intended to incorporate individually determined implications of the term "handicap" because, as noted previously, the personal meaning of the disability to the individual is the important issue in lifestyle counseling for adjustment to disability.

ADJUSTMENT

In view of the estimate that there are at least 25 million disabled individuals in the United States (Goldenson, R.M., Dunham, J.R., & Dunham, C.S., 1978) the issue of adjustment to disabilities is one of no small consequence. The ideal is for health services to regard the disabled individual in a holistic manner, not simply to "dissect the patient, distribute portions of him to appropriate repair shops, and reassemble him when all parts are in working order" (Shontz, 1975, p. vi).

The concept of general adjustment can be viewed from many perspectives (Sechrest & Wallace, 1967): the survival model focuses on adjustment to the basic levels, such as keeping alive, maintaining health, reproductiveness; the medical model emphasizes treatment of underlying causes, often to the neglect of environmental influences; the positive striving model is directed at the process of fulfilling one's self-potential, yet, paradoxically, may entail conflicts with idealism and pragmatism; and there are other, less notable, models, such as the drive reduction model, the engineering model, the social conformity model.

From the perspective of adjustment to disability, however, most of the above models, with the possible exception of the positive striving model, do not seem to be entirely satisfactory. Roessler and Bolton (1978) noted that talking abstractly about the effects of disability is important from an analytic or scientific perspective but the overriding focus in helping should be on an empathic awareness of the significance of the disability to a person's life. Moreover, Shontz (1977) concluded, after reviewing numerous studies related to the treatment of various disabilities, that:

> What has been uniformly regarded as crucial is the personal meaning of his disability to each individual client.... Virtually all of these authors have cautioned that psychological treatment must be directed toward individual situations and reactions rather than toward psychological processes that can be assumed to be constant from patient to patient. (p. 324)

At least two fundamental issues are involved in defining adjustment; they have to do with achievement versus process (Lazarus, 1969) and with frame of reference (Sechrest & Wallace, 1967). In discussing these key concepts, Roessler and Bolton (1978) noted that the achievement or final state conception of adjustment implies a final, trouble-free state, may foster unrealistically high expectations, and presumes that all problems are solvable; however, the process orientation to adjustment emphasizes how to adapt to a succession of situations and the expectation that life will not be trouble free. Also important is the frame of reference of the person assessing the level of adjustment. Essentially two frames of reference exist: the disabled person himself or an external person, such as a helping practitioner. The convergence of both frames of reference is crucial to the individual's process of adjustment.

The lifestyle approach to adjustment to disability incorporates the key factors discussed in the foregoing paragraphs. The lifestyle approach certainly respects the personalized meaning of the disability to the individual because lifestyle assessment attempts to identify the individual's general expectations of self, others, and life. Regarding the achievement versus process issue, lifestyle understanding focuses on goal-directedness, or fixed consequences to be achieved, within the context of the individual's overall pattern of movement through life. Thus, short-term goals are viewed within the perspective of overriding long-term goals.

As for internal versus external frames of reference, there is a shift, with the lifestyle approach, as the counselor assists the client in getting, psychologically speaking (Carkhuff, 1980), from where he is to where he wants to be. This entails focusing primarily on the client's frame of reference in the earlier phases with an increased blending of the counselor's frame of reference (which sometimes includes occasional nudging of the client) in the later stages. Throughout the process of lifestyle counseling for adjustment to disability, however, the counselor does not lose sight of the client's subjective, or internal, frame of reference. Because individuals are regarded, within the lifestyle framework, as being the product of both general laws and individually created laws (to be discussed more fully in the next chapter), the counselor is essentially more of an artist than a scientist in his role of attempting to understand and replicate the client's mental map.

THE HELPING PROCESS: A PERSPECTIVE

Many who apply psychological concepts to the broad field of rehabilitation perceive helping the disabled as an art. As Stubbins (1977) concluded: "Partly as a consequence of self-understanding and partly through trained judgment, they practice the helping role as an art—something difficult to define but which most practitioners agree is important in applied psychology" (p. 295).

Should those who regard the helping process, at least in its present state, as primarily a subjective art and secondarily as an objective science feel compelled to make apologies? Probably not. Lewis Thomas, regarded by some as the world's foremost scientific essayist, concluded that "The only solid piece of scientific truth about which I feel totally confident is that we are profoundly ignorant about nature" (1979, p. 73). Speaking also in terms of scientific limitations, Merleau-Ponty (1962) expressed well the importance of respecting the subjective perspective:

> I cannot shut myself up within the realm of science. All my knowledge of the world, even my scientific knowledge, is gained from my own particular point of view, or from some experience of the world without which the symbols of science would be meaningless. The whole universe of science is built upon the world as directly experienced, and if we want to subject science itself to rigorous scrutiny and arrive at a precise assessment of its meaning and scope, we must begin by reawakening the basic experience of the world of which science is the second order of expression. (p. viii)

Thus, a heightened respect for the subjective experience, which is perhaps both the means and the end of an artistic approach, may be a key factor in the overall helping process. This respect for the subjective experience is especially important in lifestyle counseling, wherein the counselor's subjective expression attempts to illuminate the patterns of the client's subjective experience.

Can lifestyle practitioners afford to lose sight of scientific research, especially the increasing number of reliability and validity studies on lifestyle assessment and outcome? Again, probably not. These contributions decrease the likelihood of deluding ourselves and our clients. Yet, we may similarly delude ourselves if we believe that, in counseling, objective influences can be the total masters of subjective ones. A complete awareness on the counselor's part of all the scientific studies ever done in counseling process and outcome will not prevent the counselor's own subjective lifestyle from oozing through the mask of objectivity into the counseling experience.

REFERENCES

Allen, T. W. The individual psychology of Alfred Adler: An item of history and a promise of a revolution. The Counseling Psychologist, 1971, 3(1), 3–24.

Amerikaner, M. J. Continuing theoretical convergence: A general systems theory perspective on personal growth and development. Journal of Individual Psychology, 1981, 37, 31–53.

Ansbacher, H. L., & Ansbacher, R. R. (Eds.). *The individual psychology of Alfred Adler.* New York: Basic Books, 1956.

Ansbacher, H. L., & Ansbacher, R. R. (Eds.). *Superiority and social interest* (2nd ed.). Evanston, Ill.: Northwestern University Press, 1970.

Bitter, J. A. *Introduction to rehabilitation.* St. Louis: C. V. Mosby, 1979.

Carkhuff, R. *The art of helping IV.* Amherst, Mass.: Human Resources Development Press, 1980.

Dunham, J. R., & Dunham, C. S. Psychological aspects of disability. In R. M. Goldensen, J. R. Dunham, & C. S. Dunham (Eds.), *Disability and rehabilitation handbook.* New York: McGraw-Hill, 1978.

Ellenberger, H. *The discovery of the unconscious: The history and evaluation of dynamic psychiatry.* New York: Basic Books, 1970.

Ellis, A. Humanistic psychotherapy. New York: McGraw-Hill, 1973.

Ford, D. H., & Urban, H. B. Systems of psychotherapy. New York: Wiley, 1963.

Goldensen, R. M. Dimensions of the field. In R. M. Goldensen, J. R. Dunham, & C. S. Dunham (Eds.), *Disability: A rehabilitation handbook.* New York: McGraw-Hill, 1978.

Goldensen, R., Dunham, J. R., & Dunham, C. S. A word to the reader. In R. M. Goldensen, J. R. Dunham, & C. S. Dunham (Eds.), *Disability and rehabilitation handbook.* New York: McGraw-Hill, 1978.

Lazarus, R. *Patterns of adjustment in human effectiveness.* New York: McGraw-Hill, 1969.

Merleau-Ponty, M. *Phenomenology of perception* (C. Smith, Trans.) London: Routledge & Kegan Paul, 1962.

O'Connell, W. E. The "friends of Adler" phenomenon. Journal of Individual Psychology, 1976, 32, 5–18.

Roessler, R., & Bolton, B. *Psychosocial adjustment to disability.* Baltimore: University Park Press, 1978.

Sechrest, L., & Wallace, J. *Psychology and human problems.* Columbus, Ohio: Charles E. Merrill, 1967.

Shontz, F. C. *The psychological aspects of physical illness and disability.* New York: Macmillan, 1975.

Shontz, F. C. Physical disability and personality: Theory and recent research. In J.E. Stubbins (Ed.), *Social and psychological aspects of disability.* Baltimore: University Park Press, 1977.

Stubbins, J. Editorial introduction (Part III). In J. Stubbins (Ed.), *Social and psychological aspects of disability.* Baltimore: University Park Press, 1977.

Thomas, L. *The medusa and the snail.* New York: Viking Press, 1979.

Wright, G. N. *Total rehabilitation.* Boston: Little, Brown, 1980.

2

STRUCTURED PROCESSES AND TECHNIQUES OF LIFESTYLE COUNSELING

Warren R. Rule

This chapter presents a somewhat structured approach to implementing the concepts of lifestyle understanding and adjustment to disability. This counseling process for adjustment to disability can be viewed as having four phases. These phases, an adaptation of the Adlerian process (Dreikurs, 1967), are Relationship, Lifestyle Investigation, Lifestyle Interpretation, and Reorientation. The initial discussion will focus primarily on procedures in an individual setting with subsequent brief discussion on adapting these procedures to a group approach.

RELATIONSHIP

The relationship phase is not actually a "phase" in the sense that it has a distinct ending. The practitioner begins the helping process by building a relationship of trust, respect, genuineness, and empathy. These

---

This chapter, "Structured Processes and Techniques of Lifestyle Counseling," from Warren R. Rule (Ed.), *Lifestyle counseling for adjustment to disability*, 1984. Rockville, MD: Aspen Systems Corporation.

and other relationship factors presumably continue to operate and provide the basis for the development of the subsequent phases.

In addition to fostering those qualities upon which a solid counseling relationship is built, the relationship phase also serves other purposes. In this phase (1) the client has the opportunity to explore himself in relationship to the disability; (2) the practitioner learns more about the client's internal frame of reference; and (3) the opportunity is provided for an exchange of specific information (e.g., medical, case history, procedural, etc.) between the practitioner and the client.

Subjective Exploration

The overriding function of client exploration, according to Carkhuff (1980), is for the individual to begin to understand where he is in relationship to where he wants to be. As part of this process of self-exploration, which is skillfully guided by the practitioner, the client is better able to clarify his inner experiencing so that he can understand himself more fully. The future-oriented, goal-directed framework of this exploration process is crucial: the here and now in relationship to the ideal future. This goal-oriented framework not only is consistent with the Adlerian view of all of man's behavior, but also is an extremely helpful approach to specificity in the counseling process itself. The client's subjectively identifying the perceived present in relation to the perceived ideal future gives the practitioner a valuable perspective as well as serves to give direction to the counseling process. At a later phase in the counseling process, these ideas can be discussed within the context of the client's overall lifestyle.

Carkhuff (1980) has developed a number of considerations that are helpful in the exploration and understanding process. These points are useful in general, yet seem to be especially applicable to practitioners who emphasize the importance of increasing awareness of another's internal frame of reference. A summary of these ideas follows.

Attending. Very basic to facilitating the exploration process is attending or giving undivided attention. Attending personally involves posturing oneself as a helper in order to communicate interest and attentiveness. Attending contextually refers to arranging the practitioner's helping environment so that it conveys open communication and support, rather than power or elevated authority.

A major component of attending is observing, because the client, often unknowingly, reveals many clues to his inner experiences through his physical behavior and appearance. Actually, the client's physical behavior is often the most fertile source of information, especially when the client's remarks are inconsistent or confusing. Energy level, posture, grooming, and nonverbal behavior are all important indices of the client's experience and level of functioning. Particularly noteworthy are discrepancies in the client's nonverbal behavior and verbal behavior. Listening is another attending skill that is extremely important. What the client says (who, what, when, where, why, and how) and how he says it (e.g., tone of voice) are keys to facilitation. The more the practitioner is able to suspend personal judgment and resist distractions, the greater will be his ability to listen for the recurrent, important themes in what the client is expressing.

Responding. The manner in which the practitioner verbally responds to the client's experiences is extremely crucial. As a result of the attending skills of accurate observing and listening, the helping person attempts to respond in a manner that expresses empathy, not sympathy. Empathy conveys the idea that the practitioner has an understanding or awareness of the client's experience and it is accomplished by responding initially at an interchangeable level with the client in terms of both feeling and content. By communicating to the client what the client has expressed, at the level of exploration the client expressed it, the practitioner is able to obtain a more accurate picture of the client's inner world. Moreover, the client is able to respond to the helper's empathic responses and this can result in further exploration or a clarification of the helper's understanding.

Interchangeable responding by the practitioner does not mean simply parroting back what the client has expressed; rather, it entails concisely expressing in a sentence the feeling state, which the client might or might not be aware of, along with a fresh understanding of the content of what the client has said. Initially, this counseling base of interchangeable responses would exist for whatever range of emotional states (e.g., anger, sadness, happiness, etc.) the client is experiencing. A working vocabulary of words and phrases that pinpoint various feeling states is essential for the practitioner.

Personalizing. After the client has explored the many dimensions of the problem, the client may be ready to move beyond interchangeable communication with the helper into deeper levels of self-understanding. Carkhuff (1980) views understanding as the next step after exploration. The readiness to do this may be signaled by sustaining self-exploratory responses without the practitioner's help or perhaps the client may make interchangeable responses with earlier remarks. At this point the helper may want to draw from the dominant theme the client has been expressing as well as from the helper's own experiences. In doing this, the practitioner will attempt to personalize the problem by helping the client understand what the client cannot do for himself that is contributing to his difficulty. (As will be discussed later, the lifestyle approach also helps the client see from a different and broader perspective what he is doing or not doing to contribute to his own difficulty.)

Thus, the issue focuses on what the individual presently is lacking or is unable to do for himself that prevents him from resolving the unwanted situation. In discussing such a deficit, the helper must be especially sensitive to the client's feeling about the deficit. In addition, the practitioner should be responsive to inconsistencies in what the client says, feels, or does as a source of useful information about what the client is unable to do for himself.

Upon reaching an awareness of this exceedingly important variable—what the client is unable to do that is contributing to the problem—the practitioner and the client are in a much better position to continue the counseling process.

As the practitioner attempts to grasp the personal meaning of the client's disability, it may be helpful to keep Shontz's (1975) broad principles in mind for viewing clients as whole, living people. These principles, while written for health professionals and not from a lifestyle perspective per se, appear generally consistent with the overall framework:

1. There are often multiple causes in life, rather than simple cause and effect relationships.
2. The person functions or attempts to function as an integrated unit.
3. The person responds to reality as he interprets it.
4. Behavior is determined by the context of the situation at the current moment.
5. Behavior maximizes construed consistency between past, present, and anticipated future experience.
6. Behavior is a function of relationships within an integrated organism-environment totality. (pp. 191–198)

Information Sharing. In addition to subjective exploration, another important component of the relationship phase is information sharing. Information sharing takes place as needed throughout the relationship phase and relates to primarily content-oriented material that has minimal emotional overtones. Information sharing would, in most cases, supplement the subjective exploration, rather than the reverse. However, it is far too easy to deal with exchanges between the helper and the client in terms of simply content; one must be prepared to respond to the emotions behind the content, even to client statements as seemingly innocuous as "information" sharing. In general, "information sharing" material might be questions and responses regarding strictly medical information, misconceptions about disability, procedural details, miscellaneous clarification, and the like. The information sharing components, which are intertwined with the subjective exploration dimension, can yield information for both the practitioner and the client.

LIFESTYLE INVESTIGATION

Prior to conducting the lifestyle investigation, Adlerian practitioners often obtain from the client information that may have a significant bearing on the subsequent lifestyle discussion. The helper explores with the client how he is functioning in the three areas of social living, sometimes referred to as the three tasks of life. Adlerians believe that everyone takes a position—with varying degrees of success or failure—on these three areas of social living: work (or school), love, and friendship. As Dreikurs (1953) notes, if one of the tasks is evaded, difficulties may ultimately unfold in the other tasks as well. The Adlerian belief is that the individual's lifestyle, including its unique strengths, weaknesses, and blind spots, functions as a coping device in all areas of life. Therefore, an increased awareness of how things are going for the client in the three main areas of life provides a fuller picture of how the client's chosen lifestyle is presently contributing to his problems or his happiness. Generally, Adlerians believe that the lifestyle becomes most apparent when the individual is experiencing stress. It is then that what has proven most useful, i.e., the lifestyle, is relied on with greater intensity.

Another procedure that some practitioners use is that of asking "The Question." This is simply asking the client what would be different if he were well or if the problem did not exist. Sometimes the answer to this question indicates for what purpose the individual is experiencing unusual difficulties, against whom or what the symptoms are directed, or against what demand or threat he is defending himself by having such a difficult adjustment.

The exploration of the three tasks of life and "The Question" normally would precede the gathering of the lifestyle information. This pre-lifestyle material might sometimes be discussed in the relationship phase, depending on appropriateness and the flow of the interaction. The demarcation points between the various stages, especially between relationship and lifestyle investigation, are not rigid; rather, one stage overlaps another until the later stage clearly emerges from the former.

The rationale for conducting the lifestyle investigation should be introduced to the client in a concise, respectful manner. An example might go something like this:

> John, sometimes it is helpful to be in touch with some pretty broad attitudes and goals that are at work in major areas of a person's life. We are talking here about important beliefs an individual has learned about himself, other people, and life that he probably is not completely aware of. One way I have found very useful in trying to help someone identify them is by taking a look at what impressions from early childhood a person is choosing to continue to believe. You and I could discuss for a while some of your early impressions and then talk about how these are operating right now, in your everyday life. Want to give it a try?

In the overwhelming majority of cases, clients are intrigued by the prospect of learning what relationship exists between early childhood and the present. This seems to hold for individuals who experienced relatively unpleasant childhoods as well as for those who experienced pleasant ones. The counselor's introductory remarks, as well as his subsequent comments, should not depict the lifestyle exploration as a mystical, murky endeavor. Rather, the emphasis ought to reflect a sharing, educational process in which relationships between the early past and present are discussed. As we have noted, Adlerians rely on the selectivity of memory as providing information that is currently useful to the individual's chosen lifestyle; accordingly, emphasis is placed on the manifest content of memory, not on symbolic meanings.

LIFESTYLE INTERPRETATION

The process itself of gathering the lifestyle information helps to cement the counseling relationship. This step, in addition to the ongoing efforts initiated during the relationship phase, provides a foundation for the practitioner and the client to discuss the client's lifestyle.

At this point, the practitioner has had an opportunity to study the client's response to the lifestyle interview. In searching for lifestyle "threads" or overriding goals the helper relies on his awareness of modest probabilities of relationship between lifestyle variables (nomothetic laws). At the same time, he is trying to make deductions and identify logical patterns that will identify individual (idiographic) laws. While looking for tentative identification of the individual's network of goals, or cognitive map, the practitioner is, in a sense, attempting to put pieces of a jigsaw puzzle together. He is wondering as he reviews the lifestyle material: "If this person has drawn these conclusions about himself, others, and life, then what kind of overriding (future-oriented) goals would he have chosen to guide him in his striving to be a coping, significant person?" In addition to seeking to identify broad, overriding goals, the counselor keeps an eye out for specific convictions that relate to the client's present problem, such as adjustment to disability.

The focus is on the person's thinking patterns, notions, and goals and only secondarily on his methods of behaving that are in the service of lifestyle goals. Most Adlerians believe that the lifestyle reveals only limited probabilities about behavior patterns, which are often more changeable than basic goals. Information on behavior used to implement lifestyle goals is primarily obtained by other modalities, e.g., discussion with the client, counselor observations, others' observations.

Once the practitioner has tentatively identified the client's lifestyle notions and goals, he shares his interpretations in a spirit of respect and exploration. He would use phrases such as "Could it be that...," "A guess that I have is...." Oftentimes, a client will respond with a "recognition reflex," a nonverbal indication that the practitioner has indeed hit a bullseye. Other times, semantic barriers are in operation and must be worked through. Occasionally, the helper misses the mark, regardless of semantic or communication barriers, and must simply return to the drawing board.

The practitioner must particularly keep in mind how the client's lifestyle operates when the client hears about his own lifestyle, e.g., those striving to please may be too agreeable, those striving for intellectual superiority may create a sparring match, etc. However, if the relationship is one of trust, if both parties are willing to cooperate and work toward understanding, agreement can usually be reached regarding major aspects of the client's lifestyle.

There are a number of frameworks for presenting lifestyle interpretations. The perspective of "I am...," "Others are...," "Life is..." is one approach. Another is to emphasize the "shoulds," e.g., "I am a person who should...," "Others are people who ought to...," "Life is a place that must..." Often it is helpful to present the material in a goal-directed framework, which denotes a future orientation, e.g., "To…" Mosak (1979) focuses on "Basic Mistakes," e.g., overgeneralizations, false or impossible goals of "security," misperceptions of life and of life's demands, minimization or denial of one's worth, faulty values. In addition, Mosak (1954) has divided lifestyle convictions into four groups: the self concept, the self ideal, the picture of the world, and ethical convictions. Another framework (Rule, 1982a) utilizes the perspective of the individual's private logic within a social context; the technique involves reframing the practitioner's interpretations in a positive and socially acceptable manner and with the imaginary context of the client's ideal self as viewed by important others. Lifestyle interpretations can also be incorporated into modalities of communication developed from other perspectives, e.g., parables and fables (Pancer, 1978), metaphors (Gordon, 1978; Rule, 1983), trance formations (Grinder & Bandler, 1981; Bandler & Grinder, 1975; Grinder, Delozier & Bandler, 1977), and Ericksonian teaching tales (Rosen, 1982).

In facilitating the interpretation process, the helper should encourage the client to take responsibility for identifying relationships between lifestyle and daily living. Sometimes clients are curious about how the practitioner arrived at the lifestyle interpretations. In response the helper may want to render brief explanations, all the while giving the client the opportunity to make the associations between past and present goals and behavior. The efforts by the counselor during the interpretation stage go a long way in enhancing client self-acceptance and feelings of OK-ness. The ripening of a positive attitude toward one's lifestyle is a key variable in the next and final phase, which focuses on the client and his difficulties.

REORIENTATION

Reorientation Goals

In the reorientation phase, the accent is on change. Upon achieving a measure of insight into the client's lifestyle, both the practitioner and the client are able to use this framework as a springboard for discussing change.

The primary goal in the reorientation phase is, of course, to help the client resolve his present difficulties. In attempting to accomplish this foremost goal, the practitioner often has in the back of his mind a number of related goals. Examples are:

1. To identify those self-serving decisions of the lifestyle that are contributing to the present difficulty by working to the client's disadvantage, and, in addition, to pinpoint those lifestyle advantages that can be used as assets in the reorientation process.
2. To assist the client in setting specific and realistic personal goals that are related to diminishing the self-defeating dimensions of the present difficulty, e.g., adjustment to disability.
3. To explore the interrelatedness of thinking, feeling, and doing. From an operational perspective, to explore the thinking processes related to the lifestyle in relationship to the associated feelings and behaviors. Although the past was utilized in order to understand the present better, the adjustment emphasis is on present responsibility for self.
4. To devise homework strategies, related to lifestyle assets wherever possible, that are a means to attaining the specified goals for change.
5. To encourage the client to believe in a significance of self that is not a function of comparisons with others or self-rankings.
6. To foster an increased other-directedness in the client. This is important because increased self-esteem seems paradoxically related to increased acceptance, empathy, and social interest in others (O'Connell, 1976).

Reorientation Strategies

Strategies for implementing many of these goals for change will be discussed below. The strategies are divided into three areas: (I) broad considerations the practitioner may keep in mind during the overall reorientation process, (2) specific goal-oriented interventions, and (3) supplemental techniques from other approaches.

Broad Considerations. The practitioner continually strives to be aware of the goal-directed nature of the client's behavior and expression of emotions. This focus characterizes the client's lifestyle goals as related to his current difficulties, his interaction with the practitioner, his decision-making procedures, and so on. As appropriate, the helper either provides the opportunity for the client to get in touch with his own goals that underlie certain behavior and feelings or he takes a more direct role by gently pointing out how the client creatively implements goals and their usefulness to his lifestyle. This awareness is conveyed to the client, not in an accusatory manner, but rather in a framework that respects the individual's creativity in devising and implementing such a goal.

The responsibility is therefore placed on the client for creating his own approach to a given situation. Moreover, the focus is kept on the (future-oriented) goals of a behavior or feeling because this reduces the likelihood that the client will feel burdened by or use to his "advantage" the "whys" or "causes" of behavior. The "whys" or "causes" reflect past, unchangeable reasons; "goals" indicate future-oriented, changeable targets. Since the helper creates an opportunity for the client to have an increased awareness of his goals, the client is less likely to pursue those goals that ultimately work to his disadvantage. (Adler is said to have expressed this point in an unforgettable metaphor: once the therapist has spit into the client's soup, the client can continue to eat the soup, but it won't taste as good.)

Sometimes it is helpful to view this change process as one of "reframing." Bandler and Grinder (1979), speaking from the neurolinguistic programming perspective, stated that "The heart of reframing is to make the distinction between intention… and the behavior.… Then you can find new, more acceptable behaviors to satisfy the same intention" (p. 138).

An awareness of the client's lifestyle enables the practitioner to consider other broad variations. The helper now has additional guidelines, as noted before, for varying his responses at critical periods. For instance, an authoritative, how-to-do-it approach may annoy a client who is heavily invested in intellectual superiority or in self-control, whereas an understanding, respectful approach would be apt to enlist cooperation more quickly. An increased lifestyle awareness may also help the practitioner recognize how different clients, with different lifestyles, may feel either encouraged or discouraged by the same behavior on the part of the helper.

The practitioner may use the lifestyle awareness to suggest change in aspects of the client's environment. These suggestions, designed to be in keeping with sensitivities inherent in the client's lifestyle, might be made to family members, medical personnel in an institution, supervisors in a work setting, and so on.

Sometimes an increased understanding of the purpose for artificial aids, such as alcohol or drugs, can result from lifestyle awareness. An individual may believe within his private logic that the artificial aid either increases the flow of his style or permits him to engage in options that are not within the flow of his lifestyle. For example, the charmer may feel more charming under the influence of drink or drugs; the self-controlled person may feel able to give up some control in his altered state.

The practitioner continually looks for opportunities to encourage the client to believe in a significance of self that is not a function of vertical rankings or comparisons with others. This awareness can be helpful to a client in learning to do a mental checkup when he experiences an unwanted negative emotion and then trying to discover how the lifestyle is dictating the message of inadequacy. This daily awareness of individual functioning can also be instrumental in avoiding future pitfalls.

In addition to encouraging the client to monitor and challenge himself on OK-ness in his daily functioning, the practitioner uses various broad strategies to accomplish the same purpose within the counseling setting. For instance, the helper may employ many uses of humor in the form of parables, fables, biography, quotations, cartoons, anecdotes. Or, the practitioner and the client may devise homework assignments designed to help the client accept himself while laughing at the exaggerated lifestyle demands he is making on himself. The use of Polaroid photographs (Rule, 1979) and nightly audiotape recordings (Rule, 1977b) has been effective.

Adler believed in the potency of humor, as Rychlak (1973) has summarized below:

> ... Adler believed in the advisability of using a series of fairly dramatic illustrations in making his point. If the therapist is too sober all he succeeds in doing is worrying the client needlessly, overvaluing the severity of the case, and establishing an authoritarian relationship. He must not make light of the client, of course, but the proper mood Adler sought was that of spontaneous cooperation in a joint effort which could assure success if they did not as therapist and client take themselves altogether too seriously. A hopeful person is not without a sense of happiness or lightheartedness, even in the face of some rather agonizing challenges. (p. 129)

Broad strategies are often necessary in facilitating change in a client who creatively uses a mental, emotional, or physical disability. These strategies are part of the intervention process for facilitation of adjustment to disability and will be discussed in detail later.

Encouragement should be a major part of the practitioner's overall attitude undergirding whatever broad strategies he selects. This important Adlerian procedure has far-reaching implications for process and outcome. As Dinkmeyer (1972) noted:

> Encouragement on the part of the counselor is comprised of both verbal and nonverbal procedures that enable a counselee to experience and become aware of his own worth. The counselor expresses faith in and total acceptance of the counselee as he is, not as he could or should be. Encouragement as defined here does not imply that the counselor rewards, bribes, or praises; it means rather that he places value on the counselee's uniqueness and humanness and indicates to him that because he is human he is of worth and value. Counselor encouragement helps to correct the counselee's mistaken assumption that he is inferior to or not as able as others. The counselor demonstrates encouragement with a strong, empathic attitude that emphasizes health rather than illness, strength rather than weakness, ability rather than inability. He completely accepts the counselee as a person of real value. (p. 177)

Specific Goal-Directed Considerations. Upon having achieved awareness of a particular lifestyle goal (or belief), the client is in a position to make a decision regarding change, continuation, and related behavior. The next step after awareness might be to identify the parameters of desired change, after which point the individual is in a position to consider various alternatives for action or nonaction. The following is a variation of a framework developed by Rule (1980) that details various goal-change orientations and suggests possible solutions:

1. The client *likes* and wants to continue this goal (and the resulting feelings). In addition, he does not wish to change a related goal dimension (situational specificity, frequency of occurrence, or felt intensity). Nor does he wish to change the behavior used to implement this goal. Moreover, for having this goal, (1) he accepts himself or (2) he rejects himself.

   Possible solutions: For (1) no solution appears to be needed. For (2) consider: (a) monitoring and/or rating thoughts, feelings, and/or sensations; (b) a rational-emotive approach (Ellis, 1974); (c) self-directed humor for self/other acceptance; (d) practitioner encouragement and humanistic sharing.
2. The client *likes* and wants to continue this goal (and the resulting feelings). In addition, he does not wish to change a related goal dimension (situational specificity, frequency of occurrence, or felt intensity). However, he does want to behave differently in order to implement the goal more effectively and not to rate self-worth in the process.

Possible solutions: (a) a rational-emotive approach; (b) self-directed humor for self-other acceptance; (c) specific cognitive self-management strategies; (d) overt behavioral strategies; (e) specific homework assignments, including utilizing community resources; (f) practitioner encouragement and humanistic sharing.

3. The client *somewhat likes* this goal (and resulting feelings). In general or in specific situations, he wishes to value the goal less or more often and/or more strongly. In addition, he wants to behave in keeping with the changed goal dimension and not rate his self-worth in the process.

   Possible solutions: (a) monitor and/or rate thoughts, feelings, and/or sensations; (b) explore and establish change goals; (c) a rational-emotive approach; (d) self-directed humor for self/other acceptance; (e) cognitive self-management skills; (f) overt behavioral strategies; (g) specific homework assignments, including utilizing community resources; (h) practitioner encouragement and humanistic sharing.

4. The client *dislikes* this goal (and the resulting feelings), yet he does not wish to change the goal or a related dimension of the goal. Nor does he wish to change the behavior used to implement the goal. But, for having this contradiction he either (1) accepts himself or (2) rejects himself.

   Possible solutions: For (1) explore no-change secondary gains and maintaining conditions in the spirit of practitioner encouragement and humanistic sharing. For (2): (a) additional self-awareness experiences; (b) monitor and/ or rate thoughts, feelings, and/or sensations; (c) explore no-change secondary gains and maintaining conditions; (d) increase decision-making skills; (e) explore and establish change goals; (f) a rational-emotive approach; (g) self-directed humor for self/other acceptance; (h) practitioner encouragement and humanistic sharing.

5. The client *dislikes* this goal (and the resulting feelings). In general or in specific situations, he wishes to value this goal much less often and/or less strongly. Yet, he does not wish to change any of the behavior that is related to the goal or rate his self-worth.

   Possible consideration: it is often more rewarding to change behavior as well (see 6 below).

6. The client *dislikes* this goal (and the resulting feelings). In general or in specific situations, he wishes to value this goal much less often and/or less strongly. Also he wants to behave in keeping

with the changed goal dimension and not rate his self-worth in the process.

Possible solutions: (a) monitor and/or rate thoughts, feelings, and/or sensations; (b) explore and establish change goals; (c) a rational-emotive approach; (d) self/other acceptance; (e) cognitive self-management skills; (0 overt behavioral strategies; (g) other specific homework assignments, including utilizing community resources; (h) practitioner encouragement and humanistic sharing.

Supplemental Techniques from Other Approaches

As we have seen, the lifestyle can provide the context within which the client's problem "deficit" is viewed. Expressed another way, lifestyle awareness can illuminate how the client's deficit (what he is wanting that he is unable to do for himself) fits into his broader life goals. Many techniques exist in addition to the Adlerian action-oriented ones. For instance, other counseling approaches, although sometimes theoretically incompatible with the overall lifestyle perspective, nevertheless offer many supplemental techniques that fit into various phases, particularly the reorientation phase. Some of these are discussed below.

Rational-Emotive Therapy (RET). The rational-emotive approach, developed by Ellis (1962, 1974), focuses on identifying and overcoming irrational thinking. It fits well into the reorientation phase of the lifestyle approach in that it helps clients reduce the intensity or frequency of identified lifestyle notions or goals that are working to one's disadvantage. In this educational approach, the counselor teaches the client how to dispute the importance that he is attributing to a real or imagined occurrence. The emphasis is on the should's, must's, ought to's, and other self-mandates that the person, often dimly consciously, upsets himself with. Both RET and the Adlerian lifestyle approach emphasize that it is desirable for self-acceptance not to be a function of achievement, comparison with others, or any form of self-rating. Moreover, both approaches assert that we mostly create our emotions rather than are possessed by them—an important counseling perspective. Additional reading in Walen, DiGiuseppe, and Wessler (1980) is suggested.

Behavioral Counseling. Behavioral counseling emphasizes learning new ways to think, feel, or act in designated situations. This essentially educational approach is especially useful in the final lifestyle reorientation phase when the client has identified a very specific problem he wants to work on. Broadly speaking, the sequence of behavioral counseling proceeds as follows: identification of problem, formulation of counseling goals, monitoring of client behavior, implementation of counseling intervention, and evaluation of goal attainment. Some useful techniques include assertive training; progressive muscle relaxation; modeling, including self-as-a-model; self- and contingency management programs; and behavioral contracting. Further information may be found in Hosford and de Visser (1974).

Gestalt Counseling. The Gestalt perspective, pioneered by Perls (e.g., Perls, Hefferline, & Goodman, 1951; Perls, 1969), focuses on awareness of what a person is sensing, feeling, and, to a lesser degree, thinking, in the present moment. The assumption is that by being challenged to draw from one's own resources, coupled with the spontaneity of the now, problems and issues that need to be dealt with will emerge into awareness. The techniques can be useful in the early phases as well as in the reorientation phase, especially in teaching clients the direct relationship between many facets of awareness and thinking processes as well as in teaching clients self-responsibility for feelings. These interventions include nonverbal awareness, fantasy, use of language, feelings (past and future as related to present centeredness), and so on. Additional discussion of the uses of Gestalt techniques within a counseling framework may be found in Passons (1975).

Miscellaneous Approaches. Sheldon and Ackerman (1974) and Lazarus and Fay (1975) offer a wide variety of techniques for the very important dimension of client homework. Transactional analysis (Berne, 1961) may provide the client with descriptive concepts of understanding interpersonal dynamics; reality therapy (Glasser, 1965) presents a systematic perspective on assuming responsibility; stress management offers helpful ideas, either from a somewhat cognitive perspective (e.g., Woolfolk & Richardson, 1978) or a more physiological vantage point (e.g., Selye, 1974) on to a broad-based eclectic orientation (e.g., Schafer, 1978). Neuro-linguistic programming (Bandler and Grinder, 1979; Dilts, Grinder, Bandler, Bandler, and Delozier, 1980) offers many techniques for structuring subjective experience.

Before concluding this section, it is worth noting that the importance of relationship factors cannot be minimized. The relationship factors, especially respect for another's rights and responsiveness to another's internal frame of reference, get the whole process moving and keep it moving. An appropriate metaphor might be that the complex interaction of relationship factors (feeling-oriented) is the key that opens the door to the dark room; the lifestyle self-understanding (thinking-oriented) creates light in the room; and the reorientation methods (action-oriented) rearrange the room and polish the furniture according to the wishes of the individual.

ADAPTATION TO GROUP SETTINGS

Lifestyle counseling, based on a holistic approach, emphasizes the interrelatedness of man to himself and to others. As such, the lifestyle approach views man as a social being who is not—although he may at times behave differently—an island unto himself. Correspondingly, the lifestyle perspective regards personal problems as basically social problems, a concept that ideally lends itself to the social setting of group counseling. The overall group process would be generally consistent with the four phases of individual counseling.

Sweeney's (1975) observations about group participation and contribution are noteworthy. In groups, participants are:

1. Inherently equal and may expect to behave as such, i.e., have a place that no one can rightfully challenge.
2. Considered to be capable of assuming responsibility for their behavior.
3. Individually understood best in a holistic, unified way as creative, purposive beings.
4. Considered as social beings meeting the same life tasks as others.
5. Capable of changing their attitudes and/or behaviors.
6. Able to help as well as be helped in the process of giving meaning to life.

Discussion during the initial meetings should explore expectations of the group members and misconceptions about group counseling. Ground rules such as confidentiality, the fact that the group is not simply "a confessional," and that members will not be forced to do anything should be covered. Moreover, at this time, logistical matters should be dealt with, such as meeting times, length (approximately two hours is recommended), duration of group, replacement of members, etc.

Relationship techniques are useful not only in the initial phase of group counseling but also as a means of maintaining the cohesiveness, meaning, and productivity of the group. Dinkmeyer, Pew, and Dinkmeyer (1979) recommend techniques such as encouragement and focusing on assets and positive feedback. In addition, facilitating participation by utilizing nonverbal cues (e.g., seating place, seating posture, facial expression, voice, hand gestures, etc.) is often beneficial. Here and throughout the whole process consideration can be given to facilitative confrontation of discrepancies in what members think, feel, and do (e.g., what was said vs. what is being said; what one is saying vs. what one appears to be feeling; what one is saying vs. what one is doing, etc.). Furthermore, much can be gained by encouraging as much here-and-now interaction as possible (except for learning about the past from lifestyle exploration) as opposed to "there and then" orientations.

In facilitating the beginning stages of lifestyle group counseling, as well as in maintaining productive relationships throughout the complete group process, leader interventions are often necessary. These interventions not only enable the group process to continue productively but also provide effective modeling for other members to emulate. Dyer and Vriend (1975) suggest that intervention may be necessary when:

1. A group member speaks for everyone.
2. An individual speaks for another individual within the group.
3. A group member overfocuses on persons, conditions, or events outside the group.
4. Someone seeks the approval of the counselor or a group member before and after speaking.
5. Someone says, "I don't want to hurt his feelings, so I won't say it."
6. A group member suggests that his or her problems are due to someone else.
7. An individual suggests that "I've always been that way."
8. An individual suggests "I'll wait, and it will change."
9. Discrepant behavior appears.
10. A member bores the group by rambling.

Insofar as group lifestyle investigation and interpretation are concerned, each group member would have—needless to say—different expectations of himself and others and would have learned different behaviors for implementing the dimly conscious goals of the lifestyle. Thus, each person's self-understanding and other group members' understanding of a given individual's private logic would be enhanced by the lifestyle approach.

The lifestyle information can be gathered by the group, a partner, or the leader and then distributed to all of the members. Then the members and the leader offer their interpretations of the group members' lifestyles in a spirit of tentative sharing and exploration. They use phrases such as "Could it be that...," "A guess that I have is...," etc. If the interpretations are in the ballpark, if the group relationship is one of trust, and if the group member and others are willing to work toward understanding, major agreement can be reached regarding major aspects of the group member's lifestyle. This procedure is continued for each member and the leader. Throughout the process, the leader and other members refer to examples from the group experience (e.g., first impressions, group exercises, etc.) that supported the lifestyle interpretation.

Because the group is a social microcosm, the lifestyle is apt to express itself in the group as well as on the outside. Thus, the group member would get feedback on how he creatively and subtly has used and is using his lifestyle in relating to others in his attempt to strive for a place of self-determined social significance. Sometimes replaying a video tape of a member's interactions with others increases this self-understanding and serves to highlight certain lifestyle behaviors that otherwise would be hard to accept. Another approach is the absurd exaggeration of lifestyle characteristics by using masquerades (Rule, 1979); the group input into determination of each individual costume as well as the group masquerade itself can result in increased self-awareness, self-acceptance, and group cohesiveness.

Lifestyle introspection, group observations and encouragement, videotaping, and the lifestyle masquerade all serve to facilitate the process of a group member saying to himself, "Hey, this is me!"

The final phase is lifestyle reorientation. Upon achieving a measure of self-awareness, the members of the lifestyle group counseling process focus on positive change that will be helpful presently and in the future. The continued emphasis is, as O'Connell (1975) noted, on personal thinking patterns or goals, not on the common stereotype of a "drive-release" group that aims simply for the expression of emotions as a curative factor. In broadening one's insight or understanding of self in relationship to others, the group members move toward achieving "outsight" or "the learned ability to see, hear, and feel along with others" (O'Connell, 1976, p. 157). Expressed in another way, the attempt is to "free them from the intoxication of a private interpretation of the world" (Ansbacher & Ansbacher, 1956, p. 348) and encourage a spirit of cooperation or "common sense versus private sense" (Ansbacher & Ansbacher, 1956, p. 253).

H. S. Sullivan (1940), whose ideas have considerable overlap with Adler's, saw the powerful relationship between the interpersonal and intrapersonal realms and concluded that one achieves mental health to the extent that one becomes aware of one's interpersonal relationships. So, during this fourth and final phase, the group member develops his goals for change and refines methods he will continue to use for change and for broadening his sense of self in relation to others.

CONSIDERATIONS REGARDING THE DISABLED

As we have seen, the lifestyle approach contends that people are social beings by nature and are inclined to establish individual self-identity by relating with and comparing self with others. The comparison process for the disabled, especially on an ongoing basis, can have severe repercussions. Usually, the resulting inferiority feeling, based on comparisons with others, is coupled with a feeling of social isolation or not belonging. As Mosak (1977) notes, a goal for the practitioner, then, should be to decrease inferiority feelings and to increase feelings of belonging. An additional dilemma resulting from comparisons involves the concept of near-normalcy. Paradoxically, clients with mild disabilities can sometimes actually have, according to Eisenberg (1977), a more difficult adjustment because they are almost normal. Consequently, these individuals may try to deny or hide the disability because it is marginal. The topics of family reaction and involvement are also self-in-relation-to-others issues, which will be discussed in detail later.

The practitioner should not overlook the implications of possibly one of the most obvious conditions imposed upon many disabled individuals—the loss of liberty. Perhaps the existence of the physical restriction is less serious than its consequences (Eisenberg, 1977). Relationships, architectural barriers, sexual adjustment, community reaction, loss of autonomy, and dependency are all factors that may be sensitive problem areas. A reverse situation can also occur in which the client relates many other problems—old and new, personal and interpersonal—to the disability. In making the disability responsible for a host of difficulties, psychosocial adjustment to the disability is correspondingly delayed.

After reviewing a variety of investigations which found that, on the average, disabled persons report lower self-esteem than nondisabled persons, Roessler and Bolton (1978) concluded that many disabled individuals' views of themselves "may militate against successful rehabilitation, unless modified through adjustment training" (p. 40).

Kir-Stimon (1977) noted a common fallacy on the part of both the client and the helper:

> That he (the client) must be either nobody or somebody worthwhile. In this either/or situation in which the severely disabled person frequently finds himself, he fails to realize that he is important simply because he exists, despite societal standards of productivity—creation, invention, even procreation. For the person with a severe disability who is labeled totally and permanently disabled and considered unable to earn his own livelihood, this becomes a distinction between being and not being. Personal unproductivity in our society is literally "un-becoming." Whereas, as a matter of fact, personal creativity need not involve a product or an object but might relate more to the very craft of living. (p. 367)

This perspective, although not written in direct support of the lifestyle counseling approach, is consistent with the encouragement of self-acceptance and the discouragement of vertical rankings, both of which are efforts that are heavily emphasized in lifestyle counseling.

Resistance

During any phase of the helping process, the practitioner may encounter resistance. Dreikurs (1967) asserts that "resistance" essentially is a discrepancy between the goals of the practitioner and those of the client. Therefore, a keen awareness of the practitioner's expectations and the client's lifestyle goals increases the likelihood of working through the resistance in a spirit of cooperation. At times, however, facilitative confrontation may be in order; Shulman (1972, 1977) has suggested helpful techniques for this purpose. Perhaps here, a wise psychological attitude in rehabilitation, as stated by Mosak (1977), is "acceptance of the patient as he is" (p. 54), which is the basis in general for all lifestyle counseling techniques.

One way to respect the client "as is," yet respond in a facilitative, useful manner to what can be broadly termed "negativism," is to use responses that combine respect for the client's present internal frame of reference with the flow of a major lifestyle goal (Rule, 1977a). Typically, in working with clients, practitioners are often stunned or baffled at expressions of client negativism. Negativism can be broadly defined as verbal and/or nonverbal expressions that convey the message that self, others, or life are at fault because one's expectations are not met. This may be expressed in the form of hostility, resentment, aggression, etc., and could be directed at the practitioner. Again, in viewing emotions as goal directed, the helper is in a better position to understand the negativism. By having an awareness of the client's lifestyle, the practitioner has insight into the goals and, consequently, how the expression of negativism is useful to the individual. The helper can act facilitatively by responding in terms of the relationship between what the person is now wanting that he is not getting, his unmet lifestyle goals, and his feelings about the deficit.

Along a similar vein, sometimes clients feel threatened because of perceived "dangers." These perceptions can greatly interfere with client cooperation. The likelihood of occurrence of each of the perceived dangers is related to the degree of correspondence to the overall individual lifestyle. The following dangers perceived by clients were noted by Shulman (1973): being defective, incurring disapproval or enmity, being ridiculed, being taken advantage of, not getting necessary help, submitting to order, having to face responsibility, and having to face unpleasant consequences. In addition, Shulman cites possible defensive patterns or forms of behavior that may be used to ward off the dangers. These devices may be at either a conscious or dimly conscious level; they may be used either almost continuously or only occasionally at a time of stress:

A. Externalization ("The fault lies outside of me")
   1. Cynicism ("Life is at fault")
   2. Inadequacy ("I'm just an innocent victim")
      a. sickness
      b. a bad background
      c. victimized by cravings and impulses
      d. possessed by demons or supernatural force
   3. Rebellion ("I can't afford to submit to life")
   4. Projection ("It's all their fault")

B. Blind Spots ("If I don't look at it, it will go away")

C. Excessive Self-Control ("I will not let anything upset me")

D. Arbitrary Rightness ("My mind is made up; don't confuse me with the facts")

E. Elusiveness and Confusion ("Don't pin me down")

F. Retreat ("Nothing ventured, nothing lost")

G. Contrition and Self-Disparagement ("Mea Culpa") and Good Intentions ("I didn't mean it")

H. Suffering ("I feel bad")
   1. Suffering as manipulation ("If you don't do what I want, I'll die and then you'll be sorry")
   2. Suffering as justification ("I have a right to my own way. Look how much I suffer when I don't get it")
   3. Suffering as self-glorification ("The amount of my suffering proves my nobility")

I. Sideshows ("I can't take care of anything else until I have slain my dragon")

J. Rationalization ("I really didn't fail")

Some Reminders

The practitioner must keep clearly in mind as he works with clients the purpose of emotions. As we know, the Adlerian viewpoint is that emotions are goal directed. That is to say, feelings are largely the by-products of our goals, which are reflected in the way we perceive, evaluate, and regard various situations. As Dreikurs (1967) noted, we need our emotions because they provide the steam and fuel for our actions. Thus, our feelings are in the service of our thoughts. This functional relationship puts responsibility on the individual for his emotions; he cannot accurately say that he lost control of them, was a prisoner of them, or the like.

Another barrier to effective understanding is the imagined distinction between "intellectual" and "emotional" insight. As Mosak (1979) asserted, this dualism can be an avoidance maneuver created by the client. Such antagonistic forces (e.g., "I know it in my head, but can't accept it emotionally") can be creations by the client in order to acceptably delay action. Thus, at a dimly conscious level, he is victimized—in his private logic—by conflicting forces that absolve him of present responsibility for taking a position on the issue at hand. Mosak (1979) suggests an exercise, referred to as the "push button" technique, for teaching a client self-responsibility for his emotions. By closing his eyes and imagining a pleasant incident, then an unpleasant incident, and then repeating the first pleasant incident, the client realizes that he can create whatever feeling he chooses simply by deciding what he will think.

In regard to the broad area of symptoms, the Adlerian approach takes the position that the main significance of the symptom lies in its service to the individual. Just as symptoms serve purposes for the person biologically, they can also serve purposes for him psychologically. According to Shulman (1973), symptoms can serve as safeguards for self-esteem or as excuses. These symptoms are viewed as being in accord with the individual's lifestyle. The use of various methods for struggling with the symptoms in order to maintain face is an example of individual lifestyle creativity. Specific examples will be discussed further in subsequent chapters.

In addition to the creative use of symptoms, individuals can employ lifestyle creativity in gamesmanship maneuvers with the counselor. Adler (1964) would usually use a countertactic, such as a paradoxical bind, a maneuver to avoid the intended power struggle, or a shrewd cultivation of the client's sense of social interest.

Lifestyle information can sometimes broaden the counselor's understanding of how a client might either react to or use a mental, emotional, or physical disability (Ansbacher & Ansbacher, 1956). An example is a client whose lifestyle is such that feelings of being significant as a person exist only when recognition is gained for being number one. Perhaps this person may be especially determined not to let a newly acquired disability stand in the way. Or, on the nonproductive side, the individual may even try to make a special mark by being the number one unmanageable client. The counselor may want to consider how a client may be using a disability. For example, a client who has a congenital disability and who was the only boy among seven sisters may well have developed many secondary gains from his disability and hopes to continue using it in this manner.

Sometimes, clients pursue what may be termed "elusive" goals. Gray-area goals such as this may be ones that are too broad, too lofty, too unclear, or incompatible with another important goal or ephemeral by nature. These elusive goals have been distilled into the three U's: Unfocused, Unrealistic, and Uncoordinated (Rule, 1982b). Sometimes, as Woolfolk and Richardson (1978) observed, when an individual is pursuing incompatible (seemingly uncoordinated) goals, especially if one of the goals is distinctly selfish or socially unacceptable, the person may experience "troublesome" emotions at a dimly conscious level. The purpose of these "troublesome" interfering emotions may be to enable the person to view himself as having altogether good intentions that were interfered with by the unwanted emotions, rather than to admit that these emotions are in the service of selfish or less-than-noble goals.

Finally, from a broader perspective, we might add that respect should be given to the client's short-term and long-term dreams. However, as Kir-Stimon suggested (1977), let the practitioner not confuse dreams and illusions with hallucination. Dreams are useful, perhaps at times necessary, as a means for achieving satisfaction, and, after all, as Trieschmann (1974) succinctly concluded, "The key to coping with one's disability is to receive enough satisfactions and rewards to make life worthwhile" (p. 558).

SUMMARY

The overall counseling process for adjustment to disability was discussed within a framework of four phases: Relationship, Lifestyle Investigation, Lifestyle Interpretation, and Reorientation. This process is based on a facilitative, cooperative relationship and emphasizes client self-awareness and self-responsibility. Contributions of selected other counseling approaches and a group approach were overviewed. In addition, attention was given to specific considerations for working with the disabled.

REFERENCES

Adler, A. *Problems of neurosis: A book of case histories.* New York: Harper & Row, 1964.

Ansbacher, H. L., & Ansbacher, R. R. (Eds.), *The individual psychology of Alfred Adler.* New York: Basic Books, 1956.

Bandler, R., & Grinder, J. *Patterns of the hypnotic techniques of Milton H. Erickson, M.D.* (Vol. 1). Cupertino, Calif.: Meta Publications, 1975.

Bandler, R., & Grinder, J. *Frogs into princes.* Mohab, Utah: Real People Press, 1979.

Berne, E. *Transactional analysis.* New York: Grove Press, 1961.

Carkhuff, R. *The art of helping IV.* Amherst, Mass.: Human Resource Development Press, 1980.

Dilts, R., Grinder, J., Bandler, R., Bandler, L., & Delozier, J. *Neuro-linguistic programming: The study of the structure of the subjective experience* (Vol. 1). Cupertino, Calif.: Meta Publications, 1980.

Dinkmeyer, D. Use of the encouragement process in Adlerian counseling. Personnel and Guidance Journal, 1972, 51(3), 177–181.

Dinkmeyer, D., Pew, W., & Dinkmeyer, D., Jr. *Adlerian counseling and psychotherapy.* Monterey, Calif.: Brooks/Cole, 1979.

Dreikurs, R. *Fundamentals of Adlerian psychology.* Chicago: Alfred Adler Institute, 1953.

Dreikurs, R. *Psychodynamics, psychotherapy, and counseling.* Chicago: Alfred Adler Institute, 1967.

Dyer, W. W., & Vriend, J. *Counseling techniques that work.* Washington, D.C.: American Personnel and Guidance Association, 1975.

Eisenberg, M. *Psychological aspects of physical disability: A guide for the health care worker.* New York: National League of Nursing, 1977.

Ellis, A. *Reason and emotion in psychotherapy.* New York: Lyle Stuart, 1962.

Ellis, A. *Humanistic psychotherapy.* New York: McGraw-Hill, 1973.

Glasser, W. *Reality therapy.* New York: Harper & Row, 1965.

Gordon, D. *Therapeutic metaphors.* Cupertino, Calif.: Meta Publications, 1978.

Grinder, J., & Bandler, R. *Trance formations.* Mohab, Utah: Real People Press, 1981.

Grinder, J., Delozier, J., & Bandler, R. *Patterns of the hypnotic techniques of Milton H. Erickson, M.D.* (Vol. 2). Cupertino, Calif.: Meta Publications, 1977.
Hosford, R. E., & de Visser, L. *Behavioral approaches to counseling: An introduction.* Washington, D.C.: APGA Press, 1974.
Kir-Stimon, W. Counseling with the severely handicapped: Encounter and commitment. In R. Marinelli & A. Dell Ono (Eds.), *The psychological and social impact of physical disability.* New York: Springer, 1977.
Lazarus, A., & Fay, A. *I can if 1 want to.* New York: Morrow, 1975.
Mosak, H. H. The psychological attitude in rehabilitation. American Archives of Rehabilitation Therapy, 1954, 2, 9–10.
Mosak, H. H. *On purpose.* Chicago: Alfred Adler Institute, 1977.
Mosak, H. H. Adlerian psychotherapy. In R. Corsini (Ed.), *Current psychotherapies* (2nd ed.). Itasca, Ill.: Peacock, 1979.
O'Connell, W. Adlerian aphorisms. The Individual Psychologist, 1976, 13, 18–28.
Pancer, K. The use of parables and fables in Adlerian psychotherapy. The Individual Psychologist, 1978, 15, 19–29.
Passons, W. *Gestalt approaches in counseling.* New York: Holt, Rinehart & Winston, 1975.
Perls, F. *Gestalt therapy verbatim.* Lafayette, Calif.: Real People Press, 1969.
Perls, F., Hefferline, R., & Goodman, P. *Gestalt therapy.* New York: Julian Press, 1951.
Roessler, R., & Bolton, B. *Psychosocial adjustment to disability.* Baltimore: University Park Press, 1978.
Rosen, S. (Ed.). *My voice will go with you: The teaching tales of Milton H. Erickson.* New York: Norton, 1982.
Rule, W. Corrective reactions to client negativism using a combined facilitative and Adlerian-based approach. Corrective and Social Psychiatry and Journal of Behavior Technology Methods and Therapy, 1977a, 23, 7–10.
Rule, W. Increasing self-modeled humor. Rational Living, 1977b, 12, 7–9.
Rule, W. Increased internal-control using humor with lifestyle awareness. The Individual Psychologist, 1979, 16, 16–26.
Rule, W. What next after self—awareness?: A rational apothecary. Rational Living, 1980, 15, 24–25.
Rule, W. Lifestyle interpretation using imagination of the ideal social self. Individual Psychology: The Journal of Adlerian Theory, Research and Practice, 1982a, 38(4), 339–342.
Rule, W. Pursuing the horizon: Striving for elusive goals. Personnel and Guidance Journal, 1982b, 61(4), 195–197.
Rule, W. Family therapy and the pie metaphor. Journal of Marital and Family Therapy, 1983, 9(1), 101–103.
Rychlak, J. F. Introduction to personality: A theory—construction approach. Boston: Houghton Mifflin, 1973.
Schafer, W. *Stress, distress and growth.* Davis, Calif.: International Dialogue Press, 1978.
Selye, H. *Stress without distress.* New York: Signet, 1974.
Shelton, J. L., & Ackerman, J. M. *Homework in counseling and psychotherapy.* Springfield, Ill.: Charles C Thomas, 1974.
Shontz, F. C. *The psychological aspects of physical illness and disability.* New York: Macmillan, 1975.
Shulman, B. H. Confrontation techniques. Journal of Individual Psychology, 1972, 28, 177–183.
Shulman, B. H. *Contributions to individual psychology.* Chicago: Alfred Adler Institute, 1973.
Shulman, B. H. Encouraging the pessimist: A confronting technique. The Individual Psychologist, 1977, 14, 7–9.
Sullivan, H. S. *Conceptions of modern psychiatry.* New York: Norton, 1940.

Sweeney, T. H. *Adlerian counseling*. Boston: Houghton Mifflin, 1975.
Trieschmann, R. Coping and disability: A sliding scale of goals. Archives of Physical Medicine and Rehabilitation, 1974, 55, 556–560.
Walen, S. R., DiGiuseppe, R., & Wessler, R. L. *A practitioner's guide to rational-emotive therapy*. New York: Oxford University Press, 1980.
Woolfolk, R., & Richardson, F. *Stress, sanity and survival*. New York: Sovereign, 1978.

Practice

I

Dealing with Resistance

3

LIFESTYLE SELF-AWARENESS AND THE PRACTITIONER: UNDERSTANDING AND REFRAMING RESISTANCE USING ANGELS AND DEVILS AS METAPHOR

Warren R. Rule

Abstract

Counseling practitioners often face client resistance, hesitating attitudes, or impasses that can be difficult to understand and to work through. The author discusses the theoretical and practical implications of an aphorism from the poet Rilke. This metaphor uses 'angels' and 'devils' to crystallize the dilemma of change from the client's perspective and relates to many significant Adlerian concepts in addition to the generic helping process.

Adlerian practitioners and others in the helping fields are committed to facilitating positive results in the lives of their clients. Regardless of

This chapter, "Lifestyle Self-Awareness and the Practitioner: Understanding and Reframing Resistance Using Angels and Devils as Metaphor," from Warren R. Rule, *The Journal of Individual Psychology* 56:2, pp. 184–91.

the individual practitioner's theoretical orientation, his or her therapeutic emphasis is most likely to be directed toward some overt or covert change on the client's part. This change will presumably lead to the resolution of the expressed problem and to an increase in the feeling of general mental health. Regrettably, the facilitative process does not always proceed smoothly nor does it always achieve this ideal outcome.

Obstacles and puzzles, both identified and incomprehensible, seem to intrude during the unfolding of the therapeutic process. A frequently targeted phenomenon by therapists and counselors is labeled as "client resistance." This phenomenon is often blamed for painfully slow progress in therapy as well as for its failure. However, in their eagerness to be a positive influence in clients' lives, helpers may lose sight of the importance for clients to maintain an internal psychodynamic balance when confronted with the threat of change. This dynamic frequently contributes to the occurrence of "resistance," that is, "a discrepancy between the goals of the therapist and those of the patient" (Dreikurs, 1967, p. 65). When resistance occurs, in terms of conscious or nonconscious therapeutic movement, the therapist's goal to lead the client somewhere psychologically is not compatible with the client's goal of maintaining or enhancing the self.

In the early 1900s, German poet and author Rainer Marie Rilke expressed a powerful metaphor regarding the enigma that pervades the conflict between confronting change and maintaining stability. In deciding not to begin psychoanalysis, he essentially concluded that: *If my devils are to leave me, I am afraid my angels will take flight as well* (Freedman, 1996; Hull, 1947). This metaphor crystallizes powerful theoretical concepts for many major, contemporary psychotherapeutic approaches in general and especially for major concepts of Individual Psychology. This aphorism, which represents many symbiotic intrapsychic relationships, can be used by Adlerian psychotherapists to develop their understanding of client resistance to change as well as to facilitate their clients' therapeutic processes.

A BROAD THEORETICAL BASE

From a broad perspective that cuts across theoretical models of psychotherapy, Ford and Urban (1998), in their recent comparative analysis, devoted considerable discussion to unifying themes in stability-maintaining and change-producing processes. They contended that, through evolution, humans have developed stability-maintaining processes that operate on a continual basis to maintain personal unity as a coping function against life's differing challenges. They further stated that "processes that protect existing states are not pathological; they are both natural and essential. However, they protect functional and dysfunctional patterns alike" (p. 161). These patterns are purposive, and indeed they are performing some function regardless of how they are judged by an outside observer. Even conflicting motivational patterns, with accompanying unwanted suffering, continue because these are the best resolution that the individual's psyche has been able to devise. Efforts by another "to alter those patterns will activate stability-maintaining processes that will defend them against change" (p. 166).

ADLERIAN APPLICATIONS

Generally and expressed in terms of the above concepts, the tasks of most therapists are (1) to respect the function and power of the stability-maintaining processes of the client and (2) to facilitate some sort of change that satisfies, circumvents, or overcomes those stability-maintaining processes. In attempting to accomplish these tasks, the broad field of counseling and psychotherapy could profit from the traditional Adlerian interest in metaphoric one-liners that insightfully express complex psychological phenomena. Adler himself used short metaphors for reframing client problems and self-responsibility. Selected brief metaphors, such as the example by Rilke, avoid the negative associations of extended psychobabble. Additionally, metaphors can be enticing yet mysterious and vague enough that clients can, upon hearing them, project their own personal meanings into their comprehension in a manner that benefits the facilitative process.

The therapeutic awareness of Rilke's potent metaphor can serve various functions, depending on the unique overriding purpose of the clinician. Sometimes it may be used by the therapist conceptually to increase his or her own understanding or as a framework to intervene strategically in other ways with the client. Frequently the metaphor itself may be introduced as a therapeutic intervention or as a prelude to a planned stage in the facilitation process. Discussed below are applications of Rilke's metaphor to some major and fundamental concepts of Individual Psychology.

Lifestyle and the Holistic Cognitive Map

Forgus and Shulman (1979) concluded that "all human motives are cognitively directed because they are filtered or mediated through the perceptual system, which directs both the structure and dynamics of personality" (p. 347). They further noted that the striving for cognitive consistency (i.e., avoiding cognitive dissonance) is the basis for resistance to change. The Adlerian concept of lifestyle, the cognitive blueprint, seeks its own confirmation, making it "difficult for us to change our points of view; our subjective bias directs how we search for reality" (p. 348). Further complicating this dilemma is that when conflict arises, one choice may preclude another: "It is not so much that we fear to eat the cake as that we want to have it and eat it too" (p. 111).

In this universal human dilemma, therefore, the unwanted devils are whatever the person consciously claims to want to get rid of within his or her perceptual field at the moment. Yet, in wishing this, the individual intuits at a deeper level of awareness that the protective angels (i.e., some of the components that contribute to the holistic nature of the self-system) would be forced to leave as well, thereby destroying the entire organizational system.

Lifestyle and the Usefulness of Symptoms

Adlerian practitioners are ever mindful of a symptom's nonconscious function to safeguard the client's self-esteem. When the "devil," discouraging behavior, is expressed by the client in the form of a symptom, the Adlerian clinician usually would view the expression as a functional attempt by the client to cope with some form of threat to his or her self-esteem. In other words, the encouraging component of the symptom is that the "angel" is the stability, predictability, and comfort that the symptom allows the client to experience while attempting to face and deal with the necessary growth required during the therapeutic process. Furthermore, Kopp and Kivel (1990) described the creativity of this relationship:

> While the client suffers from the symptom, he or she has a nonconscious investment in maintaining the symptom for the protection it affords the self-esteem and lifestyle. This threat to the self-esteem generates a fear of change. Thus, the interest in maintaining the symptoms and the lifestyle is a basic characteristic of resistance in therapy. (p. 140)

Within this conceptual framework, the protective angel is the nonconscious investment in maintaining the presence of the symptomatic devil. Because, as Adler (as cited in Ansbacher & Ansbacher, 1956) contended, a person must struggle against a symptom in order to maintain it, the very useful and quite historical struggle continues between the angels and the devils.

Lifestyle and Noble Striving

Not only is a well-intentioned angel invested, as discussed above, in maintaining the struggle with the symptom, but an angel is protectively committed to operating especially at a nonconscious level as well. Because the symptom is experienced as very unpleasant, the client regards it as a devil that must be eliminated, yet the angelic and protective process of the psyche prevents the full awareness of the broader lifestyle goal. If the angel were to take flight, the client would, as Adlerian practitioners know, be forced to look at the purpose of the symptom from the perspective of conscious common sense. At this point the client is thereby confronted with his or her own responsibility and vanity issues.

By maintaining the conflict, that is, allowing the devil-and-angel conflict to continue, the client can have the best of both worlds. In doing so, the client can also pat himself or herself on the back as a heroic angel for struggling to expel the nasty devil of a problem. If the problem really left, an opportunity to view oneself as noble would leave as well. Interpersonal gains are virtually always involved in these conflicts. Examples of the usefulness to the lifestyle of creating and maintaining these struggles can be found in Mosak (1977), Mosak and Maniacci (1998), and Shulman and Mosak (1967).

Lifestyle and the Nature of Goals

The setting and pursuit of goals themselves, regardless of whether conscious or nonconscious, have an elusive devil-and-angel dilemma inherent in their natures. As Beecher and Beecher (1966) observed:

> Every goal we set restricts us. It limits, selects, and determines the means it uses to accomplish its own ends. Any goal sets its own built-in price. What it excludes may be worth more that what it achieves. (p. 217)

The price paid for choosing to aim for a particular goal is that other possibilities are excluded. Choices are excluded by attempting to attain a selected fixed consequence of any sort. Yet, if the devil of having to be goal-directed—and thereby missing all the rest of life's bounties—were to be banished, then the protective angel of the goal-directed lifestyle pattern would take flight as well. This loss would deprive the individual of directionality in seeking a place of unique, secure significance among others. Here the metaphor enables the therapist to illustrate to the client the advantages and disadvantages of wearing blinders to get through the heavy traffic of life.

Lifestyle and Goal-Directed Movement

A chosen and valued lifestyle goal not only has a price attached because of its being an exclusory, generic goal, but it also virtually always has a severe price that is paid because of the "shadow" side of whatever goal that is chosen. In the previous section, the disadvantage pertained to what was not selected because of its being outside of the goal. Here the downside is inherent within the breadth of usefulness of the goal itself. Although the lifestyle functions as a unified whole, the implementation of the lifestyle in differing environmental contexts can yield contrasting degrees of satisfaction or worthwhile interpersonal benefits. This "duality" of usefulness is an evaluation of outcome rather than a function of individual process of movement. Thus, the individual lifestyle has an inherent duality of use for most people, and probably the best a person can hope for is to minimize—through awareness—the shadow-like or negative side. The lifestyle that works to a person's advantage in one context also works to his or her disadvantage in another context. The same lifestyle that provides the individual's greatest strengths also provides the greatest weaknesses. The chosen lifestyle that is responsible for the person's best successes is also responsible for the person's worst failures (Rule, 1982, 1984). This flip-side of a lifestyle goal often operates at a more vague level of awareness than the side that pursues the desired outcomes.

The usefulness of the goal tends to be a function of context and vanity. It is almost as if the real goal purposely does not have an identifiable label in the individual psyche: When the pursuit of it brings what is desired, the individual is proud of it and gives it positive identification. When it does not work out so well, the person labels it as a negative characteristic (or makes an excuse or does not become completely aware of it at all) and wishes to be rid of it. However, the ambiguity of the major lifestyle goal is useful: Ambiguity is a protective angel because, if one allowed the entire goal "to leave," the truly advantageous uses of the goal would "take flight" as well. Thus, it is quite useful for this goal to remain not understood or nonconscious (Dreikurs, 1967).

All behavior and goals are useful within the schema of an individual's lifestyle perceptions, including those implemented within a socially constructive context. This positive choice results from the implementation of the advantageous side of the lifestyle goals. This usage is often more self-actualizing, and it tends to be more deeply satisfying to the person in the long run. However, a cruel irony exists when the individual is confronted with a crisis situation. The person uses disadvantageously (in terms of outcome) the lifestyle goal with increasing intensity and frequency in a desperate attempt to cope. This effort is often precisely the same disadvantageous use of the lifestyle goal that brought on the crisis situation to begin with. Sadly, the person nonconsciously clings tenaciously to the self-defeating patterns (i.e., the devils) to keep the good uses of the same patterns (i.e., the angels) from taking flight as well. Thus, what appears as a false dichotomy to the external observer is, from the subjective perspective of the individual, quite consistent and holistic.

Lifestyles and Tasks of Life

This patterned, goal-directed movement is used unilaterally by the individual to address the life tasks: the occupational task, the social task, and the sexual task (Adler, 1931/1998). A patterned, goal-directed movement of any sort is likely to bring differing results in different contexts. Expressed another way, the implementation of a lifestyle goal, with its inherent disadvantageous blind-side, cannot be expected to yield equally satisfying results in addressing the problems of life. In therapy, the devil-angel metaphor can be used to illustrate the trade-offs of using a given lifestyle to solve differing life tasks. Consequently, discussion of this dilemma with the client can highlight the importance of developing newer and more flexible approaches to dealing with life's challenges.

The unenlightened individual seems to sense, at a vague level of appreciation, that keeping this broad lifestyle goal, including its devilish downside, is the best chance of creating a place of secure significance at least somewhere. So, if one were to focus on its disadvantageous use in some of the life tasks, the awareness might cause the whole goal "to take flight." The client is unlikely to find it useful to become consciously aware of the patterned down-side of his or her chosen movement until a trusting, respectful relationship is established. This occurrence enables the client to explore and accept the "whole" self.

CONCLUDING REMARKS

In making the decision to discuss Rilke's metaphor as a part of the therapeutic process, the psychotherapist should exercise discretion. For instance, clients adhering to very fundamental religious beliefs may find the metaphor to be sacreligious. Furthermore, clients taking exceptionally little responsibility for themselves might be inclined to use the metaphor to feel even more helpless because of what they would interpret as the convergence of these "external forces." At any rate, the clinician would be well served, when explaining the relevance of this metaphor to a client, to emphasize that "These are devils and angels that you have created." Much can be gained by a mutual discussion and exploration by the therapist and client regarding the symbiotic roles of the devils and angels within the issue at hand. The therapist should avoid, however, assigning morally judgmental identities to particular behaviors. Because the value of a value is evaluated by another value, the facilitative process is enhanced when the therapist guides the client in identifying his or her bottom line values.

This metaphorical intervention may be incorporated into or supplemented by related therapeutic techniques. Kopp and Kivel (1990) offered strategies for circumventing client resistance and impasses, and Kopp (1995) discussed the potency of using client-generated metaphors as a therapeutic strategy. Traditional Gestalt approaches (e.g., Passons, 1975; Perls, 1969; Polster & Polster, 1973) offer holistic therapeutic procedures for resolving conflicts between two "opposing" poles, especially those based on introjection. Mosak and Maniacci (1998) described many interventions and tactics that also relate to these issues. Finally and not insignificantly, the therapist may want to ponder the implications of Rilke's metaphor for his or her own practice of counseling and psychotherapy.

REFERENCES

Adler, A. (1998). *What life should mean to you.* (C. Brett, Trans.). Center City, MN: Hazelden. (Original work published 1931.)

Ansbacher, H. L., & Ansbacher, R. R. (Eds.). (1956). *The Individual Psychology of Alfred Adler.* New York: Basic Books.

Beecher, W., & Beecher, M. (1966). *Beyond success and failure.* Richardson, TX: Beecher Foundation.

Dreikurs, R. (1967). *Psychodynamics, psychotherapy, and counseling.* Chicago: Alfred Adler Institute.

Ford, D. H., & Urban, H. B. (1998). *Contemporary models of psychotherapy: A comparative analysis* (2nd ed.). New York: Wiley.

Forgus, R., & Shulman, B. (1979). *Personality: A cognitive view.* Englewood Cliffs, NJ: Prentice-Hall.

Freedman, R. (1996). Life of a poet: Rainer *Marie Rilke. New York: Farrar, Straus, & Giroux.*

Hull, R. F. (1947). *Selected letters of* Rainer *Marie Rilke.* New York: Brunner/Mazel.

Kopp, R. R. (1995). *Metaphor therapy.* New York: Brunner/Mazel.

Kopp, R. R., & Kivel, C. (1990). Traps and escapes: An Adlerian approach to understanding resistance and resolving impasses in psychotherapy. *Individual Psychology: The Journal of Adlerian Theory, Research, & Practice, 46,* 137–145.

Mosak, H. H. (1977). *On purpose.* Chicago: Alfred Adler Institute.

Mosak, H. H., & Maniacci, M. P. (1998). *Tactics in counseling and psychotherapy.* Itasca, IL: F. E. Peacock.
Passons, W. R. (1975). *Gestalt approaches in counseling.* New York: Holt, Rinehart & Winston.
Perls, F. (1969). *Gestalt therapy verbatim.* Moab, UT: Real People Press.
Polster, E., & Polster, M. (1973). *Gestalt therapy integrated: Contours of theory and practice.* New York: Brunner/Mazel.
Rule, W. (1982). Lifestyle interpretation using imagination of the ideal social self. *Individual Psychology: The Journal of Adlerian Theory, Research and Practice, 38,* 338–342.
Rule, W. (Ed.) (1984). *Lifestyle counseling for adjustment to disability.* Rockville, MD: Aspen Systems.
Shulman, B. H., & Mosak, H. H. (1967). Various purposes of symptoms. *Journal of Individual Psychology, 23,* 79–87.

4

CORRECTIVE REACTIONS TO CLIENT NEGATIVISM USING A COMBINED FACILITATIVE AND ADLERIAN-BASED APPROACH

Warren R. Rule

In most correctional settings—both institutional and in the field—the practitioner is often at a loss in dealing productively with negativism, hostility, resentment, aggression, etc. A combined approach utilizing psychiatrist Alfred Adler's life style concept and a facilitative-response framework can possibly enhance communication in the many phases of correctional rehabilitation.

One of Alfred Adler's main contributions to psychiatry was a concept termed "Life Style." Although this term has been borrowed from Adler and has various contemporary uses, the original concept may be defined as the "superordinate organizational pattern which directs

This chapter, "Corrective Reactions to Client Negativism Using a Combined Facilitative and Adlerian-Based Approach," from Warren R. Rule, *Corrective and Social Psychiatry and Journal of Behavior Technology Methods and Therapy*, 23:1, pp. 7–10.

behavior" (Shulman, 1973, p. 43). This "law of movement" (Ansbacher & Ansbacher, 1956, p. 195) is characterized by an overriding goal, which is supplemented by subgoals; in addition, this holistic network of dimly conscious goals is developed by the individual before age six in an effort to develop guiding principles for coping with life. The child does this while gathering information from a host of variables (e.g., sibling interaction and competition, parental expectations and modeling, etc.) in the attempt to move from a position of feeling inferior, in the sense of not being "enough," to a position of coping with a feeling of significance and belonging. In this effort, the individual learns behaviors that are goal-directed, i.e., implemented for a purpose, and in keeping with the subjectively determined life style.

Relying on the selectivity of memory, Adlerian practitioners question the client about the mildly determining influences of early childhood. Dreikurs and colleagues (1967) developed a questionnaire which focuses on the life style variables of self description, family constellation characteristics, parental influences, and early recollections. After this effort to pin down the client's subjective impressions of early years. the therapist attempts to distill from the information an overriding theme which, Adlerians believe, is reflected (based on the selectivity of memory) in the individual's present outlook on life. This theme, around which accompanying notions and goals are organized, may be helpful to the client's self-understanding and to the therapist in facilitating the psychotherapeutic process.

Adler believed, as stated previously, that all behavior is goal-directed and, consequently, may be viewed in terms of its usefulness to the individual in the context of one's life style. This approach can be applied to specific and global behaviors and—particularly important for the purpose of this discussion—negativism. Negativism is broadly defined here as verbal and non-verbal expressions which convey the message that self, others, or life are at fault because one's expectations are not met. Negativism can be expressed in various disguises, depending upon the hidden intended impact; it can appear sometimes as hostility, disappointment, resentment, aggression, discouragement, frustration, inadequacy, etc.

In the following paragraphs, three examples will be discussed in order to illustrate how an awareness of even an extremely abbreviated version of the life style could be beneficial in better understanding a client's internal logic and, consequently, how the expression of negativism is useful to the individual.

Client #1: A male who has a brother five years older, a sister three years older, and a brother two years younger. John describes himself as not having been very close to any sibling before age six and viewed the parents as spoiling all the siblings except him. His two earliest memories:

1. I remember the time our neighbor said to me and my friends that he would give 25 cents to whomever knew the name of the capitol of our state. I said the right answer the same time George did. Mr. Jones acted like he didn't even hear me and gave the 25 cents to George. Felt?—Very mad at this unfair treatment.
2. One day I didn't want to go to school and threatened to run away. Parents said you're going to go whether you want to or not. Felt?—Frustrated—They made me do something I didn't want to.

It can be seen in the above life style information that the client had the least favorable birth order position in terms of unearned specialness. John competed with (in the sense of striving to find a place of unique significance) all his siblings, each of whom had a position of built-in specialness: The "first-born," "the girl," and "the baby." The parents—at least in his view—spoiled the others more than him. Both early recollections supplement this outlook of "unfairness-collecting" and expecting others to undermine him. Adlerians believe that a general unifying theme such as this, based on the selectivity of memory, is probably reflected in this client's present outlook as he moves through life.

Client #2: A female, who is the youngest of three, has two older brothers. Sally describes both brothers as having liked and protected her before age six. She was "the apple of her father's eye," and mother was viewed as a good mother "who always did little things for us." Her two earliest memories:

1. I recall a surprise birthday party when I was three. My family and friends were all there. I had a wonderful time. Felt?—Excited and pleased that they went to so much trouble for me.
2. I remember playing in the yard one time. A big dog came up and barked at me. I sat down and cried until Dad came out and chased it away. The ice cream made me feel a lot better.

Even in the above limited sampling of life style information, a guess about a theme can be made. Sally probably concluded as a child that she was quite an important person: she was the "baby" of the family, "the girl," and apparently received much pampering from parents and brothers. The early recollections confirm and expand this line of thinking in that others go to extra lengths to insure her happiness and protect her. Accordingly, the client presently may tend to regard herself at a dimly conscious level of awareness as somewhat of a "crown princess" who places much responsibility on others for her happiness and well-being.

Client #3: An only child, who remembers being a follower and well-liked by playmates. George's father left the home shortly after his birth, and his mother was described as always praising what he did and encouraging him to be a good boy. Two aunts, who also lived in the home, were remembered as being kind and interested in him and what he did. His first two early recollections:

1. My cousin from out of town was visiting us. When we were playing, he got mad and hit me. At the dinner table I told his mother that he hit me and to show him that I forgave him I gave him one of my cookies. Felt?—Proud—She liked what I said.
2. In the first grade, I got an "A" on a spelling test. I had learned all the words by heart the night before. Mom was very happy. Felt?—Happy because she was pleased.

The brief sampling of life style material cited above seems to reflect the importance to George of striving to please and win approval, especially from authority persons. A possible way of putting this style into practice is subtly to use his goodness to elevate himself over others as a means of securing a place of significance.

VARYING THE THERAPEUTIC APPROACH

For each of the three clients discussed above, it cannot be predicted with certainty what specific behaviors the clients will use in later life in accordance with their styles; however, guesses can be made as to some of their guiding goals for interacting with people. An increased awareness of these guiding goals may help the therapist better understand the client and possibly enable the client to reach a better understanding of self; in addition, this awareness could be an aid in working through stumbling blocks as they present themselves in the psychotherapeutic process. For instance, imagine that during therapy, each of these three clients begins expressing negativism, as defined previously, in one form or another. In attempting to explore this with these clients in the conventional manner, the therapist is still not satisfied that he has achieved a workable understanding; this could be due to a host of variables, e.g., continuing client resistance, the client's poor verbal skills in expressing innermost feelings, the client's giving superficial responses, the client's unwillingness to be vulnerable by exploring the issue, etc. It may be at this point that an increased awareness on the therapist's part of some of the subjective guidelines that the clients are using in their life styles can reveal what the expressed negativism is intended to accomplish for them, i.e., what are they wanting that they are not getting.

Client #1, John, who has a tendency to collect unfairnesses and seems sometimes to expect to be victimized, is understandably apt to overreact to the slightest provocations. This tendency may best be handled by the therapist outlining in an honest, firm fashion for the client those areas which are open for discussion and may be changed based on his input and those areas which are pretty much fixed. The therapist may want to develop further this emphasis on the non-productivity of complaining by gently and firmly ignoring complaints in these areas. This firm position could be tempered by a therapist making an increased effort to be responsive to the client's feelings of vulnerability in those areas that are subject to change and negotiation. Whereas for John, in view of his life style, the negativism may have been intended to communicate to the therapist that "You, the system, and life are not going to take advantage of me!" the very same negative behavior expressed by Client #2, Sally, in the context of her tendency to want to be recognized as a "crown princess," may be designed to convey, "Recognize my specialness, therapist, you are not doing enough for me!" Upon guessing this purpose for her negativism and confirming it with the client, the therapist may choose to structure just what the therapeutic role entails and what responsibilities she is to be held accountable for in the psychotherapeutic process. The therapist may also want to arrange homework assignments of gradually increasing difficulty to assist the client in learning how to be more responsible for self.

With Client #3, George, who seems heavily invested in striving to please and in winning approval from important people, the same overt negativism may mean "I'm not getting enough feedback that what I'm doing is OK!" Upon considering this, the therapist could choose to vary the therapeutic approach and encourage the client more often, even for very minor accomplishments. Responsiveness to the confrontation itself is recommended, since it is more risky to express negativism to an authority person for this client than, for example, Client #1, John. Thus, these examples hopefully illustrate how one type of behavior, which is simply "negative behavior" to the casual observer, may have much more individual meaning, when considered from a facilitative Adlerian framework, than meets the eye.

VARYING THE THERAPEUTIC RESPONSES

From more of a here-and-now perspective, a prior knowledge of aspects of the client's life style can be helpful in facilitatively coping with sudden negativism expressed by the client. This understanding might be particularly helpful in suddenly-occurring situations, as well as in those having long-term implications such as discussed above. For example, perhaps the most dramatic and intense expression of negativism in the counseling session is a display of temper. Mosak (1972, p. 240) states that there are only two major reasons for temper. "One reason is to announce to the world, 'I want to have my own way. You better do it or I'm going to intimidate you.'... The other reason is right-eous indignation. 'I'm the custodian of the right, and how dare you do something as wrong as that.'" These global purposes might be kept in mind by the therapist as he attempts to understand just how the client defines and refines either of these general purposes in accordance with one's own life style.

Whereas temper displays are often very striking forms of expressing negativism, other more subtle methods of negative display are used. Regardless of the degree of intensity expressed, the individual is rarely apt to feel sincerely at fault. The client usually cannot recognize the individualized purpose for the negativism; rather, the client is much more likely to subjectively feel driven to behave in a negative manner—the other person or something outside of self is responsible for the fighting (Beecher, 1949). In reacting to the client's demonstration of temper or other displays of negativism, therapist responses which generate meaningful self-exploration on the client's part may well be the most productive, particularly if the exploratory emphasis is on the purpose for one's behavior.

Using a combined facilitative and Adlerian-based framework for focusing on the client's goals, the therapist can respond to the client in terms of where the client is in relation to where he wants or needs to be. Responses of this nature emphasize the relationship between the client's life style goal "deficit" and the immediate goal which underlies the expression of negativism. This method of responding, an Adlerian-based variation of a model for facilitative responding developed by Carkhuff (1973), combines three concepts: (1) the therapist's understanding of the client's life style "deficit"; (2) the therapist's awareness of how the client feels about this deficit; and (3) the therapist's attempting to identify the client's hidden goal which underlies the expression of negativism. The "deficit" theme is stated in terms of how the client's overriding life style goal presently contributes to a feeling of unmet expectations; this is expressed in the context of "you cannot," "you won't," "you are unable," etc. Using this reference point, the counselor is able to venture a guess as to the client's immediate goal; i.e., the intended impact of the negativism—regardless of how cleverly disguised the demand on the environment is. Finally, the response might be rounded out by indicating a respect for the client's feeling about not getting what he believes is needed from the environment.

In regard to responses such as these, two assumptions are in order. First, depending on the situation, the therapist should be reasonably certain that the client is not within his right as a person and client in expecting the environment to be responsive. For example, sometimes the role of the therapist involves doing for the client what the client cannot do for himself and even involves at times manipulating the environment for the client. Second, a facilitative base of communication should be present. This may well include: mutual respect; client agreement as to the therapist's conclusions concerning the client's life style; and client ability to process therapist responses in an exploratory manner. Some examples of Adlerian-based facilitative responses, using the above discussed three components, are given in the following paragraphs.

For a client who uses "control over others" as an overriding life style goal for coping with life, the therapist could respond to unreasonable negativism by saying something like, "Could it be that you're pretty disappointed with yourself because you can't be in control right now and you want to bully me into giving in to you?"

For the client who uses "pleasing" as the major measure of a sense of self-worth and who is struggling to choose a course of action, the counselor might want to respond to sudden negativism by saying something on the order of "I'm wondering if you're upset because you are unable to have a guarantee of approval if you go ahead with this idea and you want me to give you reassurances that it's OK."

For the client whose life style is characterized by displaying inadequacy in order to avoid responsibility, the counselor may choose to disarm the negativism by stating, "I think that you are being very unfair to me. My guess is that you want to make me feel guilty because you aren't getting the special help and treatment that you would like. I can understand, though, how confusing it is to expect something and not get it."

In each of the above examples, the therapist would be expected, in fairness to the client, to follow through on whatever impact this disarmament had, e.g., exploring how the client's life style is contributing in other ways to the problem at hand, discussing how the client feels about it, or considering alternatives which would provide better ways of getting what is desired from the therapist and environment.

REFERENCES

Ansbacher, H. L., & Ansbacher, R. (Eds.). *The Individual Psychology of Alfred Adler.* New York: Basic Books, 1956.

Beecher, W. (1949). Oblique hostility. *Individual Psychology Bulletin, 7*, 51–74.

Carkhuff, R. R. (1973). *The Art of Helping* (2nd ed.). Amherst, MA: Human Resource Development Press.

Dreikurs, R. (1967). *Psychodynamics, Psychotherapy, and Counseling.* Chicago: Alfred Adler Institute.

Mosak, H. H. L. Life style assessment: A demonstration focused on family constellation. *Journal of Individual Psychology, 28*, 232–247.

Shulman, B. H. (1973). *Contributions to Individual Psychology.* Chicago: The Alfred Adler Institute.

II

Mental Health Therapy

5

THE EARLIEST RECOLLECTION: A CLUE TO PRESENT BEHAVIOR

Warren R. Rule

Early recollections have intrigued professionals in the helping fields for nearly a century. In addition to the primarily statistical, taxonomic, and perceptual studies that have been completed, two of the major perspectives on early recollections have been that of Sigmund Freud and Alfred Adler.

Freud viewed early recollections essentially as screen memories which cover up infantile sexual conflicts, murderous fantasies, or trauma. The emphasis was on his theory of repression and the process of free association to discover the latent meaning of early memories.

In contrast to Freud's infantile amnesia point of view, Adler's perspective was that early recollections are much more present-oriented and much more revealing than concealing. Adler viewed early recollections as revealing fundamental aspects of the individual's current view of life. He was convinced that the person selects or chooses to retain at the conscious level those few early experiences that best summarize one's own current attitudinal frame of reference. Thus, the individual uses the memories as reminders of what to expect from self, others, and life.

In helping chemically dependent clients, I have found Adler's perspective on early recollections to be exceptionally helpful as a tool for exploratory discussion of interpersonal role expectations and of possible related future stress situations.

KEY POINTS

Many advocates of the Adlerian perspective believe that the earliest recollection is the most important in understanding the individual because it serves as the first crystallization for the person of what to expect in the present. Experienced practitioners, however, usually gather as many as six of the person's earliest memories, believing that early recollections supplement, rather than contradict, each other.

Listed below are other important considerations in understanding an early recollection:

- When gathering the earliest memory, a simple question will suffice, e.g., "Could you tell me your earliest specific memory? Maybe closing your eyes and visualizing it will help."
- The emphasis in interpretation is on the subjective perspective, especially from a social or interpersonal vantage point.
- Virtually all early memories contain omissions and distortions; therefore, they are regarded primarily as constructions rather than reproductions.
- Emphasis should be given to those early memories (or dreams) that can be visualized as a specific incident (not an event that occurred again and again).
- Seemingly insignificant early recollections are as important as the dramatic ones.
- The memories that occurred before age 7 or 8 are the most useful.
- Feelings about the remembered event should be included.
- Early recollections, as well as all behavior, are useful and goal-directed. Thus when a person's fundamental outlook in life really changes, early recollections are likely to change (in content, emotional tone, remembering new early memories, forgetting former early recollections) to reflect the changed orientation and outlook.

INTERPRETATION

Understandably, the more training and experience the practitioner has, the more that will be obtained from the earliest memory or memories. However, fruitful results can be obtained by those relatively new to the technique if it is handled in a spirit of tentative exploration, respect, and broad interpersonal interpretation.

In one application of this technique to individual or group counseling and the recovery process, exploratory discussion can be directed around two key issues:

1. "How does the role in the earliest recollection relate to the person's preferred interpersonal role today?"

A good possibility exists that the person is currently taking a sensitive position on the interpersonal role in the early recollection. This sensitive position could be expressed as a direct relationship from the early recollection to the present (the remembered role is an ideal to measure up to, i.e., "I should strive to be like...") or as an indirect relationship (the role is to be avoided, overcome, or compensated for, i.e., "I should strive to avoid...").

At any rate, the role in the early recollection can be expected to "touch a tender nerve"—one way or the other—in the person's present interpersonal world.

Examples of these interpersonal roles include: moving away from, toward, or against others; acting upon, observing, being acted upon; leader or follower; superior or inferior; giving or receiving; alone or in a group; center stage or overlooked, competent or inadequate, appealing or unappealing, encouraged or discouraged, and so on. The interpretation emphasis is placed more on the subjective outlook of the person rather than on the actual behavior itself.

2. "In the view of the interpersonal self-message in the earliest recollection, what stress situations in the future would render this person most vulnerable to a chemical relapse?"

The key issue to discuss is the everyday interpersonal circumstances under which the self-programmed role would be painfully thwarted or unfulfilled, possibly resulting in a relapse in the recovery process. It is important for us to keep in mind that virtually all self-roles whether images to strive for or to overcome have blind spots or pitfalls. So, in daily living, when the heat is on, a person is most likely to rely on time-tested patterns of expectations for self, others, and life. Expressed another way, the lifestyle (a term, incidentally, originally coined by

Adler) becomes most apparent when stress is on the individual. Along a related dimension, it comes as no surprise to us that intensive stress often increases the temptation of a person's returning to time-tested patterns of substance abuse.

It is important to note that people are generally not fond of most kinds of negative stress, yet our unique individual reactions to stressors vary and are considerably related to our images of ourselves. Insight into our images of our interpersonal selves can often be obtained from the earliest memory. From these role interpretations, possibilities of interpersonal vulnerability can be explored.

Examples of role vulnerability to stress include: the passive pleaser (the role in early memory) who is severely criticized (the current interpersonal vulnerability); the artful dodger who is trapped; the observer who is finally forced to act; the leader who is dethroned; the charmer who loses some magic; the excitement seeker who is floundering in boredom; the victim who is forced to accept self-responsibility; the hero or the sufferer who loses admirers; the superior one or the perfect one who really screws up; the inferior one who finally succeeds; and so on.

Once awareness is achieved for a person, alternative coping strategies in the potentially stressful situations can be explored, such as contacting a partner, relaxation, imagery, rehearsal, assertion, self-paradoxes, etc.

SOME CAUTIONS

The earliest recollection can yield helpful information, yet the technique can be abused. Whether individually or in a group setting, the emphasis in discussing early recollection interpretations must be non-dogmatic and respectfully explorative (e.g., "A guess I have is…" "Could it be that…" 'You're in the driver's seat in correcting me about this possibility…').

The helper or group member is not to be a diagnostician or an analyst. Rather, he or she should be an encouraging partner who uses a technique that seems to be pulled from the past, but is really grounded in the present, in order to assist with the future. The emphasis is definitely not on whys, drives, personality flaws, skeletons from the past, or lame excuses. Instead, the emphasis is on gaining an awareness of a time-tested self-message that may have a bearing on one's long-term recovery process.

6

LIFE-STYLE INTERPRETATION USING IMAGINATION OF THE IDEAL SOCIAL SELF

Warren R. Rule

Adlerians place much emphasis on the life-style concept as a means of understanding an individual. The life style has been defined as the "superordinate organizational pattern that directs behavior" (Shulman, 1973, p. 43), and the practitioner can draw from as many as eight avenues (Lombardi, 1973) in attempting to learn about an individual life style.

Upon reviewing a client's life-style information and then achieving a workable understanding of a client's life style, the practitioner is subsequently faced with the next big phase, interpretation to the client. Often this interchange takes the general form of a sharing process in which the practitioner tentatively presents his/her impressions in an I-Thou fashion. After this, the client accepts, clarifies, or rejects the practitioner's notions; presumably the client has the final veto power. After substantial agreement is reached, the counseling process moves into a discussion of how the life style is contributing to the presenting problem, key decisions, future stress situations, etc.

The purpose of this paper is to discuss a variation of the somewhat typical interpretation process that usually boils down to, "I, the knowledgeable practitioner, am going to make some guesses about you, the needful client." The intention here is to discuss a slightly different approach, one that enables the confrontation inherent in the usual interpretative approach to be expressed in a more indirect and, perhaps for some clients, in a more thought-provoking manner. Essentially, this approach entails positively reframing the practitioner's conclusions about the client's life style into the individual's imagined ideal self as viewed by important others.

Using this method, the practitioner would have the client vividly imagine himself/herself in a social situation—at work or at a family gathering, for example—preferably involved in whichever task of life the client is having the most difficulty with. Then, the practitioner might say something like, "Bob, several people there are looking at you and thinking: 'Bob is so unique; he certainly goes all out, yet he still accomplishes so many different things—I wonder how he does it all!' Is this a general conclusion that you would like others to form about you?"

THEORETICAL FOUNDATIONS

Adlerian psychology focuses on the individual's private logic within a social context. It also asserts that a person strives to measure up to an imagined ideal self in relation to others and thereby to learn a unique place of respect. Thus, the individual's sense of identity and corresponding self-worth are greatly influenced by one's fictive image of how he/ she should be perceived by important others. Consistent with this Adlerian theoretical perspective, the interpretative approach discussed in this paper encourages the client to create in his/her imagination a meaningful social situation in which others are affirming the individual's ideal self. Consequently, the client imagines his/her life style striving in a less general and more reality-based context than would occur if the person were presented with an abstract concept. The underlying communication emphasis itself is somewhat different in this variation of the interpretation process. Instead of the standard practitioner-to-client delivery, the responsibility for the delivery of the interpretation is now shared between the practitioner and imagined important others. By experiencing the interpretation in this context, the client is less apt to view the practitioner in a forthrightly confrontational manner. As a result, this indirect presentation might permit more genuine self-exploration by those clients who, for whatever purposes, tend to overreact or struggle against the practitioner's direct interpretations.

LIFE-STYLE EXAMPLES

In using this approach, the practitioner should limit the words that the client's important others are "thinking" to one succinct sentence. This sentence, whether a central life-style theme or a variation, should express the self-servingness of the life-style dimension in a positive, socially acceptable manner. This is understandably so because in reality (and for the purpose of this interpretative approach) individuals usually want to be viewed by important others in appealing—rather than pathological—terms.

Listed below are examples of illustrative life-style themes that could be expressed within the framework of this approach. These examples were adapted for this paper from life styles (expressed in brackets) taken from a typology developed by Mosak (1971), who cautioned that predictions about which behavior will correspond with a given life style must be made in terms of probabilities rather than certainties. Additionally, Mosak (1979) emphasized that the uniqueness of the individual is violated by typologies, which should be viewed as strictly didactic contributions. Also noteworthy is that each of these themes could be expressed in many different ways while still maintaining a positive, socially acceptable flavor. As discussed earlier in this paper, the practitioner would make introductory remarks regarding the client's imagined social setting and encourage the client (e.g., Bob) to imagine vividly the important others who are looking at him and thinking:

Bob is so unique; he

- really has a way of handling people and coming up with whatever he's after! ["getter"]
- certainly goes all out, yet he still accomplishes so many different things—I wonder how he does it all! ["driver"]
- sure is able to stay on top of things in his life! ["controller"]
- is exactly on the mark—I can't remember the last time he was off base on something! ["needs to be right"]
- really is a cut above the ordinary and does everything so well! ["needs to be superior"]

- sure has the remarkable desire to make everybody happy! ["pleaser"]
- truly has the understanding and integrity of a saint! ["needs to be good" and/or "morally superior"]
- sure is able to give 'em hell! ["opposes everything"]
- certainly has the worst luck! What black cloud is going to find him next? ["victim"]
- really amazes me in how he's able to shoulder such burdens! ["martyr"]
- is so sweet—I just love being around him! ["baby" and/or "charmer"]
- sure does know his limits and isn't too proud to ask for help! ["inadequate person"]
- is really sharp and has a way of cutting right through to the heart of things! ["avoids feelings"and/or "needs to be intellectually superior"]
- certainly lives his life to the fullest—never a dull moment! ["excitement seeker"]

IMPLEMENTING THE TECHNIQUE

After introducing this possible dimension of the ideal social self to the client, the practitioner may want to add something like, "Is this the main way you'd like important people in your life to see you?" or "Is this a conclusion that you'd like others to form about you?" Possibly, the occurrence or absence of a "recognition reflex" would reflect the accuracy of the interpretation of the life-style theme. Also a question that can be very helpful is "What would you change about this picture of you to make it more accurate?"

As Mosak (1968, 1979) has observed, themes other than the central theme exist for each individual. Accordingly, this one-sentence format could be used to express a central as well as a qualifying, even paradoxical, theme. (For example, "Martha is so unique, she is really able to be totally independent whenever she wants yet have others give her help and tender loving care on demand.")

Some clients, upon having dimensions of their ideal social selves successfully affirmed, may need to be reminded especially that life-style awareness involves choice. That is to say, the acceptance by the client of the results of this method (or any method) of life-style interpretation does not mean the person is locked into this fictive ideal and should necessarily continue always to use it as a guiding light. The advantages and disadvantages of using this acknowledged social ideal of self should be discussed in relation to other important factors, such as the presenting problem, one's short-term and long-term goals, constructive or non-constructive behavior, etc.

Sometimes the practitioner may need to clarify specific points related to unique life styles. He/she may want to point out the difference between having the personal ability to accomplish something—to please others, for example—and choosing to strive for it as an overriding goal. Also, perhaps the social context of the ideal self would need to be discussed—for example, the degree of applicability of the term others (significant others, or most others, or all others, etc.). The practitioner should be mindful of how a client's life style influences the manner in which the client processes and responds to interpretation of the life style; a person who is heavily invested in pleasing others may react to the assessment process considerably differently than one who values intellectual superiority or one who struggles against others.

A number of variations of this approach may be explored. Revealing information can result from discussing with the client what is the most appealing compliment he/she likes to hear. Perhaps a ranking or rating system involving examples similar to those discussed above could yield helpful information from either a practitioner or a research perspective. Other variations might be developed by using the imagination of the ideal social self within the context of other techniques: personality priority assessment (Pew, 1976; Ward, 1979); poetry therapy (Sanchez, 1976); parables and fables (Pancer, 1978); self-modeled humor through exaggerated masquerades (Rule, 1979) and audio recordings (Rule, 1977); tombstone inscriptions (Shulman, 1973); and so on.

In summary, this paper discussed a technique that is based on the individual's private logic within a social context. The technique involves reframing the practitioner's interpretations in a positive and socially acceptable manner and within the imaginary context of the client's ideal self as viewed by important others. This interpretative focus can be varied in accordance with life-style uniquenesses and may be supplemented by other techniques.

REFERENCES

Lombardi, D. Eight avenues of life style consistency. The Individual Psychologist, 1973, 10, 5–9.

Mosak, H. The interrelatedness of the neuroses through central themes. Journal of Individual Psychology, 1968, 24, 67–70.

Mosak, H. Lifestyle. In A. Nikelly (Ed.), *Techniques for behavior change.* Springfield, III.: Charles C Thomas, 1971.

Mosak, H. Mosak's typology: An update. Journal of Individual Psychology, 1979, 35 (2), 192–195.
Pancer, K. The use of parables and fables in Adlerian psychology. The Individual Psychologist, 1978, 15, 19–29.
Pew, W. *The number one priority.* Monograph, International Association of Individual Psychology. Munich, Germany, August 1, 1976.
Rule, W. Increasing self-modeled humor. Rational Living, 1977, 12, 7–9.
Rule, W. Increasing internal control using humor with lifestyle awareness. The Individual Psychologist, 1979, 16, 1626.
Sanchez, F. Poetry therapy in the assessment of fictive goals. The Individual Psychologist, 1976, 13, 22–25.
Shulman, B. *Contributions to Individual Psychology.* Chicago: Alfred Adler Institute, 1973.
Ward, D. Implications of personality priority assessment for the counseling process. The Individual Psychologist, 1979, 16, 12–16.

7

PURSUING THE HORIZON: STRIVING FOR ELUSIVE GOALS

Warren R. Rule

I saw a man pursuing the horizon;
Round and round they sped.
I was disturbed at this;
I accosted the man.
"It is futile," I said, "You can never —"
"You lie," he cried,
And ran on.

—Stephen Crane

Counselors are often confronted with client goals that seem to be, at varying levels of awareness, elusive to either the counselor or the client. The above poem, written nearly a hundred years ago, accurately reflects the conflict involved in contrasting perceptions of an individ-

This chapter, "Pursuing the Horizons: Striving for Elusive Goals," reprinted from Warren R. Rule, *Personnel and Guidance Journal,* 61(4), 1982, pp. 195–197. © ACA. Reprinted with permission.

ual's goal. Counselors are often confronted with a similar dilemma. Many expect themselves, on one hand, to be basically empathic and supportive of an individual's goals. Whereas, on the other hand, some counselors have difficulty in exploring with the client those goals that seem, either at a conscious or intuitive level, to be inherently elusive. This "elusive" quality of a goal may be the result of a number of properties: Possibly the goal is too lofty, or is too broad, or is incompatible with another important goal; perhaps the goal itself is unclear, or possibly the goal is ephemeral by nature. For the purpose of this article these variables are distilled into the three U's, Unfocused, Unrealistic, and Uncoordinated, and will be discussed later. Discussion will first be given to the broader issue of the place of goals in human behavior and counseling.

THE PERVASIVENESS OF GOALS

Goals, or purposes, are the energizing fabric of daily living. Adler noted that we are unable to think, feel, or act without the perception of some goal (Ansbacher & Ansbacher, 1956). This goal directedness or purposiveness of humankind can be related to the powerful determination to maintain and enhance the self. Parallels exist in the plant and animal kingdoms as well. Humans, while not always fully conscious of their goals, create them in order to give direction to the various forms of movement in life, such as physical, psychological, and social. Subsequently, a goal, which may be generally defined as a fixed consequence to be attained in the future, is a major, if not the major, influence on emotions and behavior.

Counselors traditionally have been keenly aware of the importance of using a goal-oriented framework in conceptualizing and conducting the helping process. For instance, Carhhuff (1980) has emphasized the importance of being aware of where the client is in relation to where the individual wants to be. Behavioral counselors usually focus on the necessity for specifying operational goals in counseling and employ various monitoring strategies to develop and determine the degree of achievement of chosen counseling goals.

The discussion in this article will not center around how better to achieve target goals, nor will the emphasis be on resolving classical approach-approach, avoidance-avoidance, approach-avoidance conflicts in which the goals are specifically and consciously identified (e.g., becoming a doctor or a lawyer, staying with or leaving a lover). In contrast to discussing issues related to these relatively black-and-white goals, the concentration here will be on identifying considerations related to the more elusive "gray area" goals, the three U's: Unfocused, Unrealistic, and Uncoordinated.

UNFOCUSED GOALS

At the opening of one of his most famous addresses, "A House Divided," Abraham Lincoln succinctly expressed a potent concept (Sandburg, 1960): "If we could first know where we are, and whither we are tending, we could better judge what to do, and how to do it."

Awareness is helpful with certain unfocused goals, such as those that are unidentified, yet very functional. Many individuals are unaware of the goal-directed nature of their behavior, especially in a stressful situation. Exploration of this by the counselor and client, and particularly acceptance of this phenomenon by the client, can sometimes be a significant step. This step can increase the awareness that the individual does indeed contribute to one's own difficulties. Often related to this is the lack of conscious awareness of the pervasiveness of a pattern of overriding goals in an individual's life. The "life-style" concept, developed by Adler and refined by his proponents (e.g., Ansbacher & Ansbacher, 1956; Dreikurs, 1967; Mosak, 1977; Shulman, 1973) denotes the organizational consistency of the goals used in individual coping. An increased identification of one's life-style goals frequently increases the client's sense of self-responsibility and, subsequently, may expand the individual's present and future range of choices.

Awareness itself is not always helpful for some unfocused goals. For instance, another type of unfocused goal involves situations in which the individual is clearly aware of the behavior used to implement the goal; yet counselor and client are genuinely at a loss in understanding what is behind the behavior. Sometimes, as Watson and Tharp (1977) note, intermittent reinforcers or avoidance maneuvers could conceivably be involved. In terms of counseling procedure here, perhaps the identification of the precise self-serving goal is relatively unimportant. The energy of the counselor and client may be made better use of by focusing on changing the unwanted behavior itself, rather than chasing the goal on the horizon. Thus, in this situation, perhaps the unfocused goal is wisely accepted as being elusive.

In addition to deciding whether the identification of an unfocused goal is facilitative or not, the counselor may encounter another problem in focusing: goals that are too broad. Goals that are too broadly identified or defined can be barriers to both counseling process and outcome. Goals that are too broad (e.g., "to feel better," "to be important") can be frustrating to pursue and lend themselves to disappointment. Counselors with a behavioral orientation have developed procedures for breaking down and monitoring the attainment of broad goals (e.g., Hosford & de Visser, 1974; Mahoney & Thoreson, 1974; Watson & Tharp, 1977).

Another kind of difficulty related to unfocused goals involves clients who are goal-ridden. These individuals attempt to deal with so many goals at once that they are unable to focus on and achieve most or all of them, thereby setting themselves up for feelings of "not-enoughness" or inadequacy. Sometimes people like this have a driving or a getting approach to life; sometimes secondary gains may be involved, for example fear of failure, display of good intentions, and so on. Establishing priorities in a systematic fashion can be helpful, especially if accompanied by meaningful exploration of self-expectations.

UNREALISTIC GOALS

The exhortation, "Your reach should exceed your grasp," written by the poet Robert Browning, is a message we receive in many forms. Yet, should we consciously set goals beyond our ability to achieve them? In order to keep going, do some of us really need "pipe dreams," as poignantly portrayed in Eugene O'Neill's play "The Iceman Cometh"? Who is to say? Maybe the goals are not so unrealistic after all.

In considering this thorny question, the counselor, unless very careful, can drift easily into the role of a soothsayer who assumes the mystical ability of prediction. At the other extreme, the laissez-faire counselor would be perfectly comfortable allowing the client to chase the goals on the horizon. It is hoped the counselor can find a balance between the two extremes.

Two suggestions may be considered in attempting to achieve a balance. The first suggestion is for the counselor to assist the client in putting the elusive goal ("elusive" according to the suspicions of either the counselor or the client) within the context of broader goals in the client's life. Gaining an awareness of what goal is served by pursuing an elusive, "unrealistic" goal can provide the client with an expanded choice. The previously discussed Adlerian life-style approach is exceedingly helpful in putting goal relationships into perspective. The second suggestion is for the counselor and client to devise exploratory and homework strategies that will yield more information for the client to base a decision on. This practical, external orientation supplements the abstract, internal orientation of the first suggestion. The homework strategies could entail bibliotherapy (e.g., autobiographies and biographies), talking with individuals who have achieved the valued goal, writing an imaginary daily log as if one had achieved the goal, and so on. Thus the client, having learned more about internal and external expectations and standards, is apt to decide better how unrealistic the goal is.

The above discussion of unrealistic goals is directed toward goals that are both relatively specific and focused in the client's consciousness. Another group of unrealistic goals exists which are somewhat broader, more unfocused, and subtly very powerful in their influence. The intense pursuit of this type of elusive goal may lead to sharp disappointment or gnawing self-doubt. These goals, heavily reinforced by contemporary values, can sometimes be put into clearer perspective for clients. The aforementioned suggestions are helpful, but more emphasis here probably needs to be placed on the counselor and client exploring the individualized meaning to the client of this kind of goal.

Examples of these goals, often having an elusive quality as well as having a host of individual meanings, include: happiness, perfection, progress, rationality, being Number One, and self-actualization. The pursuit of happiness is often not very happy. As Woolfolk and Richardson (1978) observe, happiness is a transitory experience, not a final state; happiness as a goal often results in stress, leading to worry over finding it, losing it, and the unpredictable future. Preoccupation with happiness rarely leads to happiness. The goal of perfection is certainly an elusive goal. Living in an imperfect, often unfair world is difficult for those who are mesmerized by the quest for perfection. Ellis (1971), in fact, believes that striving for perfection is the root of most human problems. The broad goal of progress is paradoxical because it usually involves having the goal of worshipping the achievement of other goals. Encouraged by technology and pleasure-seeking, the goal of progress, as Woolfolk and Richardson (1978) note, demeans the past and the present while revering the future. The goal of rationality is somewhat irrational because the unpredictable world is inhabited by humans who seem to have a biological tendency to think irrationally (Ellis, 1971); a more balanced goal is to believe that it is desirable to strive to be more rational while accepting the inevitable irrationality. The goal of being Number I is for most people as rewarding as simply chasing the horizon. Most do not arrive at this transitory state; those few who do often feel unfinished because of the ephemeral nature of being king of the mountain. The goal of self-actualization, which has an irresistible quality for many in the helping professions, is indeed elusive when viewed as an outcome. When savored as a process, a means to a nonexistent end, the pursuit of the goal takes on different meaning: the pursuer now focuses on enjoying the changing sunlight from the elusive horizon. So, in exploring the pros and cons of unrealistic goals, the client can become aware of broader perspectives that lead to expanded choices. For ultimately it is the client who decides the personal meaning of impossible when choosing to dream the impossible dream.

UNCOORDINATED GOALS

Uncoordinated goals are roughly divided here into two groups: those probably really uncoordinated and those seemingly uncoordinated. The first group, probably really uncoordinated goals, may be characterized by a situation in which an individual is pursuing two or more essentially incompatible goals. The person in effect is trying to run in two or more directions at once. Consequently, the achievement of one or all of the goals, plus the accompanying sense of satisfaction, is elusive.

In this case, many clients are basically unaware of the relatively incompatible nature of their selected goals. Examples of these (Woolfolk & Richardson, 1978) are wanting to rise to the top of one's work without exerting extra effort or displeasing anyone in the process; and wanting to have abundant freedom in one's life, yet have children. One solution is for the counselor and client to explore priorities. Giving one priority more weight than another or putting one priority in a different time frame can sometimes help overcome the incompatibility of such uncoordinated goals. Also, as Krumboltz and Thoreson (1969) have indicated, rarely are choices limited to simply two alternatives.

Sometimes uncoordinated goals are involved when an individual adopts a goal that is incompatible with a more broadly based personality or life-style goal. The stress expert Seyle (1974) uses the example of a racehorse personality who attempts to adopt a major goal incompatible with the self, a situation that results in increased stress. The consideration of choosing goals that are in flow with one's life-style currents is a very significant one. Some counselors, in their eagerness to encourage clients to pursue specific goals or behavioral objectives, tend to overlook this potential incompatibility and are sometimes puzzled by the disappointing results. Along a similar vein, dissimilar (uncoordinated) goals between client and counselor may well be the basic cause of what has been labeled "resistance" on the client's part (Dreikurs, 1967).

The second group of uncoordinated goals consists of goals that seem to be uncoordinated but probably really are not. This inconsistency sometimes occurs within the individual in the sense that the person creates what appears to be an inner conflict in order to pursue an ulterior, usually face-saving, goal. The individual, although probably not fully aware of the ulterior goal that the conflict serves, is aware of the unpleasantness and the ambivalence. Thus the ambivalence or "yes...but" conflict (Adler, 1934) can be in the service of a variety of ulterior, yet distinctly self-serving, goals. Examples are, according to Mosak and LeFevre (1976) who also discusses resolution strategies, the avoidance of the responsibility of making a decision, the opportunity to place blame on others if they make the decision, keeping a bad situation with minimal guilt, being regarded by self and others as struggling heroically, and increasing the likelihood of creating other useful symptom. Other possible examples of the usefulness of seemingly incompatible goals, which serve the broader goal of safeguarding self-esteem, can sometimes be found in a range of situations, such as the conflicts among intellect and emotions, procrastinations, fear of failure, various physical symptoms, and so on. One of O'Connell's (1975) approaches is to recognize and to reframe the individual creativity involved in the endeavor and to rechannel the creativity toward conflict resolution.

RELATED CONSIDERATIONS

By being mindful of client goals, both elusive and nonelusive, the counselor increases the likelihood of staying in touch with the client's movement. An added benefit to this orientation is that the client is regarded as having the responsibility for choosing to maintain or to change goals. The freedom implied in the future-orientation of a goal is in contrast to the deterministic approach of being possessed by past, uncontrollable drives. Additional reading on strategies and special concerns related to goal-directedness may be found in Mosak (1977). The previously discussed three U's, Unfocused, Unrealistic, and Uncoordinated goals, provide a framework that, while somewhat overlapping, may be helpful in identifying and putting into perspective many elusive goals. A healthy respect should be maintained, however, for the elusive goals that are beyond our abilities to clarify and resolve totally. Perhaps the most influential example is the self-ideal which, when contrasted with present perception of self, generates inferiority feelings, a necessary compensatory motivation for movement from birth to death (Dreikurs, 1967). Perhaps, then, one should wisely accept at least part of the feelings of "not enoughness" resulting from the pursuit of the elusive goal of the self-ideal. As Gertrude Stein reportedly concluded, "We find when we get there, there's no there, there."

REFERENCES

Adler, A. Lecture to the Medical Society of Individual Psychology, London, May 17, 1934. Individual psychology pamphlets, 1934, No. 13, pp. 11–24.
Ansbacher, H., & Ansbacher, R. The Individual Psychology of Alfred Adler. New York: Basic Books, 1956.
Carkhuff, R. The art of helping IV. Amherst, Mass.: Human Resources Development Press, 1980.
Dreikurs, R. Psychodynamics, psychotherapy, and counseling. Chicago: Alfred Adler Institute, 1967.
Ellis, A. Growth through reason. Palo Alto, Calif.: Science & Behavior Books, 1971.
Hosford, R., & de Visser, L. Behavioral approaches to counseling: An introduction. Washington, D.C.: APGA, 1974.
Krumboltz, J., & Thoreson, C. Behavioral counseling: Cases and techniques. New York: Holt, Rinehart & Winston, 1969.
Mahoney, M., & Thoreson, C. Self control: Power to the person. Belmont, Calif.: Wadsworth Pub. Co., 1974.
Mosak, H. On purpose. Chicago: Alfred Adler Institute, 1977.
Mosak, H., & Le Fevre, C. The resolution of intrapersonal conflict. Journal of Individual Psychology, 1976, 32, 19–26.
O'Connell, W. Action therapy and Adlerian theory. Chicago: Alfred Adler Institute, 1975.
Sandburg, C. The most enduring memorial to Lincoln. In R. Newman (Ed.), Lincoln for the ages. New York: Doubleday, 1960.
Seyle, H. Stress without distress. New York: Lippincott & Crowell, 1974.
Shulman, B. Contributions to individual psychology. Chicago: Alfred Adler Institute, 1973.
Watson, D., & Tharp, R. Self-directed behavior (2nd ed.). Belmont, Calif.: Wadsworth Pub. Co., 1977.
Woolfolk, R., & Richardson, F. Stress, sanity, and survival. New York: Sovereign Books, 1978.

8

LIFESTYLE SELF-AWARENESS AND THE PRACTITIONER

Warren R. Rule

For even saintly folks act like sinners
Unless they have their customary dinners.

Many practitioners in the helping professions would like to believe that the above quotation, from Bertolt Brecht, does not pertain to them. In fact, some seem to believe, either consciously or dimly consciously, that functioning as a helping practitioner somehow cleanses the lifestyle into saintly purity.

A great deal has been written in the lifestyle literature about the usefulness of lifestyle methods for helping clients. Extremely little has been written on how the practitioner can help himself using the lifestyle method, and, in doing so, become a more effective counselor. This dearth of literature makes one wonder if the fact has been too often overlooked that the client and the counselor are both human beings

This chapter, "Lifestyle Self-Awareness and the Practioner," from Warren R. Rule (Ed.), *Lifestyle counseling for adjustment to disability*, 1984. Rockville, MD: Aspen Systems Corporation.

whose lifestyles work at times to the disadvantage of self and others. The purpose of this chapter is first to highlight the importance of overall practitioner self-awareness, second, to discuss lifestyle implications for the counseling role, and, finally, to explore action considerations.

PRACTITIONER SELF-AWARENESS

The benefits of increased practitioner self-understanding appear to be considerable. Appell (1963) asserted that the most important dimension in the counseling relationship is counselor self-understanding. Passons (1975) concluded that:

> … it is recognized that the person of the counselor is the essential instrument in his work. Stripped of all professional accouterments and rhetoric, who the counselor is remains the primary factor in his functioning. His values, beliefs, needs and other personal characteristics permeate everything he does in his many functions as a counselor. (p. 4)

Shoben (1962) stated that the counselor is well-served if he has insight into himself and his counselor frame of reference because the choice of any given counseling perspective is a reflection of one's own personality. Lister (1964) concluded that one's personal theory of counseling is heavily influenced by one's hypotheses regarding effective and satisfying human relationship in general. He noted that:

> Each beginning counselor has already spent years formulating hypotheses about himself and others and the nature of the world in which he lives. In the broadest sense, the counselor's personal theory refers to the hypotheses he has come to view as reliable guides to satisfying human relations. Although many such hypotheses are largely implicit and inarticulate, they nevertheless constitute patterns for counseling behavior or personality theory. For example, the student whose experience has led him to believe that his effectiveness in human relations requires that he prevent others from getting the upper hand is apt to maintain tight control of topics covered in the counseling interview.… If a student believes that people are basically trustworthy and capable of responsible behavior, he will probably have a higher threshold for the perception of "clear and imminent danger" than the student who has found others untrustworthy and irresponsible. (p. 209)

Passons (1975) contends that a congruence must exist between the counselor as a person and his theory of counseling. Moreover, attempts by others or by himself to impose theory that does not fit will result in a state of dissonance. Thus, Passons (1975) recommends that the first step in formulating a personal theory is for the practitioner to attain a high level of awareness of his philosophical beliefs, values, needs, etc. Without this awareness, the base of his personal theory may be shaky. In addition, as the counselor becomes more aware of himself, he endangers his ability to evaluate other theories of counseling in terms of their appropriateness to him. As Shoben (1962) has concluded, if there were a theory that was "right" for every counselor, there would not be so many of them.

LIFESTYLE IMPLICATIONS FOR THE COUNSELING ROLE

Aside from the issue of how the lifestyle works to an individual's advantage and disadvantage in one's personal life, which will be touched on below, the issue of how a person's lifestyle relates to his work as a counselor is an intriguing, and hopefully beneficial, concern. It may be remembered that, according to Adlerian theory, the lifestyle that one has formed as being useful for coping with life in general will also be the same lifestyle used for coping with the life task of work. This area of "work" includes one's activities and thoughts on matters such as relating to clients, colleagues, and supervisors. Also included are eagerness to experiment with different counseling approaches, reaction to client noncooperation, telephone conversations, organization of daily activities, internal evaluation of job success, etc.

From the perspective of counselor-client interaction, counselor lifestyle notions, attitudes, and goals can both enhance and detract from the counseling relationship. For instance, the counselor who has concluded at a dimly conscious level that intellectual superiority is the way to go in life may well alienate clients (by abstractions, big words, oratories, etc.) who aren't on an intellectual wave length for solving problems. Yet he may help those clients who are very similar or who rely too heavily on other methods in coping with difficulties. Similarly, a counselor whose style is heavily laden with mandates of self-control may be able to keep a level head during a client's nonproductive emotional outbursts yet fail to provide a spontaneous, emotionally warm model for clients who may profit immensely from such a counselor. Related to this is the counselor who treats himself as if he should control others. He can help clients who need structure in the counseling process but may antagonize those clients who are also like this or who simply want to make their own decisions. Furthermore, the counselor who is heavily invested in being right and avoiding being wrong may well have the tendency to be overly stubborn, or even engage in seemingly irrelevant behaviors such as repeating himself frequently (to make sure his ideas are fully understood)—thereby impressing some clients with his rightness, but annoying others.

In addition, the counselor who has learned at a vague level of consciousness that he only feels OK when he is getting constant approval can possibly help some of those clients who profit from his extra efforts to please them. Yet this notion can work to his disadvantage if he avoids confrontation when appropriate or if he is too hard on himself for not getting the desired amount of approval-assurance from certain clients. The counselor who displays moral superiority or goodness-togetherness may be encouraging as a well-intentioned person to some clients. But he might create an image of saintliness to some other clients and, in doing so, inadvertently create discouragement. In addition, the counselor who has concluded at a vague level of apprehension that OK-ness means driving and striving for a place of special importance can find many of his clients "unmotivated" who do not share this intense conviction. But, on the other hand, he may be able to spur on successfully some other clients who need a shot in the arm or who relate well to the counselor's projection on them. Additional examples abound.

An important point is that counselors are both people and counselors. They therefore have broad notions about self, others, and life that can and do creep into the counseling role by thought, word (as well as silence), and deed. Obviously, the same holds true for clients—they are both people and clients. In terms of compatibility between counselor and client, some research studies, e.g., Gerler (1958), Carson and Heine (1962), Mendelsohn and Geller (1965), have indicated that counselors and clients who are either very similar or very dissimilar on personality variables are generally less apt to do as well together as are counselors and clients who are neither too similar nor too dissimilar. Possibly too much reinforcing empathy is going on at one extreme and not enough at the other. Although these findings do not warrant the status of an ironclad rule, the practicing counselor may want to keep an eye on this variable when compatibility difficulties seem to be occurring.

Because all behavior—including "helping" behavior—is regarded as being goal directed, a lifestyle question that may be worth exploring for the practitioner is "What does 'helping' do for me?" Related to lifestyle notions regarding self and others, a host of purposive, self-serving possibilities may exist, such as increasing rightness, fostering praise, encouraging redemption, nurturing control, guaranteeing an audience, ensuring importance, granting goodness, recharging batteries, bestowing specialness, heightening self-elevation, and so on.

ACTION CONSIDERATIONS

Many believe that characteristics of the lifestyle become most apparent when the individual is experiencing some stress or when life is not going his way. A thought that may be worth pursuing, based on one's lifestyle notions, is: "What do I keep telling myself about myself when things have not worked out for me?" Similar to Ellis's (1971) rational-emotive approach, the task is to pinpoint and to challenge the self-message that has a "should" or a "must" attached to it.

A practitioner could also make a concerted effort to work into his everyday thinking the Adlerian belief in the goal-directed nature of behavior. This might be particularly helpful as this phenomenon relates to characteristics the counselor does not quite understand about his manner of approaching some of his work activities. By stretching the imagination a little, the counselor may be able to make the connection between a lifestyle notion and a hard-to-understand behavior or behavior pattern that is in the service of that notion. Examples of this are the constant apologies and expressions of good intentions for one whose lifestyle notions dictate pleasing and winning approval, or possibly the power and/or recognition demands that underlie a quick temper, or the avoidance-of-failure purpose beneath the feeling of being unable to concentrate when beginning a task. Sometimes much can be learned by viewing an "unwanted" behavior or feeling as a safeguard for self-esteem.

During the helping process, the counselor may profit by becoming more aware of his initial experience of a negative thought or feeling (e.g., frustration, anger, anxiety, boredom, etc.) or visceral reaction and using this awareness as a "triggering device" for self-exploration. By attempting to match up the initial negative experience with what one suspects are some of his lifestyle notions, the counselor is better equipped to take a more accurate look at what is going on and then to act accordingly—ideally for the ultimate benefit of both the client and the counselor.

The counselor may want to consider his guesses as to some of his lifestyle notions from the perspective of how this awareness can be used to build upon strengths. By guessing in which direction one's energy is inclined to flow, the counselor may choose to capitalize upon and enhance those aspects that work to his advantage and minimize those that work to his disadvantage. For example, if control over the environment is a strong dimension in one's lifestyle notions, a consideration is to sharpen one's organizational skills some more or even concentrate on administrative efforts. If intellectual mastery is prominent, one could explore those counseling approaches that emphasize cognitive problem solving. If putting others in one's service is a dominant theme, maybe the counselor can increase his skills in areas that could be naturally self-fulfilling, such as public relations or employer development.

The mental act of encouraging oneself can often lead to gratifying results. By subvocalizing something like "You're still OK even when you are not… e.g., perfect, Number One, pleasing everyone, in control, right," can help move oneself off the vertical plane of comparisons and onto a more satisfying horizontal plane of accepting the various parts of the self that one continually keeps on trial.

Having identified what one suspects is a lifestyle notion or goal underlying a problem area, one is then able to take a stand on one or several of the following actions: (1) to accept how the lifestyle notion or goal is working, yet want to learn different, more effective ways of behaving in order to implement the goal more satisfactorily; (2) to desire to reduce the felt intensity of a lifestyle notion or goal by attempting to change one's thoughts, e.g., mental self-discipline, self-encouragement, internal challenging, self-rewards and punishments, etc.; (3) to desire to reduce the felt intensity of a lifestyle notion or goal by attempting to behave in ways that are counter to the goal, e.g., learning new behavior, doing more or doing less of already learned behavior; (4) to decide not to decide to do anything. It's worth emphasizing that individual lifestyle goals are dimensions that a person takes a sensitive position on. Both the behavior that is a function of this sensitivity as well as the sensitivity itself can be altered. People—including counselors—can change!

Many types of action steps exist for those willing to take the necessary risks. For example, telling a client about one's own lifestyle notions can be risky, e.g., "I've got a tendency to want… (to be right about, to control, approval for, etc.) things, so let me step back from this so my bias doesn't get in your way," yet it can yield surprising dividends. Or an individual can even try taking a small creative risk when things are not going so well when it is suspected that one's own lifestyle is contributing to the difficulty. One way to do this is to laugh fully at oneself by vividly imagining a ridiculously exaggerated version of a lifestyle notion. Examples are: for a counselor who treats himself as righteously perfect—a white robe, halo, angel wings, surrounded by a dazzled, yet humble, congregation; for one who demands of himself that he be a number-one achiever—a king's crown, a battleax, ribbons and medals, perched atop a throne while competitors and servants bow and do homage from below.

Additional homework considerations can be found in an excellent book by Lazarus and Fay (1975) entitled *I Can If I Want To*. Although not written from a direct lifestyle point of view, it provides many helpful strategies for changing thoughts and behaviors.

The process of using the lifestyle approach, either in part or totally, can be further enhanced by sharing in a group setting with fellow practitioners. In this manner, the group members can provide additional validity checks as well as vicariously learn from their fellow group members.

OVERALL STRESS MANAGEMENT

Stress is a key factor in everyone's life. Here, too, the counseling practitioner is no exception, because stress is a significant part of the individual's professional and personal life. As discussed previously, the lifestyle, with all its advantages and disadvantages, is at work in all areas of living.

Schafer (1978) has provided a useful concept of stress management that is consistent with lifestyle self-awareness: "Managing stress wisely means knowing what amount of stress is right for you and keeping control of the pace of your life so you neither stagnate nor are overwhelmed with too much to do" (p. 20).

Stress has been viewed as a bodily response and as a perception. Selye (1974) defines stress as "the nonspecific response of the body to any demand made on it" (p. 14). Woolfolk and Richardson (1978) regard stress as "a perception of threat or expectation of future discomfort that arouses, alerts, or otherwise activates the organism" (p. 9). Both views are helpful in understanding the broad range of ways in which stress operates.

In the physical realm the innate fight or flight response, which we inherited from our primitive ancestors, results in many bodily changes when stimuli coming in are interpreted as threatening. The pupils enlarge so that we can see better, hearing becomes acute, blood pulsates through the head to stimulate thought processes, heart and respiratory rates increase to energize the system, and so forth. Most contemporary threats, however, cannot be dealt with in a fight or flight manner, as could ancient threats of fierce animals or savage competitors. Thus, this programmed response to stress can take a bodily toll over the years and is said to contribute to symptoms including heart attacks, headaches, colitis, and allergies.

Other realms are closely connected to the physical realm. The emotional realm and the behavioral realm are descriptive types that can be related to the physical and to the cognitive realms. The emphasis in this chapter is on the cognitive realm. It is this realm that, for the individual, seems to assess the degree of "awfulness" of the perceived threatening stimuli; this assessment, in turn, appears to contribute to the nature of response in the physical, emotional, and behavioral realms. In addition, the cognitive realm seems to lend itself best to self-awareness and self-management strategies that are consistent with the lifestyle conceptual frame-work.

Not all stress is negative. Stress can be both pleasant and unpleasant (Rule, 1986). Selye (1974) defines unpleasant, negative, or intense stress as distress. Prolonged distress can result in damaging wear and tear on the mind or body, destructive behavior toward others, or interference with everyday living. Individuals vary in their comfort zones of stress and degree of desired stimulation from stress.

Thus, awareness of individual lifestyle vulnerability, along with the accompanying awareness of personal sensitivity to various types of stressors, can be particularly beneficial. This may be especially helpful when one is confronted with personally threatening experiences. For example, some of the major experiences that can lead to distress, according to Schafer (1978), are overload; understimulation; absence of meaning; role conflict, including personal desires conflicting with the expectations of others, expectations associated with one role conflicting with expectations associated with another role, and different expectations of a single role conflicting with each other; role ambiguity; transitions; loss; unfinished business; "negative" life scripts; and a perceived gap between ideals and reality.

Schafer (1978) organizes the main personal approaches to managing stress into three areas:

1. Managing your stressors—controlling the pace of your life.
2. Managing your stress filter—taking care of yourself so that stressful events will have minimal harmful effect on mind and body and developing personal qualities that will soften the impact.
3. Managing your coping response—coping with distress constructively so it will be reduced rather than increased; i.e., live with the

distress, withdraw from the stressor, relate to the stressor differently, change the stressor, or accept the situation and thereby lower the stress.

In one of his most famous essays, "A House Divided," Abraham Lincoln (Sandburg, 1960), master of the metaphor, concisely expressed a potent concept that speaks to the heart of lifestyle self-awareness, action considerations, and stress management: "If we could first know where we are, and whither we are tending, we could better judge what to do, and how to do it" (p. 33).

Related to this, Shoben (1962) has observed that the counselor who "knows himself" and can use his theoretical tools flexibly is indeed fortunate. He further concludes that the "counselor who achieves this kind of honesty in dealing with his cognitive self is likely to enjoy a sense of personal growth that is denied to others" (p. 621).

So, in response to the question "Why should I concern myself with an increased awareness of biased lifestyle notions? After all, I am completely free to choose what I want to think and do," the Adlerian suggestion might be to look for a common attitude or pattern of movement that ties together those features of your working style that you want to change. For in doing so, you may well be really exploring the hidden notions influencing "where you are" in relation to "where you want to be." Aided by this self-insight, you now have an increased opportunity to plot a straighter course or even to change the destination.

SUMMARY

Very little has been written in the counseling literature on the disadvantages of the counselor's lifestyle. The benefits of increased practitioner self-awareness seem to be useful in human interaction as well as in developing one's personal approach to counseling.

The counselor's lifestyle is likely to operate at a dimly conscious level in ways that are both advantageous and disadvantageous to the client. Exploring the question of "What does helping do for me?" may yield worthwhile results for the practitioner.

Action considerations that result from practitioner self-awareness may take many directions: self-disputing, identifying blind spots, focusing on triggering cues, building upon strengths, challenging vertical comparisons, creating goals and behavioral strategies for change, humorous self-confrontation, peer feedback in a group setting.

In addition, the practitioner may profit by incorporating into his self-awareness a place for overall stress management.

REFERENCES

Appel, M. L. (1963). Self understanding for the guidance counselor. *Personnel and Guidance Journal, 43*, 143–148.
Carson, R. C., & Heine, R. W. (1962). Similarity and success in therapeutic dyads. *Journal of Consulting Psychology, 26*(1), 38–43.
Ellis, A. (1971). *Growth through reason*. Palo Alto, CA: Science & Behavior Books.
Gerler, W. (1958). *Outcome of psychotherapy as a function of client-counselor similarity.* Dissertation Abstracts, 18, 1864.
Lazarus, A., & Fay, A. (1975). *I can if I want to.* New York: Morrow.
Lister, J. (1964). The counselor's personal theory. *Counselor Education and Supervision, 3*, 207–213.
Mendelsohn, G. A., & Geller, M. H. (1965). Effects of counselor-client similarity on the outcome of counseling, *Journal of Counseling Psychology, 10*(1), 71–77.
Passons, W. (1960). *Gestalt approaches in counseling*. New York: Holt, Rinehart, & Winston.
Rule, W. R. (1986). *Lifestyle counseling for adjustment to disability.* Rockville, MD: Aspen.
Sandburg, C. (1960). The most enduring memorial to Lincoln. In R. Newman (Ed.), *Lincoln for the ages*. New York: Doubleday.
Schafer, W. (1974). *Stress, distress and growth*. Davis, CA: International Dialogue Press.
Selye, H. (1974). *Stress without distress*. New York: Signet.
Shoben, E. J., Jr. (1962). The counselor's theory as a personality trait. *Personnel and Guidance Journal, 40*, 617–621.
Woolfolk, R., & Richardson, F. (1978). *Stress, sanity, and survival*. New York: Sovereign.

III

School Counseling

9

ADLERIAN METHODS IN SCHOOL PSYCHOLOGY

Warren R. Rule

In recent years, the ideas of Alfred Adler have been receiving considerable attention. This rebirth is characterized by an increasing number of Adlerian practitioners, counseling centers, educational offerings, and publications. The Adlerian framework for understanding individuals and corresponding Adlerian counseling techniques can contribute to the effectiveness of the school psychologist. First, discussion will be directed to assumptions regarding the nature of man. Then, the techniques having a direct bearing on the work of the school psychologist will be presented: the Adlerian life-style approach and Adlerian counseling approach with children.

This chapter, "Adlerian Methods in School Psychology," from J. Cull & L. Golden (Eds.), *Psychotherapeutic Techniques in School Psychology,* 1984. Courtesy of Charles C Thomas, Publisher, Springfield, IL.

NATURE OF HUMANITY

Counseling professionals are wise to explore their assumptions regarding the nature of man. After all, those in the business of assisting individuals to cope, to change, to enjoy themselves more, or to become self-actualized ought to have an awareness of their assumptions about the complex creature that they are trying to help. The Adlerian therapeutic approaches are based on a well-integrated framework for understanding the nature of humanity. This framework itself can be viewed as a solid base for the school practitioner who views himself/herself as therapeutically eclectic.

Adler believed that each of us develops a life-style during childhood that exerts a major influence on our thoughts, feelings, and behavior throughout life. In fact, Alfred Adler coined the term "life-style" more than fifty years ago. His definition of the concept focused heavily on the core of personality, particularly on the individual's unique cognitive map. This "life-style" concept can be defined as the pattern of dimly conscious notions or goals that a person uses for interacting with others and for measuring self-worth.

With regard to characteristics of the life-style, Adlerians believe that all behavior, including thought and emotion, is goal directed. Even though one may be consciously aware of the purpose for thinking or acting in a certain fashion, most of the time one is unaware of unique self-concerned goals that, at a dimly conscious level, underlie actions, thoughts, and feelings.

In describing this phenomenon, "purpose" may be substituted for the term "goal." The point is that behavior is a function of one's ideas about consequences to be obtained in the future. Hence, this overriding pattern of goal-directed thinking is subtly at work in all segments of daily living: in the way the person handles school, in the choice of clothes to wear, in the choice of friends, in successes and failures, etc. Furthermore, this holistic pattern of goals is organized around the subjectively determined concept of the ideal self that the individual created during childhood years. The person, in his/her private logic. continually moves through life with this ideal self as a reference point and, almost as if wearing blinders, strives to become like the ideal self. Thus, individuals operate as if they will only have a sense of significance in the eyes of others and have a real feeling of security when they live up to the ideal self.

Adlerians believe that childhood conclusions drawn about self, others, and life before age six largely contribute to these present internalized guidelines that the individual uses in striving. These conclusions seem to be drawn from the experience built into the person's first social group, the family, and take into account characteristics such as family constellation, including siblings' age differences, ordering of sexes, alliance groups, and developmental areas. In addition, parental influences and expectations, family atmosphere, peers, and neighborhood all contribute to the biased slice of life from which the child must generalize. Much emphasis is placed on the psychological territory the individual chooses to stake out in an attempt to feel "others take notice of me when I am like this." This feeling of significance, or belonging, can occur from being "the best," or even sometimes "the worst," in areas such as academic accomplishments, toughness, athletic ability, critical mindedness, etc. Each sibling, Adlerians believe, will move in a different overall direction in these areas or sometimes may attempt to overtake a sibling in an area.

Through trial and error, not only do individuals learn from an early age what goals will be most apt to help them move toward a place of significance, but they also learn which kinds of behavior are most useful in implementing the goals. Understandably, people also learn behaviors in keeping with the often dimly conscious goals of the life-style that safeguard their sense of self-esteem. Generally speaking, then, the life-style allows the person to evaluate, to understand, to predict, and to control experience (Mosak & Dreikurs, 1973).

LIFE-STYLE APPROACH

The life-style assessment technique is most properly used with adolescents and adults (sometimes parents need to be counseled on an individual basis as part of the family counseling process). Techniques for assessing the goals of children will be covered in the next section.

Life-style assessment generally fits into a four-step sequence of helping. The first stage focuses on exploring the relationship, understanding the client's problems, and explaining how the client is coping with the various tasks of life. Life-style investigation is the second stage. Psychological disclosure and discussion of the life-style is the third. The fourth stage is reorientation.

In answer to the question, How does one determine what an adolescent's or adult's life-style is?, Adlerian thinking rests on the premise that the memory is selective. As Dreikurs (1967) indicated, people operate on an economy principle by selectively using their memories and abilities in accordance with their individual purposes. Hence, our memories of early childhood reflect the most important attitudes, notions, expectations, convictions, and goals that crystallized during this formative period. Adlerians believe that these early recollections reflect those firm ideas that are embedded in the client's present outlook. In making use of this phenomenon, the practitioner is able to gather life-style information by pointed questions and, in so doing, to reconstruct the important aspects of the client's early environment.

Dreikurs (1967) developed a life-style questionnaire that covers the significant areas of concern. Based on personal memories of early childhood before age six or seven, areas of life-style information include describing the self and siblings, sibling rankings on possible areas of competition (e.g., displaying intelligence, trying to please, having own way, etc.), sibling interrelationships, parents and parental influence, the family atmosphere, and early recollections and dreams.

Adlerians emphasize the family constellation by attending to the person's position of birth as related to sibling age differences, ordering of sexes, uniqueness, and alliance groups. Shulman (1973) listed five basic positions: only, eldest, second, middle, and youngest child. Each position has several modest probabilities of stereotyped characteristics. The practitioner considers and refines these hypotheses in accordance with the direction of movement reflected by the other life-style variables.

For example, the first-born child most often is subject to parental expectations and authority. Mindful of losing his/her place of importance as eldest child, the individual may be inclined to identify with established parental values and might be determined to be the number-one achiever. On the other hand, the eldest may become discouraged by what the child considers as unfair treatment or unreasonable expectations. As a result, the individual may develop a fatalistic, rebellious outlook. Therefore, in the eldest child's situation or position, the life-style may perhaps be related to a stance—pro or con—of cooperating with or rebelling against parental authority and expectations.

Much importance is given to the client's early recollections, memories, and dreams. The Adlerian belief is that there are no chance memories. From thousands of experiences to which the individual has been exposed in early childhood, only those recollections are remembered that coincide with present outlook on life. Consequently, the individual's early recollections show the same patterns; they are reminders the person carries around regarding personal limits and the meaning of circumstances (Ansbacher & Ansbacher, 1956). Generally, when asked, individuals can remember at least six specific incidents that occurred during their childhoods. Each recollection, viewed by the practitioner in the context of the feeling about the remembered incident, reflects a current expectation about life. Each recollection supplements and rounds out the outlook reflected by the other early recollections and life-style variables.

The complete life-style questionnaire can take as many as several hours to collect information, or an abbreviated version may be used. The choice depends on several factors, such as the availability of time and the purpose of gathering data. Understandably, if more information is gathered, then a greater probability of accurate and well-rounded results can be expected.

Some examples of commonly observed life-style themes are cited by Mosak (1971), who cautioned that a wide array of behaviors may be used to implement each of these mental frameworks on a daily basis. He also believed that only probable behavioral hypotheses can be made. Examples of these themes include gaining possession, driving, controlling, always being right, being the center or the best, pleasing, being admired for moral superiority, opposing, being victimized, being a martyr, being the baby or a charmer, being inadequate, being intellectually superior, and being the excitement seeker.

The amount of experience and familiarity with life-style variables are certainly determining factors in how much information the counselor can obtain from life-style material. Additional reading may enable the practitioner to gather at least a general idea of an individual's overriding life-style, which would be further clarified by discussion with the client. References for further reading may be found in a comprehensive Adlerian bibliography by Mosak and Mosak (1975).

A heightened awareness of a person's life-style can enhance the therapeutic process. The life-style information-gathering process and the interpretation process can help to cement the therapeutic relationship. Additionally, the life-style can give the school practitioner guidelines or suggestions for change in the client's environment. Life-style information can sometimes broaden the helper's understanding of how a client is likely to react to or use a mental, emotional, or physical disability. Moreover, the use of artificial stimuli, e.g., drugs and alcohol, offers a productive perspective regarding individual life-styles.

Outcomes can be focused on either general or specific terms. Regarding a more general outcome, the focus can be helping the client discover how his/her life-style is contributing to the present problem. In addition, sometimes the client can be encouraged to do situational checkups by expressing a negative emotion and then to try to discover how personal life-style dictates a feeling of nonsignificance. There is also much to be gained by helping the client become aware of the advantages of his/her life-style. This is especially helpful in increasing self-esteem as well as in personal and career planning.

In focusing on specific outcomes, the school practitioner may want to combine the Adlerian approach with other counseling frameworks that encourage specificity in process and outcome, e.g., behavioral, rational-emotive. This expanded approach might entail using the life-style as a guideline to help the client increase or decrease the number of times that he/she responds in an already learned manner. Or, possibly, the helper may want to assist the client in learning new ways to think, feel, or behave to benefit the natural currents of his/her life-style. Additional discussion of this approach may be found in Rule (1980).

The acquisition of knowledge obtained from the life-style approach is by no means limited to clients. An increased awareness of the school practitioner's own life-style and how it is at work in his/her personal and professional life on a daily basis can be a significant asset.

The life-style approach may be handled on an individual basis or in a group setting. One positive aspect of the group setting, in addition to efficient utilization of the school practitioner's resources, is that the group members are able to point out and validate relationships between individual behavior in and out of the group and individual life-style goals. Furthermore, the encouragement process of the group is a factor of no small significance. O'Connell (1975), Sweeney (1975), and Dinkmeyer and Muro (1971) offer innovative suggestions for group work.

COUNSELING CHILDREN

Counseling school-age children can be conducted with individuals or in a family counseling approach. Often it is desirable to involve whichever of the parents will become involved in family counseling, simply because parental behavior is so influential in the child's life. Another specific individual who has an impact on the child's development is his/her teacher.

A basic assumption in the Adlerian framework is that a misbehaving child is a discouraged child. Misbehaving children are often unsure of their place among others and believe that they can get a feeling of significance by pursuing goals that are not socially productive.

Adlerians generally believe that a misbehaving child is likely to be pursuing one or more of four goals. The characteristics of these four common goals of misbehavior, as discussed in an excellent manual by Walton and Powers (1974), are as follows:

Goal 1: Attention. The child believes that he/she is only OK when making his/her presence felt. Behaviorally, the child may be "hyperactive," noisy, clowning, exceedingly talkative, etc. The personal reaction of the affected person to this behavior is to feel annoyed or put upon. When corrected, the child stops—only briefly. Often the best solution is to ignore the inappropriate attention-seeking behavior and to help the child earn recognition in a productive way.

Goal 2: Power. The child thinks that he/she should be the boss or at least should not be bossed. In terms of behavior, the child is apt to be defiant, aggressive, bossy, subtly disobedient, prone to use the power of tears, etc. The personal reaction of the affected person is to feel frustrated or angry. When corrected, the misbehavior is likely to continue or even escalate. Frequently, the best solution is to step out of the power struggle, because it takes two people to fight. Moreover, the child's aid can be elicited in cooperative endeavors.

Goal 3: Revenge. The child attempts to hurt others, especially when hurt himself/herself. Behaviorally, the child may be viewed as brutal, mean, or violent. The affected person is likely to react by feeling hurt by the revengeful behavior. When corrected, this behavior becomes retaliatory or more violent. One solution is to get through to the significant other(s) who may well be using hurtful (verbal or physical) approaches in disciplining the child. In addition to engaging the child in helpful activities, sometimes the goal of hurting can be discussed in an atmosphere of friendliness.

Goal 4: Inadequacy. The child thinks that he/she cannot measure up and wants very little expected of him/her. In terms of behavior, the child may give up easily or will not try, yet is rarely a discipline problem. The personal reaction of the affected person is to feel helpless. The child is likely not to respond when corrected. Regarding solutions, the accent should be on encouraging whatever positive contributions are made, perhaps lowering standards, and minimizing discussion of expectations.

Adlerian practitioners, in working with parents and teachers, provide additional guidelines for handling the child. These guidelines focus on identifying mistaken approaches as well as on suggesting improvements (Walter and Powers, 1974; Dreikurs and Goldman, 1967).

- Avoid pampering and overprotection. Both approaches are votes of nonconfidence in the child's ability to work things out. Do not do for a child what he/she can do alone. Overresponsible parents may inadvertently produce irresponsible children.
- Avoid the autocratic approach. This suppression method conveys the message that the child must be forced to do whatever is right. Democratic cooperation and sharing is preferable. This is particularly important in dealing with adolescents.
- Avoid reward and punishment. By modeling this autocratic system of interaction, some children become reward "demanding," others may feel the right to punish others in return. It is better to allow natural consequences (direct results of the child's behavior) to occur and to arrange logical consequences (the situation is arranged so the child experiences the logical results of behavior).
- Regard homework as the child's responsibility. By staying away, the parent conveys to the child that it is his/her responsibility.
- Act rather than talk in a conflict. If a power struggle develops, withdraw. Do not fight, but do not surrender; it takes two to fight.
- Do not interfere in children's fights. By resolving conflicts, children learn the give and take of social living. Additionally, by not interfering, the parent avoids taking sides. If the fight becomes too noisy or disruptive, the logical consequence is for the children to settle their dispute outdoors.
- Distinguish between realistic and great expectations. Unreasonable expectations are insisting that the child be "the best," and conveying the message to the child that "you are not good enough as you are."
- Experiment with a Family Council. Weekly, the family can discuss issues related to the household in a cooperative spirit. In this democratic atmosphere, the chairmanship could be rotated.

In addition to counseling with children and families, some school practitioners with an Adlerian orientation choose to organize parent education groups. The primary purpose for these groups is for parents to learn more effective methods for understanding and coping with their children. Family counseling demonstrations are sometimes conducted as a part of the educational and sharing experiences. The time-tested book *Children: The Challenge* (Dreikurs and Soltz, 1964) is often used to supplement the discussion.

As a supplement to counseling with children. Adlerian practitioners frequently consult with teachers. With misbehaving children, the emphasis is on the previously discussed principles. Particular attention is paid to the goal-directed nature of behavior and to the four common goals of misbehavior. Additionally, Adlerians often recommend uniting the class and having group discussions whenever possible, acting more and talking less, creating logical consequences instead of punishment, and fostering the often-neglected process of encouragement. Additional reading in this area may be found in Dreikurs (1968) and Dinkmever et al. (1979).

SUMMARY

The work of the psychologist in a school setting may be enhanced by the incorporation of Adlerian ideas and techniques into one's psychotherapeutic repertoire. The Adlerian framework of viewing the nature of humanity offers a well-integrated eclectic perspective. The life-style approach, which initially focuses on the past as a means to understand the present better, often yields extremely helpful information about an adolescent's or adult's dimly conscious life goals. In addition, the Adlerian approach offers many guidelines and techniques for helping children in the home and school.

REFERENCES

Ansbacher, H. & Ansbacher R. (Eds.). The Individual Psychology of Alfred Adler. New York: Basic Books. 1956.

Dinkmever, D. & Murc, J. Group counseling: theory and practice. Itasea, Ill.: F. E. Peacock, 1971.

Dinkmeyer, D., Pew, W., & Dinkmeyer, D. Adlerian counseling and psychotherapy. Belmont, Calif.: Wadsworth, 1979.

Dreikurs, R. Psychodynamics, psychotherapy, and counseling. Chicago: Alfred Adler Institute, 1967.

Dreikurs, R. Psychology in the classroom (2nd ed.). New York: Harper & Row, 1968.

Dreikurs, R. & Goldman, M. The ABC's of guiding the child. Chicago: North Side Unit of Family Education Association, 1967.

Dreikurs, R. & Soltz, V. Children: the challenge. New York: Hawthorne Books, 1964.

Mosak, H. Lifestyle. In A. Nikelly (Ed.), Techniques for behavior change. Springfield, III.: Charles C Thomas, 1971.

Mosak, H. & Dreikurs, R. Adlerian psychotherapy. In R. Corsini (Ed.), Current psychotherapies. Itasca, Ill.: F. E. Peacock, 1973.

Mosak, H. & Mosak, B. A bibliography for Adlerian psychology. Washington, D.C.: Hemisphere, 1975.

O'Connell, W. Action therapy and Adlerian theory. Chicago: Alfred Adler Institute, 1975.

Rule, W. What next after self-awareness: A rational apothecary. Rational Living, 1980, 15, 24–25.

Shulman, B. Contributions to Individual Psychology. Chicago: Alfred Adler Institute, 1973.

Sweeney, T. Adlerian counseling. Boston: Houghton Mifflin, 1975.

Walton, F. & Powers. R. Winning children over. Chicago: Practical Psychology Association, 1974.

10

ADLERIAN METHODS: CASE STUDY

Christopher Ovide and Warren R. Rule

The Adlerian psychotherapist does not approach the child as a single entity but conceives the child as part of a social environment. Rather than being exclusively concerned with the child's inner dynamics or manifest behavior, the Adlerian counselor works with the child, parents, siblings, school personnel, and significant others who influence the child's perception and interpretation of the world. The following case is illustrative of the use of Adlerian methods in a school setting.

David, a fourth grade student, was referred for counseling by his teacher, who believed that his misconduct in class and learning difficulties were a result of emotional problems. She described David as "very troubled." To avoid bias, the psychologist chose not to consult the child's school file or the teacher for background information prior to the first interview. Such bias would have reduced much of the session to confirming the data in the child's file and the teacher's impressions.

This chapter, "Adlerian Methods: Case Study," from J. Cull & L. Golden (Eds.), *Psychotherapeutic Techniques in School Psychology*, 1984. Courtesy of Charles C Thomas, Publisher, Springfield, IL.

The psychologist's goal for the first meeting with David was to establish rapport with him and to begin the diagnostic process that would help orient the psychotherapeutic process. The psychologist planned to use relationship-building techniques, such as active listening and empathic reflection in combination with Adler's diagnostic interview questions (Ansbacher & Ansbacher, 1956), to achieve these goals.

David was asked why he thought his teacher had referred him to counseling, and he replied that it was probably because he "drove her crazy." He explained that he talked to others at inappropriate times, asked the teacher too many questions, and could not stay in his seat, and added that he was "just a bad kid." From these statements the psychologist considered it likely that David was operating from what Dreikurs (1967) described as a mistaken goal of being perceived as powerful. Through his actions, David was showing his teacher that she could not control him and that he could, through his misbehavior, control the classroom environment. His actions also included elements of negative attention-getting behavior and hinted at revenge-seeking tactics. The psychologist decided that a more formal lifestyle analysis might yield helpful information, although this analysis is usually employed with older persons.

At the end of the first session, David was told that his parents would be contacted and a conference requested. David stated that his father was overseas on military duty but his mother would be available to attend, although she probably would choose to decline. When David added that his mother's lack of caring was of no importance to him, the earlier impression of the existence of a power-oriented goal with strong feelings of revenge on others was reaffirmed.

Following the first session, both mother and teacher were contacted. David's teacher described him as a likeable, but exasperating, child who could not remain still. She said he was prone to outbursts of talking to others, talking to himself, laughing and talking excessively loud, and flare-ups of temper with physical attacks on his classmates. In addition, David's academic work was inconsistent, with periods of exceptional performance and periods of poor work and study habits. She had tried to schedule conferences with his mother but reported that David's mother believed it unnecessary because David was "sick." The mother had told the teacher that David was hyperactive and was taking medication but that it did not seem to help very much. The teacher tried to remedy some of the problems David presented in the classroom by giving individual attention to his scholastic work; moving his desk to the front of the class; giving him special, responsible tasks and errands; and rewarding and praising his good behavior. She had no success with any of these techniques and often found that David's behavior worsened as a result of her efforts. Punishment was used as a last resort.

David's mother confirmed that he was on medication for hyperkinetic behavior. Since this had failed to slow him down, she believed nothing could be done to help her son. She agreed to meet with the psychologist, however. During the sessions, the counselor learned that David had been diagnosed at five years old to be hyperactive and had been on and off various medications since that time, with little improvement. At home David was said to be continuously active and aimless in his activity—quarrelsome, physically and verbally abusive to his older sister, and uncooperative in refusing to obey directions from his mother. The mother stated that both David and his sister, Susan, knew they were adopted children. She felt David's behavior had become worse since she and her husband had experienced marital problems the year before and thought David might not believe that her husband was out of the home only until his tour of duty was over.

His mother's method of disciplining David at home was to spank him, to take away privileges, and to restrict him to the house or to his room. She characterized her daughter as the "exact opposite" of David—helpful, cheerful, cooperative, and exceptionally successful in school. His mother believed that most of David's school problems were a result of his being held back a year in the fourth grade by the same teacher he had at present. She believed his teacher had decided David was not intelligent and that the teacher had a personal dislike for him.

In the second session with David, his family constellation was investigated using the lifestyle format suggested by Ansbacher and Ansbacher (1956) and Dreikurs (1967). David and his sister were the only children in the family, and he was unaware of any attempts of his parents to have their own children or to adopt another child. David described himself as "happy, anxious, bad, always into trouble," while he saw Susan as "smart and good," doing everything she should. In comparing himself to his sister, David believed her to be harder working, more successful in school, more helpful, more conforming; he saw himself as more intelligent and rebellious. Susan tried to please others more than he, and she generally succeeded. David was more critical of himself and others, more selfish and insistent on having his own way. David reported Susan actually got her own way most often and that Susan had higher standards of achievement and behavior.

David thought his mother and father catered to him more often than to Susan. Neither of the children was punished very often, according to David, although in the last few years his mother had been restricting him to the house when his behavior was particularly bad. He still threw temper tantrums, after which he usually was sent to his room. After punishing him, though, David's parents usually gave him what he demanded.

David believed Susan had more friends than he; accordingly, she was very popular, but no one liked him. When they were younger, he and Susan played together much of the time, but lately Susan was devoting most of her time to her friends. In his relationship with his peers, David thought of himself as an outsider; he was always on the fringes of groups and never felt included in activities. He said that he had no close friends, and although others did not dislike him, they rarely liked him. He implied that he felt unimportant, unnoticed, and unrecognized.

David's parents quarreled openly and often, causing David a great deal of fear each time this occurred. His main concern was that if they separated, neither would want him. In his opinion, his father, a quiet, friendly man, loved Susan more than David. On the other hand, David was his mother's favorite. David described his mother as very emotional, sometimes very attentive and affectionate, at other times cool and aloof. She was always going places and seemed very busy.

The process of gathering information about family constellation and early recollections, in addition to yielding valuable life-style data, serves as a mechanism for building rapport. In interpreting David's family constellation, the psychologist observed that David exhibited some characteristics that sometimes denote the youngest child, e.g., an expectancy to be cared for, an eagerness to make one's presence felt. David's older sister was very successful in maintaining her place of established superiority. In doing this, however, she discouraged David in his efforts to strive toward useful areas of personal achievement. As such, David was a child who was familiar with failing at achieving positive recognition from others. He had grown to expect defeat in most of what he attempted to do; also he had concluded that he could be noticed by others only when he annoyed or angered them. His mother was always on the go, constantly busy, and this angered him, making him feel as if she had neither time nor interest for him. His principal method of operation—continuous activity—may have been adopted from his mother's (unintended) message that she was always busy and hence had no time to be with him.

In the following session, the client's early recollections were explored. In very young children, early recollections may not be helpful, and many Adlerian counselors avoid them. Early recollections can occasionally prove useful in establishing more specifics about the client's style of life for those individuals at the stages of late childhood to early adolescence.

David's earliest remembrances occurred at about three-and-one-half years of age and took place in his front yard. His parents were working in the yard when a sports car drove up and stopped. Excited by its sudden appearance, David called out to his parents to look at the car. He was disappointed when no one noticed his cries. When the car loudly sped away, the disturbance caused his parents to look up, angrily, and to discuss the driver.

In his second recollection. David recalled going to a neighbor's home with his mother and sister for a visit. During lunch, his mother and her friend left the two children in the kitchen to eat and had their lunch alone in the living room. David got up from the table and went in with his mother. She told him to go back to the kitchen with his sister and to be nice and quiet. David went back into the kitchen but began to fight with his sister, who chased after him. His mother came in and stopped the situation. David was scolded for not obeying and later was admonished by his father.

In a third recollection, David remembered being in a clinic waiting room. Susan was very ill, and his mother had taken her to the doctor. David felt bored and asked his mother to read one of the books in the office to him. She explained that his sister was ill and she had to take care of her. David got down from his chair, went up to other people in the waiting room, picked up and threw down magazines and books, jumped on empty chairs, and played loudly on the floor. His mother tried to stop this behavior, but he persisted. He was scolded later at home by both parents.

An overriding theme in these early recollections began to emerge. David attempted to involve himself with others, generally in a positive manner, but the results of his efforts were negative. David was successful, however, in obtaining the attention of people when he was misbehaving. The dynamics involved in the roar of a speeding sports car and the disruption David created in the clinic waiting room yielded an increased understanding of David's hyperactivity. David's early recollections also showed a concern with adults and authority figures, rather than peers. (His only interaction with a peer was to involve his sister in a fight in order to achieve the recognition of adult figures.)

Once information on David's life-style was obtained, David's teacher and mother were asked to attend a joint conference. His father, still on overseas assignment, could not attend. In this conference, the psychologist explained some of his insights of David's life-style to the teacher and mother. A method of giving David adequate encouragement and recognition was discussed as were methods of using logical consequences to help reduce or eliminate David's more troublesome behavior. The psychologist also suggested that he be recognized for positive behavior, by verbal expression, and that his opinions on various home and classroom issues be sought. For disruptive behavior, the suggestion was made that peer group pressure be used as a logical consequence of his actions in the classroom, together with facing the logical consequences of his behavior both at home and in the classroom. David's mother was encouraged to attend an Adlerian child guidance study group, but she declined. She was then asked to consult with the psychologist when problems arose in controlling David's behavior.

In sessions with David thereafter, a solid relationship was developed using the gradual interpretation of David's life-style. Initially, his feelings of not being accepted were explored, together with his idea that adults and powerful people were the only important individuals. David was assigned several tasks to help involve him with children his own age. His success in these assignments led to an increased social awareness of people his own age, as well as a realization that people are important whether they are powerful or not. His own self-acceptance and self-concept was also increased. Focusing on this aspect of his life-style caught David off guard. For perhaps the first time in his life, his excessive activity and short attention span was not of utmost concern to those working with him. By interpreting David's use of hyperactive behavior as a method of feeling secure and as a way of keeping others, important others, aware of him, the counselor was helpful in increasing David's awareness.

As David solidified a position of acceptance with his peers and received encouragement from his teacher, his hyperactive behavior began to decrease in school. His work improved slightly, and his attention span improved considerably. At home, David's behavior did not measurably change in quality. His mother continued to find many of his efforts to capture her attention irritating and annoying. Yet, his hyperactivity seemed to disappear. The psychologist suggested that David's medication be discussed with his physician and it was consequently reduced. Within forty-five days of the first counseling session, David's medication was discontinued. There was no increase in activity level when the medication was eliminated, and the quality of his behavioral activity improved. David's homework assignments continued to be sporadic and of inferior quality. This suggested ongoing difficulty in the home, hence David's mother was contacted and family counseling was suggested. His mother refused, saying he was doing much better and she was satisfied with his progress.

David was seen by the psychologist once every two weeks for the remainder of the school year. He was also included in a guidance group that was held for several of his classmates on an eight-week basis. Serious disruption in his family occurred when David's mother filed for a legal separation from his father. This resulted in some recurrence of David's previous behavior for a brief period. Subsequently, he was able to deal effectively with the difficulties and continued to exhibit gains in his scholastic work. David remained free of medication for the school year and, on follow-up, the summer thereafter. His parents eventually reconciled, and the family remained intact. David was promoted to the fifth grade, his achievement having risen to the mid–fifth year level.

REFERENCES

Ansbacher, H. L. & Ansbacher, R. W. (Eds.). The Individual Psychology of Alfred Adler, New York: Basic Books, 1956.

Dreikurs, R. Psychodynamics, psychotherapy; and counseling. Chicago: Alfred Adler Institute, 1967.

IV
Rehabilitation

11

LIFESTYLE AND ADJUSTMENT TO DISABILITY

Warren R. Rule

Many assumptions and issues are involved in the relationship between lifestyle and adjustment to disability. First of all, it is very likely that the practitioner cannot avoid being influenced by his assumptions regarding the nature of man. The conscious and dimly conscious beliefs that the helper holds about man's personality development and nature will influence his method of intervention. Moreover, this will be subtly in operation regardless of whether the disability is congenital or acquired. The practitioner's beliefs as to whether man is determined by his past or freely chooses from moment to moment, whether he is basically driven by instincts or is shaped by his environment, whether an individual creates his feelings or is possessed by his feelings, and so on, all unavoidably influence how one goes about helping others. Getting in touch with the dimensions of one's personal "personality theory" can be a worthwhile first step. Subsequently, the individual who has made this self-inventory is in a better position to supplement or even change

This chapter, "Lifestyle and Adjustment to Disability," from Warren R. Rule (Ed.), *Lifestyle counseling for adjustment to disability*, 1984. Rockville, MD: Aspen Systms Corporation.

his beliefs as a result of considering more formalized personality theories.

An approach to understanding personality based on the concept of the Adlerian lifestyle provides a holistic framework for viewing disability. It is both substantial and broad based enough that it could have appeal to practitioners with an eclectic orientation. This approach, along with variations, may be helpful to the practitioner because an increased awareness of the individual lifestyle may be a key to understanding his own perception of and reaction to disability.

ADLERIAN LIFESTYLE

As we noted in Chapter 1, Adler believed that each individual develops a "lifestyle" during his childhood years that exerts a major influence on his thoughts, feelings, and behavior throughout life. Adler coined this term more than 50 years ago and he developed this concept over a span of a quarter of a century. Shulman (1973) summarized the lifestyle as:

> a superordinate organizational pattern that directs behavior. By means of selective perception, cognition, memory, etc., it codifies rules for characteristic attitudinal positions. It becomes the intervening variable between efficient cause and effect, between stimulation of the outside world and the responsive behaviors of the person. It is formed early in childhood and is self-reinforcing through selectivity. It is self-consistent, coherent, and unified. It is constant; it does not change from time to time or situation to situation, though it is not necessarily rigid. It can be recognized by its repeated appearance as a theme in the life history of even everyday behavior of an individual. It develops through trial and error and is influenced by physical, developmental, cultural, and familial factors. It is a necessary rule for coping behavior, to bring order into one's relationship with the challenging and confronting world. It is therefore of critical significance to the clinician who wishes to understand the "whys?" of human behavior. (p. 44)

The focus is not on the feelings or behavior that a person uses as he moves through life; rather, the emphasis is on the pattern of goal-directed thinking. Let us examine further some of the important assumptions upon which the lifestyle concept rests.

The Holistic Nature of Man

A basic assumption that fits securely into the perspective of the psychosocial adjustment of the individual is Adler's belief about the wholeness of the individual. A person's wholeness, or "holistic" nature, is irreducible; to break up the personality or fragment it into parts is to destroy the wholeness and thereby undermine the understanding of the individual. A person cannot be dissected without losing some understanding of the pattern or theme that runs through his life. Adler used an analogy from music: music cannot be fully appreciated by studying each note itself—one needs to have the context of the other notes in order to experience the melody.

Adler chose the term "lifestyle" to depict this holistic pattern that is greater than the sum of the parts. The assumption that the unit (the individual) is indivisible is important, particularly for understanding the relationship of an individual to disability. This is so because the way in which individuals organize themselves as whole people influences their perceptions of themselves and others and has a large bearing on their goals and behavioral interactions with others.

Heredity and Environment

Adler was strongly convinced of the creative power of the individual, believing in "soft determinism" as opposed to "hard determinism" (Ansbacher & Ansbacher, 1956). He stated:

> Do not forget the most important fact that not heredity and not environment are determining factors. Both are giving only the frame and the influences which are answered by the individual in regard to his styled creative power. (p. xxiv)

Dreikurs, who was probably Adler's foremost student in the United States, observed that:

> The genetic emphasis on heredity factors is equally mechanistic as the behavioristic analysis of environmental influences. Even the efforts to describe the interrelationships between heredity and environmental influences on the development of the personality structure result in a mechanistic picture of a struggle between antagonistic or supplementary forces. (1967, p. 168)

A closely related issue is that of lifestyle as a cause of behavior or a determiner of behavior. Shulman (1973) noted that the lifestyle is a "cause" of behavior in the sense that Aristotle discussed the causa formalis, the "ordering or patterning of relationships that leads to specific results" (p. 18). Shulman further concluded that the lifestyle acts as a "determiner" in the sense that it limits, as does any law, and it governs in terms of directing overall line of movement and providing feedback that serves to reinforce or inhibit the movement.

Cause-and-effect thinking can sometimes work to the practitioner's disadvantage when applied to life issues other than the validity of the lifestyle concept. The following passage, although not written from an Adlerian perspective, richly illustrates the limitations of mechanistic cause-and-effect thinking when used as a framework for understanding the complexity of life's flow:

> "What is fate?" Nasrudin was asked by a scholar.
> "An endless succession of intertwined events, each influencing the other."
> "That is hardly a satisfactory answer. I believe in cause and effect." "Very well," said the Mulla, "look at that." He pointed to a procession passing in the street.
> "That man is being taken to be hanged. Is that because someone gave him a silver piece and enabled him to buy the knife with which he committed the murder, or because someone saw him do it; or because nobody stopped him? (Ornstein, 1972, p. 75)

Social Context

Adler believed that man is a social being and that behavior can only be fully understood in a social context. Ansbacher and Ansbacher (1956) noted that Adler's approach could properly be referred to as a "context" psychology. He regarded personal problems basically as social problems. Related to this assumption about man's social nature is the idea that in each of us there exists the desire to belong. Expressed in another way, each of us strives to have a place of significance in the eyes of others. The goal of obtaining a "place of somebodyness" is handled differently by different people. Correspondingly, a congenital or acquired disability would be handled differently by different lifestyles because both the perceived "place of somebodyness" and the social context would vary from person to person.

Broadly speaking, the goals a person pursues and the behaviors an individual learns can be indirectly related to the innate desire to enhance oneself within a social context. Thus, in attempting to understand another person, a workable framework would be: "How is this person seeking to be known by others?" The answer has obvious implications for the psychosocial adjustment of an individual with a disability. Another Adlerian assumption, the goal-directed nature of behavior, further increases our understanding of the social implications of disability.

Goal-Directedness

Adler believed that all behavior, including emotions, is goal directed. Stated another way, everything we do has a purpose and is a function of our ideas—both conscious and dimly conscious—about consequences to be obtained in the future. Behaviors that seemingly cannot be explained become more understood as the goal or purpose comes to light. So, even though at times we are consciously aware of the purpose of thinking, feeling, or acting in a certain fashion, most of the time we are unaware of our unique self-concerned goals that are in operation at a dimly conscious level. We are not aware of how pervasively lifestyle goals are at work in our daily life: in the way we interact with others, in our choice of friends or consumer products, in our sense of accomplishment or vulnerability, in the viewpoint we take toward the implications of disability, etc.

Thus, the individual seems to operate from a subjective mental framework and is not always fully conscious of his goals. In understanding someone, the focus must be on the person's subjective or internal frame of reference. This seems necessary because the individual's perceptions, including his inner biases influencing his perceptions, determine his behavior more than "reality" does. Furthermore, the individual organizes his perceptions into expectations that influence his personal goals.

It is noteworthy that a wide range of behavioral patterns is usually available to the individual for any given lifestyle conclusion or "characteristic attitudinal position" (Shulman, 1973). The lifestyle approach asserts that people can, in fact, change in major ways; however, the sensitive position on a lifestyle notion may be the common thread that runs through the "changes" a person regards himself as having made throughout the span of his life. These behavioral changes, even seemingly major ones, may actually be variations of the same theme. Or, expressed another way, these changes could be different creative behavioral implementations—in response to changing environmental situations—of the same lifestyle conclusions that the person continues to take a sensitive position on. Mosak (1958) illustrates some of the different behavioral implementations a person could use who has taken a sensitive position on the lifestyle conclusion "Life is dangerous":

> Such a person, behaviorally, may see danger where none exists. He may exaggerate the dangers of life. He may retreat from these perceived dangers with anxious or phobic behavior. Or he may call upon certain defense mechanisms to cope with the omnipotent threat. In the compulsive individual, for example, one observes reliance upon ritual and feelings of omnipotence and the necessity to control as response to danger. Many compulsives are preoccupied with death because this is the greatest threat—the one force which cannot be controlled. Hypochondriacs may exaggerate each body symptom as expressing their conviction that life is fraught with danger. Other individuals may develop into towers of strength or become dependent upon or identify with "strong" people or groups in order to minimize the dangers of life. Still others may actually court or provoke personal disaster in order to confirm their basic attitude. Some flirt with danger in order to prove that they possess a charmed life. While these reactions do not exhaust the repertoire available to people who feel that life is dangerous, they do serve to exemplify the variety of reactions which are possible within a single dimension of an individual's perceptual frame of reference. (p. 306)

Thus, the individual creativity is ever present as the person moves through life. In terms of bringing together the relationships of these different concepts, the following broad generalizations may be useful: from a sensitive position on lifestyle conclusions (e.g., I am…, others are…, life is…) the individual creates both dimly conscious goals and conscious goals to guide him through life; emotions are the energizers that transform the goals into behavior.

Subjectively Striving to Overcome

Adler believed that this pattern of lifestyle goals is organized around the subjectively determined concept of the ideal self, much of which the individual created during childhood years. The person, in his private logic, continually moves through life with this self ideal as a general reference point. Almost as if the individual is wearing blinders, he strives—at a dimly conscious level—to become like the imagined ideal self. Subsequently, the person seems to treat himself at a vague level of awareness as if he will only be truly OK or have a total sense of significance in the eyes of others and have a real feeling of security when he lives up to the ideal self. Thus, this network of lifestyle goals is patterned after an ideal concept of self. It provides the main thrust for the lifestyle that enables each of us to move, on a daily basis and throughout our lives, from a position of dimly felt inferiority or noncoping to a position of overcoming or coping.

Adler believed that this pattern of goals is organized around a single "fictional final goal." This concept has been criticized for its simplicity (e.g., Ford & Urban, 1963), but from the practitioner's vantage point adopted in this book, the significance lies in the concept that a pattern of complementing major goals flows in a unified direction; the issue of whether or not one goal slightly edges out the rest is somewhat academic.

Commensurate with the goal-directed nature of behavior, the individual is able, by his own standards, to move from the felt minus state of non-enoughness to the felt plus state of enoughness. As the individual moves through life, it seems that he never quite gets "there" or is absolutely and totally satisfied.

Adler believed that early conclusions drawn before approximately age six or seven go a long way toward determining the dimly conscious goals that comprise the lifestyle. These conclusions appear to be drawn from experiences related to the person's first social group, the family. Approximately age six or seven can be chosen as a general cutoff primarily because at that period the child is beginning to become enmeshed in a school setting; i.e., the individual has begun to broaden the range of influences received from his first social group, the family, to those of the next social group, the school. Adlerians assert that the childhood conclusions drawn about self, others, and life approximately before age six or seven largely contribute to the internalized guidelines that the person uses in his present striving. The child creatively uses heredity and environment as tools from which he molds a lifestyle.

The early conclusions that become goals of the lifestyle are drawn from a host of childhood impressions and experiences. Exceedingly important is the family constellation, including siblings' development, age differences, ordering of sexes, alliance groups, etc. Moreover, parental influences and expectations, family values and atmosphere, peers, and neighbors all contribute to the biased slice of life that is the only slice of life the child has available to generalize from.

Considerable emphasis is placed, in attempting to understand a person's lifestyle, on the psychological "territory" the individual chose to stake out as his own in an attempt to feel "others take notice of me when I am like this." This sense of self-significance or belonging can be manifested in a variety of outlets, e.g., being the best, the worst, the charmer, the tough one, etc. Each sibling, Adlerians hypothesize, will move in a different overall direction in these areas or may even try to overtake a sibling in a chosen area.

Individuals learn at an early age, through trial and error, not only what goals will be most apt to help them move toward a place of significance, but they also begin to experiment with which kinds of behavior are most useful in implementing the goals. Not surprisingly, individuals also learn behaviors, including emotions, in keeping with the dimly conscious goals of the lifestyle that safeguard their vulnerabilities and sense of self-esteem. Generally speaking, then, the chosen lifestyle allows individuals to evaluate, to understand, to predict, and to control experience (Mosak, 1979a).

Adler's approach to understanding the nature of man can be used, either in whole or in part, as a basis for a broadly eclectic approach to counseling. His concepts have influenced many in the helping professions, as discussed in the previous chapter, and his ideas have been of interest to some from other professional disciplines. The anecdote below is one such example:

> I remember this incident mostly because I used to think to myself, "It must be wonderful to be someone like Adler. You'd never have to worry about whether you were intelligent or not." This incident opened my eyes to the fact that everyone, no matter who you are, questions their intelligence and needs reassurance from time to time.
>
> Adler was coming to dinner at my father's house one night. He rang the doorbell. We opened the door. He walked in, and without any greeting, stood there with the most beaming smile and said in his slow speaking way, "I have a new (long, drawn out and softly accented) follower. Guess who?" Of course none of us could guess. And he said, very slowly, and beaming all the time, "Albert Einstein."
>
> He had received a letter from Einstein, who had attended one or more of his lectures, stating that he (Einstein) considered Adler's Individual Psychology to be the most scientific and closest to the truth for today. (Matteson, 1977, p. 48)

LIFESTYLE ASSESSMENT

The lifestyle assessment technique has traditionally been used with adolescents and adults. Some Adlerians, however, have experimented with lifestyle techniques for children.

Sources of Lifestyle Information

There are a number of ways by which the practitioner can learn more about an individual's lifestyle. Some of these sources of information are very broad and some are relatively narrow; others draw from readily available data and others require the gathering of additional information. Lombardi (1973) discusses eight different avenues that yield information about the consistent and patterned lifestyle:

1. Case history data—knowing about subject
2. Psychological interviewing—talking to subject
3. Expressive behavior—observing subject
4. Psychological testing—measuring subject
5. Family constellation—social influence on subject
6. Early recollections—subject's meaning of life
7. Grouping—interacting with subject
8. Symptomatic behavior—subject's tell-tale signs. (p. 6)

While the most ideal approach is to obtain information from all of the above avenues, oftentimes the practitioner must expediently settle for less. Perhaps one of the most widely used procedures for learning about an individual's lifestyle entails using a lifestyle assessment form. Several versions exist, one of the most popular being the form originally deve-loped by Dreikurs (1967). This form, which has since been modified by other practitioners to suit individual preferences, has incorporated several of the above-listed avenues for obtaining lifestyle information. The section below will expand on the nature of this somewhat structured approach to obtaining lifestyle information. Two variations of the Dreikurs form, a long and an abbreviated form, are included.

Significance of Early Memory

Memory is selective. As Dreikurs (1967) observed, people operate on an economy principle by selectively using their memories in accordance with their individual purposes. Thus our memories from early childhood serve as anchoring orientation points, reflecting the most important conclusions, expectations, and goals that crystallized during this formative period. Adlerians believe that these early impressions and memories reflect those firm ideas that are embedded in the individual's present outlook. So, in utilizing the selectivity of memory phenomenon, the helping practitioner is able to gather lifestyle information by asking the client significant questions and, as a result, is able tentatively to reconstruct important aspects of the client's early environment. Once this is accomplished, the helper can look for themes in the remembered early environment that reflect the dimly conscious notions and goals the client is presently using.

Based on the client's memories (both real and sometimes imagined) before approximately age six or seven, areas of lifestyle information include descriptions of self and siblings, sibling rankings on possible areas of competition (e.g., intelligence, pleasing, having own way, athletics, appearance, temper, etc.), sibling interrelationships, parents and parental influence, family values and atmosphere, relationship to peers, and specific early recollections and dreams.

Family Constellation

Particular emphasis is given in the Adlerian lifestyle approach to family constellation from a psychosocial perspective. Accordingly, attention is directed to sibling age differences, ordering of sexes, favoritism, uniquenesses, alliance groups, development of patterns of siblings, how client felt about his position, etc. Only-born children are often compared with playmates.

Shulman (1973) listed five basic positions: only, eldest, second, middle, and youngest child. Different variations and combinations for these basic positions exist. Each basic position has several very modest probabilities of stereotyped characteristics attached to it. The helper considers and refines these tentative hypotheses in line with the direction of movement reflected by the other lifestyle variables. For example, sometimes first-born children (both oldest and only-born) have taken a sensitive position in their early lives on mandates, e.g., "shoulds," "musts," and "ought to's." This heightened sensitivity may have been the result of strong parental expectations. Or, it might have been influenced by the conclusion that one is only OK when one "achieves" in life (hence the usefulness of mandates as stimulators). A host of possible influences may have contributed to this sensitivity to "shoulds." For the purpose of illustration, we will assume below that a consistent pattern of this characteristic has emerged from the rest of the lifestyle information, including the early recollections.

How is an awareness of this pattern or any other pattern helpful to the practitioner? The practitioner can explore how this particular sensitivity is useful to the client in his own unique lifestyle as he moves through life. Does he use it to align himself with authority or established values? Does he strive to be Number One by setting lofty—perhaps unreasonable—"shoulds" for himself? Does he passive-aggressively resist most of life's mandates? The emphasis for the practitioner would be on relating patterns of lifestyle movement, which are grounded in childhood conclusions, to difficulties that the client is presently experiencing. Expressed another way, the practitioner is interested in helping the client get in touch with how his lifestyle is contributing—however consciously—to his problems.

This same flexible process of lifestyle analysis would be used to validate or reject tentative hypotheses the helping practitioner would have in mind about an individual with respect to position in the family constellation. For instance, some youngest borns sometimes strive to be charmers, others choose a pattern of irresponsibility with the expectation that others should step in and help them, some are eager to be the boss, others—particularly from big families—seek to outdo the preceding siblings and become top-notch achievers, and so on. In working with a youngest-born client, the Adlerian practitioner might look for these and/or related patterns, fully keeping in mind that while very modest stereotypes of family constellations exist, the individual is unique in his lifestyle development. Since early influences on the child can be so varied, the modest probabilities of family constellation may or may not be confirmed. The lifestyle interview is designed to pinpoint many of these other early influences so that the practitioner can digest and refine them in the process of bringing the client's lifestyle into sharper focus.

Specific Early Recollections

In rounding out the lifestyle understanding, much importance is given to the client's early recollections, memories, and dreams. Adlerians believe that there are no chance memories. That is to say, from the thousands and thousands of experiences to which an individual has been exposed in early childhood, only those recollections are remembered that coincide with one's present outlook on self, others, or life. Thus, the person's early recollections reflect the same patterns; they are reminders the individual carries around regarding personal limits and the meaning of circumstances (Ansbacher & Ansbacher, 1956).

Generally speaking, individuals can remember, when asked, at least six specific incidents that occurred during their early childhood. Each early recollection, when considered in the context of the accompanying feeling about the remembered incident, reflects a current expectation. Adlerians focus on the manifest content of the early memory, not on hidden, symbolic meanings. Moreover, each recollection supplements and rounds out the outlook reflected by the other early recollections.

Adlerian practitioners generally believe that the individual is the product of both individual "laws" and general "laws." In other words, a person is the result of individual laws that he created for himself and the result of general laws that apply to all people or specified groups of individuals. So, in seeking to understand more fully another person, the practitioner keeps an eye on both individual (idiographic) and general (nomothetic) understanding.

The Lifestyle Interview

The lifestyle interview can take several hours to complete or a shorter interview can be conducted. Several variables are involved here, such as time availability and the purpose for performing a lifestyle analysis. If a greater amount of information is gathered, the likelihood is increased of obtaining more accurate and well-rounded results.

Some examples of different lifestyle themes are cited by Mosak (1971), who cautioned that predictions cannot be made as to what behavior will coincide with a given lifestyle. In addition, Mosak (1976b) emphasized that the uniqueness of the individual is violated by typologies, which should be viewed as strictly didactic contributions. Examples of these themes are controlling, getting, driving, always being right, pleasing, being the center or the best, being admired for moral superiority, being against, being the baby or a charmer, being victimized, being intellectually superior, being an excitement seeker, being a martyr, etc.

If these examples appear to have a distinct self-serving flavor, several points might be kept in mind. First, individuals want to move from a position of dimly felt inferiority to a position of significance. The labels given to the themes reflect the powerful determination to enhance the self. Second, the lifestyle works to one's advantage as well as one's disadvantage. These themes can be channeled on the socially useful side of life and truly enhance others as well as the self. Third, the creativity of the individual is ever present in choosing the subtle as well as the more obvious ways the lifestyle is implemented.

The question of the reliability and validity of the lifestyle approach is not to be taken lightly. Discussion of studies related to these issues may be found in sources such as Allen (1971), Kern, Matheny, and

Patterson (1978), and Mosak (1979a). Birth-order research has generated over 500 studies and the bulk of the significant results have been discussed by Forer (1976) and Sutton-Smith and Rosenberg (1970). Early recollections have been the subject of increasing research studies; many of those having Adlerian application are discussed by Mosak (1958, 1977), Olson (1979), and Taylor (1975). A comprehensive bibliography by Mosak and Mosak (1975) is a useful reference for most of these studies. Statistical research can make a contribution in the study of nomothetic, or general, laws as related to the lifestyle approach; however, the idiographic laws, which the individual created for himself as dimly conscious guidelines for moving through life, are more difficult to study with statistical methods.

Experience and familiarity with lifestyle variables and assessment are understandably significant factors in determining how helpful the approach is to the practitioner. Further reading, in addition to supervision, would provide a solid start.

LIFESTYLE FACTORS AND DISABILITY

In considering the utility of the Adlerian lifestyle approach as a means to better understand adjustment to disability, it is important to keep in mind that "lifestyle" awareness is just as applicable to disabled groups as to "normal" groups. Reviews (e.g., Dunham and Dunham, 1978; English, 1974) of relevant investigations have concluded that few, if any, personality differences exist between the disabled and the normal population. The lifestyle analysis would seem to have as much merit for understanding the "personality" of a disabled individual as a nondisabled person. In addition, once a measure of lifestyle understanding is achieved between the practitioner and the client, exploration can be devoted to the extremely important issue of the relationship between the client's lifestyle and his disability. The focus would be on how the client's lifestyle notions and goals are contributing to—or undermining—adjustment to the disability.

Other Theoretical Perspectives

In comparison to some of the other major theories that attempt to explain psychological reaction to disability, the lifestyle approach seems to have some distinct advantages. The psychoanalytic theory is so grounded in the total determinism of early childhood that it does not appear to have the flexibility of the "soft determinism" of the Adlerian approach. Though definitely emphasizing the importance of early childhood, Adler strongly believed that the individual creatively molds, while exercising a measure of free choice, his lifestyle from environment and heredity. Correspondingly, one's reaction to disability was viewed by Adler as being less deterministic than the psychoanalytic position.

Proponents of the "Body Image" theory or the "Social Role" theory, as discussed by English (1974), would perhaps find their method of assessing reaction to disability enhanced by the lifestyle technique. Briefly stated, the "body image" theorists place much importance on those attitudes individuals have toward themselves and others with regard to physical characteristics. The "social role" theorists emphasize that people interact according to learned role expectations, including how to behave in a sick or disabled role. A heightened awareness of the more broadly based basic lifestyle notions and goals, which have a psychosocial foundation, would enhance or supplement the results obtained by focusing on either the individual's perceptions of body image or his disability role expectations.

Shontz (1977) regarded the "interpersonal" theoretical ideas as probably being the best developed (e.g., Barker and Wright, 1953; Wright, 1960). These ideas, which overlap with the "Social Role" theory discussed above, emphasize the values assigned to the disability and body by self and others and use descriptive concepts such as spread, value loss, containment of disability effects, etc. Shontz also noted other perspectives: motivation theories, e.g., Maslow (1954), who emphasized level of needs; crises theory, involving stages or cycles of the crisis experience; comparison level theory, which focuses on level of payoff or reinforcement; stress theory, which attempts to relate physiological and psychological processes; and attitudes toward disability.

Attitudes toward Disability

Negative attitudes toward the disabled often contribute to the difficulties faced by them. Although the emphasis here is on the personal meaning of the disability to the individual, the following conclusions drawn by Roessler and Bolton (1978), based on reviews by Barker, Wright, Meyerson, and Gonick (1953) and Siller (1976), are worth noting:

> First, attitudes toward disabled persons are typically unfavorable, despite what most people say when asked. Second, negative attitudes toward the disabled result in real barriers and restricted opportunities; again, prejudice produces discrimina-

> tion against disabled persons. Third, the unfavorable attitudes held by nondisabled persons may influence disabled persons' views of their worth.... Fourth, disabled persons often live with unfavorable attitudes from a very early age because even their parents may have difficulty treating them normally. (p. 11)

Adlerian Implications

A heightened awareness of the more broadly based basic lifestyle notions and goals, which act as a psychosocial filter for the individual, may enhance or supplement whatever results are obtained using the theoretical perspective discussed in the preceding two sections.

Several of Adler's concepts have sometimes been inconsistently and/or superficially discussed in the disability literature. Adler's student, Rudolf Dreikurs (1967), was aware of the increasing misunderstanding of Adler's concepts in the health field and he published a paper, originally appearing in 1948, in which he attempted to qualify Adler's ideas, especially as they relate to disability.

The concept of organ inferiority, developed very early in Adler's career, is a main source of confusion in the rehabilitation field, especially as it is related to the concept of compensation. Since originally developing the idea of organ inferiority ("organ" meaning any physically identifiable part of the body) and compensation, Adler considerably modified and expanded his ideas during the next 25 years. In this evolutionary process, the concept moved toward and contributed to the sociopsychological orientation of the lifestyle approach as the basis of behavior and away from the earlier emphasis on the physical realm as being the basis of behavior. Unfortunately, many reviewers focused on the earlier emphases, thus missing Adler's refined—and more useful—concepts.

Regarding those individuals with a disability, Adler believed that the creativity of the individual is foremost and that concepts predicting rigid, deterministic reactions to disability were useless. For instance, he believed that a number of possible responses exist, depending on lifestyle variables of the individual: courageous compensation; despair leading to retreat; a protective, hesitating attitude. Dreikurs (1967) observed that the courageous response converts the difficulty into a blessing, the despairing response can mean retreat into disability, and the neurotic response says, "How much better could I do if I had not this disability!" (p. 174).

In regard to the aforementioned evolutionary stages of Adler's thinking, Rychlak (1973) noted that:

> It was this belief in the multiplicity of response to organic inferiority which gave Adler his first inkling that the patient as an interactional person contributed something subjectively to the situation in which he found himself. Illness was not a simple cause-effect business. (p. 99)

Dreikurs further attempted to clarify the confusion related to the uses of the term "inferiority." The words "inferiority," "inferiority feelings," and "inferiority complex" are often not differentiated in the literature. The following passage (Dreikurs, 1967) distinguishes the usages of these terms, which have an important bearing on psychosocial adjustment and lifestyle:

> Inferiority can refer to any objective inadequacy in function or in status. But it does not necessarily produce an inferiority feeling. A person may be weak, deficient or of low status without any realization of inferiority. On the other hand, an inferiority feeling may exist without any real inferiority. The decisive factor in the dynamics of inferiority feelings is the person's assumption of being inferior, either physically, socially, or in comparison to his own goals and standards. This assumption may not always be expressed on a conscious or verbal level as the individual may not be fully aware of it.... Only the inferiority feeling can stimulate a compensation on the part of the individual. The situation is different in regard to biological inferiorities and organ deficiencies, because the whole organism takes them into consideration and may, therefore, prompt biological compensations and over compensations, without any necessary awareness by the individual. The term "Inferiority Complex" applies to an entirely different psychological mechanism. A discouraged individual may use a real or assumed deficiency for the purpose of special benefit, generally as an excuse or an alibi for nonparticipation and withdrawal, or as a means to get special services or consideration. This is the only type of inferiority of which the individual is fully aware, as he tries to impress others and his own conscience with the magnitude of his defects. The "Inferiority Complex" does not lead to any compensation. It is a deadlock for any further development. (pp. 175–176)

In terms of purposes served within various lifestyles, "inferiority" is a somewhat objective assessment or comparison, "inferiority feelings" have been present in everyone at various times and influence future development, and "inferiority complex" is a fatalistic reaction to a very difficult situation without attempting to correct or improve it.

Adjustment to Disability

The concept of disability brings a variety of thoughts to the minds of individuals in both the general public and the helping professions. Some of these thoughts are based on reality, others are grounded in stereotypes, and more than a few are fallacies. Let us first note several misconceptions related to personality and disability (primarily physical). The first widely held belief is that specific disabilities are associated with specific types of personality. Another frequently held viewpoint is that different types of disability cause specific personality reactions. A third common assumption is that severity of disability is directly related to degree of psychological impairment. Extensive reviews of the literature by Shontz (1977) and Roessler and Bolton (1978) indicated that all of the above-stated beliefs are misconceptions that have virtually no solid research support. Shontz (1977) observed that:

> No authority claims that disability never affects personality; individual reactions frequently are profound and intense. What is denied is the systematic and universal correlation of type or degree of disability with type or degree of personality adjustment. (p. 334)

Thus there is a broad scope of reactions to disability. Persons with the same disabilities may have entirely different responses. This phenomenon as well as Shontz's conclusions, based on a review of the literature, that "basic personality structure appears to be remarkably stable even in the face of serious somatic change" (p. 345) are both consistent with the lifestyle approach to disability, which focuses on the individual meaning of the disability to the person.

In terms of this important issue of individual versus general approaches, Roessler and Bolton (1978) concluded that:

> Hence, an individual-by-individual approach to adjustment to disability is important. However, generalizations, if they are not binding, help in providing both an explanation for what one is observing and a framework for a theoretical understanding of adjustment and disability that leads to hypotheses about new ways to serve the disabled. (p. 18)

Brief summaries are listed below of various generalizations related to adjustment to disability. These generalizations should be viewed as tentative considerations that may or may not apply to an individual lifestyle:

- Wright (1977) asserted that basically four issues exist in overcoming emotional barriers to adjustment: (1) enlarging the scope of values, which entails extending one's horizons beyond the disability and the self; (2) subordinating physique, involving the elevation of values other than physique; (3) containing disability effects, which entails preventing the spread of the disability limitations into nondisability-related areas; and (4) upholding asset evaluation, involving a focus on the positive or basic requirements, and on nonjudgmental standards of comparison.
- Kübler-Ross (1973) developed a five-stage theory that relates to adjustment to death, yet has a direct parallel to adjustment to disability: denial ("No, not me"), rage and anger ("Why me?"), bargaining ("Yes, me, but..."), depression ("Yes, me"), acceptance.
- Gunther (1969) observed that the somewhat orderly process of adjustment to disability generally involves the following stages, which may vary in duration: shock, partial recognition, initial stabilization, regression, and resolution of the regression phase.
- Eisenberg (1977) noted that, in addition to the use of defense mechanisms, which are employed by everyone (the common ones used by individuals with disabilities being withdrawal, denial and repression, projection, displacement, regression, rationalization), misconceptions about disability and adjustment should be considered. These include such misconceptions as the expectation of excellence in compensatory efforts, obtaining inner peace through suffering, adjustment by disowning a defective body part, and waiting for a miracle cure.
- Siller (1976) observed that noteworthy long-term reactions to traumatization, particularly as related to spinal cord-injured persons, could be: passivity; dependency, including pseudoindependent phenomena (e.g., obstinacy, inappropriate confidence, inability to accept appropriate offers of help, and unrealistic goal setting); aggression; and compensation.
- Thompson (1982) has drawn parallels between Erikson's life continuum of eight distinct stages and adjustment to severe disability, such as spinal cord injury. The stages are infancy, autonomy, initiative, industry, adolescence, identity, generativity, and integrity. In

each stage it is assumed that there is a danger-unsuccessful development pushes the person toward the opposite, or negative, pole.

- Cohn (1961) isolated stages that she regards as somewhat fluid points on a continuum rather than as discrete categories. These stages of adjustment refer to permanently disabled persons whose physical conditions are not likely to improve appreciably: shock ("This isn't me"), expectancy of recovery ("I'm sick, but I'll get well"), mourning ("All is lost"), defense (healthy: "I'll go on in spite of it"), neurotic (marked use of defense mechanisms to deny the effects of the disability), adjustment ("It's different, but not 'bad'").
- Falek and Britton (1974), in a review of studies on human reaction to stress, isolated a sequence of responses that enable a person to regain a "psychological steady state": denial (behavioral focus including being stunned or dazed, refusing to accept information, insisting there has been a mistake, not understanding what has been said); anxiety and fear (possibly expressed in the form of generalized nervousness, overactivity, irritability, headaches, fatigue, insomnia, loss of appetite, somatic complaints); anger and hostility; depression; equilibrium.
- Roessler and Bolton (1978) listed variables affecting rehabilitation outcome, which is very closely related to reaction to disability: person variables (organismic variables, behavioral competencies, self-regulatory systems and plans, expectancies, encoding and personal constructs, subjective stimulus values); environmental variables; nature of disability; cultural factors in rehabilitation; and interaction position.

The above generalizations may be useful when considered within a lifestyle perspective. In terms of generalizing about generalities, Shontz's (1975) observation, although specifically directed toward physical illness, has implications for the broad range of disabilities:

> The broadest view recognizes that suffering in physical illness is the resultant of physiological, subjective (cognitive, emotional), and environmental influences, all operating together. The relative importance of each, and the relations among them, differs among persons and conditions and may be understood only by close study of each individual and his situation. (p. 271)

SUMMARY

The lifestyle often provides an increased understanding of an individual's dimly conscious cognitive map regarding self, others, and life. This information, when viewed in the context of the goal-directed nature of thinking, feeling, and behaving, can provide a useful perspective on the individual's adjustment to disability.

Lifestyle factors were discussed as they relate to disability, other theoretical perspectives, and Adlerian implications. In addition, generalizations were considered that relate to the broad area of adjustment to disability.

REFERENCES

Allen, T. W. The Individual Psychology of Alfred Adler: An item of history and a promise of a revolution. The Counseling Psychologist, 1971, 3(1), 3–24.

Ansbacher, H. L., & Ansbacher, R. R. (Eds.). The Individual Psychology of Alfred Adler. New York: Basic Books, 1956.

Barker, R. G., & Wright, B. A. The social psychology of adjustment to physical disability. In J. F. Garrett (Ed.), Psychological aspects of physical disability (Rehabilitation Services Series No. 310). Washington, D.C.: Office of Vocational Rehabilitation, Department of Health, Education, and Welfare, 1953, pp. 18–22.

Barker, R. G., Wright, B. A., Meyerson, L., & Gonick, M. R. Adjustment to physical handicap and illness: A survey of the social psychology of physique and disability (Rev. Ed.). New York: Social Science Research Council, 1953.

Cohn, N. K. Understanding the process of adjustment to disability. Journal of Rehabilitation, 1961, 27(6), 16–18.

Dreikurs, R. Psychodynamics, psychotherapy, and counseling. Chicago: Alfred Adler Institute, 1967.

Dunham, J. R., & Dunham, C. S. Psychosocial aspects of disability. In R. Goldenson, J. Dunham, & C. Dunham (Eds.), Disability and Rehabilitation Handbook. New York: McGraw-Hill, 1978.

Eisenberg, M. Psychological aspects of physical disability: A guide for the health care worker. New York: National League of Nursing, 1977.

English, R. W. The application of personality theory to explain psychological reactions to physical disability. In J. Cull & R. Hardy (Eds.), Rehabilitation techniques in severe disability. Springfield, Ill.: Charles C Thomas, 1974.

Falek, A., & Britton, S. Phases in coping. Social Biology, 1974, 21(1), 1–7.

Ford, D. H., & Urban, H. B. Systems of Psychotherapy. New York: Wiley, 1963.

Forer, L. The birth order factor. New York: McKay, 1976.

Gunther, M. Emotional aspects of spinal cord injury. In D. Ruge (Ed.), Spinal cord injuries. Springfield, Ill.: Charles C Thomas, 1969.

Kern, R. M., Matheny, K. B., & Patterson, D. A case for Adlerian counseling: Theory, techniques, and research evidence. Chicago: Alfred Adler Institute, 1978.

Kübler-Ross, E. On death and dying. In E. Wyschogrod (Ed.), The phenomenon of death. New York: Harper & Row, 1973.

Lombardi, D. N. Eight avenues of life style consistency. The Individual Psychologist, 1973, 10(2), 5–9.

Maslow, A. H. Motivation and personality. New York: Harper & Row, 1954.

Matteson, P. Excerpt on "Friends and Community." In G. J. Manaster, G. Painter, D. Deutsch, & B. J. Overholt (Eds.), Alfred Adler: As we remember him. Austin, Tex.: North American Society of Adlerian Psychology, 1977.
Mosak, H. H. Early recollections as a projective technique. Journal of Projective Techniques, 1958, 22(3), 302–311.
Mosak, H. H. Lifestyle. In A. Nikelly (Ed.), Techniques for behavior change. Springfield, Ill.: Charles C Thomas, 1971.
Mosak, H. H. On purpose. Chicago: Alfred Adler Institute, 1977.
Mosak, H. H. Adlerian psychotherapy. In R. Corsini (Ed.), Current psychotherapies (2nd ed.). Itasca, Ill.: Peacock, 1979a.
Mosak, H. H. Mosak's typology: An update. Journal of Individual Psychology, 1979b, 35(2), 192–195.
Mosak, H. H., & Mosak, B. A bibliography for Adlerian psychology. Washington, D.C.: Hemisphere, 1975.
Olson, G. Early recollections: Their use in diagnosis and psychotherapy. Springfield, Ill.: Charles C Thomas, 1979.
Ornstein, R. E. The psychology of consciousness. San Francisco: Freeman, 1972.
Roessler, R., & Bolton, R. Psychosocial adjustment to disability. Baltimore: University Park Press, 1978.
Rychlak, I. E. Introduction to personality and psychotherapy: A theory-construction approach. Boston: Houghton Mifflin, 1973.
Shontz, F. C. The psychological aspects of physical illness and disability. New York: Macmillan, 1975.
Shontz, F. C. Physical disability and personality: Theory and recent research. In J. Stubbins (Ed.), Social and psychological aspects of disability. Baltimore: University Park Press, 1977.
Shulman, B. H. Contributions to Individual Psychology. Chicago: Alfred Adler Institute, 1973.
Siller, J. R. Psychological situation of the disabled with spinal cord injuries. Rehabilitation Literature, 1969, 30, 290–296.
Siller, J. R. Attitudes toward disability. In H. Rusalem & D. Malikin (Eds.), Contemporary vocational rehabilitation. New York: New York University Press, 1976.
Sutton-Smith, B., & Rosenberg, B. G. The sibling. New York: Holt, Rinehart & Winston, 1970.
Taylor, J. Early recollections as a projective technique: A review of some recent validation studies. Journal of Individual Psychology, 1975, 31(2), 213–218.
Thompson, D. D. In psychosocial redevelopment: Erikson's model. In J. Lott, J. Owens, & W. Wilson (Eds.), A holistic approach to employment for persons with spinal cord injury. Fishersville, Va.: Virginia Spinal Cord Injury System, 1982.
Wright, B. A. Physical disability—A psychological approach. New York: Harper & Row, 1960.
Wright, B. A. Issues in overcoming emotional barriers to adjustment in the handicapped. In R. P. Marinelli & A. E. Dell Orto (Eds.), The psychological and social impact of physical disability. New York: Springer, 1977.

12

A HOLISTIC GROUP APPROACH TO OFFENDER REHABILITATION

Warren R. Rule

In correctional rehabilitation, an increasing interest has been developing in experiential group approaches that are in keeping with the concepts of holistic rehabilitation. In holistic rehabilitation, a man is viewed as a complex being who is a creative thinking, feeling, and doing creature. The interrelatedness of these characteristics is an overriding concern in holistic understanding. Moreover, this interrelatedness is not only a concept that describes the individual's intrapersonal self but also applies interpersonally as well. Since individuals are viewed as basically social beings, the process of holistic rehabilitation particularly focuses on social contexts such as group counseling. Thus, group counseling enhances the focus on both self-interrelatedness and other interrelatedness—a condition that increases the probabilities of productive self change.

This chapter, "A Holistic Group Approach to Offender Rehabilitation," from L. Hippchen (Ed.), *Holistic Approaches to Offender Rehabilitation*, 1982. Courtesy of Charles C Thomas, Publisher, Springfield, IL.

Perhaps an important consideration that should precede a discussion of the process of group counseling is the need for an increased awareness of the counselor's assumptions regarding the nature of man. After all, if the group counselor is interested in employing holistic rehabilitation principles and is attempting to change individuals so that they can cope with society's demands more effectively, then this helper ought to have an increased awareness of his assumptions about this complex being that he is trying to help. If the group counselor has a lack of awareness of his own notions or lacks somewhat of a workable framework of understanding, then his personal biases operating at a dimly conscious level could work to his group members' disadvantage. Regardless of the group counselor's avowed orientation, his assumption as to whether man is basically driven by instincts or is shaped by his environment, whether he is determined by the past or freely chooses from moment to moment, whether an individual creates his feelings or is possessed by his feelings, and so on, all help influence how he goes about helping others. Consequently, discussion below will be given to a particular holistic approach to understanding the nature of man and to broad assumptions related to criminal behavior. Following this, discussion will be given to the goals and process of holistic group counseling for offender rehabilitation.

UNDERSTANDING THE NATURE OF MAN

In a holistic approach to rehabilitation, the focus should be on a broad, yet flexible, model for viewing the nature of man. An approach to understanding that seems to fit particularly well into an eclectic perspective is the Adlerian lifestyle approach. This approach, developed by Alfred Adler (Ansbacher and Ansbacher, 1956) is becoming an increasingly popular framework for understanding individuals.

One of the major assumptions about man in the Adlerian perspective is that he is a social being and that his behavior can only be fully understood in a social context. In fact, Adler regarded personal problems basically as social problems. Another assumption regarding man's social nature is that in each of us there exists the desire to belong. Another way of expressing this social characteristic is that each of us strives to have a place of significance in the eyes of others. This goal of obtaining a "place-of-somebodyness" is handled differently by different people. Some individuals strive to gain a place of belonging on the productive or useful side of life; others—for various purposes—have chosen to strive to achieve to "be somebody" on the nonproductive or antisocial side of living. Regardless of the goals a person pursues or the behaviors learned by the individual, they can be indirectly related to his innate desire to enhance himself within a social context. So, in attempting to understand another person, the appropriate framework appears to be: "How is this person seeking to be known by others?" This assumption of belonging has strong implications for holistic understanding of the individual and of the offender, especially since rehabilitation using a group counseling process is viewed as a springboard to reentry into other social involvements outside the penal institution.

Another basic assumption that fits securely in a holistic rehabilitation perspective is the wholeness of the individual. A person's wholeness, or "holistic" nature, is irreducible; to fragment the personality or break up the person into parts is to destroy this wholeness and thereby undermine the understanding of the individual. Adler used an analogy from music in that music cannot be fully appreciated by studying each note itself—one must have the context of the other notes and the melody. Similarly, an individual cannot be dissected without losing some understanding of the theme or pattern that runs through his life. Thus Adler chose the term "lifestyle" to depict this holistic pattern that is greater than the sum of the parts. This assumption seems to be an important one in understanding people, because the way in which individuals organize themselves as whole people influences their perceptions of themselves and others as well as their goals and behavioral interactions with others.

Another important Adlerian assumption about the nature of man is that all human behavior, including emotions, has a purpose. Behaviors that seemingly cannot be explained become more understood, once the purpose or goal comes to light. Stated another way, everything the person does is a function of his ideas about consequences to be obtained in the future. Adler noticed that people seem to operate from a subjective framework and are not always fully conscious of their goals. In understanding someone, the focus must be on the person's subjective or internal frame of reference. This is so because the person's perceptions, including his inner biases influencing his perceptions, determine his behavior more than "reality" does. Thus, the individual organizes his perceptions into expectations that influence his personal goals.

Since Adler viewed behavior as being goal-directed and the lifestyle as holistic, he felt that each person has an overriding goal around which all his "subgoals" are organized in a holistic fashion. This goal and its supplemental goals provide the main thrust of movement for the lifestyle that enables each of us to move from a position of dimly felt inferiority or non-coping to a position of overcoming or coping. Using this approach of understanding behavior as being goal-directed, Adlerian group counselors are interested in what use the person is making of his heredity and past experiences.

Because it is extremely important for each person to cope with the previously discussed innate desire to belong, each individual strives toward a subjectively determined place of significance that is related to conclusions drawn from the person's early childhood. These early conclusions, from which an individual continues to operate, are based on the biased sample of life that he experienced as a child. These early conclusions become convictions (e.g., I am…; Others are…; Life is.…) that guide the person through life and on which goals are based. Through trial and error, not only do individuals conclude which goals will be most apt to help them move toward a place of significance but they also learn which kinds of behavior are most useful in implementing the goals.

Understandably, people also learn behaviors, in keeping with the goals of the lifestyle, that safeguard their sense of self-esteem. Thus, the lifestyle is essentially an individual's unique mental framework for measuring self-worth as a function of interaction with others. The lifestyle allows the person to evaluate, to understand, to predict, and to control experience (Mosak and Dreikurs, 1973).

Some examples of commonly observed lifestyle themes are cited by Mosak (1971), who cautioned that a wide array of behaviors may be used to implement on a daily basis each of these mental frameworks and only probable behavioral hypotheses can be made. Examples of these themes include getting, driving, controlling, always being right, being the center or the best, pleasing, being admired for moral superiority, being against, being victimized, being a martyr, being the baby or a charmer, being inadequate, being intellectually superior, and being the excitement seeker.

If these examples seem to have a somewhat self-serving connotation, three points should be kept in mind: (1) striving for a sense of significance, (2) functioning in the tasks of life, and (3) individual variations.

First, from early childhood to the present, individuals eagerly want to move from a position of dimly felt inferiority to one of coping with a sense of significance. In this effort, especially in early childhood, a tendency to intensify and generalize those guidelines that seem to be the most useful exists. As a result, the labels given to these themes depict the powerful determination to enhance the self.

Second, it is helpful to realize that the same style is used in coping with the three main tasks in life: (1) interpersonal relationships with family and friends, (2) work or school, and (3) relationships with the opposite sex (Dreikurs, 1967). In these areas, a person's lifestyle leads to both failures and successes and functions to his disadvantage as well as advantage. For instance, an overriding goal of striving to become the best can work to a person's advantage as measured by prestige, income, and the social contribution that may have resulted from accomplishments. Yet the same lifestyle that led to these subjectively perceived successes may work to a person's disadvantage if the individual neglected family, avoided pursuits in which excellence was not guaranteed, treated others ruthlessly, or became a criminal in his effort to become the best.

Third, it should be emphasized that each lifestyle expresses itself individually in very subtle ways as well as in the obvious ways that would be expected of a stereotypical lifestyle. A person who relies on getting as a means of feeling significant can use such common, socially appropriate behaviors as returning often to a smorgasbord table, developing fast reading skills, smugly enjoying a large savings account in a bank, and working very hard to make sure desired rewards are gained. Each behavior is in line with the goal of getting as a major means of coping in life. Another person may have learned, however, socially inappropriate means of getting, such as stealing, beating the system, being the tough guy in order to intimidate, being the shrewd master mind, etc. Of course, other lifestyles can use these same behaviors. There is some overlapping among various lifestyles, although there seems to be a greater probability that certain lifestyles will be more likely to use certain behaviors than others. The creativity of the individual is ever present in choosing among various alternatives in order to implement the goals of the lifestyle.

Lifestyle Understanding

In answer to the question "How do you determine what a person's lifestyle is?" Adlerian thinking rests on the premise that the memory is selective. As Dreikurs (1967) indicated, people operate on an economy principle by selectively using their memories and abilities in accordance with their individual purposes. Hence, our memories of early childhood reflect the most important attitudes, notions, expectations, convictions, and goals that crystallized during this formative period. Adlerians believe that these early recollections reflect those firm ideas that are embedded in the person's outlook. In making use of this phenomenon, the practitioner is able to gather lifestyle information by pointed questions and, in so doing, to reconstruct the important aspects of the person's early environment.

Dreikurs (1967) developed a lifestyle questionnaire that covers the significant areas of concern. Based on personal memories of early childhood before age six or seven, areas of lifestyle information include description of self and siblings, sibling rankings on possible areas of competition (e.g., intelligence, trying to please, having own way, etc.) sibling interrelationships, description of parents and parental influence, the family atmosphere, and early recollections and dreams. The use of this form in the group counseling process will be discussed later in the chapter.

Adlerians emphasize the family constellation by attending to the person's position of birth as related to sibling age differences, ordering of sexes, uniqueness, and alliance groups. Shulman (1973) listed five basic positions: only, eldest, second, middle, and youngest child. Each position has several modest probabilities of stereotyped characteristics attached to it. The practitioner considers and refines these hypotheses in accordance with the direction of movement reflected by the other lifestyle variables.

For example, the firstborn child is often the most subject to parental expectations and authority. Mindful of losing his place of importance as eldest child, the individual may be inclined to identify with established parental values and might be determined to be the number-one achiever. On the other hand, the eldest may become discouraged by what the child considers as unfair treatment or unreasonable expectations. As a result, the individual may develop a fatalistic rebellious outlook. Therefore, in the eldest child's situation or position, the lifestyle may perhaps be related to a stance—pro or con—of cooperating with or rebelling against parental authority and expectations.

Much importance is given to the person's early recollections, memories, and dreams. The Adlerian belief is that there are no chance memories. From thousands of experiences to which the individual has been exposed in early childhood, only those recollections are remembered that coincide with present outlook on life. Consequently, the individual's early recollections show the same patterns; they are reminders the person carries around regarding personal limits and the meaning of circumstances (Ansbacher and Ansbacher, 1956). Generally, when asked, individuals can remember at least six specific incidents that occurred during their childhoods. Each recollection, viewed by the practitioner in the context of the feeling about the remembered incident, reflects a current expectation about life. Each recollection supplements and rounds out the outlook reflected by the other early recollections and lifestyle variables.

The complete lifestyle questionnaire can take as many as several hours of information collecting or an abbreviated version may be used. The choice depends on several factors, such as the availability of time and the purpose of gathering lifestyle information. Understandably, if more information is gathered, then a greater probability of more accurate and well-rounded results can be expected.

Lifestyle and Crime

An Adlerian approach would emphasize that criminal acts serve different purposes for different individuals. Moreover, these criminal acts could be viewed as being on the useless, as opposed to useful, side of social living. For instance, a person whose lifestyle is characterized by "getting" may have learned, depending on other lifestyle variables, that criminal acts, e.g. stealing, are a means of enhancing this lifestyle and the accompanying rating of self-worth. In addition, a lifestyle of "controlling others" may lend itself, depending on other variables, to organized approaches to crime. Also, the person who is heavily invested in measuring his self-worth by being Number One in his undertakings, may have discovered that since he cannot be Number One in useful endeavors then possibly he will strive to be Number One in a chosen area of crime. Many more examples could be cited; however, the important point is that crime can serve different purposes for different lifestyles. Further discussion will be given later in the chapter to the importance of assisting the offender in exploring the purpose (not the whys) of criminal behavior for him. The question becomes: "What is the future consequence related to his self-ideal that he is striving to attain?"

Practitioners using Adlerian principles generally believe that an individual is the product of both individual "laws" and general "laws." In other words, a person is the result of individual laws that he created for himself and the result of general laws that apply to all human beings or to specified groups of individuals. Consequently, in seeking to better understand another person, an Adlerian practitioner keeps an eye on both individual (idiographic) and general (nomothetic) understanding. In regard to the holistic rehabilitation of an offender, the Adlerian would explore the individual laws that the offender created for himself by using the previously discussed lifestyle format. In addition, the group counselor would attempt to be mindful of generalizations that could characterize many other offenders.

Insofar as generalizations are concerned, Adler (Ansbacher and Ansbacher, 1956) contended that there are several considerations that could be kept in mind when working with those who have a history of crime. He believed that some offenders may never have experienced "social interest" (an empathically evaluative attitude toward others or feeling of "weness" in the world). This possibility of low social interest has strong implications for the goals of group counseling. Furthermore, Adler claims that many offenders experienced childhood as a "pampered" child. He did not mean "pampering" in the sense of material goods or luxury—often the reverse of this was the case; rather, he meant that the pampered child concluded that he was important merely because of his existence, without making any effort to earn the esteem of others. This attitude of expecting easy satisfaction or unearned recognition can lead to difficulties with others. When difficulties occur, others are found to be at fault by the formerly "pampered" individual—not himself.

Adler further noted that unlike several other types of disorders, criminals have as a group a high degree of "activity" or tendency to "act upon" life. This activity, unfortunately, is thrown on the useless side of life, rather than on socially useful endeavors. Thus an Adlerian group approach would hope to redirect this high propensity for activity toward ultimately more satisfying and socially productive concerns. It can be remembered from previous discussion that Adler believed that all personal problems are social problems. Accordingly, crime may be regarded not as an isolated thing in itself, but as an attitude toward social living. So, the holistic approach in group counseling is enhanced by focusing on the offender's social relatedness—within the group and within the society that presumably he will sometime reenter.

GOALS OF HOLISTIC GROUP COUNSELING

In holistic group counseling for offender rehabilitation, the goals of the group process and outcome focus on the interrelatedness of man to himself and to others. In regard to man's interrelatedness to himself, the holistic approach views man as a creative thinking, feeling, and doing creature; this perspective provides a major basis for the goals of holistic group counseling. In reference to man's interrelatedness to others, the holistic approach sees man as a social being who is not—although he himself at times may believe differently—an island unto himself; this perspective also provides a major basis for the goals of holistic group counseling.

In this context, the goals of holistic group counseling may be viewed from two perspectives: the individual and the group. However, it is paradoxical that the goals of these two perspectives cannot be totally separated.

From the frame of reference of the individual's goals for himself, the goals of holistic group counseling may be tentatively stated as follows:

1. To explore the interrelatedness of thinking, feeling, and doing. Operationally speaking, to explore lifestyle and related thinking processes and the feelings and behaviors that flow therefrom.
2. To identify those self-defeating dimensions that ultimately work to one's disadvantage and those assets that ultimately work to one's advantage.
3. To set specific and realistic personal goals that are related to diminishing the self-defeating dimensions.
4. To set up "homework" strategies, which are to be implemented both within the institution and ultimately outside of the institution, that are the means to attain the personal goals.
5. To enhance self-acceptance and self-esteem by an increased awareness of one's lifestyle advantages and by "homework" strategies for building on lifestyle strengths.
6. To recycle this process as needed.
7. To use successful reentry into society, after discharge, as the ultimate criterion of success of holistic group counseling.

From the frame of reference of the individual as a member of the group, a facilitative atmosphere must exist in order that the above-stated individual goals can be achieved. Thus, the overriding goal of the group in terms of social interrelatedness can be tentatively stated: to create an atmosphere of belongingness that facilitates self-exploration, reality testing, encouragement, risk-taking, self-acceptance, and self-change.

So it seems that the goals of holistic group counseling are interwoven goals that are related to individual responsibility and to responsibility to the group. In the next section, discussion is given to procedures for reaching these goals.

THE PROCESS OF HOLISTIC GROUP COUNSELING

In a holistic group approach to offender rehabilitation, thought should first be given to selection of group members. This variable is related to the nature of interaction of the group as well as to the ultimate success of group counseling. Hare (1962) has identified six major characteristics that have a bearing on the interaction process; these characteristics of group interaction are discussed below in the context of the selection process.

1. The personality characteristics of the members have an obvious influence. In terms of selection, Yalom (1975) recommends heterogeneity in regard to variety of personality characteristics, yet homogeneity in reference to level of psychological functioning or adjustment. Perhaps in offender groups a variety of personalities and offenses with relatively similar levels of "emotional health" would be desirable. Some research (e.g. Rule and McKenzie, 1977, 1975) indicates that early recollections can sometimes be used to determine group composition.
2. Social characteristics of the group members, e.g., age, socioeconomic level, etc., would be difficult to control. A related characteristic, however, is the issue of volunteering as a group member. Preferably, the offenders would have volunteered as group participants, although it is quite possible that secondary gains, e.g., parole enhancement, would be major factors in some of their decisions to volunteer. The least desirable is a situation in which all participants are required to be in the group.
3. The size of the group is primarily a function of leader preference. A range of between six and twelve would seem appropriate. A desirable number, especially for major life exploration, appears to be approximately eight.
4. The task of the group is primarily educational in nature. The overriding focus is learning more about oneself and learning different ways of thinking, feeling, and behaving. In attempting to accomplish this task, the accent is on facilitation, not punishment. This is an important operational distinction within a penal institution. If punitive measures become a norm in the group, they may well be viewed by some of the offenders as a challenge, a trial of strength. This means would serve to reinforce in their private logic that power is the key, i.e., "We'll see who is stronger! We'll see who can hold out longest!" (Ansbacher and Ansbacher, 1956:420).
5. The communication network is relatively unstructured. Insofar as the group leader and group members are concerned, it is one of an educational consultant/counselor to students/clients; at other times the whole group could have a communication network that

would be one of sharing among equals. Hopefully, communication of superior to inferior posture would be minimized.

6. The leader is presumably an individual who has led counseling groups in the past and is particularly familiar with Adlerian practice and theory. It is also highly desirable that the leader have an awareness of his own lifestyle in order that he minimize projection onto group members (Rule, 1976). Furthermore, the addition of a coleader would be especially helpful to the group process as well as provide a different model for the group members. As the group process progressed, the expectation would be that the leader(s) would exert less direct influence as the members assumed increasing responsibility for themselves and for the group.

Those who approach group counseling from a broad Adlerian perspective divide the helping process into four phases (Dreikurs, 1967): Relationship, Lifestyle Investigation, Lifestyle Interpretation, and Reorientation. These phases provide a handy structure for the holistic group counseling process; therefore, the contribution of each phase will be discussed in subsequent paragraphs.

Relationship

Actually the relationship phase is not a "phase" in the sense that it has a distinct ending. The group begins by building trust, respect, empathy, genuineness, which are necessary components of a meaningful group; however, these and other relationship factors continue to operate and provide the basis for the unfolding of the subsequent phases.

The initial group meetings provide the opportunity for developing norms for the group and can be viewed by the members as somewhat of a prelude. Carkhuff (1977) states that the helping process should begin by the exploration of feelings and reasons for feelings on the part of the group members. Then, he believes, the process should flow into understanding and, then, action; however, the helper must first "prove" his ability to enter the client's frame of reference by demonstrating his empathic ability to the client. This exploration process, which is a part of the relationship phase of helping, increases the probability that both the group leader and the individual member are aware of the dimensions of the member's presenting problems.

In this initial phase of holistic group counseling, a discussion of the purposes of the group and a structuring process is in order. At this point, the leader would discuss the purposes for meeting, give a general overview of the group process and provide some "ground rules." Insofar as purposes are concerned, the previous discussion in this chapter on the holistic group approach to rehabilitation is a source of discussion material. In addition, Sweeney's (1975) following assumptions about group participation and contribution are noteworthy; participants are:

1. inherently equal and may expect to behave as such, i.e., have a place that no one can rightfully challenge.
2. considered to be capable of assuming responsibility for their behavior.
3. individually understood best in a holistic, unified way as creative, purposive beings.
4. considered as social beings meeting the same life tasks as others.
5. capable of changing their attitudes and/or behaviors.
6. able to help as well as be helped in the process of giving meaning to life.

Further discussion could be given here to expectations of the group members and misconceptions about group counseling. Ground rules such as confidentiality, the fact that the group is not simply "a confessional," and that members will not be forced to do anything could be discussed. Moreover, at this time, logistical matters could be handled such as meeting time, length (approximately two hours is recommended), duration of group for certain members, replacement of members, etc.

Since, as Cull and Hardy (1975) note, the offender is often a person who has isolated himself somewhat from others, the leader cannot always expect meaningful early participation. Modeling of desired behavior by the leader is helpful. Furthermore, warm-up exercises, depending upon leader preference and his early "feel for" the group, can be implemented. Dyer and Vriend (1975) have suggested several examples of these beginning exercises. Members can simply introduce themselves; or, they can introduce themselves after having written down first impressions of the other members (to be shared later); possibly, each member can finish a sentence stem, e.g., "What no one ever understood about me is —" or "I'm different from most people in that I —," or "The thing about myself that I would most like to change is —".

Relationship techniques are useful not only in the initial stage of group counseling but also as a means of maintaining the cohesiveness, meaning, and productivity of the group. Dinkmeyer et al. (1979) recommend techniques such as encouraging and focusing on assets and positive feedback. In addition, facilitating participation by utilizing nonverbal cues (e.g., seating place, seating posture, facial expression, voice, hand gestures, etc.) is recommended. Further consideration includes facilitative confrontation of discrepancies in what members think, feel, and do (e.g., what was said versus is being said; what one is saying versus what one appears to be feeling; what one is saying versus what one is doing, etc.). Moreover, much can be gained by encouraging as much here-and-now interaction as possible (except for the past learning from lifestyle exploration) as opposed to "there and then" orientations. This especially applies to long discussions of past judicial factors related to the incarceration of the members.

In facilitating the beginning stages of holistic group counseling as well as in maintaining productive relationships throughout the complete group process, leader interventions are often appropriate. These interventions not only sometimes enable the group process to continue productively but also provide an effective modeling for other members to emulate. Dyer and Vriend (1975) suggest that intervention may be necessary when:

1. a group member speaks for everyone.
2. an individual speaks for another individual within the group.
3. a group member focuses on persons, conditions, or events outside the group.
4. someone seeks the approval of the counselor or a group member before and after speaking.
5. someone says, "I don't want to hurt his feelings, so I won't say it."
6. a group member suggests that his or her problems are due to someone else.
7. an individual suggests that "I've always been that way."
8. an individual suggests "I'll wait, and it will change."
9. discrepant behavior appears.
10. a member bores the group by rambling.

The importance of relationship factors cannot be minimized. In subsequent sections, discussion will be given to lifestyle procedures for enhancing self-understanding and to action methods based on that self-understanding. Yet, the relationship factors, particularly respect for others' rights and responsiveness to another's internal frame of reference, get the process moving and keep it moving. A holistic analogy might be that the complex interaction of relationship factors (mostly identified by feeling) is the key that opens the door to the dark room; the lifestyle self-understanding (thinking) creates light in the room;

and the reorientation (action) methods polish and rearrange the room according to the wishes of the individual.

Lifestyle Investigation

As noted in the above analogy, this phase of the group process results from movement from somewhat of a "feeling" orientation to a "thinking" orientation. At this point the focus is on gathering information related to the lifestyles of the group members.

Using the lifestyle information form (Dreikurs, 1967) discussed previously, the leader can use a questionnaire (fill-in-the-blank) format; can break the group into pairs, with each partner interviewing the other; or, he can obtain the information privately on a one-to-one basis. If time does not permit the gathering of complete lifestyle information for every member, an abbreviated version or even simply several early recollections can be helpful.

In soliciting this early childhood information from the group members, the overriding purpose is to reconstruct the members' first social groups from which they formed conclusions about themselves, others, and life. Adlerians believe, as noted before, that people remember only those things from the early past that are useful in providing guidelines for expectations in the present. It is important that the group members understand the purpose of employing the lifestyle as a means of self-exploration and potential behavior change. Furthermore, information related to individual functioning past, present, and in the projected future (upon leaving the institution), as related to the previously discussed three tasks of life, is obtained. The functioning in the tasks of life provides a context for lifestyle understanding.

Later in the group process, the lifestyle self-understanding will assist the group members in attempting to identify the individual purpose(s) related to personal problems, criminal behavior, or whatever concern the individual may want to explore. Upon achieving an awareness of one's purpose (imagined future consequences that one is striving to attain), the individual is in a better position to learn how to implement the goal more effectively or to alter it. It may be, however, that the exploration during the first or Relationship Phase did not bring into sharp enough focus a personal problem or concern for the group member to relate to his lifestyle goals. In this event, supplemental exercises can be used that can illuminate areas of concern. Dyer and Vriend (1975) discussed several strategies that may be helpful: writing an oral letter to someone with whom the member has "unfinished business";

creating an oral fantasy in which the individual is doing or having anything he desires—here the member becomes aware of some of his values as well as profits from group feedback; role shifting in which members role play each other, after having drawn names from a hat, and the group later attempts to guess who was being played—this exercise provides a means of understanding others' perceptions of them; projecting oneself ten years in the future and receiving group feedback (this could be modified to three months, one year, or five years after discharge). Many additional selfawareness exercises may be found in Pfeiffer and Jones (1974).

Thus, the group member in this second phase, Life-Style Investigation, is attempting to look inward. He is focusing on looking at himself through sharing lifestyle information and is continuing the self-exploration begun during the first phase that results from group involvement. In the next phase, the selfexploration continues, yet the emphasis is upon accepting "this is me."

Lifestyle Interpretation

In this third phase, the focus is on working towards an understanding of and accepting one's lifestyle goals. The learning from the previous group experiences and exercises are tied in so that the group member obtains a holistic self-understanding that is the result of one's past lifestyle information, one's assessment of present lifestyle functioning in the three tasks of life, one's personal assessment of the group experiences so far, and the feedback of the other group members regarding their perceptions of the member and his lifestyle functioning.

By this point, the leader has gathered lifestyle information for each member and has studied each set of information, searching for lifestyle "threads" or overriding goals. In doing this for each member, the leader is attempting tentatively to identify each individual's network of goals or "cognitive map" (Mosak and Dreikurs, 1973) that forms the lifestyle plan. Guidelines for interpretation of lifestyles can be found in Shulman (1973), Mosak (1977), Ansbacher and Ansbacher (1956), Eckstein et al. (1975), Sweeney (1975).

In the following paragraphs, two examples will be discussed that illustrate how an awareness of even an extremely abbreviated version of the lifestyle could be beneficial in better understanding a group member's private, internal logic.

GROUP MEMBER #1: As a child, John had a brother five years older, a sister three years older, and a brother two years younger. John describes himself as not having been very close to any sibling before age six and viewed the parents as spoiling all the siblings except him. His two earliest memories:

1. I remember the time that our neighbor said to me and my friend that he would give 25 cents to whomever knew the name of the winner of the World Series last year. I said the right answer the same time George did. Mr. Johnson acted like he didn't even hear me and gave the 25 cents to George. Felt? Very mad at the unfair treatment.
2. One day I didn't want to go to school and threatened to run away. Parents said you're going to go whether you want to or not. Felt? Frustrated—they made me do something I didn't want to.

It may be seen in the above lifestyle information that the client had the least favorable birth order position in terms of unearned specialness. John competed with (in the sense of striving to find a place of unique significance) all his siblings, each of whom had a position of built-in specialness: The "firstborn," "the girl," and "the baby." The parents—at least in his view—spoiled the others more than him. Both early recollections supplement this outlook of "unfairness collecting" and expecting others to undermine him. Adlerians believe that a general unifying theme such as this, based on the selectivity of memory, is probably reflected in this client's present outlook as he moves through life.

GROUP MEMBER #2: William, who was the youngest of three, had two older sisters. He describes both sisters as having liked and protected him before age six. William was "the star of his father's eye," and mother was viewed as a good mother "who always did little things for us." His two earliest memories:

1. I recall a surprise birthday party when I was three. My family and friends were all there. I had a wonderful time. Felt? Excited and pleased that they went to so much trouble for me.
2. I remember playing in the yard one time. A big dog came up and barked at me. I sat down and cried until Dad came out and chased it away. The ice cream made me feel a lot better.

Even in the above limited sampling of lifestyle information, a guess about a theme can be made. William probably concluded as a child that he was quite an important person: he was the "baby" of the family, "the boy," and apparently received much pampering from parents and sisters. The early recollections confirm and expand this line of thinking in that others go to extra lengths to insure his happiness and protect him. Accordingly, the person presently may tend to regard himself at a dimly conscious level of awareness as somewhat of a "crown prince" who places much responsibility on others for his happiness and well-being.

In the above two examples, different examples of lifestyle "themes" can be seen. Insofar as the group members are concerned, each group member would have different expectations of himself and others and would have learned different behaviors for implementing the dimly conscious goals of the lifestyle. Each person's self-understanding and other group members' understanding of a given individual's private logic would be enhanced by the lifestyle approach.

In the group, the group leader would share his interpretations of the group members' lifestyles in a spirit of tentative sharing and exploration. He would use phrases such as "Could it be that__?", "A guess that I have is__," etc. Consequently, if the group leader's interpretations are sound and well phrased, if the group relationship is one of trust, and if the group member and others are willing to work toward understanding, major agreement can often be reached regarding major aspects of the group member's lifestyle. This procedure would be continued for each member. Throughout the process, the leader and other members would refer to examples from the group experience (e.g., first impressions, group exercises, etc.) that supported the lifestyle interpretations.

Since the group is a social microcosm, the lifestyle is apt to express itself in the group as well as on the outside. Thus, the group member would get feedback on how he creatively and subtly has used and is using his lifestyle in relating to others in his attempt to strive for a place of self-determined social significance. Sometimes replaying a video taping of a member's interactions with others increases this self-understanding and serves to highlight certain lifestyle behaviors that otherwise would be hard to accept.

The lifestyle introspection, the group observations and encouragement, the possible video taping, all serve to facilitate the process of a group member saying to himself, "Hey, this is me!" In the following section, discussion will be given to broadening this understanding and to learning methods of self-enhancement and change.

Lifestyle Reorientation

Upon achieving a measure of self-awareness, the members of the holistic group counseling process focus on positive change that will be helpful presently and in the future. The continued emphasis is, as O'Connell (1975) notes, on personal thinking patterns or goals, not on the common stereotype of experiencing a "drive-release" group that aims for simply the expression of emotions as a curative factor. In broadening one's insight or understanding of self in relationship to others, the group members move toward achieving "outsight" or "the learned ability to see, hear, and feel along with others" (O'Connell, 1975:157). Expressed in another way, the attempt is to "free them from the intoxication of a private interpretation of the world" (Ansbacher and Ansbacher, 1956:348) and encourage a spirit of cooperation or "common sense versus private sense" (Ansbacher and Ansbacher, 1956:253). During this fourth and final phase, the group member develops his goals for change and refines methods he will continue to use for change and for broadening his sense of social interest. These goals for change are often closely related to an increased awareness of lifestyle goals.

In working on this positive change, the leader and other members must sometimes remind a member that a dimension of his lifestyle is presently working to his disadvantage. This process, referred to by Adler as spitting in the person's soup so it will not taste as good, has many applications. If a group member overuses the expression of negative or hostile remarks, others' awareness of his lifestyle can provide guidelines for responding to him (Rule, 1977a). An increased awareness of the lifestyle of a group member can possibly provide insight into alcohol and/or drug abuse; the charmer may feel more charming under the influence, whereas the person who is heavily invested in control may enjoy more control when drinking, if only in altered fantasy. Furthermore, the lifestyle can be an aid in the vocational decision-making process, particularly in building on lifestyle strengths. Moreover, a heightened awareness of the group members' lifestyles may be beneficial to the group leader in regard to how different members may feel either put down or enhanced by the same action (Rule, 1978).

As a reminder that the significance of behavior lies in the consequences, a helpful perspective is discussed by Adler in regard to the self-servingness of "uncontrollable" symptoms for someone who chooses the antisocial side of life:

> ...on the useless, antisocial side of life, his increased inferiority feeling incites him toward a goal of personal superiority, or the semblance of superiority, generally looked for at the expense of

> others. The most serviceable moods and affects for this purpose, such as fear, rage, sadness, and guilt feeling, show in their own dynamics the tense attempt to advance from "below" to "above," from an increased inferiority feeling towards superiority over the other, the opponent. Thus, in each expressive movement, one can observe, in addition to the degree of social interest, the individual striving towards superiority.... They (criminals) have turned away from the real problems of life and are engaged in shadowfighting to reassure themselves of their strength. (Ansbacher and Ansbacher, 1956:255)

In trying to understand and encourage group members, the focus is best kept on the purpose of behavior. This is a different slant than zeroing in on the "whys" of behavior. The "whys" reflect past, unchangeable reasons; "purposes" indicate future-oriented, changeable targets. Using this purpose, or goal-directed orientation, the leader and group members cooperate in trying to help a member decide how his unique lifestyle is contributing to his personal problems. Upon figuring out how his lifestyle goals feed into his difficulties, the group member can establish goals for change and strategies for implementing the goals for change. Whenever possible, the member's lifestyle strengths should be capitalized upon.

In formulating personal goals and strategies for change, group members should keep one eye on the present and the other eye on the future outside of the institution. When planning a strategy for change, the recommendations should be as specific and identifiable as possible. In focusing on specific outcomes, the group counselor may want to use the lifestyle as a framework for helping the group member increase or decrease the number of times the member behaves in an already learned manner; possibly, the group may help the member learn an entirely new way to behave. This approach probably works best when related to present or future situations in the group member's life. Following are some examples of these procedures.

The first category of uses involves situations in which the group member likes how the lifestyle goal(s) is (are) operating in the situation and is content with the level of intensity experienced yet is not happy with the behavior used to implement the goal(s). Rather than learning a totally new way of behaving, the member may need only to increase or decrease behavior that already has been learned. To explain the importance of increasing the occurrence of a behavior in accordance with the flow of the lifestyle, the group counselor may say something like "George, we've discussed how you are unhappy and sort of depressed when you are on work release and that you can't figure out what's behind this feeling. I noticed that you agreed very much with the lifestyle goals we checked out with you. Since we discovered how extremely important it is for you to be liked and accepted, I can imagine how tough it is for you to be a newcomer among a bunch of strangers. Let's talk about some things you can do on the job that will help you get accepted quicker; for instance, how about increasing the number of times you strike up a conversation with people there that you don't know?"

Perhaps a specific behavior might be decreased in occurrence in order to serve the group member's lifestyle better. For example, another member, similar to the one who measures self-worth by how much he is able to please, may want to learn to reduce inconsiderate behaviors, such as monopolizing conversation, butting in, or talking endlessly, in order to hasten acceptance. Sometimes a totally new behavior must be learned in order to serve the lifestyle goal better. If a very confrontive member is heavily invested in being right and avoiding being wrong as a means of feeling significant, this person may profit from learning totally new behavior that is associated with merely being assertive rather than being offensively aggressive. A job supervisor may well be offended by the member's aggressive method of delivery and may respond defensively rather than listen carefully to the intended message.

The second category involves helping the group member to increase or to reduce an occurrence of a behavior or even to learn a new way of behaving in order to lessen the experienced intensity of a goal. This is a possibility when the member wants to change an aspect of lifestyle self-messages. A member may have become aware of a personal tendency towards intellectual superiority and togetherness that may be annoying to others in some situations. This person may want to behave directly opposite to the usual method of attempting to impress others with insight and of asking leading questions by making an effort to ask genuine information-seeking questions and to seek advice honestly when not in the know. By doing this repeatedly, the group member is apt to reduce the felt intensity of the goal in these situations. This reduction may be a result of experiencing the benefits of this new way of behaving or realizing that the consequences of behaving in this manner are not so disastrous as originally imagined. Thus, the person continues to allow the lifestyle flow to work in areas that provide genuine benefit; yet the person does not allow it to work disadvantageously in situations in which different behaviors produce results that are ultimately more satisfying.

From a more general vantage point, perhaps the group member does not like the vertical direction in which the lifestyle seems to point at times. If so, the group could encourage the member to believe in a significance of self that is not a function of comparisons or rankings. Significance is not attained only when the person is being number one in the eyes of others, being right, being charming, or whatever the person uses to measure self-worth. This global awareness can be meaningful to a member who learns situationally to do a mental checkup on experiencing a negative emotion and then tries to discover how personal lifestyle is dictating a feeling of non-significance. This awareness of how the individual functions in the lifestyle on a daily basis also can be instrumental in avoiding future pitfalls. This procedure would be especially helpful for those who have difficulty thinking through a tendency to quickly display emotions. Cull and Hardy (1975) have noted that often offenders have difficulty handling impulsive behavior.

As Dyer and Vriend (1975) contend, some resistance is to be expected. People want to hold onto what has been a part of them and has worked for them. The idea of giving up thought patterns, behaviors, etc. can be threatening, and the admission of needing to accept new ways of thinking and behaving can be viewed as further evidence of inadequacy. The inherent risk and personal threat involved in this process can present virtually insurmountable barriers to change. This understandable difficulty in changing points up the necessity for the leader's and group members' support and encouragement.

Other group counseling theories have perspectives that can enhance a holistic approach to offender rehabilitation. The rational-emotive approach (e.g., Ellis, 1973) fits nicely into this fourth phase of Reorientation. This approach assists the individual in looking at his thought sequences; rather than focusing on the activating event, the person learns how to check out and dispute what he tells himself about the importance of the event, an approach that is similar to the Adlerian approach.

Another group approach that has helpful techniques to offer is the behavioral counseling approach (e.g., Hansen et al., 1976). This method relies heavily on learning principles as a means of self-change. Emotional, operant, social, and cognitive learning strategies are tailored to the member's goals for change. Helpful strategies are shaping, written behavior contracts, modeling, assertiveness training, and role playing. Assertiveness training and role playing are especially meaningful in offender rehabilitation. Sometimes, offenders need to learn to handle themselves assertively in particular situations, rather than aggressively or passively. The technique of role playing, of which assertiveness training is a part, is very helpful in learning how to handle oneself more effectively in any of the three tasks of life.

Other approaches also have contributions to make. Gestalt counseling (e.g., Passons, 1975) offers techniques for confronting one's own inner resources and for becoming aware of a more unified self. Transactional Analysis (e.g. Berne, 1966) has developed descriptive terms that simplify some of the complexities of the group interaction process. Humor is an emerging technique for facilitating the process of change. Ellis (1977) and O'Connell (1975) have discussed the importance of this and offer suggested techniques; some research (e.g., Rule, 1977b, 1979) indicates that humor can be combined with lifestyle awareness with beneficial results.

As stated earlier, the adjustment of the offender upon leaving the institution must be the ultimate criterion of success in holistic rehabilitation. Accordingly, as the group approaches completion or as a particular member moves closer to departure from the institution, the emphasis should be directed on future-needed information and skills. Decision-making skills, diet and nutrition, and adjustment skills are examples of possible considerations. An often neglected, yet extremely important focus is in the avocational or leisure area. The likelihood of altercation is apt to greatly increase during the person's uncommitted time. McDowell (1976) presents ideas for handling this critical time dimension and Rule and Stewart (1977) discuss leisure counseling from a lifestyle perspective.

Perhaps an appropriate concluding exercise for the group would be the fantasy reunion exercise (Dyer and Vriend, 1975). The group imagines that it is meeting again one year later (or a specific amount of time after all the members are released from the institution). Each member then describes at length his fantasy of what his life has been like since the group terminated. Thus, the final group meeting becomes somewhat of an informal "commitment" session, one in which the members make indirect—and hopefully optimistic—social contracts with their peers to accomplish specific goals in the future.

SUMMARY

In a holistic group approach to offender rehabilitation, the emphasis is on man as a social being. This method of helping focuses on the interrelatedness of thinking, feeling, and behaving. The unifying theme of the lifestyle concept provides a workable framework for increasing self-understanding and group understanding. When supplemented with other methods, the lifestyle approach enhances the holistic group counseling process of exploration, understanding, and action.

As a result of the holistic group process, the member becomes more aware of self in relationship to others. This awareness, along with self-strategies for change, provides the individual with an expanded sense of freedom of choice. The offender is then in a better position to decide whether to flow enjoyably with his own natural currents or, at times, ultimately to benefit by going against the flow.

REFERENCES

Ansbacher, Heinz L. and Rowena R. Ansbacher (1956). The Individual Psychology of Alfred Adler. New York: Harper & Row.

Berne, Eric (1966). Principles of Group Treatment. New York: Oxford University Press.

Carkhuff, Robert R. (1977). The Art of Helping III. Third Edition. Amherst, Massachusetts: Human Resource Development Press.

Cull, John G. and Richard E. Hardy (1975). Counseling Strategies with Special Populations. Springfield, Illinois: Charles C Thomas.

Dinkmeyer, Don C., W. L. Pew, and Don C. Dinkmeyer, Jr. (1979). Adlerian Counseling and Psychotherapy. Monterey, California: Brook/Cole.

Dreikurs, Rudolf (1967). Psychodynamics, Psychotherapy, and Counseling. Chicago, Illinois: Alfred Adler Institute.

Dyer, Wayne W. and John Vriend (1975). Counseling Techniques that Work. Washington, D.C.: The American Personnel and Guidance Association.

Eckstein, Daniel, Lee Baruth, and David Mahrer (1975). Life Style: What It Is and How To Do It. Henderson, North Carolina: Mother Earth News.

Ellis, Albert (1973). Humanistic Psychotherapy. New York: McGraw-Hill Book.

Ellis, Albert (1977). "Fun as Psychotherapy." Rational Living 12 (No. 1):26.

Hansen, James C., Richard W. Warner, and Elsie M. Smith (1976). Group Counseling: Theory and Process. Chicago, Illinois: Rand McNally College Publishing.

Hare, A. Paul (1962). Handbook of Small Group Research. New York: The Free Press.

McDowell, Chester F. (1976). Leisure Counseling: Selected Life Style Processes. Eugene, Oregon: University of Oregon Press.

Mosak, Harold H. (1971). "Lifestyle." Pages 77–81 in Arthur G. Nikelly (ed.), Techniques for Behavior Change. Springfield, Illinois: Charles C Thomas.

Mosak, Harold H. (1977). On Purpose: Collected Papers of Harold H. Mosak, Ph.D. Chicago, Illinois: Alfred Adler Institute.

Mosak, Harold H. and Rudolf Dreikurs (1973). "Adlerian Psychotherapy." Pages 35–83 in Raymond Corsini (ed.), Current Psychotherapies. Itasca, Illinois: F. E. Peacock.

O'Connell, Walter E. (1975). Action Therapy and Adlerian Theory. Chicago, Illinois: Alfred Adler Institute.

Passons, William R. (1975). Gestalt Approaches in Counseling. New York: Holt, Rinehart & Winston.

Pfeiffer, J. William and John E. Jones (1974). A Handbook of Structured Experiences for Human Relations Training (Volumes II and V. San Diego, California): University Associates.

Rule, Warren R. (1976). "Exploring Counselor SelfAwareness Using a Variation of the Adlerian Life Style Approach." Richmond, Virginia: Virginia Commonwealth University Rehabilitation Monograph Series (No. 2: Fall).
Rule, Warren R. (I977a). "Corrective Reactions to Client Negativism Using a Combined Facilitative and Adlerian-based Approach." Corrective and Social Psychiatry and Journal of Behavior Therapy Technology Methods and Therapy, 23 (No. 1):710.
Rule, Warren R. (1977b). "Increasing Self-Modeled Humor." Rational Living, 12 (No. 1):79. 1978 "Rehabilitation Uses of Adlerian Life Style Counseling." Rehabilitation Counseling Bulletin, 21 (No. 4):306–316.
Rule, Warren R. (1979). "Increased Internal Control Using Humor with Life Style Awareness." The Individual Psychologist, 16:16–21.
Rule, Warren R. and Donald H. McKenzie (1977). "Early Recollections as a Variable in Group Composition and in Facilitative Group Behavior." Small Group Behavior, 8 (No. 1):75–82.
Rule, Warren R. and Donald H. McKenzie (1978). "Life Style Characteristics in Early Recollection and Observable Group Behavior." Small Group Behavior, 9 (No. 3):417–424.
Rule, Warren R. and Morris W. Stewart (1977). "Enhancing Leisure Counseling Using an Adlerian Technique." Therapeutic Recreation Journal, 11 (No. 3):87–93.
Shulman, Bernard H. (1973). Contributions to Individual Psychology. Chicago, Illinois: Alfred Adler Institute.
Sweeney, Thomas J. (1975). Adlerian Counseling. Boston, Massachusetts: Houghton-Mifflin.
Yalom, Irving D. (1975). The Theory and Practice of Group Psychotherapy. Second Edition. New York: Basic Books.

V

Leisure Counseling

13

AVOCATIONAL COUNSELING FOR LIFESTYLE ADJUSTMENT

Warren R. Rule

Slightly over a hundred years ago, former U.S. President James A. Garfield expressed an intriguing observation:

> We may divide the whole struggle of the human race into two chapters.... First, the fight to get leisure; and then the second fight of civilization—what shall we do with our leisure when we get it. (National Geographic Society, 1975, p. 33)

This conclusion, if even only partially true, reflects the immense importance, frequently overlooked, of leisure in our lives. Sometimes avocational counseling is used to seek an answer to this question of "what shall we do with our leisure when we get it." However, before we explore this action-orientation, some definitions and concepts need to be clarified.

This chapter, "Avocational Counseling for Lifestyle Adjustment," from Warren R. Rule (Ed.), *Lifestyle counseling for adjustment to disability*, 1984. Rockville, MD: Aspen Systems Corporation.

"Avocational counseling," as defined here, is a broad term that relates to how individuals spend their nonworking time. The process of avocational counseling varies according to the purpose for which it is intended; there can be several different emphases. Avocational counseling can be tailored to leisure enjoyment, stress management, retirement planning, time management, lifestyle enhancement, specific self-change strategies, as well as to adjustment to disability, etc. In this chapter, the focus will be on avocational counseling for adjustment to disability and leisure satisfaction.

Much confusion surrounds the definition of concepts used to describe activity related to the passage of time. As Bolles (1978) notes, nonworking time can be broken into personal care time, sleep, house and family care, and free time. The leisure enjoyment of free time will be emphasized in this chapter because disabled individuals, particularly severely disabled individuals, are often confronted with much free time.

In considering the issue of leisure enjoyment of free time, the practitioner is faced with yet another question: just how does the concept of "leisure" fit into or relate to free time? There seems to be no one definition of leisure. It can be free time, an activity that is freely chosen, a state of mind, playfulness, the spirit with which one does anything, lifelong enjoyment, realizing self-actualization potential, etc. For the purpose of the present discussion, "leisure" refers to a freely chosen activity that one truly enjoys. As a result of engaging in this activity, a person may or may not—depending on many variables—experience additional benefits that are by-products of the activity (e.g., a generalized flow, a spirit of engaging life, an enriched state of mind, etc.).

In an effort to put these various terms into perspective, the relationships may be expressed as follows: avocational counseling varies according to the broad functional goals that the individual has for all or part of his nonworking time; a person's free time is a slice of his nonworking time; and leisure is most often an enjoyable activity that is part of someone's free time. However, sometimes a by-product of leisure activity is a leisurely attitude or spirit of satisfying playfulness that can generalize into daily living. Furthermore, for the purposes of this chapter, avocational counseling views leisure as either a means to an end or as an end in itself, depending on the purpose of the avocational counseling.

THE NEED FOR LEISURE ENJOYMENT

The need for leisure enjoyment is apparent from many perspectives. For the first time in the history of civilization, huge groups of people in the industrially advanced countries no longer have to preoccupy themselves with work as the overriding concern in their existence (Morrow, 1981). A century ago the average workweek was approximately 72 hours; today it is almost one half that, leaving a great deal of nonworking time. Compton and Eddy (1981) estimate that this comprises 225,000 hours of a person's total life space. Sad to say, many choose the path of least resistance by becoming locked into ultimately unsatisfying activities such as obsessive television watching, frequent substance abuse, and so on. In addition, increasing numbers of individuals are doubting that the "Protestant Work Ethic" yields worthwhile dividends of happiness. The tilt of the social landscape indicates—for better or for worse—that many people indeed feel entitled to fun and happiness.

Trieschmann (1974) observed that "The key to coping with one's disability is to receive enough satisfaction and rewards to make life worthwhile" (p. 558). However, the process of finding leisure satisfaction can be difficult and complex for the disabled. Within the context of society's apparent preoccupation with fun, happiness, and beautiful people, the disabled individual must often contend with one of his most obvious conditions—the loss of some liberty. As Eisenberg (1977) notes, the fact of physical restriction may well be less serious than its consequences (e.g., relationships, barriers, dependency, etc.). So, the disabled person often has an abundance of nonworking time in addition to a somewhat restricted range of choices in deciding what to do with this time.

COUNSELING APPROACHES FOR ENHANCING LEISURE ENJOYMENT

The counseling process for enhancing leisure enjoyment is, as McDowell (1976) observed, more complex than simply matching a person to an activity. In this section, we will consider procedures in the counseling process that relate to increased leisure enjoyment for the client. The focus here will be on leisure enjoyment that the individual can experience outside of an institutional setting; recreational activities within an institutional setting will be deemphasized. As may be guessed, the procedures used in the counseling process for enhancing leisure enjoyment do not necessarily flow in a systematic, orderly fashion. However, a pattern will generally unfold in the following sequence: exploratory discussion of the problems associated with free time, assessment, analysis, and action.

Exploratory Discussion

Difficulties with leisure enjoyment are often expressed implicitly, rather than explicitly. It is unusual for a client to state forthrightly, "I am experiencing difficulty with my leisure enjoyment." The practitioner should be alert to hidden messages that are attached to feelings, thoughts, and behavior. Several examples are given by McDowell (1976):

1. Expressed feelings—about boredom, procrastination, guilt anxiety, obsessions, uncertainty, unsureness, flightiness, social isolation, and so forth.
   Affective content in client responses may include the following phrases—"I hate the thought of this coming weekend," "I feel so guilty being away from the kids and enjoying myself," "I'm quite depressed in my free time," "I'm always so anxious and uncertain when it comes to planning my days off."
2. Expressed thoughts and interpretations—about leisure involvement, social relationships, and behavior.
   Cognitive content in client responses may include the following phrases—"I don't know what to do with my time," "I'd like to but…," "I'm bored," "I feel so obligated," "My wife and I don't have any common interest," "Work takes my mind off myself," "I can't stand doing nothing," "Just sitting around gets on my nerves," "I'm always wasting time," among many others.
3. Maladaptive behavior the client wishes to alleviate—"chronic" television watching, sleeping, or drinking. (p. 55)

As a part of the exploration process, the practitioner would want to discuss several factors with the client. They might include how the passage of time relates to the lifestyle tasks of life: social, occupational, and relationship to opposite sex. Especially for the disabled, particular consideration might be given to personal and medical care as related to free time. Along this vein, some disabled individuals may be so preoccupied with the limitations imposed by their disabilities that they greatly reduce their range of choices. Others may be somewhat inefficiently spending so much effort with self-maintenance use of time that they believe themselves to be too busy for extended leisure enjoyment. Consequently, as a part of the process of enhancing an individual's leisure enjoyment, sometimes the focus for some clients must shift from dealing with too much free time to carving out individual blocks of time for leisure enjoyment.

Assessment

Having identified a perceived sensitivity to how one deals with the passage of time, the practitioner can proceed into the phase of assessment. Assessment generally involves a process of gathering information related to how the person is presently functioning (i.e., thinking, feeling, or doing) or how the person would like to function. The next phase after assessment, analysis, involves the attempt to synthesize this information into meaningful conclusions that lead to action-oriented goals.

The tools for assessment may be loosely categorized into two groups: standardized and nonstandardized. The standardized instruments are administered according to prescribed directions, scored uniformly, and interpreted in reference to specific norm groups. The nonstandardized tools are less structured and are not designed with standardized conditions in mind.

Standardized. The *Leisure Activities Blank* (LAB) was developed by McKechnie (1975). This self-administered instrument identifies activity factors and is based on 120 recreational activities. The respondent indicates the extent to which he has been involved in the activity in the past or to which he expects to participate in it in the future. The norm group represents a relatively affluent segment of society, a feature which is said to provide a "recreation-ideal." However, comparisons with such a privileged group could lead to confusing inferences on the part of many clients.

The *Leisure Interest Inventory* (1969), developed by Hubert, determines preferred leisure activities based on five typologies: sociability, games, art, mobility, and immobility. This self-administering test forces choice among 80 groups of these activities.

A number of leisure assessment tools, both standardized and nonstandardized, have been developed for use with target populations. Many of these instruments are evaluated by Wehman and Schleien (1980) in terms of testing criteria such as norm referenced vs. criterion referenced, reliability, validity, ease of administration, etc. These include Davis's (1957) Recreational Directors' Observational Report (Psychiatric); Joswiak's (1975) Leisure Counseling Assessment Instruments (Developmentally Disabled); Wessel's (1976) I Can (TMR—Children); Knox, Hurff, and Takata's (1974) Deaf-Blind Assessment (Deaf-Blind, Birth-Adolescence); Williams and Fox's (1977) Minimum Objective System (Severely Handicapped); Cousins and Brown's (1979) Recreational Therapy Assessment (Nonambulatory Adult); and others.

In addition to the examples of leisure instruments selected above, a number of interest tests have been developed. These instruments, while developed primarily for vocational counseling, sometimes have helpful implications for avocational counseling and leisure satisfaction. The Strong-Campbell Interest Inventory (Campbell & Hansen, 1981) consists of over 300 items. In addition to including basic interest scales and general occupational scales, it shows how similar respondents' interests are to the interests of people working in a wide range of occupations. The Kuder Preference Record–Vocational (Kuder, 1960) consists of triads of items for which the respondent indicates the activity he would like to do the most and the one he would like to do the least. Scores are provided for the following interest clusters: outdoor, mechanical, computational, scientific, persuasive, artistic, literary, musical, social service, and clerical. Another interest inventory is the Self-Directed Search, developed by Holland (1972). This tool is self-administered as well as self-interpreted. The respondent determines his own scores or occupational clusters from the areas of realistic, investigative, artistic, social, enterprising, and conventional.

Nonstandardized. A number of nonstandardized tools and information-gathering assessments can be used for leisure purposes. Perhaps the most basic nonstructured technique, yet one that is easily overlooked in the practitioner's eagerness to assess the client, is simply to ask the client what he enjoys the most. Sometimes this response leads to very fruitful information.

A number of interview procedures and questionnaires exist that are designed to elicit specific information on variables related to an individual's use of leisure. Edwards (1977) has developed the Constructive Leisure Activity Survey, which is devoted to broad classifications of leisure activity. McDowell (1976) has formulated a somewhat more general interview process. Lewinsohn, Munoz, Youngren, and Zeiss's A Pleasant Events Schedule (1978), while originally developed as a treatment device for depression, has broader applicability for overall leisure. Closely related information can be obtained through the Reinforcement Survey Schedule (Cautela & Kastenbaum, 1967). If "values" seem to be the desired avenue of exploration, Simon, Howe, and Kirschenbaum (1972) offer many exploratory procedures. Overs and Page (1974) have developed the Avocational Title Card Sort as a means of assisting the individual in prioritizing preferences for activities.

Sometimes difficulties in leisure enjoyment result from broader personal issues than the inability to identify or give priority to satisfying leisure activities. In certain leisure-related problems as well as in other personal problems, Lazarus and Fay (1975) suggest encouraging the client to identify those things he really likes versus what he believes he should like. Another approach they recommend is to request that the client list the things he quit doing because he could not do them perfectly. They suggest that helpful information may also be obtained by asking an individual to identify his unrewarding habits.

Other self-monitoring procedures can be used in order to identify and explore areas of the client's daily living. One approach is to keep an hourly log of activities during the day. This may be accompanied by a subjective assessment of the emotion attached to each activity. Possibly a rating scale can be used as a means of determining the degree of satisfaction enjoyed by each activity. The recording of fantasies and daydreams can also sometimes yield fertile information about one's idealized leisure activities.

The flow of time can be regarded as having three dimensions: past, present, and future. Some leisure difficulties can be resolved by focusing on variables in only one time frame. Yet, leisure exploration can sometimes be enhanced by exploring the relationship of factors in an additional time frame or even in all three time frames (Rule & Jarrell, 1980). Sometimes, past currents of thinking, feeling, and behavior flow into the present and then the flow is redirected from present awareness to a recycled past. Possibly the flow of present awareness might be, on other occasions, channeled toward imagined future destinations. Or perhaps at times, the past currents are, for various purposes, allowed simply to flow toward future destinations, by passing present awareness.

The Adlerian lifestyle approach, discussed in previous chapters, can often yield helpful information about this relationship. The past has a large bearing on the individual's present, and because behavior seems to be goal directed, the past influences the future as well. Very significantly, the lifestyle approach can play a major role in determining a client's difficulties with leisure satisfaction and, as a result, can be useful in both the assessment and analysis phases (Rule & Stewart, 1977). By yielding information on the client's dimly conscious goals regarding self, others, and life, the lifestyle can shed light on dimensions of leisure difficulties that need further exploration and resolution. Thus the lifestyle can serve as an indicator of which assessment instruments may be useful in providing leisure information. In addition, this approach can be used as a framework for interpreting the assessment results in the next phase, analysis.

Analysis

Once the practitioner has the assessment results before him, he proceeds to study and synthesize the information. Initially the practitioner relies on his past experience and intuition in providing direction; later in the analysis, the client's reactions to the assessment information and to the practitioner's interpretations become the overriding focus.

As Neulinger (1974) notes, leisure has one and only one essential criterion, the condition of perceived freedom. In other words, the activity must be carried out freely in order to be considered a leisure experience. He further discusses other dimensions that have a bearing on leisure activities: motivation for the activity and the goal of the activity. The motivation issue entails whether or not the satisfaction gained from the activity results from engaging in the activity itself (intrinsic motivation) or from the result of some payoff from the activity (extrinsic motivation). In regard to the goal dimension, the activity with an instrumental goal may be pursued for the sake of achieving another, final goal; whereas an activity meeting a final goal represents the end result. The client's presenting difficulties with leisure would, of course, be the determining factor in selecting which activities satisfy the requisite conditions of motivation and goal orientation. For some clients, the assessment instruments express the results in terms of specific activities; other assessment procedures, as noted previously, identify broad interests that must, in turn, be converted into specific activities.

In the process of helping clients identify or experience satisfying leisure activities, the practitioner can expect to encounter varying degrees of difficulty in analyzing profiles. The assessment results can yield several areas of high interest or activity clusters that come as a delightful surprise to the clients, who then immediately take action steps. As can be imagined, the majority of leisure involvements do not proceed this smoothly. Edwards (1977) provides some ideas for analyzing the results of those individuals whose profiles are more difficult; the following is a summary of her suggestions:

1. No main interest, few "no interests," and many medium interests. The focus should be on practical activities, thereby reducing the range to consider. An activity could be found that combines as many of the client's interests as possible, because a single interest is unlikely to be satisfying enough for this kind of person.
2. Too many main interests. This seems to be a common pattern. Individuals are so enthusiastic about so many pursuits, try to do them all, and, as a result feel unfulfilled. A key seems to be prioritizing a few for the present while saving some for the future.
3. No high interests, many "no interests," very few medium interests. A not-too-unusual profile for the severely disabled. The practitioner should look for a new twist to a medium interest that the person does not know about. Volunteer work is

sometimes successful. Pursuing the classified ads in the phone book can possibly give leisure direction. Individuals in this category are often reluctant to try the unknown, so the helper should be prepared to use encouragement liberally in addition to suggesting practical solutions.

4. High interest that shows up only once. These "random highs" are not confirmed by the other instruments or sources of information. The focus should be on trying to fit the random high in with another interest or pattern of interests. This may serve to reinforce a more obvious interest.
5. Atypical interests. Sometimes the instruments will not have a broad enough range. Practitioner intuition, based on a large field of experience, is important here. Sometimes those persons seeming to be in this category may be honestly lazy and not wanting to do anything during their leisure time.

Regarding the perspective of work and leisure, Bolles (1978) suggests that "the principle of alternating rhythm" be considered. He contends that leisure should complement one's work. The person should identify his oldest and most enjoyed skills. If one's work does not satisfactorily utilize these skills, the person could choose leisure activities that will. If the individual's job does satisfactorily use his skills, then the person can use his leisure time to explore and develop his newest and potentially most enjoyable skills. This principle of alternating rhythm has obvious implications for the disabled client who is no longer able to engage in his chosen work. Perhaps leisure pursuits could be selected that would employ those skills and interests that were satisfied by his previous work. In regard to related considerations, Overs, O'Conner, and DeMarco (1974) offer helpful guidelines on the relationship between various activities and limitations imposed by disabilities. Bolles (1978) has also developed a helpful "leisure map" based on Holland's (previously discussed) six areas of interest.

The practitioner should be ever alert for the appearance of inconsistencies during the sharing of this analysis process with the client. Inconsistencies can appear in many forms and, when explored, can result in very valuable insights: discrepancies between client fantasies or fears of an activity and the reality of it; a high-interest area accompanied by a strong negative reaction; a low-interest area accompanied by a strong positive reaction; a discrepancy between what the client says as compared with his behavior; inconsistencies between ability and interest; discrepancies between practicality and interest; etc. Often, as Edwards (1977) asserted, emphasizing specifics might be a productive way of breaking down many of the above inconsistencies. Then the practitioner can deal with specific solutions. For instance, by learning specifically what a person expects to gain from an activity, the practitioner may be able to suggest an imaginative substitute for the person whose leisure aspirations appear to greatly exceed his abilities.

The Adlerian lifestyle approach can yield helpful information in the analysis stage. In addition to providing helpful assessment information, the lifestyle can reflect the standards of satisfaction the person uses. Furthermore, pitfalls in decision making can perhaps be avoided by an increased awareness of a client's lifestyle. For example, in trying new leisure activities, some clients may be more vulnerable than others. Failure experiences can be growth producing for some clients; for others, they can be devastating.

Action

In the final phase, reconsideration must be surely given to the goal for avocational counseling with a particular individual. If the goal for the counseling involvement is to increase leisure enjoyment, then the activities recommended as the result of exploration in the assessment and analysis phases will usually be ends in themselves. If the overriding goal for avocational counseling is for the activities to be instrumental in bringing about change in other dimensions of a person's life, then the activities may be viewed as means to an end, an end that may not be leisure related (to be discussed further below). The distinction here may determine the activities selected, how the individual will feel about and respond to the activities, and what course of action is to be taken in pursuing the activities.

The main emphasis in this chapter has been on avocational counseling for leisure satisfaction. In this approach the basic purpose is to help the individual become involved in enjoyable activities. This process often entails not only recommending activities to the client but also specifying ways and places for becoming involved with the activities. Edwards (1977) suggests maintaining a comprehensive activity file. This file, organized by major leisure categories, would include community resources, sources of leisure information, newspaper clippings, schedules, book lists, etc. By utilizing this extensive file, the practitioner is in a better position to recommend convenient alternatives for the client. Edwards suggests that activities can be organized in terms of those that a person can do alone, those to be enjoyed with significant others, and those that can be pursued with people outside of one's social network.

Occasionally, the client will need to seek out additional information on his own. Additional reading may be assigned at the library. Sometimes this client may benefit by talking to individuals who are happily engaged in the activities under consideration. Perhaps observing some of the activities can be instructive. The more responsibility the client takes for exploring and selecting the activities, the greater the chances are that the client will ultimately find them satisfying.

In the process of exploring the ways and places of leisure activities, the practitioner may need to explore with the client what activities he will deemphasize or eliminate in order to accommodate the newly chosen ones. Perhaps an overall time-management plan will be necessary so that a pleasant flow of events is achieved. Lakein (1973) offers some helpful time-management tips. This area may be particularly critical for severely disabled individuals with many self-maintenance concerns or those with huge blocks of uncommitted time.

Barriers. In the action phase of helping in which the client explores what to do and how and where to do it, the practitioner should be mindful of obvious and not-so-obvious barriers to leisure satisfaction. Edginton, Compton, and Hanson (1980) suggest consideration of the following broad categories of barriers to leisure fulfillment: attitudinal, communicative, consumptive, temporal, sociocultural, economic, health, leisure values and skills, and experiential. Inconsistent and conflicting goals can also serve as functional barriers (such as wanting security and adventure at the same time).

Two of the most sabotaging psychological barriers to leisure satisfaction are high standards and procrastination. High standards or perfectionism can easily prevent a person's enjoyment of a leisure activity. The individual may feel he has never done well enough, or he may be afraid of failure, or perhaps will expect too much of others' involvement. With the second barrier, procrastination, the person might be telling himself any one of many irrational messages (Ellis & Knaus, 1977) in order to postpone an encounter with the activity. Either one of these two barriers is apt to exist not only in a person's approach to leisure but in other dimensions of his life as well. The understanding gained from the Adlerian lifestyle approach may be helpful here.

Self-Management. A vocational counseling can be directed toward purposes other than leisure satisfaction. One such purpose is self-management. In this approach the goal of the enjoyable activity is instrumental in nature, i.e., the goal of the activity is secondary to or is a means to achieving another goal. This primary goal relates to self-change in a dimension of the person's life that is not necessarily directly leisure related.

Examples of this application might include the process of a recovering substance abuser quickly becoming involved in a pre-selected leisure activity when he finds himself weakening in his efforts to abstain from the self-defeating chemical. Another use involves a client selecting an enjoyable leisure setting or activity for the purpose of trying out risky behaviors, e.g., assertiveness, interacting with the opposite sex, etc. Also, an individual who is vulnerable to depression could, upon recognition of cues signaling the onset of a depressive state, enmesh himself in an absorbing leisure pursuit. Furthermore, a unifying leisure activity may help in solidifying a potentially disintegrating family. The unifying thread in this use of leisure is that the pleasant quality of the activity will take the rough edge off of an otherwise very difficult process.

Often in this approach, satisfying activities are viewed in terms of their relationship to the person's target behaviors for change. Activities may be judged in regard to their ability to elicit certain behaviors or their likelihood of reinforcing certain behaviors. In this approach, the strategy is to use contingency management in order to help the individual achieve the desired behavior change; a strong emphasis is on specific goals and performance criteria. Activities, events, and experiences are thus valued for their reinforcing properties. Rimm and Masters (1979) have divided these reinforcers into five categories: material, social, activity, token, and covert. The use of pleasant activity and experiences in this manner is thus usually a part of a broader counseling strategy. Indeed, Karoly (1980) observed that "positive contingency control may well be the most versatile tool in the realm of behavior change" (p. 225). Additional reading in the use of these techniques may be found in Watson and Tharp (1977), Rimm and Masters (1979), Kanfer and Goldstein (1980), Mahoney and Thoreson (1974), Thoreson and Mahoney (1974), and Goldfried and Merbaum (1973).

Follow-up is an important final step in the action phase. The practitioner and the client should devise a procedure that indicates to what degree the client's goals were met. This may take the form of subjective ratings, logs, tallies, reports, observations, etc. Specificity in follow-up should be encouraged as much as possible. The emphasis, however, must ultimately be on the client's perceptions, because leisure satisfaction is by nature a very subjective experience.

Stress Management. Somewhat related to self-management strategies is the emerging area of stress management. Satisfying leisure activities have a definite place in an overall stress management plan for adjustment to disability.

A stressor can be viewed as "any demand on your mind or body" (Schafer, 1978, p. 27). All stressors seem to cause wear and tear. However, "pleasant" stress seems to cause less harm to the mind and body than does "unpleasant" stress. Stressors may also be few or many in a person's life. Some disabled people may suffer from too few stressors and, as a result, be understimulated, whereas other individuals may be overwhelmed with stressors at work (e.g., high-pressure sales, certain hospital work) or during "nonworking" time (e.g., mothers with small children, compulsive gamblers, active job seekers, etc.).

Another significant factor that is related to avocational counseling is the dimension of newness versus familiarity. It seems that, in general, the greater the amount of new stressors, as opposed to familiar ones, the greater will be the impact on the individual. From a somewhat different, yet related, perspective, von Bertalanffy (1968), a general systems theorist, contends that systems need both maintenance and change in order to function satisfactorily. However, individuals seem to vary in the degree of needed personal balance between these and related factors. As Selye (1974) has observed, some people are stress seekers and some are stress avoiders.

From an avocational counseling perspective, then, it is sometimes helpful to explore with a disabled client what is his own "comfort zone" (Schafer, 1978) of stress. In terms of amount of stimulation for this zone, one person may require a wide range (2 to 8 on a scale ranging from 1 to 10), another individual may feel he must always be on the go (a range of 7 to 10), and a third person may get very tense at the hint of a lot of stimulation (a range of 1 to 5). This will, of course, vary among lifestyles. Perhaps the stereotypic lifestyle of "excitement seeker" would lean toward one extreme, whereas the "inadequate" lifestyle would be found near the other.

In terms of stress management and leisure activities, the practitioner may, at times, want to respect the "comfort zone" of the disabled client. At other times, particularly if secondary gains are involved with the client's comfort zone, the practitioner may want to be instrumental in expanding, raising, or lowering the limits of the zone—what is comfortable for some individuals may not necessarily be healthy for them.

SUMMARY

Avocational counseling can be used for many different purposes. In adjustment to disability, avocational counseling is often directed toward leisure satisfaction. The primary goal here is for the selected activities to be freely chosen and enjoyable in and of themselves. The issue of freedom in choosing activities is an important one for the disabled. This seems so because these individuals sometimes have plenty of "free time" while, paradoxically, having their freedom of choice of activities somewhat limited by the nature of their disabilities. The practitioner must be especially mindful of the obvious and not-so-obvious barriers to leisure satisfaction. The suggested sequence of avocational counseling phases are exploratory discussion, assessment, analysis, and action.

REFERENCES

Bolles, R. N. The three boxes of life. Berkeley, Calif.: Ten Speed Press, 1978.

Campbell, D. P., Hansen, J. C. Manual for the SVIB-SCI1 (3rd ed.). Stanford, Calif.: Stanford University Press, 1981.

Cautela, J. R., & Kastenbaum, R. A reinforcement survey schedule for use in therapy, training, and research. Psychological Reports, 1967, 20, 1115–1130.

Compton, D., & Eddy, J. Developing leisure behavior: Education, counseling, and therapeutic recreation. Counseling and Human Development, 1981, 13(6), 1–16.

Cousins, B., & Brown, E. Recreation therapy assessment, Jacksonville, Fla.: Amelia Island JCFMR, 1979.

Davis, J. Recreational directors observation report: Occupational therapy: Principles and practices. Springfield, Ill.: Charles C Thomas, 1957.

Edginton, C. R., Compton, D. M., & Hanson, C. J. Recreational leisure programming: A guide for the professional. Philadelphia: Saunders, 1980.

Edwards, P. B. Leisure counseling techniques. Los Angeles, Calif.: University Publishers, 1977.

Eisenberg, M. Psychological aspects of physical disability: A guide for the health care worker. New York: National League for Nursing, 1977.

Ellis, A., & Knaus, W. J. Overcoming procrastination. New York: The Institute for Rational Living, 1977.

Goldfried, M. R., & Merbaum, M. (Eds.). Behavior change through self-control. New York: Holt, Rinehart & Winston, 1973.

Holland, J. L. Professional manual for the self-directed search. Palo Alto, Calif.: Consulting Psychologists Press, 1972.

Hubert, E. The development of an inventory of leisure interests. Doctoral dissertation, University of North Carolina, 1969.

Joswiak, K. Leisure counseling program materials for the developmentally disabled. Washington, D.C.: Hawkins and Associates, 1975.

Kanfer, F. H., & Goldstein, A. P. (Eds.). Helping people change (2nd ed.). New York: Pergamon Press, 1980.

Karoly, P. Operant methods. In F. H. Kanfer & A.P. Goldstein (Eds.), Helping people change (2nd ed.). New York: Pergamon Press, 1980.

Kuder, G. F. Administrator's manual: Kuder preference record. Chicago: Science Research Associates, 1960.

Lakein, A. How to get control of time and your life. New York: Signet, 1973.

Lazarus, A., & Fay, A. I can if I want to: New York: Morrow, 1975.

Lewisohn, P. M., Munoz, R. F., Youngren, M. A., & Zeiss, A. M. Control your depression. Englewood Cliffs, N.J.: Prentice-Hall, 1978.
Mahoney, M. J., & Thoreson, C. E. Self-control: Power to the person. Monterey, Calif.: Brooks/Cole, 1974.
McDowell, C. Leisure counseling: Selected lifestyle processes. Eugene, Ore.: Center of Leisure Studies, 1976.
McKechnie, G. Leisure activities blank. Palo Alto, Calif.: Consulting Psychologists Press, 1975.
Morrow, L. Essay: What is the point of working? Time, May 11, 1981, pp. 93–94.
National Geographic Society. We Americans. Washington, D.C.: National Geographic Society, 1975.
Neulinger, J. The psychology of leisure. Springfield, Ill.: Charles C Thomas, 1974.
Overs, R. P., O'Conner, E., & DeMarco, B. Avocational activities for the handicapped. Springfield, Ill.: Charles C Thomas, 1974.
Overs, R. P., & Page, C. M. Avocational title card sort. Milwaukee, Wisc.: Curative Workshop of Milwaukee, 1974.
Rimm, D. C., & Masters, J. C. Behavior Therapy (2nd ed.). New York: Academic Press, 1979.
Rule, W., & Jarrell, G. Time dimensions in leisure counseling. Journal of Leisurability, 1980, 7, 3–8.
Rule, W., & Stewart, M. Enhancing leisure counseling using an Adlerian technique. Therapeutic Recreation Journal, 1977, 11(3), 87–93.
Schafer, W. Stress, distress and growth. Davis, Calif.: International Dialogue Press, 1978.
Selye, H. Stress without distress. New York: Signet, 1974.
Simon, S. B., Howe, L. W., & Kirschenbaum, H. Values clarification: A handbook of practical strategies for teachers and students. New York: Hart, 1972.
Takata, N. Play as exploratory learning. Los Angeles: Sage Publishers, 1974.
Thoreson, C. E., & Mahoney, M. J. Behavioral self control. New York: Holt, Rinehart & Winston, 1974.
Trieschmann, R. Coping with disability: A sliding scale of goals. Archives of Physical Medicine and Rehabilitation, 1974, 55, 556–560.
Von Bertalanffy, L. General systems theory. New York: Braziller. 1968.
Watson, D. L., & Tharp, R. G. Self-directed behavior: Self-modification for personal adjustment (2nd ed.). Belmont, Calif.: Wadsworth, 1977.
Wehman, P., & Schleien, S. Relevant assessment in leisure skill training programs. Therapeutic Recreation Journal, 1980, 14(4), 9–21.
Wessel, J. I can physical education program. Northbrook, Ill.: Hubbard Scientific Co., 1976.
Williams, W., & Fox, T. Minimum objective system. Burlington, Vt.: University of Vermont, Center on Developmental Disabilities, 1977.

14

ENHANCING LEISURE COUNSELING USING AN ADLERIAN TECHNIQUE

Warren R. Rule and Morris W. Stewart

A recent furor has occurred in the area of leisure counseling. The culmination of these efforts and concerns were expounded upon at the 1976 National Recreation and Park Congress held in Boston, Massachusetts. A mini-institute on leisure counseling addressed personnel considerations (Fain, 1976) and the presentation of a leisure counseling model (Peterson, 1976), with a panel of respondents offering critical insight into each topic. Much concern was expressed for a struggling identity in leisure counseling.

It must be agreed that skepticism and caution will serve as a sounding board for the profession; however, this will not alter the continual growth and development in the area. Expansion of knowledge through information sharing will enhance the professional understanding. One may cling to clichés such as "a little knowledge is more dangerous than none," but it is beyond imagination how a profession

---

This chapter, "Enhancing Leisure Counseling Using an Adlerian Technique," from Warren R. Rule and Morris W. Stewart, *Therapeutic Recreation Journal,* 11(3), pp. 87–93.

can bury its head in the sand when the momentum exists without direction. It is necessary to alter this course through research, writing, training, and pragmatic application. The contention and theme prevalent throughout the remainder of this paper will be to provide insight and additional possibilities so that those electing to pursue leisure counseling may be better able to serve the client's best interest via a larger reservoir of resources.

Leisure counselors are looking for swift, useful techniques that can possibly enhance the counseling process and outcome. In helping a client, the leisure counselor sometimes chooses to rely on data obtained from devices such as activities indices, interest inventories, even regression equations and various other quantified instruments. In selecting these tools the practitioner is hoping to use nomothetic formulations, i.e., laws of general validity, and is attempting to apply them to the individual client. When the leisure counselor focuses on the client's uniqueness by studying the person's background, by fostering an I-Thou encounter, or by responding emphatically to the client, the emphasis shifts toward seeking idiographic (individual) formulations, i.e., laws which are particular to the individual case.

Certainly, both types of formulation contribute to the success of leisure counseling. Wilson (in Overs et al., 1974, p. vii) sums up well this combination stating that the major tool in avocational counseling is the computer, yet avocational counseling's "special expertise is the warm, human element of an understanding counselor." The Adlerian technique of utilizing a client's early memories as a means of better understanding the person's present outlook in life is a method that can foster an open and meaningful counseling relationship. Furthermore, this technique, which focuses primarily on idiographic understanding, can strengthen leisure counseling outcomes.

Alfred Adler developed a concept for understanding the individual that he termed "life style." This term can be understood to mean the mental guidelines a person uses for interacting with others and for measuring self worth. Adler believed that everyone strives toward a subjectively determined place of significance which is a function of the conclusions drawn from one's early childhood. These early conclusions about self, others and life are based on the biased sample of life that children have experienced. These notions guide one through life, and upon them our goals and behavior are based. Moreover, one is not always fully conscious of the biased notions that continually become reindoctrinated and reprogrammed.

UNDERSTANDING EARLY RECOLLECTIONS

A major Adlerian method of gaining some insight into an individual's life-style notions about self, others and life is to obtain and interpret the person's early memories. The Adlerian belief is that there are not any "chance memories." From the thousands of experiences to which the individual has been exposed in early childhood, only those recollections are remembered which coincide with one's present outlook on life. The individual's recollections (ER) show the same pattern; they are reminders of one's own limits and the meaning of circumstances (Ansbacher & Ansbacher, 1956).

Generally individuals can remember, upon being asked, at least six specific incidents which occurred before six or seven. Each recollection, when viewed by the practitioner in the context of the feeling about the remembered incident, reflects a current expectancy about life. The early recollections do not contradict each other; each supplements the outlook reflected in other early recollections. Furthermore, the concern is not with whether or not the remembered event actually occurred, since the individual is apt to omit or distort details in accordance with innate biases. If the event can be mentally visualized, as on a movie screen, it is considered an early recollection (Mosak, 1958).

Researchers from various frames of reference have found that relationships exist between early recollections and specific personality characteristics (e.g., Waldfogel, 1948; Chance, 1957; Lieberman, 1957; McCarter, 1957; Charry, 1959; Grey, 1959; Tolar & Fazzone, 1966; Mosak, 1969; Pustel, Sternlicht, & Siegel, 1969; Wolman, 1970). In addition, early recollections have been found to be related to certain vocational choices (Holmes & Watson, 1965; Manaster & Perryman, 1974).

In leisure counseling, probably three to six early recollections would provide a sufficient starting point for client self-exploration. For example, the leisure counselor could introduce and justify the gathering of the early recollections by saying:

John, it may be helpful for us to explore some of the notions and expectations that are at work in your daily life. In discussing some of them, maybe we can find ways to keep them front working to your disadvantage in your leisure pursuits. It seems that just about all of our major attitudes have both advantages and disadvantages built into them. One way to better understand these vaguely conscious attitudes is to take a look at an individual's earliest memories. It seems that the earliest memories can give an indication of a person's present attitudes and expectations about life.

After having gathered the client's earliest recollections, the leisure counselor can privately spend a little time jotting down several tentative interpretations to be explored later with the client. In attempting to pin down a general, tentative understanding of the early recollections, probably the best means is to study each one individually, then try to gain further understanding by determining how the early recollections supplement each other. In viewing each one, the focus is best kept on capturing the personal and interpersonal conclusions that the client inferred from the remembered incident. In other words, these early lessons in expectations can be viewed in the overriding context of current expectations for self, others, and life.

ILLUSTRATION

As an illustration, an individual's three earliest recollections are given below, followed by general tentative interpretations:

> ER #1—I remember when my brother had just been born and word was sent back from the hospital. I said to the rest of the family, "We have a baby brother!" Felt? I felt proud.
>
> ER #2—One time I remember sitting by myself in the back yard playing with a moss-covered rock. I enjoyed handling it and the feel of the surface. Felt? Contented; curious.
>
> ER #3—I remember how I used to hate wearing to school a particular hat that my mother insisted I wear. As I rounded the corner I would stick it in my pocket. One day I must have done it too soon because my mother saw me and told the family and others about it later. They all laughed. Felt? Defiant in doing it; pleased that they liked it.

The interrelation of the ERs and the individuality of each contributes to the total scope and understanding. Using the previously mentioned "I am..."Others are...," "Life is...," framework, tentative interpretations may be as follows:

* I am a resourceful person who is capable of self-control.
* Others are apt to admire my goodness.
* Life is a place where one should cleverly arrange and maintain a place of importance.

These interpretations are, of course, viewed as springboards for client self-exploration and for discussion and modification. It should be kept in mind that internalized guidelines such as these are at work in the many aspects of our lives, including our approach to leisure. Furthermore, one tends to measure self-worth by how much one is able to live up to these self-mandates. Some other examples, using variations from Mosak (1971), can be related to themes such as: to be the "best," to present oneself as inadequate, to struggle and to win, to gain special consideration for a burden or the black cloud overhead, to win approval at all costs, to gain recognition, to create excitement, to be right and avoid being wrong, to control others, to impress others with one's mental ability, to get as much as one can from others and life, to show one's goodness is beyond reproach, to put others in one's service. As can be noticed, these ideas are self-serving and have implications for leisure decision-making, the leisure counseling process, and leisure counseling outcomes.

Discussed below are some specific dimensions to look for in interpreting early recollections that might be particularly helpful in leisure counseling:

1. What is the perception of the environment? Some examples are (Lieberman, 1957): threatening emotionally, threatening physically, rejecting, friendly, frustrating, nurturing.
2. What degree of social interest is shown? Examples are: selfish greed at one extreme; unselfish group-mindedness at the other extreme.
3. What degree of activity is involved? For instance: What is involved when the person acts on the environment or is acted on by the environment? How does a positive or a negative outcome influence the acted on–acted upon dimension? Did the purpose (or expectation) for acting or not acting pay off? What subjective guideline might be kept in mind as a result?
4. When another individual or when individuals are mentioned in an ER (e.g., father, mother, sibling, etc.), usually the generalization is made to people in general (e.g., others; and if a pattern presents itself—men, women, authority figures, etc.).
5. The most vivid part of the ER is often the focus that reveals overriding message from the ER.
6. Specific considerations (Ansbacher & Ansbacher, 1956);
   a. Recollections of dangers and accidents, as well as punishment, often disclose the exaggerated tendency to keep in mind particularly the hostile side of life.

b. The recollection of the birth a brother or sister frequently reveals a sensitivity to losing a place of importance.
c. The recollection of the first visit to school, kindergarten, etc., can indicate a keen interest in the excitement of newness and new situations.
d. Several recollections (a pattern), particularly involving a mother or other individual persons in a friendly atmosphere, may suggest a liking for special treatment.
e. Recollections of misdeeds which have been committed usually point to an effort to keep them from occurring again.
f. An indication of interest, such as visual, auditory, motor, sensory, etc., can be checked out for vocational or avocational purposes.

7. Specific avocational criteria can be used, such as the social-psychological factors listed by Overs, O'Conor, and DeMarco (1974): aesthetic, utilitarian, creative, pre-patterned, abstract or concrete, group effort or individual effort, structured or unstructured, supervised or unsupervised, opportunity or little opportunity for recognition.

FACILITATING LEISURE EXPLORATION

In the case of the above-discussed individual, what considerations could be explored simply using his early recollections? Using Overs et al.'s (1974) classification system of avocational activities, one might guess that this person would not relate particularly well to games, unless of an intellectually challenging nature. For the same reason, sports may well not be to his liking; additional reasons for dislike may be the difficulty involved in establishing a place of recognized importance and the lack of autonomy because of the rules and regulations. Art and music activities, educational (especially reading) and cultural activities, nature and craft activities may be more to his liking in view of the opportunity for curiosity, self-control, sense of individual resourcefulness, opportunity for creativity and sensory (visual, tactile) experience. Factors seem to lean for and against the enjoyment of collection activities, thus making it difficult to guess. Insofar as organizational and volunteer activities are concerned, the opportunity to be admired and a feeling of autonomy may well depend on whether a place of recognized importance is secured—it appears quite unlikely that he would be content if he were "just one of the troops."

An awareness of these life-style notions and how they relate to one's approach to leisure could be helpful in another way. Assume that the above person is already into a leisure pursuit—even one that is somewhat enjoyable but he does not feel quite satisfied. This approach could be used to explore with him what it is that he is wanting that he is not getting. Then, variations or alternatives could be explored.

In discussing these relationships with the client, the leisure counselor must emphasize the importance of sharing ideas. In subjective interpretations of any nature, the possibility certainly exists for inaccurate inferences. If the communication channels are open, the probability is increased that this form of self-understanding will enhance-leisure decision-making. Introductory phrases by the counselor such as "Could it be that…" or "A guess that I have is…" can foster the desired atmosphere of mutual exploration. In discussing these life-style notions with the client, the counselor is moving toward the leisure self-concept which, as described by McDowell, "consists of the self as seen by the self, the self as seen by others and the self as one would like to be" (1974, p. 99). The counselor may well want to explore how the client puts into practice behaviorally these notions in daily living. Operationally, it seems that a person's thinking goes something like, "If this is the way I am, others are, and life is, therefore I should have certain goals and should behave in a certain way."

Fain (1973) has indicated that in leisure counseling a useful question is, "Why do you do or would like to do a certain thing?" (p. 5). An Adlerian approach, giving this question a different twist, would emphasize the goal-directed nature of human behavior. Alteration of the question may be, "For what purpose do you do or would like to do a certain thing?" Moreover, understanding the life-style notions would help answer the question.

A tentative understanding of these life-style notions by both counselor and client can be helpful in avoiding potential pitfalls in decision-making. For some clients failure experiences can be growth producing; for others, they can be devastating. In addition, exploring and understanding these notions can have beneficial by-products in leisure counseling such as providing a helpful framework for guessing how a client will react to a newly acquired disability. Also client avoidance maneuvers and procrastinations can be viewed in a different light. Furthermore, the counselor may be in a better position to make recommendations to other professionals who are working with the client. As an added bonus, the leisure counselor is better informed and can now be more emphatic during the counseling process and can tailor responses more to the goals of the client, e.g., Rule (1978).

FACILITATING BEHAVIOR CHANGE

Oftentimes a well-fitted leisure pursuit for a client is the primary goal of leisure counseling. Yet on other occasions, the counseling goal is therapeutically broader—using leisure as a means of changing specific behaviors in other areas of the client's life. This may be handled individually by the counselor or by working closely with other professionals. Thus, it seems that the leisure counselor is in a position to use leisure either to help the client flow more enjoyably with the natural currents in his life or to help the client to go against some of the natural currents in his life in order to bring about a behavior change.

If the client's life-style notions are compatible with the intended counseling strategy for behavior change, chances of success would seem to be greater. For example, a counseling strategy related to leisure may be for the client to reinforce himself with a positive reward after having successfully performed a behavior in line with the desired self-change. This and other behavioral self-control approaches are discussed in Mahoney and Thoresen, 1974; Thoresen and Mahoney, 1974; Goldfried and Merbaum, 1973. To supplement these approaches the leisure use of early recollections can be used to help confirm the potency of the positive reinforcer selected by the client. Similarly, information contained in early recollections can be used to help decide on leisure activities in which the client can take beneficial interpersonal risks. It would seem to be safer to rehearse the desired behaviors first in a pleasurable leisure setting and then focus on the more anxiety-laden situations, such as interactions with friends, family members, or co-workers. These tentative life-style notions may also be used as guidelines for increasing or reducing in frequency already-learned behaviors as well as for learning entirely new behaviors (Rule, 1976).

Finally, early recollections may shed some light on whatever the client is thinking that may be maintaining the gap between the leisure discrepancy described by McKechnie (1974) of what one does versus what one would like to do. Those entering into the area of leisure counseling must maintain a broad approach to the process with the hope that further understanding and an expansion of knowledge will serve to facilitate the effectiveness of the client's behavioral change. The preceding discussion would offer yet another technique for the leisure counselor.

REFERENCES

Ansbacher, Heinz L., & Ansbacher, Rowena (Eds.). The Individual Psychology of Alfred Adler. New York: Basic Books 1956.

Chance, J. E. Some Correlates of Affective Tone of Early Memories. Journal of Consulting Psychology, 1957, 21, 203–205.

Charry, J. B. Childhood and Teenage Memories in Mentally Ill and Normal Groups. Unpublished doctoral dissertation. Columbia University, 1959.

Fain, Gerald S. Leisure Counseling: Some Personnel Considerations. Paper Presented at the Mini-Conference on Leisure Counseling, National Recreational and Park Association Congress, Boston, 1976.

Fain, Gerald S. Leisure Counseling: Translating Needs Into Action. Therapeutic Recreation Journal, 1973, 7, 5–9.

Goldfried, Marvin R., & Merbaum, Michael (Eds.). Behavior Change Through Self Control. New York: Holt, Rinehart & Winston, 1973.

Grey, L. Utilization of the Earliest Childhood Recollection in Detecting Maladjustment Among Junior College Students. Unpublished doctoral dissertation, University of Southern California, 1959.

Holmes, David S., and Watson, Robert J. Early Recollection and Vocational Choice. Journal of Consulting Psychology, 1965, 29, 486–488.

Lieberman, M. G. Childhood Memories as a Projective Technique. Journal of Projective Techniques, 1957, 21, 32–36.

Mahoney, Michael J., and Thoresen, Carl E. Self Control: Power to the Person. Monterey, California: Brooks/Cole Publishing Company, 1974.

Hamster, G. Y., & Perryman, T. B. Early Recollections and Occupational Choice. Journal of Individual Psychology, 1974, 30, 232–237.

McCarter, R. E. Affective Components of Early Recollections. Unpublished doctoral dissertation, Princeton University, 1961.

McDowell, Chester F. Toward a Healthy Leisure Mode: Leisure Counseling. Therapeutic Recreation Journal, 1974, 8, 96–104.

McKechnie, George E. Psychological Foundations of Leisure Counseling: An Empirical Strategy. Therapeutic Recreation Journal, 1974, 8, 4–10.

Mosak, Harold H. Early Recollections as a Projective Technique. Journal of Projective Techniques, 1958, 22, 302–311.

Mosak, Harold H. Early Recollections: Evaluation of Recent Research. Journal of Individual Psychology, 1969, 25, 56–63.

Mosak, Harold H. Lifestyle. In Arthur Nikelly (Ed.) Techniques for Behavior Change. Springfield, Illinois: Charles C Thomas, 1971.

Overs, Robert P., O'Connor, Elizabeth, and DeMarco, Barbara. Avocational Activities for the Handicapped. Springfield, Illinois: Charles C Thomas, 1974.

Peterson, Carol. Leisure Counseling: What Is It and into What Context Does It Fit? Paper Presented at the Mini-Conference on Leisure Counseling, National Recreational and Park Association Congress, Boston, 1976.

Pustel, G., Sternlicht, M., & Siegel, L. Pleasant Versus Unpleasant Early Childhood Recollections of Institutionalized Adolescents and Adult Retardates. Journal of Clinical Psychology, 1969, 25, 110–111.

Rule, W. R. Exploring Counselor Self-Awareness Using a Variation of the Adlerian Life-Style Approach. Virginia Commonwealth University Rehabilitation Monograph Series, Vol. 2, 1976.

Rule, W. R. Corrective Reactions to Client Negativism Using a Combined Adlerian and Facilitatively-Based Approach. Corrective and Social Psychiatry and Journal of Behavior Technology Methods and Therapy, 1978.

Tolar, A., & Fazzone, R. A. Early Memories as Indicators of Ego Functioning. Psychological Reports, 1966, 19, 979–983.
Thoreson, C. E., & Mahoney, M. J. Behavioral Self Control. New York: Holt, Rinehart & Winston, 1974.
Waldfogel, S. The Frequency and Effective Character of Childhood Memories. Psychological Monographs, 1948, 62, No. 4 (whole No. 291).
Wolman, R. N. Early Recollections and the Perceptions of Others: A Study of Delinquent Adolescents. Journal of Genetic Psychology, 116, 157–163.

VI
Counseling Uses of Humor

15

INCREASED INTERNAL-CONTROL USING HUMOR WITH LIFESTYLE AWARENESS

Warren R. Rule

In a best-selling book, Dyer stated that "perhaps the single most outstanding characteristic of healthy people is their unhostile sense of humor" (1976, p. 214). An investigation by O'Connell (1960) indicated that the well-adjusted person has a greater appreciation for humor than the less-adjusted person. From a clinical perspective, some practitioners, e.g., Shelton and Ackerman (1974), advocate the therapeutic use of evocation of humor as a state incompatible with anxiety and Ellis (1976) emphasized humor as a means of challenging irrational beliefs. Recently in Wales, the world's first International Symposium on Humor was held. Adler made frequent use of humor (Ansbacher & Ansbacher, 1956) and those endorsing Adlerian ideas (e.g., O'Connell, 1975; Olson, 1976) employ humor in psychotherapy.

The ability to find humor in and to laugh at one's own biased expectations of self, others, and life, when these notions are working to one's

This chapter, "Increased Internal-Control Using Humor with Lifestyle Awareness," from Warren R. Rule, *The Individual Psychologist* 16:3, pp. 16–21; published by The Adler-Dreikus Institute of Human Relations.

disadvantage, would seem to enhance personal growth. This ability could well exist less frequently than is generally imagined, e.g., O'Connell's (1969) findings suggest that the ability to produce humor was not closely related to its appreciation. Possibly the ability to generate self-humor can be encouraged and learned by a continued exploration and development of creative therapeutic approaches. Kadis & Winick (1973) have found selected cartoons to be an effective means of facilitating the therapeutic process. They define the cartoon (p. 106) as "a stylized drawing, often of people in a social situation, which exaggerates their foibles." Shulman (1973) has used dramatic confrontation in group psychotherapy by having group members respond to another member's life style demands on them in an exaggerated manner, e.g., treating a member like an inadequate baby or another member like a splendid princess. Related to these approaches, the focus of the present investigation is on the absurd exaggeration of individual life styles, using masquerades and photography, as a means of increasing self-awareness and self-acceptance. The emphasis here is on a technique employing humor which may be helpful in the practice of counseling and psychotherapy.

Alfred Adler developed a concept for understanding the individual that he termed "life style." This term may be understood to mean the pattern of dimly conscious guidelines or goals a person uses for interacting with others and for measuring self-worth. Adler contended that everyone strives toward a subjectively determined ideal of respect-from-others which is a function of the early childhood conclusions drawn about self, others, and life. These conclusions or notions are, of course, biased by variables unique to each person such as family values, birth order, interaction patterns, parental modeling, and other childhood experiences. These somewhat biased notions continue to guide an individual through life and upon them goals and behavior are based. The life style, or "cognitive map" (Mosak & Dreikurs, 1973, p. 74), creates self-reinforcing biased expectations and accompanying selective perceptions which work well for the individual some of the time, but not as well on other occasions. An increased awareness of these biased expectations that underlie one's goals and behaviors can be helpful as a person moves through his daily life. The therapist relies on the selectivity feature of memory as reflecting indications of childhood conclusions that presently are being used as guidelines for coping.

The process of helping a person to increase this level of insight in everyday life frequently can be quite challenging and difficult, as is the case with most cognitively oriented therapeutic approaches. The following quasi-experiment was an exploration of a humor-based method for enhancing self-awareness and self-control, as well as an effort to lend credence to this technique from a practitioner's vantage point. The research hypotheses were that (a) internal locus of control would increase and that (b) negative feeling states related to self would decrease, when the subjects had been involved in self-directed-humor exercises.

METHOD

The experimental group consisted of nine students enrolled in a seminar emphasizing the use of the Adlerian life style approach in counseling. The selection of the control group of nine, also from the same graduate program, was based on the matched variables of sex and demonstrated scholarship. Three males and six females comprised each group.

Four weeks prior to the completion of the seminar, both groups were given a variation of Rotter's Internal-External Control Scale (Rotter, Chance & Phares, 1972). Rotter's scale indicates the degree to which an individual feels in control of his own destiny or feels controlled by external circumstances. This variation consisted of changing the forced choice nature of the fifty-eight items to that of a semantic differential in which the respondent was asked to circle the number (1–9) which best represented the degree of believing or disbelieving each statement. This format was changed in order to reflect more sensitively pre-post test changes in locus of control. The groups were not significantly different upon pre-testing ($t = .38$).

The second criterion was frequency of negative feeling states. Each day for one week, the subjects, using wrist golf counters, were requested to tally negative emotions or mental states (e.g., anxiety, anger, confusion, etc.) they would prefer experiencing less strongly or less often. After the subsequent two-week period, at which time the experimental group engaged in their self-directed-humor exercises, both groups repeated tallying negative feeling states for a one-week period. In a three-month follow-up, both groups were asked to again tally negative feeling states for one week and to retake the modified Rotter Scale.

On the evening prior to the beginning of the two-week experimental period, the experimental group assembled for the photographing of the life style masquerades. The determination of each individual life style was the result of group input using the format developed by Dreikurs (1967). Preceding this period, feedback was expressed by the group in the Adlerian framework of biased notions about self, others, life and of goals and behaviors used to implement these notions. In the determination of a group member's life style, the individual had the responsibility of ultimately deciding which of the suggested life-style characteristics were accurate. The choice of the exaggerated life-style masquerade was likewise the result of group-individual interaction with the individual making the final costume choices. During this evening, polaroid photographs were made of each of the masqueraded group members.

Highlights of the self-serving characteristics of each life style and of the exaggerated masquerade features were as follows: (a) life style: to be "gooder than good" along with charm, achievement orientation, and the use of silent suffering as an approach-avoidance motivator; masquerade: a prima donna pose and a charming, solicitous smile, a basket of overflowing goodies, a huge sunburst, and an umbrella embellished with her name; (b) to be a mysterious observer-sage while obtaining special treatment through subtle tactfulness: a seductive pose, an all-knowing facial expression, clad in many veils and in Far-Eastern attire; (c) to be on top of others by outdoing them, along with attempts of intellectual superiority and grandiose intimidation: perched atop a ladder in a matador's outfit, complete with sword in one hand and a book in the other; (d) to please others in an ongoing effort to measure up while expecting tender-loving-care in return: midway up a ladder, clothed in a choir boy's robe and a halo, clutching a yardstick and a picture of an attractive, understanding woman; (e) to maintain autonomy of self through achievement, control of others, guarding private sensitivity: stepping upward, grimacing from a mouse trap on one hand and having puppet-like controlling strings in the other hand while wearing a blouse imprinted with a computer keyboard; (f) to be recognized as a charming queen by using sweetness, generosity, and propriety: a regal pose and a smile complemented by a queen's crown, basket of gifts and sugar in one hand and a pair of binoculars in the other; (g) to collect and savor the pleasures of life, sometimes through smooth and clever manipulation: slouched in a chair while wearing a yachtman's hat and smoking a pipe, a game box in one hand and girlie magazine in the other; (h) to drive and strive for a place of importance in the eyes of others, particularly through the use of attention resulting from achievement and from sharing knowledge: leaning forward and beckoning attention, clad in a racing cap, scarf, gloves, and with a red heart on a eye-catching outfit, plus a scholarly book in hand; and (i) to be recognized as gallant and strong, especially by handling more than one's share and by being independent: a Caesar-like pose with head tilted back, wearing a cape, sword, and flowers while holding a football helmet on which a message proclaims, "Let me… I can manage."

With the polaroid photograph attached to a cardboard fold-out resembling a passport, each person was instructed to complete a prescribed procedure before each meal for two weeks. The procedure was first to record on the fold-out the number of situations in which negative feeling states were experienced since the last meal. Then, for each situation, the person was requested to look at the exaggerated self-ideal picture and try to figure out how the life style contributed to the unwanted negative feeling or mental state. The emphasis was placed on exploring the "shoulds and should nots" that were at work. The number of situations in which the life style was discovered to be working to one's disadvantage were then recorded on the fold-out. Finally the individual was required to:

> Select one situation (from those in which you discovered your life style at work) that you would like to change the most. Then vividly imagine yourself during this situation pausing or really laughing at yourself for letting this self-ideal work to your disadvantage. Picture yourself actually smiling or even uproariously laughing and saying to yourself subvocally, "You're still OK (John), even when you don't make these exaggerated expectations of yourself."

If the individual was unable to identify a situation in which a negative feeling was experienced and it was suspected that things since the last meal really were not that satisfactory, the person was to punish himself for lack of awareness by not drinking any liquids with the meal.

RESULTS AND DISCUSSION

In regard to increases in internality, based on the Locus of Control instrument, there was a significant difference (p. 10, t =1.52) between the experimental and control groups on the post-testing. The results were significant even when the individual with the highest increase in the experimental group was assigned the mean value for the remainder of the group.

Aside from the statistical restrictiveness resulting from the use of a small sample in this investigation, this modest level of significance would seem to be noteworthy in view of the apparent difficulty in changing such a global criterion (locus of control) in a relatively brief time span.

There was no significant difference between the experimental and control groups in decreasing negative feeling states. This lack of significance characterized the pre- and post-comparison (t =.009) and the pre- and three-month follow-up comparison (t = .414).

The possibility exists that either an extended period of the humor exercises or specific structured homework assignments were needed to decrease the overall frequency of negative feeling states. Another influential factor is that none of the individuals engaged in this experiment for the expressed purpose of solving personal problems. Yet, from the perspective of ongoing daily functioning, the heightened awareness of the contribution of one's life style to personal problems, accompanied by an increased humorous acceptance of self, may well have been beneficial. For instance, from a practitioner's perspective, it is interesting to note that the experimental group found that 73.4% of the negative feeling states (N=634) which were recorded during the two-week period could be related to the exaggerated life style characteristics.

The procedure of humorously exaggerating individual characteristics through masquerading to enhance self-acceptance and other-acceptance can be used in many types of group approaches. An atmosphere of cohesiveness and trust greatly facilitates this process. Furthermore, the participation of the leader in the exaggerated masquerade is desirable. As can be imagined, the gathering for photographing the masqueraded group members is highly charged with a spirit making and Gemeinschaftsgefühl.

Additional uses of this method of using humor (Kadis & Winick, 1973) could be to: penetrate resistance, reduce anxiety, reflect one's own life situation, avoid the maneuvers of a group member whose verbosity is unproductive, communicate to a person who responds to visual images rather than verbal input, and illuminate an individual's self-defeating defenses. Thus, this facilitative use of humor would seem to be a useful technique for the practitioner in both individual and group settings.

REFERENCES

Ansbacher. H. L., & Ansbacher, R. (Eds.) The Individual Psychology of Alfred Adler. New York: Basic Books, 1956.

Dreikurs, R. Psychodynamics, psychotherapy and counseling. Chicago: Alfred Adler Institute, 1967.

Dyer, W. Your erroneous zones. New York: Funk & Wagnalls, 1976.

Ellis, A. Presentation at the national convention of the American Psychological Association. Washington, D.C., September, 1976.

Kadis, A. L., & Winick, C. The cartoon as therapeutic catalyst. In Mosak, H. H. (Ed.) Alfred Adler: His influence on psychology today. Ridge Park, N.J : Noyes Press, 1973.

Mosak, H. H., & Dreikurs, R. Adlerian psychotherapy. In Corsini, R. (Ed.) Current psychotherapies. Itasca, Ill.: Peacock, 1973.
O'Connell, W. Action therapy and Adlerian theory. Chicago: Alfred Adler Institute, 1975.
O'Connell, W. The adaptive functions of wit and humor. Journal of Abnormal and Social Psychology, 1960, 61, 263–270.
O'Connell, W. Creativity in Humor. Journal of Social Psychology, 1969, 78, 237–246.
Olson, H. The use of humor in psychotherapy. The Individual Psychologist, 1976, 13, 1.
Rotter, J., Chance, J., & Phares, J. Applications of a social learning theory of personality. New York: Holt, Rinehart & Winston, 1972.
Shelton, J. L., & Ackerman, J. M. Homework in Counseling and Psychotherapy. Springfield, Ill.: Charles C Thomas.
Shulman, B. Contributions to Individual Psychology. Chicago: Alfred Adler Institute, 1973.

16

INCREASING SELF-MODELED HUMOR

Warren R. Rule

Creative uses of humor in counseling and psychotherapy have been explored from many perspectives. Research by O'Connell (1960) suggested that the well-adjusted person has a greater appreciation for humor than the less-adjusted person. Jackson (1963) described an approach for absurdly exaggerating suspiciousness with paranoids. Shelton and Ackerman (1974) recommended the evocation of humor as an important part of paradoxical intention. Exaggeration therapy (van den Aardweg, 1972) has been used with homosexuals. Kadis and Winick (1973) considered selected cartoons as having many therapeutic advantages. In conveying insight to clients, Alfred Adler (Ansbacher & Ansbacher, 1956) made frequent use of humor.

The ability to find humor in and to laugh at one's own exaggerated notions and illusions of super-specialness certainly seems an asset. Moreover, an increased awareness, accompanied by humor, of these biased expectations of self, others, and life when they are working to one's disadvantage would seem to enhance personal growth. However,

---

O'Connell's (1969) findings suggested that the ability to produce humor is not closely related to its appreciation. Furthermore, the process of helping a person to generate self-humor, or, for that matter, self-insight in general, can sometimes be quite challenging when applying the cognitively oriented therapeutic approaches. Perhaps Adler's pioneering concept that psychotherapy is education, expressed and strongly endorsed by Ellis (1973), has implications for encouraging the production of self-directed humor.

Much similarity exists between the Adlerian and RET approach to understanding behavior, e.g., the belief that the various forms of behavior are cognitively created and that individuals tend to rate their behaviors and then equate the rating with personal self-worth. A major difference in emphasis is that Adlerians focus on the individual's childhood as a means of gaining an understanding of present biased notions or irrational beliefs.

Adler's term "life-style" may be understood to mean the pattern of dimly conscious notions or goals a person uses for interacting with others and for measuring self-worth. These beliefs and goals are said to be a function of childhood variables such as birth order, sibling interaction patterns, family values, parental modeling, and other childhood experiences. These early conclusions remain with the individual as long as they are useful in maintaining and enhancing a subjectively determined ideal of coping. One framework for conceptualizing these biased beliefs, which are the basis for goals and behavior, has been expressed by Shulman (1973) in terms of "I am...," "Others are...," "Life is...." In attempting to understand characteristics of an individual's life-style, Adlerian practitioners question the client regarding the above-mentioned childhood variables and rely on the selectivity feature of the client's memory to reflect indicators of childhood conclusions that presently are being used as guidelines for coping.

The following quasi-experiment was an exploration of a humor-based technique which is a combination of Adlerian and RET approaches. The hypotheses were that (a) frequency of undesirable negative self/other thoughts and feeling states would decrease, and (b) ratings of disliking self for negative self/other thoughts would decrease.

METHOD

The subjects consisted of 10 students enrolled in a seminar emphasizing the use of the Adlerian life-style approach in counseling. Four were males; six were females. During the latter portion of the course, the students were asked to keep for one week a daily log (to be recorded each night) of undesirable negative self/others thoughts and feeling states (e.g., anxiety, anger, confusion, disappointment, etc.). The guideline was: if "this is not the way I would like to think or feel" then record the situation in the log and assign a rating of 1 to 5 to it (1 = very mildly dislike myself for thinking this way; 5 = extremely dislike myself for thinking this way).

The experimental period began at the beginning of the next week and lasted for two weeks. The daily assignment during this period related to each individual's understanding of one's own life-style notions. The determination of each individual life-style resulted from group input. The life-style questionnaire primarily used was developed by Dreikurs (1967). Each member gave feedback to each person in the group using the previously mentioned format of "I am…, "Others are…," "Life is…." To offset the inevitable semantic barriers encountered in this or any interpretative process, each individual had the responsibility of combining and distilling the various interpretations into one that was most personally meaningful.

Examples of actual life-style notions were: I am a charming princess; others are expected to treat me with tender loving care; life is a place that should be a bowl of cherries. I am a person who must have self-control; others are expected to admire my goodness; life is a place where one should cleverly arrange and maintain a place of importance. I am a person who should avoid displeasing at all costs; others are going to accept me if I keep them aware of my fragility; life focuses on shortcomings. Additional self-mandates were related to themes such as: controlling others, injustice-collecting, making one's presence felt, getting one's way while maintaining a low profile, enjoying heavy burdens, getting goodies by the illusion of pleasing, being on top of others through achievement.

Each evening for two weeks, each person was asked to do the following: (a) Review in your mind the day's activities and choose the situation in which you most strongly experienced a negative self/others thought, i.e., the most intensely undesirable mental state or feeling. (b) Using the framework of "I am…," "Others are…," "Life is…" that you selected, try to relate variations of these beliefs to the undesirable mental state that you experienced today and then complete the spaces on one of the accompanying sheets. (c) Read the page into your tape recorder; as you read, embellish and spice it with as much humor and self-aggrandizing as possible. (d) Play it back to yourself three times. Listen as intently as possible as you allow yourself to become amused with your-self. Allow yourself the luxury of chuckling or even bursting into gales of laughter at yourself! (e) Close your eyes for approximately 15 seconds and vividly imagine yourself smiling or laughing at yourself during the actual situation that occurred. (f) Each night rate from 1 (very little) to 5 (extremely) the number which best expresses the degree to which you were able to concentrate or "get into" this exercise.

Each of the accompanying sheets referred to above in part (b) consisted of the following fill-in-yourself format:

> Today I was in a situation in which I… My self-elevating belief was that I should…
>
> Furthermore, I even expected that others (or another person) would (or ought to have, or will)…
>
> I don't, however, always want to keep measuring my self-worth when things don't go my way and demanding (either publicly or privately) that others be exactly like I expect them to be. Therefore I am going to say, "Tough Shit"!!! (or a related expression)—it's not that awful when life is (or is not)…

During the explanation, tape-recording was demonstrated, emphasizing the importance of tailoring the introductory phrases on the format to one's unique situation and the importance of using humor, childishly self-centered voice inflections, and light-hearted profanity. The fleeting rational belief was omitted in order to highlight exclusively the buffoonery inherent in the irrational thinking of others.

The use of humorous exaggeration in the logs and in the tape-recordings was an educational self-modeling process intended to increase self-awareness and self-acceptance. The process of modeling as a powerful method of learning is well documented (e.g., Bandura, 1969). In this study, by listening to their own recorded voices, the individuals were modeling their ideal selves who were expressing and believing the "tough shit" rationale; furthermore, the modeled ideal selves were demonstrating self-acceptance by creating a humorous attitude towards the irrationality. Research by Hosford (1974) and Hosford and de Visser (1974) suggests much potential for the self-as-a-model technique, which is similar to rational-emotive imagery (Ellis, 1973).

After this experimental two-week period, the subjects repeated for one week the log-keeping that had been done during the pre-experimental week.

RESULTS AND DISCUSSION

The mean number of undesirable self/other thoughts and feelings decreased from 34.2 to 19.0 from pre- to post-period, a significant difference (t = 2.12, p .05, one-tailed), thus supporting the first hypothesis. It appears that the self-modeled humor exercise had an impact on the self-monitored thoughts and feelings. It is unclear what influence, if any, the process of self-monitoring itself had on the findings, and this question could be the focus of a future study.

The second hypothesis was not supported. Average ratings decreased from 2.87 to 2.67, indicating some reduction in degree of disliking for oneself, but the difference is not statistically significant (t = 1.11, n.s.).

Probably some of the unacceptable thoughts and feelings were unique to each person and were not apt to diminish without specific attention, such as challenging irrational beliefs or concentrated homework assignments. The subjects' motivation for changing undesirable thoughts/feelings was different from that of clients who seek assistance with specific and intense personal problems. Yet, the subjects seemed to have taken the procedures seriously, as most of them report having concentrated on and "got into" the exercise moderately well. While a more carefully controlled study is very desirable, these results suggest that this humor-based technique of self-modeling appears to be educationally useful as an awareness and self-acceptance procedure.

REFERENCES

Ansbacher, H. L. & Ansbacher, R. (Eds.). The Individual Psychology of Alfred Adler. New York: Basic Books, 1956.

Bandura, A. Principles of behavior modification: New York: Holt, Rinehart & Winston, 1969.

Dreikurs, R. Psychodynamics, psychotherapy, and counseling. Chicago: Alfred Adler Institute, 1967.

Ellis, A. Humanistic psychotherapy: the rational-emotive approach. New York: Julian Press, 1973.

Hosford, R. E. Self-as-a-Model: possibilities for counseling? Unpublished manuscript, University of California, Santa Barbara, 1974.

Hosford, R. E. & de Visser, L. Behavioral approaches to counseling. Washington, D.C.: APGA Press, 1974.

Jackson, D. A suggestion for the technical handling of paranoid patients. Psychiatry, 1963, 26, 305–307.

Kadis, A. L. & Winick, C. The cartoon as therapeutic catalyst. In Mosak, H.H. (Ed.), Alfred Adler: His influence on psychology today. Ridge Park, N.J.: Noyes Press, 1973.

O'Connell, W. The adaptive functions of wit and humor. Journal of Abnormal and Social Psychology, 1960, 61, 263–270.

O'Connell, W. Creativity in humor. Journal of Social Psychology, 1969, 78, 237–241.

Shelton, J. L. & Ackerman, J. M. Homework in counseling and psychotherapy. Springfield, Ill.: Charles C Thomas, 1974.

Shulman, B. Contributions to Individual Psychology. Chicago: Alfred Adler Institute, 1973.

Van den Aardweg, G. J. A grief theory of homosexuality. American Journal of Psychotherapy, 1972, 26, 52–68.

Research

I

Empirical Considerations

17

SELF-ACTUALIZATION: A PERSON IN POSITIVE MOVEMENT OR SIMPLY AN ESTEEMED PERSONALITY CHARACTERISTIC?

Warren R. Rule

The term "self-actualization" has often been applied in a varied, perhaps imprecise, manner. The assumptions for investigating self-actualization are discussed from the perspective of three considerations: (1) the self as a group statistic; (2) the self as static; and (3) the self that should be successfully good. A brief framework for self-actualization variables is offered. Implications are considered for investigating the concept within and outside of the context of psychological science.

"'Tis neither this nor that, but both—and more"

This chapter, "Self-Actualization: A Person in Positive Movement or Simply an Esteemed Personality Characteristic?," from Warren R. Rule, Handbook of Self-Actualization, Special Issue of the *Journal of Social and Personality*, 6(5), pp. 249–264.

The above quote can be related to the complexity involved in evaluating the positive nature of an individual unfolding self, i.e., research that investigates self-actualization. The anonymous nature of the source of the quote is appropriate here, too, because it reflects the anonymous, or forgotten, nature of the holistic "self" in some of the research on self-actualization (S/A). Expressed another way, a number of those interested in S/A research (discussed later) have a more narrow perspective of S/A than is conceptualized in this paper. The focus here is on a goal-oriented actualization of the self.

The proposed framework for conceptualizing S/A from a research perspective involves at least two variables, X and Y, and, in more sophisticated research, a third variable, Z. The variable X represents measures related to concepts of self of which the individual either has, or is capable of having, a degree of self awareness or self imagery. These concepts of self could exist in the real or imagined time frames of the past, present, and future. The variable Y represents a goal, or purpose, of which the individual may or may not have self awareness/ imagery and could also be viewed within the contexts of past, present, and future. The assertion in this paper is that basic S/A research should at least investigate the relationship between variables X and Y and that each of these variables should occur in a different time frame. Research of a more complex nature would incorporate variable Z, the behavior or emotion that precedes, intervenes between, or follows either X or Y. Variable Z could occur in the same real or imagined time frame as either X or Y, or it could occur in the remaining time frame that X and Y do not each represent. (This framework will be discussed more fully in a later section.)

From a developmental vantage point it is necessary to discuss how this self-goal framework dovetails into some of the existing contributions to the S/A literature. Several limitations and strengths, from the perspective of the proposed framework, will be discussed under the following four headings: (1) the self as a group statistic? (2) the self as a static, frozen in time? (3) the self that should be successfully good? and (4) implications for psychology. A unifying theme throughout these sections of the paper will be the importance of researchers using the term "self-actualization" more judiciously.

THE SELF AS A GROUP STATISTIC?

> "I am not fond of the word psychological. There is no such thing as the psychological. Let us say that one can improve the biography of the person."

The above observation, attributed to Sartre (1980, p. 64), highlights the importance of the perspective of the individual holistic self. A major contention of the proposed framework for researching S/A is that the "self" must be broader than simply an individual "personality characteristic," particularly one which is selected by the researcher because it seems to represent for everyone in the entire sample a measure of goodness, success, optimal functioning, mental health, valued living, or whatever seems to be an appropriate correlate of S/A. It is tempting, however, to define the self very narrowly, i.e., as one part of a group, whose performance is measured on a specific variable. Thus, the same very small slice, as determined by the researcher, is taken from each of however many selves that constitute the sample (no consideration is given to the difference in how connected to or how important this small slice is to each of the selves). A collective slice of selves is then calculated, i.e., measures of central tendency, numbers representing the variability of the slices, etc., which in turn is compared with another collective slice of the selves from a different group of selves (the dependent variable, the control group, the norm group, etc.). Ultimately, an overall statistic is obtained which gives the researcher the level of probability of accuracy of the relationships of the measurements of the very small slices of selves for this sample. Usually the prudent researcher finally cautions, in summary, that these probabilities of conclusions cannot be generalized to other samples of selves.

Whatever happened to the integrity of each of the selves in this melting pot? The above-described "personality characteristic" approach is not unique to S/A investigations and has a familiar place in the broader field of behavioral science. Yet these studies do have a contribution to make to S/A building blocks, particularly when used with other research procedures, e.g., meta-analysis, factor analysis, that point the way to possible large patterns or clusters. Or, reviews of these studies may shed light on concepts related to S/A, e.g., the healthy personality (Vinacke, 1984).

The definition of what constitutes the "self" is indeed a thorny conceptual issue, and, from the S/A perspective, quite a number of investigators have addressed its importance (e.g., Schwitzgebel, 1961; Bayne, 1977). As Adler concluded (Ansbacher & Ansbacher, 1956), a person cannot be dissected without losing much of the understanding of the pattern or theme that runs through the self; similarly, music cannot be fully appreciated by studying each note itself—one needs to have the context of the other notes in order to experience the melody.

The possibility of somehow capturing a "total self" in S/A research is probably unrealistic in view of the host of metaphysical, epistemological, and axiological issues that surround the scientific perspective (more on this later). However, perhaps a more realistic research expectation, when using the term "self' in S/A research, is to capture—using Adler's metaphor—at least more than one note in the melody. Thus, the term "concept of self' (referred to initially as Variable X) would include not simply a single note selected by the researcher, but at least another note — even if this second note were no more than an indication of how relevant the first note is to the subject's experience of the self. The most elementary measurements here would be instruments such as self-report inventories based on a Likert Scale format in which the researcher determines the variable and the subject assesses the degree of relevance to the self. More notes in the melody might be included in assessment, by more sophisticated instruments such as the Strong-Campbell Interest Inventory (Hansen & Campbell, 1985), which seems curiously underutilized in S/A research. A more holistic, idiographic concept of self may be obtained by the Adlerian Lifestyle approach (Mosak, 1989; Powers & Griffith, 1988; Shulman & Mosak, 1988).

In sum, when researchers use the term "self-actualization," the "self' should at least be construed more fully (and expressed more appropriately) than simply a subject's score on a standardized scale of measurement as it compares to a one-time norm group's performance on the same scale.

THE SELF AS STATIC, FROZEN IN TIME?

"The impish attempt to paint the color of the wind"

We may wonder, as in the above definition of poetry (Bodenheim, 1970, p. 441), if those interested in S/A research are not really like poets in their attempt to paint the wind of "actualization" in self-actualization. The term "actualization" denotes growth, process, change, unfolding, evolving, transcending, movement from a here to a there or a there to a here—anything but a single measure at a frozen point in time of a changing, global phenomenon.

Indeed, this orientation, often termed "growth," is conceptually at the core of most approaches to self-actualization (Corsini, 1977). Associated with the belief that individuals are capable of a growth-orientation is usually the assumption that people are also goal-oriented. Goals, or purposes, are the basic orientation and fabric of daily living (Rule, 1982).

> Adler noted that we are unable to think, feel, or act without the perception of some goal (Ansbacher & Ansbacher, 1956). This goal directedness or purposiveness of mankind can be related to the powerful determination to maintain and enhance the self. Parallels exist in the plant and animal kingdoms as well. Humans, while not always fully conscious of their goals, create them in order to give direction to the various forms of movement in life, such as physical, psychological, and social. Subsequently, a goal which may be generally defined as a fixed consequence to be attained in the future, is a major, if not the major, influence on emotions and behavior. (p. 195)

This second variable, goals (labeled variable Y in the present S/A framework), are viewed in this proposed framework as being a function of the broader concept(s) of self (variable X). Yet, considerable difficulty exists in measuring individual goals as linked to a unique concept of self, using most standardized psychological tests. Here again, with these instruments the quest is for nomothetic (general) laws, i.e., how an individual compares, based on performance at the time, with the collective performance of a norm group taken at another point in time. The result of this form of assessment appears to be a quite frozen and restricted sample of the goal-directedness, or future-orientation, of the individual. Furthermore, Mosak (1989), in discussing the overall merits of the Adlerian lifestyle approach to assessment, which combines the nomothetic and the idiographic (individual) approaches, notes that the labels derived from psychological tests are "static descriptions and ignore the movement of the individual. They describe what the individual has, but not how he or she moves through life" (p. 96).

As noted previously, the proposed X (concept of self) and Y (goal) framework states that each one must exist, in reality or in imagery, in different time frames. This condition increases the likelihood that individual movement, i.e., here-to-there, there-to-here, which is the essence of actualization, will be addressed as opposed to research on frozen personality correlates, i.e., here-here, there-there.

The importance of focusing on the process of psychological movement becomes even more salient when related variables are considered, such as individual differences in the experience of time itself

(Hall, 1984), the possibility that self-transcendence is a major part of self-actualization (Frankl, 1966), or that self-actualization may really be ephemeral (Rule, 1982):

> The goal of self-actualization, which has an irresistible quality for many in the helping professions, is indeed elusive when viewed as an outcome. When savored as process, a means to a nonexistent end, the pursuit of the goal takes on different meaning: the pursuer now focuses on enjoying the changing sunlight from the elusive horizon. (p. 196)

The paradox in viewing goals from a lifespan perspective is that the attainment of a goal, regardless of the level of awareness, seems to result in creation of another. This changing effect appears to be undergirded by a lifelong pattern of, as Adler observed (Ansbacher & Ansbacher, 1956), moving from a felt-minus-state to a felt-plus-state from birth to death. Or, as Gertrude Stein reportedly noted, "We find when we get there, there's no there, there."

Possibly the balance of the time frames has been influenced by Western civilization's developments. More specifically, maybe contemporary thinking in self-actualization has been overshadowed by society's emphasis on progress. Encouraged by technology and the pursuit of pleasure, as Woolfolk and Richardson (1987) have observed, the broad goal of progress usually has the goal of worshipping the achievement of other goals while demeaning the past and present and worshipping the future.

In regard to proposed research procedures, the previously cited Adlerian lifestyle approach offers promise for assessing individual goals, as do observational and individual narrative methods; yet, validity, reliability, and other research issues often haunt primarily idiographic assessments. Single-case research can be revealing. Letters and biographies may offer contributions, especially when systematically and reliably assessed by several raters. More nomothetic instruments, such as goal-attainment inventories and purpose-in-life assessments offer more general contributions. Further development of the Time Competence scale of the Personal Orientation Inventory (Shostrom, 1984) might be useful.

Welch, Tate, and Medeiros (1987) compiled 1158 references related to self-actualization which they believe represent most of the self-actualization literature. Ninety-one of these are organized under the heading "Instruments." Fully four-fifths of the 91 investigated various relationships of the Personal Orientation Inventory (Shostrom, 1984).

Most of the remaining one-fifth reported on other standardized tests. An evaluation of the pros and cons of any individual instrument is outside of the scope of this paper; the point is that much room exists for the exploration of other forms of assessment.

In addition to the careful development of other standardized tests, increased attention could be paid to a developmental approach when researching S/A. It is useful to explain the process of individual changes, not only within the self but also within the lifespan of which the self is a part. Various methods that could be used more frequently to assess S/A change include the cross-sectional method, longitudinal method, and sequential methods.

THE SELF THAT SHOULD BE SUCCESSFULLY GOOD?

> "Do not forget the most important fact that not heredity and not environment are determining factors. Both are giving only the frame and the influences which are answered by the individual in regard to his styled creative power."

Adler was convinced, as the quote (Ansbacher & Ansbacher, 1956, p. xxiv) suggests, of the creativity of the individual in developing a lifestyle which could be directed in the socially useful or useless sides of life. However, individual creativity, perhaps the energizer of self-actualization, expresses itself in many, many ways which may be considered as socially useful or productive. Perhaps over-heralded, however, by S/A theorists and investigators are those individual qualities or endeavors that are labeled as important self-actualizing contributions only if they have a "noble," "good," or "successful" character about them, e.g., Maslow's (1964) "superior person"; Rogers' (1963) "fully-functioning self."

This perspective, more often than not, favors the recognizably fortunate and accomplished. This undercurrent is reflected by the connotation of the following key words used in the aforementioned 1158 entry computer search (Welch et al., 1987): "self-actualization, fully functioning self, adequate personality, productive personality, mature personality, personality integration, self-fulfillment and self-realization" (p. x).

As Krasner and Ullmann (1973), speaking from a behavioral perspective, have noted, "we evaluate the value of a value by another value" (p. 491). If indeed this is so, the value by which "self-actualization" has usually been evaluated is successful goodness. This implied linkage between self-actualization and achievement-laden values has concerned others as well, e.g., self-actualization and elitism (Buss, 1979), self-actualization and competence (Patterson, 1974).

In sum, it is rather peculiar that the greater interest in S/A movement has been on positive change as primarily a vertical process. Expressed another way, the bottom-line value seems to imply that worthwhile growth only occurs when one moves from a "less-than" to a "more-than," or, stated in interpersonal (group sample) terms, has "outdone" some "less-thans" in the measurement of the selected variable(s). Furthermore, this vertical mentality usually esteems, as examples of self-actualization, the performance of those "at the top," those enjoying peak performance, or at least those heading in that upward direction.

More S/A research could be completed in other relatively unheralded areas of positive movement. Although expressed in somewhat oversimplified categories and terms, below are listed types of self-actualizing movement other than those which are markedly vertical and top-heavy but which also contribute to greater satisfactory functioning for the individual:

1. *Movement toward others.* The emphasis here is on measures of interpersonal connectedness, empathy, bonding, appeal as a model, interpersonal risk-taking or courage, social interest or other forms of "horizontal" movement. This type has the potential to become "vertical" movement, especially if the individual views this quality as a noble achievement.
2. *Movement from the "low" to the "medium" range.* As opposed to movement that progresses from low to high, medium to high, or, in other words, "peak-oriented" movement, this area of semi-vertical movement investigates self-actualization that may occur when, for example, a person with a severe disability achieves a quite remarkable level of adjustment which should be judged only "the norm" by traditional criteria or comparisons. Other self-actualizers could be high school or college students with very modest intellectual abilities who milk their abilities dry as they achieve "only" close to the norm.
3. *Movement downward from high to low.* For some individuals, self-actualization growth occurs when a superiority complex or superiority perceptions of oneself actually lowers, thus rendering the person less burdened with self-importance and more truly connected with other people. The general field of helping and human behavior is not lacking in members who might well benefit from this descending movement.

4. *Movement back and forth.* This movement, one step forward and one step backward, is the classic "yes … but" conflict (Adler, 1934) and can be in the service of a variety of ulterior, yet distinctly self-serving (and perhaps self-actualizing), goals. These creative excuses and self-deceptions serve useful purposes, e.g., avoidance of responsibility, placing blame, keeping a bad situation with minimal guilt, being noticed for struggling heroically, creating beneficial symptoms (Mosak and LeFevre, 1976), that can be part of an individual's grand and self-actualizing strategy, although operating at a dimly conscious level of self-awareness.
5. *Movement that follows an unpredictable zig-zag pattern.* Campbell (1988), the world-renowned mythologist, has spoken of the importance of fording and following one's "bliss," i.e., doing in life what one desires, independent of others' expectations. The unpredictable and erratic struggles inherent in this type of quest seem to be worthy of research which places a premium on optimum functioning.
6. *No movement.* This state of seeming non-movement entails a sort of accepting the self as is. Grotz (1983), from a historical perspective, has noted that our ancestors had a much keener acceptance of their personal limits—with accompanying self-satisfaction—than those caught up in today's mentality of moreness. Perhaps this self-imposed "lack" of movement, or self acceptance of "what is" (resulting not necessarily from an inward journey), is enormously empowering for some individuals and is worthy of research. Interestingly enough, the observation has been made by this writer that many of the most "alive" (self-actualized?) persons are those who unabashedly accept themselves and their limits, despite the fact (or because of the fact?) that they appear to concern themselves very little with the conventional measures of vertically-oriented self-actualization, such as achievement, success, or recognized goodness.
7. *Movement inward.* These include a host of possibilities that have potential for self-actualizing movement inward, e.g., spirituality, mediation, Gestalt exercises, trance induction, etc. This inward growth is available to unheralded ordinary people and is all-too-often overlooked by the research of behavioral scientists. The novelist John Michener (1962) eloquently expresses the importance of this journey:

> For this is the journey that men make: to find themselves. If they fail in this, it doesn't matter much what else they find: Money, position, fame, many loves, revenge are all of little consequence, and when the tickets are collected at the end of the ride, they are tossed into a bin marked FAILURE. But if a man happens to find himself — if he knows what he can be depended upon to do, the limits of his courage, the position from which he will no longer retreat, the degree to which he can surrender his inner life to some woman, secret reservoirs of his determination, the extent of his dedication, the depth of his feeling for beauty, his honest and unpostured goals — then he has found a mansion which he can inhabit with dignity all the days of his life. (p. 169)

The above types of movement, outside the realm of traditional success or vertical movement, underscore the importance of defining the parameters of what is meant by the term "self-actualization." Perhaps the conceptual overlap with "happiness" needs to be sorted out. Possibly, just as M. Erickson (Haley, 1973) did not believe in abstract overall happiness and instead sought out individuals' specific meanings, so will behavioral scientists conclude that self-actualization is basically an abstract and empty concept when devoid of individual meaning. Perhaps paradoxes are involved in the understanding of self-actualization, just as they seem to be a part of fathoming some of the concepts of happiness (Rule, 1983).

IMPLICATIONS FOR PSYCHOLOGY

> "Rodney Dangerfield is a popular comedian whose trademark is the plaintive cry, 'I don't get no respect!' In a way, this is aligning summary of psychology's status in the public mind." (Stanovich, 1986, p. 58)

The "broad brush" usage of the term "self-actualization" in psychology does not contribute to increasing the chances that psychology will disinherit the above-cited dubious distinction from the public's view or even from the minds of other scientists. Conceptually, more critical thinking and dialogue are needed in the fundamental areas of scope and terminology (e.g., Geller, 1984; Welch et al., 1987).

At present, researchers would probably be wise to use the term "self-actualization" more judiciously. The dilemma seems to be, in keeping with the scientific tradition, one of precision. As discussed previously, the fullness of the term could be most accurately reflected by regarding self-actualization as a process in which the self is holistic, moving, and not necessarily successful, superior, or "good." Perhaps even the phrases "characteristic of self-actualization" or "correlate of self-actualization" are descriptive if subjects are simply being evaluated at a given point in time on a personality test, yet these phases seem preferable to the process term "self-actualization."

Personality tests in general, unfortunately, may have somewhat of a limited contribution to research on self-actualization, as defined in this paper. Tyler (1984), a pioneer in the testing movement, has concluded that most personality tests are not designed to reveal: (1) positive or admirable qualities; (2) the ego control system a person is using, in spite of measured maladaptive tendencies; (3) the unique structure of a person's world (some projective tests may do this, to a degree, but interpretation is difficult), and (4) uniquely individual gifts or handicaps.

Broad subjects that may lead to fruitful results with further refinement include S/A and the self-ideal discrepancy (Mahoney & Hartnett, 1973), realism as a cognitive indicator of S/A in temporality (Lomranz, Medini, & Aschuach, 1982), and S/A and the meaning of critical experience (Rizzo & Vinacke, 1975). Furthermore, measuring the results or signs of the meaning of goal-directedness itself over periods of time may be very interesting.

Special difficulties exist for the scientific approach of psychology in the investigation of S/A, as defined in this paper. Discussed below are some of the unique conceptual, assessment, and methodological challenges for variables X (concept of self), Y (goals), Z (behavior or emotions), and the issue of differing time frames.

Concept of Self

Perhaps a more precise term is needed other than "the self." What are the parameters of the self? Is awareness of the self really necessary? (e.g., Cangemi & Englander, 1974; Cangemi & Martray, 1975). Joseph Campbell (1988), previously cited expert on mythology, studied the myths of divergent worldwide cultures that have existed for thousands of years. He was stunned by the uniformity of the myths, e.g., the hero's journey (very interesting from the S/A perspective) and drew the overriding conclusion that an invisible plane exists underneath the visible plane. If this is possibly so, how can S/A researchers accurately speak of a total self or even a major concept of self? Should a study of a culture's myths, such as the hero's journey, be necessary before the S/A behavioral scientist can appreciate the sense of self in that culture?

Closer to the "visible plane" are a testee's responses to personality tests, such as often used to measure S/A. The cognitions used to provide a sample of behavior for the psychologist may not really be unique to the "self' of the testee. In a recent U.S. District Court ruling, Judge P.N. Leval concluded:

> All intellectual creative activity is in part derivative... There is no such thing as a wholly original thought or invention. Each advance stands on building blocks fashioned by prior thinkers. (Sachs & Scott, 1990, p. 87)

Goals

Measuring individual goals, or purposes, reasonably accurately is a difficult enough venture for the behavioral scientist. The endeavor becomes exceedingly more complicated by the variable of awareness. In S/A research, should only those goals that the subject is aware of, i.e. operational ones, be investigated? Should consciousness of the striving or the quest be assessed? Should S/A investigators grudgingly accept their scientific limits in attempting to measure the inherent unfolding, organismic process that Rogers (1961) speaks of (and which may have implications for Campbell's "invisible plane") and, instead, direct their energies toward goals that can be specified? Yet, if the fullness of the concept of S/A is to be taken seriously, it is doubtful that the nonconscious processes can be ignored. Sometimes, psychodynamically speaking, an individual's self-esteem does not find it useful to be aware of a particular goal, especially if the awareness will force a person to come face to face with responsibility or vanity issues. This "mental mischief" is very likely to be at work at different times, for different people, in their self-actualizing movement.

So, a voice from over 200 years ago, before the scientific revolution had blossomed, reminds us that "The heart has its reasons which reason knows nothing of" (Pascal, in Barlett, 1980, p. 300).

Behavior or Emotions

Quite probably, this variable (Z) lends itself more readily to the scientific perspective than do variables X, Y, or the contextual issue of time. The relative specificity of behavior, and to a lesser extent, emotions, provides more opportunity for operational definitions and measurement than do the more diffuse concepts of self or goals. As noted previously, this type of research is more complicated than that which investigates the relationship between variables X and Y. Variable Z could either precede, intervene between, or follow either X or Y; Z could also occur in the same real or imagined time frame as either X or Y or it could occur in the remaining time frame that X or Y do not represent. Although a variety of combinations exist, examples are included in Table 17.1.

TABLE 17.1

Past	Present	Future	(Explanation)
	X	YZ	(Relationship between a present concept of self **and** expected feeling after **attainment\non-attainment** of goal)
ZY	X		(Relationship between past behavior used to **attain\not-attain** goal and a present concept of self)
Z	X	Y	(Past feeling or behavior as related to present concept of self **and an** expected future goal)
X	Y	Z	(A past concept of self as related to **present goal and** expected feeling or behavior)

Each of these examples, as can be noted, has variables in at least two different time frames, the purpose of which is central to investigating S/A movement. In reference to S/A group or single-case research methodology, each one of the variables X, Y, or Z could function as either independent or dependent variables, in accordance with the research design.

Time

The contextual dimensions of time, labeled in past, present, and future, are haunting ones for the S/A investigator who is concerned with the implications of a temporal here-to-there or a there-to-here. Small consolation can be taken by behavioral scientists, however, in that many physical scientists, on one hand, and more abstract scholars, on the other hand, regard time as the greatest mystery in the universe. Most humbling perhaps is that nobody really knows what it is. As Goudsmit and Clairborne (1966) have written about time:

> What we cannot do, oddly enough, is define it. To the psychologist, time is an aspect of consciousness, the means by which we give order to our experiences. To the physicist time is one of the three fundamental qualities—the other two are mass and dis-

> tance—in terms of which he can describe anything in the universe. To the philosopher time is still other things. Yet these learned men, though they may write books about time, can none of them define it in a way satisfactory to one another, or even to themselves. (p. 9)

Perhaps reflection upon the dimension of time itself, or even how time embraces the process of S/A, should be left to those not heavily invested in the contributions of the Newtonian scientific method, such as those from disciplines that have more faith in that which cannot be observed.

A Skeletal Proposal for an Elusive Framework

Self-actualization may have arguably been an underpinning for the development of the third force in psychology, humanistic psychology (Welch et al., 1987). Yet, it seems that the methodology of a lot of research on self-actualization is still plagued by the deterministic ghosts of the first force (Freudian) in the form of the self as a battleground of disparate parts and of the second force (Behavioral) in the form of the self as parts that constitute essentially a mechanical robot. This conceptualization, that the individual can be divided into component parts, increases the quest in self-actualization research for nomothetic (general) laws as opposed to idiographic (individual) laws.

Most of the previously discussed variables, i.e., concept of self, goals, behavior or emotions, the time context, seem difficult enough to assess independently of each other. When these variables become interactive with each other, as in self-actualizing movement, the researcher's task becomes more arduous.

The nature of (self-actualizing) movement itself, as defined by this paper, presents even more investigative problems. The proposal here is that when each of the discussed variables is in self-actualizing movement, it is in the process of becoming a part of the ground from which it had previously been a figure (as in the classic figure-ground relationship). Thus, the variable in S/A movement is losing its unique specificity and is merging with the ground that previously provided its contrast. Accordingly, the independent and unique concept of self (the figure) is in the process of blending into a broader, perhaps more spiritual, plane (the ground), such as Campbell's invisible plane which was discussed earlier. Second, if the assumption can be made that the usefulness of most personal goals is for broader psychosocial significance and security (Adler, 1934), then in S/A movement the goal (figure) becomes less self-centered and more other-centered (ground)—a process which most great religions have been advocating for thousands of years. Third, the self-serving properties of a behavior or an emotion (figure) would fluidly blend into the total self (ground), an acceptance that would occur regardless of its degree of "success" or "failure." Thus, it would not "stand out" and be given special importance in relation to overall self-worth, or, as Ellis (1973) recommends, an action or a feeling would not be used to rate self-worth. Fourth, in regard to the issue of time, the self-actualizing person would often have an experience of the moment (figure) in which it lost its specificity and was processed as timelessness (ground). This figure-ground merger as been expressed by St. Augustine as "the eternity of the moment" and, more recently, as a loss of time-consciousness or a "peak experience" by Csikszentmihalyi (1975).

Science's Slice of the Pie

Possibly science's slice of the total S/A pie of understanding is really considerably smaller than would be otherwise desired. Perhaps some behavioral scientists have taken too seriously the poet Robert Browning's admonition that "your reach should exceed your grasp."

Just as science is a discipline that values its tradition of precision, so should behavioral science be more precise in what it attempts and what it cannot attempt. Blatant declarations of what is not being measured would seem to have an undisputed place in S/A research. Furthermore, maybe the term "self-actualization" (as used in this paper) is too broadly imprecise and a more qualifying phrase is needed (e.g., "characteristic of S/A," "correlates of X and Y"). Or perhaps the term should only rarely be used in empirical research.

The controlled procedures of behavioral science have a place in beginning to understand S/A. However, when investigating a phenomenon as deeply personal as self-actualization, perhaps Merleau-Ponty's (1962) perspective is worth pondering:

> I cannot shut myself up within the realm of science. All my knowledge of the world, even my scientific knowledge, is gained from my own particular point of view, or from some experience of the world without which the symbols of science would be meaningless. The whole universe of science is built upon the world as directly experienced, and if we want to subject science itself to rigorous scrutiny and arrive at a precise assessment of its meaning and scope, we must begin by reawakening the basic

> experience of the world of which science is the second order of expression. (p. viii)

The possibility also exists that science, at least as it is presently developed, is incapable of ever knowing where to begin to slice the S/A pie of understanding. Maybe other, less quantifiable, slices are bigger than we think, such as the contributions of the poets, novelists, playwrights, songwriters, artists, philosophers, or even the subjective testimonials of everyday people trying to realize their dreams.

In discussing other dreams, such as those related to the religion of science, R. Jastrow, a noted scientist, offers a thoughtful metaphor (1978):

> For the scientist who has lived by his faith in the power of reason, the story ends like a bad dream. He has scaled the mountains of ignorance; he is about to conquer the highest peak; as he pulls himself over the final rock, he is greeted by a band of theologians who have been sitting there for centuries. (p. 116)

REFERENCES

Adler, A. (1934). Lecture to the Medical Society of Individual Psychology, London, May 17, 1934. Individual Psychology Pamphlets, No. 13, 11–24.

Ansbacher, H. L., & Ansbacher, R. R. (1956). The Individual Psychology of Alfred Adler. New York: Harper & Row.

Bayne, R. (1977). What does self mean in the term self-actualization. Bulletin of the British Psychological Society, 30, 213–214.

Bodenheim, M. (1970). In E.E. Brussel (Ed.), Dictionary of quotable definitions. Englewood Cliffs, NJ: Prentice-Hall.

Buss, A. R. (1979). Humanistic psychology as liberal ideology: The socio-historical roots of Maslow's theory of self-actualization. Journal of Humanistic Psychology, 19(3), 43–45.

Campbell, J. (1988). The power of myth/Joseph Campbell with Bill Moyers. New York: Doubleday.

Cangemi, J. P., & Englander, M. (1974). From self awareness to self-actualization. College Student Journal, 8, 88–92.

Cangemi, J. P., & Martray, C. (1975). Awareness: A psychological requisite for actualizing personality. Psychology, 12(3), 44–49.

Corsini, R. J. (1977). A medley of current personality theories. In R.J. Corsini (Ed.), Current Personality Theories (329–431). Itasca, IL: F.E. Peacock.

Csikszentmihalyi, M. (1975). Beyond boredom and anxiety. San Francisco: Jossey-Bass.

Ellis, A. (1973). Humanistic psychotherapy: The rational emotive approach. New York: McGraw Hill.

Frankl, V. E. (1966). Self-transcendence as a human phenomenon. Journal of Humanistic Psychology, 6(2), 92–106.

Geller, L. (1984). Another look at self-actualization. Journal of Humanistic Psychology, 24(2), 93–106.

Goudsmit, S., & Clairborne, R. (1966). Time. New York: Time.
Grotz, G. (1983). The furniture doctor. New York: Doubleday.
Haley, J. (1973). Uncommon therapy. New York: W.W. Norton.
Hall, T. E. (1984). The dance of life: The other dimension of time. New York: Doubleday.
Hansen, J. C., & Campbell, D. (1985). Manual for the SVIB-SCII (4th ed.). Palo Alto, CA: Consulting Psychologists Press.
Jastrow, R. (1978). God and the astronomers. New York: W. W. Norton.
Krasner, L., & Ullmann, L. P. (1973). Behavior influence and personality: The social matrix of human interaction. New York: Holt, Rinehart, & Winston.
Lomranz, J., Medini, G. & Aschuach, R. (1982). Realism as a cognitive indicator of self-actualization in temporality. Journal of Psychology, 110(1), 53–62.
Mahoney, J., & Hartnett, J. (1973). Self-actualization and self-ideal discrepancy. Journal of Psychology, 85(1), 37–42.
Maslow, A. H., (1964). The superior person. Transaction, 1, 17–26.
Merleau-Ponty, M. (1962). Phenomenology of perception (C. Smith, Trans.). London: Routledge & Kegan Paul.
Michener, J. (1962). The fires of spring. New York: Random House.
Mosak, H. H. (1989). Adlerian psychotherapy. In R. J. Corsini & D. Wedding (Eds.), Current psychotherapies (4th ed.). Itasca, IL: F. E. Peacock.
Mosak, H. H., & Le Fevre, C. (1976). The resolution of intrapersonal conflict. Journal of Individual Psychology, 32, 19–26.
Pascal, B. (1980). In J. Barlett (Ed.), Familiar Quotations. Boston: Little, Brown & Co.
Patterson, C. H. (1974). Beyond competence: Self-actualization as an integrative concept. Counseling Psychologist, 4(4), 82–86.
Powers, R. L., & Griffith, J. (1988). Understanding lifestyle: The psycho-clarity process. Chicago: The American Institute of Adlerian Studies.
Rizzo, R., & Vinacke, E. (1975). Self-actualization and the meaning of critical experience. Journal of Humanistic Psychology, 15(3), 19–30.
Rogers, C. R. (1961). On becoming a person. Boston: Houghton Mifflin.
Rogers, C. R. (1963). The concept of the fully functional person. Psychotherapy: Theory, Research, and Practice. 1, 17–26.
Rule, W. (1982). Pursuing the horizon: Striving for elusive goals. Personal and Guidance Journal, 61(4), 195–197.
Rule, W. (1983). Exploring paradoxes of happiness in offender therapy. International Journal of Offender Therapy and Comparative Criminology, 27(2), 119–124.
Sachs, A., & Scott, G. (1990, April 30). Foul weather for fair use: A wave of copyright suits puts scholars on the defense. (With reporting by) Time. pp. 86–87.
Sartre, J. P. (1980). In Voices: The art and science of psychotherapy. Journal of the American Academy of Psychotherapists, 15(4), p. 64.
Schwitzgebel, R. (1961). The self in self-actualization. Psycholigica, 4, 163–169.
Shostrom, E. L. (1964). An inventory for the measurement of self-actualization. Educational and Psychological Measurement, 24(2), 207–218.
Shulman, B. H., & Mosak, H. H. (1988) Manual for lifestyle assessment. Muncie, IN: Accelerated Development.
Stanovich, K. E. (1986). How to think straight about psychology. Glenview, IL: Scott, Foresman & Co.
Tyler, L. E. (1984). Testing the test: What tests don't measure. Journal of Counseling and Development, 63, 48–50.
Vinacke, W. E. (1984). Healthy personality: Toward a unified theory. Genetic Psychology Monographs, 109(2), 279–329.
Welch, I. D., Tate, G. A., & Medeiros, D. C. (1987). Self actualization: An annotated bibliography of theory and research. New York: Garland.

Woolfolk, R. & Richardson, F. (1978). Stress, sanity, and survival. New York: Sovereign Books.

II

Therapeutic Relationships

18

CONTEXTUAL INFLUENCES ON PRODUCTION OF EARLY RECOLLECTIONS

Joseph M. Bauserman and Warren R. Rule

Summary: This investigation focused on whether selected elements of the context in which early recollections are collected can contaminate the recollections. The independent variables were examiner's style (warm or cold), presence or absence of the examiner, and order in which the examiner was present. Ten examiners collected six early memories from 60 subjects. Three raters evaluated the early memories on six scales; in addition, they established satisfactory rater reliability. Analysis of variance showed subjects with warm examiners produced significantly more solitary memories and less vivid ones. Theoretical and research implications were discussed.

The importance of therapeutic context in understanding mental processes has been an increasing concern in the theoretical literature.

This chapter, "Contextual Influences on Production of Early Recollections," from Bauserman, J. M. & Rule, W. R. Use of subjective information in scientific psychology: II. Contextual influences on production of early recollections. *Perceptual and Motor Skills*, 1988, 66, 823–828.

Psychodynamic and systemic theorists have postulated that contextual influences are both profound and subtle. Probably the earliest to indicate a sensitivity to the ongoing, dyadic interaction in therapy was Ferenczi (1925, 1950). Others have continued to explore these issues and related ones from the 1920s to the present (Reich, 1945; Heimann, 1945; Racker, 1957; Sullivan, 1953; von Bertalanffy, 1966; Whitaker, Felder, & Warkentin, 1965; Bateson, Jackson, Haley, & Weakland, 1968; Haley, 1973; Bandler & Grinder, 1975; Langs, 1975, 1979; Scheflen, 1978; Bowen, 1978; Searles, 1979a, 1979b). Professional interest, however, has been primarily theoretical and clinical as opposed to research.

In view of the number of professionals who incorporate some form of projective technique into the assessment phase of their work, this study sought to investigate selected dimensions of the interactional component operating in the production of projective data. The projective technique selected was early recollections due to its pioneering stature (Adler, 1927) and to its relative purity in that it requires virtually no external stimuli (as opposed to the Rorshach or TAT) and very little skill on the collector's part.

In hundreds of studies early recollections from a variety of perspectives have been investigated and related to a host of variables. The range extends from validity and reliability studies on to personality and vocational-choice relationships as well as on to various experimental designs. A dearth of research information exists, however, on the interactional component in the collection of early recollections. Related to this, Bach (1952) theorized about the influence of the current context on the production of memories. Purcell (1956) found memory function related to personality structure and the dynamics of the moment. Quay's (1959) research indicated that the number of family-oriented memories could be influenced by reinforcement. Yet Hedvig (1961), studying stability, found no effect when the collection of early memories was preceded by either success or failure experiences and by contact with friendly, neutral, or hostile examiners.

The main hypotheses in this investigation were: Do elements of context such as (1) examiner's style, (2) presence or absence of examiner, and (3) order of presence and absence of examiner influence subjects in the production of early memories?

METHOD

Examiners

The 10 examiners who collected data were volunteers selected from a graduate counseling class at a southeastern university. Out of 15 volunteers, 10 were selected based on their scores (5 highest and 5 lowest) on the Rokeach Dogmatism Scale (Rokeach, 1980). The five highest were +27, –2, –5, –11, –12, and the five lowest were –33, –43, –43, –51, –56. Four of the examiners were women and one was a man for each of the two groups.

Because one of the independent variables in this examination was the style of the examiner, it was necessary to select examiners who could more congruently adopt a particular style. The two styles were warm/receptive and cold/administrative. The presumption was that the relatively more dogmatic of the examiners would be better able to sustain a colder, more businesslike manner throughout the data collection process. Cold examiners were told to be task focused and to communicate in the "blank screen" manner of the classical analyst, a manner devoid of self-expression or affect insofar as possible. They were to provide instructions and not respond to additional solicitations for more structure other than to read the instructions again. Warm examiners were to read exactly the same instructions but to relate to the subject in a warm, personable manner, gently deflecting any questions about the instructions and apologetically returning to repeating the instructions. Examiners were trained in paracommunications to enhance their natural styles so that they were both predisposed to and trained in their style. Regarding assessment of examiner's styles, the three raters (discussed subsequently) used in scoring the early memories were able to distinguish between the two groups of examiners by listening to them give instructions on cassette recordings. All three raters were able to identify the five examiners in each group.

Subjects

The sample of 60 students was from the same southeastern university. Each examiner was responsible for locating six volunteer subjects from outside the personal circle of family and friends. Graduate students were 16 of the subjects and 44 were undergraduates (36 women and 24 men in all). No subject was well known to an examiner.

Procedure

All examiners were provided three blank 90-min. cassettes with instructions to tape all interactions using one side of a tape per subject. They were also given six blank sets of verbal instructions used to record the tape recollections. Each set was coded so that the examiner knew the proper model to use. The code letters W and C indicated warm or cold, followed by the code letters P or A indicating whether the examiner was to be present or absent for the collection of the first three recollections. The examiner, if present, simply read the instructions and taped the first three memories, instructing the subject on the use of the tape recorder for recording the second set of three in the examiner's absence. The examiner, if absent for the first three, instructed the subject to follow the written instructions and to notify the examiner when the first three memories were recorded so that the examiner could return to record the last three.

The examiners were instructed to transcribe the memories verbatim from the tape to the form, from which the memories were typed onto the rating sheets. The numbers 1 to 360 were randomized by computer and a number was assigned to each memory and an accompanying rating sheet.

Raters and Rating Scale

Three raters were used to rate the memories. All were experienced counselors who had previous experience with the therapeutic use of early memories. They were instructed to make their ratings based on manifest content as opposed to a theoretical interpretation (e.g., Adlerian or psychodynamic).

The rating scale designed for this investigation utilized a nine-point continuum, similar to scales designed by Hedvig (1961) with early memories and Beavers-Timberlawn (Lewis, Beavers, Gossett, & Phillips, 1976) for the purpose of family assessment. The first scale was ranked along a continuum marked by the polarities pleasant and unpleasant and was designed to be a global assessment of the overall tone of the memory. In a memory with both positive and negative aspects, both were considered in the overall score. The second scale, with the extremes of interpersonal and solitary, was designed to measure the social aspects of the scale. The presence of people and the importance of the people was considered. The third scale, from interpersonal (positive) to interpersonal (negative), was meant to describe the relationship climate, from joyful to painful. Again, positive and negative aspects were to be considered and balanced. The fourth scale, from active to passive, described the subject's style in the memory and how instrumental was the subject in what was going on. The fifth scale, from most vivid to least vivid, described the richness of description of the memory, the amount of verbal evidence that this memory had vitality for the subject. The sixth scale, from secure to threatening, described the overall context in which the memory occurred, including the setting, people, and events.

RESULTS

Pearson product-moment correlation was used to assess the relationship between raters on a scale-by-scale basis. As anticipated, all correlations were .50 or above (12 out of 18 at r=.70). The overall correlations between raters across scales and memories were .68, .69, and .66.

The main hypotheses were: do the elements of context, i.e., examiners' style, presence or absence of examiner, and order or examiners' presence and absence, influence subjects in the production of early memories? The null hypothesis was that there will be no statistically significant relationship between these independent variables and raters' scores ($p = .05$).

Six separate analyses of variance were calculated for present vs. absent and for absent vs. present and six for warm vs. cold. The results showed two scales with significant effects of examiners' style. Warm examiners received more solitary memories and cold examiners received more interpersonal memories (Scale 2) ($F_{1,58} = 17.00$, $p < .001$). The means were 4.26 (warm) and 3.67 (cold) ($SS = 10.46$). Warm examiners received less vivid memories and cold examiners received more vivid memories (Scale 5) ($F_{1,58} = 5.93$, $f' < .02$). The means were 4.68 (warm) and 4.09 (cold); $SS = 10.48$. No other variables or interactions yielded significant effects.

DISCUSSION

The finding that subjects with warm examiners were rated as providing significantly more solitary and less vivid memories than subjects with cold examiners is somewhat supportive of Bach's contextual notion about the interpersonal nature of childhood memories and their functional role in achieving reduction of adult tension. These findings do not appear to support Freud's (1960a, 1960b) concept of the screen memory, i.e., a defense against something within but, rather, the subject's productions seemed to be a reaction to an external perception.

Unknown is whether the subjects produced entirely different early memories than they would have given in more neutral circumstances or whether they merely modified or embellished their "standard" early memories in response to contextual factors. The first possibility would not support Adler's (1927) contention that early memories have a consistent pattern so long as the lifestyle remains unchanged. The second possibility, on the other hand, supports the Adlerian assertion that people are goal-directed social beings (their lifestyle goals are at work even in how they present their early memories to others); on the other hand, however, some difficulty exists in theoretically explaining the uniformity of the reactiveness of the individual lifestyles to the contextual styles.

One caution comes from the fact that the examiners were all students in a graduate counseling class, and no student was, by nature, markedly cold and business-like. It is possible that the results could be influenced by the likelihood that the students were not congruently cold and that subjects were reacting to incongruent communication.

An unanticipated and inexplicable finding was the consistently low rater correlations found on the fifth memories, and, to some extent, the second memories. These memories would have been the middle of a set of three, but neither subjects nor raters would have known this.

In terms of implications, a number of research issues can be raised, such as other effects resulting from the nature of the examiners' style, whether cold examiners contaminate the field more than warm examiners, whether non-conscious material is communicated or whether the contexts of testing and therapy have different effects.

REFERENCES

Adler, A. (1927) The practice and theory of Individual Psychology. New York: Harcourt, Brace, World.

Bach, C. R. (1952) Some diadic functions of childhood memories. Journal of Psychology, 33, 87–98.

Bandler, R., & Grinder, J. (1975) Patterns of hypnotic techniques of Milton Erickson, M.D. Vol. 1. Cupertino, CA: Meta Publ.

Bateson, G., Jackson, D. D., Haley, J., & Weakland, J. (1968) Toward a theory of schizophrenia. In D. Jackson (Ed.), Communication, family, and marriage. Vol. 1. Palo Alto, CA: Science and Behavior Books, pp. 31–54.

Bauserman, J. M. (1984) A study of contextual influences on the production of early recollections. Unpublished doctoral dissertation, University of Virginia, Charlottesville.

Bowen, M. (1978) Family therapy in clinical practice. New York: Jason Aronson.

Ferenczi, S. (1950) Further consideration of the technique of psychoanalysis. London: Hogarth.

Ferenczi, S., & Rank, O. (1925) The development of psychoanalysis. New York: Nervous and Mental Disease Publ.

Freud, S. (1960a) Childhood memories and screen memories. Collected papers. Vol. 3. New York: Basic Books.

Freud, S. (1960b) Screen memories. Collected papers. Vol. 5. New York: Basic Books.

Haley, J. (1973) Uncommon therapy. New York: Norton.

Hedvig, E. B. (1961) A study of the effects of immediately preceding experiences upon early childhood recollections. Dissertation Abstracts, 21, 2784.

Heimann, P. (1981) On countertransference. In R. Langs (Ed.), Classics in psychoanalytic technique. New York: Jason Aronson, pp. 139–142.

Langs, R. J (1975) The therapeutic relationship and deviations in technique. International Journal of Psychoanalytic Psychotherapy, 4, 106–141.
Langs, R. J. (1979) The interactional dimension of countertransference. In L. Epstein & A. Feiner (Eds.), Countertransference. New York: Jason Aronson, pp. 71–104.
Lewis, J., Beavers, E., Gossett, J., & Phillips, V. (1976) No single thread. New York: Bruner Mazel.
Purcell, K. (1956) Memory and psychological security. Journal of Abnormal and Social Psychology, 47, 433–440.
Quay, H. (1959) The effect of verbal reinforcement on the recall of early memories. Journal of Abnormal and Social Psychology, 59, 254–257.
Racker, H. (1957) The meanings and uses of countertransference. Psychoanalytic Quarterly, 26, 303–357.
Reich, W. (1945) Character analysis. New York: Orgone Institute Press.
Rokeach, M. (1960) The open and closed mind. New York: Basic Books.
Scheflen, A. (1978) Communications aspects of schizophrenia. In M. Berger (Ed.), Beyond the double bind. New York: Bruner Mazel, pp. 125–154.
Searles, H. (1979a) Countertransference and related subjects. New York: International Universities Press.
Searles, H. (1979b) The countertransference with the borderline patient. In J. Le-Boit & A. Capponi (Eds.), Advances in psychotherapy of the borderline patient. New York: Jason Aronson, pp. 309–346.
Sullivan, H. S. (1953) The interpersonal theory of psychiatry. New York: Norton.
Von Bertalanffy, L. (1966) General systems theory and psychiatry. In S. Arieti (Ed.), American handbook of psychiatry. Vol. 3. New York: Basic Books, pp. 705–721.
Whitaker, C., Felder, R., & Warkentin, J. (1965) Countertransference in the family treatment of schizophrenia. In J. Boszormenyi-Nagy & J. Franco (Eds.), Intensive family therapy. New York: Harper & Row, pp. 323–341.

19

ASSOCIATIONS BETWEEN PERSONAL PROBLEMS AND THERAPEUTIC INTERVENTIONS AS REFLECTED BY VARIABLES IN EARLY RECOLLECTIONS AND GENDER

Warren R. Rule

Of at least 500 studies conducted on the psychological meaning of early recollections, other than taxonomic studies, the bulk of the research is based on assumptions related to the thinking of Adler or Freud. Increasing interest has been shown (e.g., Reichlin & Niederehe, 1980) in the Adlerian perspective. Adler's assumptions, which undergird the present study, assert that the manifest content of early memories is related to the present life-style of the individual and can be used for diagnostic and facilitative purposes (e.g., Adcock & Ross, 1988; Bruhn, 1985; Farrell, 1984; Himelstein, 1980; Watkins, 1985).

Investigators have also been eager to apply these assumptions to how early recollections (ERs) can be used to understand client expectations and experiences of the therapeutic process itself. For example, Mosak (1965) explored the prediction of the relationship of the client to the psychotherapist from ERs. Manaster (1982) investigated the ERs of counselors and clients. Bauserman and Rule (1988) studied the contextual influences on the production of ERs. Binder (1980) concluded that the memories clients choose to share with their therapist reflect their experience of present needs and stresses. The prediction of self-disclosure and style was investigated by Barrett (1983). Chesney, Fakouri, and Hafner (1986) studied ERs as an indicator of which alcoholics would be willing to continue treatment. Von Korff (1987) investigated the referential activity between therapist and client using client ERs.

The present exploratory study was directed toward the pre-therapeutic phase, that of individual and gender attitudes and expectations about personal problems and therapy as reflected in selected ER variables.

METHOD

Subjects

The subjects in the sample consisted of 118 students from a university in the middle Atlantic region. They were enrolled in sections of a required sophomore-junior level course in a school of community affairs. The variability of the socioeconomic background and age was quite probably greater than would be expected in university undergraduate courses. The gender was approximately equally divided.

Procedure.

Survey. The instructions on the survey requested that the subject write a description of one's earliest recollection. Emphasis was given in the directions to: be as specific as possible; not include a 'report' (a memory of an incident that happened many times); include a memory that one is not absolutely sure occurred or regardless of how insignificant it may seem; only describe one that happened before age eight; include feelings, even mixed ones; include the names of other people there; describe the most vivid part; include what happened before and afterward along with accompanying feelings; attempt a guess at one's purpose of behavior; and state the approximate age of occurrence. For further description of the specifics, see Rule (1984).

ER Variables and Ratings. Each of the nine ER variables (described below) was presented to the three raters as a 1–7 Likert Scale. Each rater was asked to circle the most appropriate number, ranging from

"1" (no, none) to "4" (both, cannot say) on to "7" (very strong). The nine variables were selected by the investigator as among those personal characteristics which seem to be valued as measures of healthy personal adjustment by at least several of the major counseling theories (Adlerian, Personal-Centered, Rational-Emotive, Behavioral, and Gestalt). The scales differentiated between the internal frame of reference of the subject (six scales) and the behavior of the subject (two scales) or the behavior of others (one scale); this distinction appears to be an important one in ER ratings (Altman & Rule, 1980). The one through nine scales and accompanying rater definitions are:

A. Internal frame of reference of subject: Use of logic or reason.

B. Internal frame of reference of subject: "Should" expectations of self, others, or life. (Note: This is an irrational "rigid" message on what to do, think, or feel; expressed another way, it is an imperative, a demandingness, a "must," an "ought to," a "have to.")

C. Internal frame of reference of subject: Self-confidence versus inferiority.

D. Internal frame of reference of subject: Awareness of feelings—self or others.

E. Internal frame of reference of subject: Pleasantness outcome.

F. Internal frame of reference of subject: Level of curiosity (eagerness or openness to learning).

G. Behavior of subject: Active versus passive (Active—initiating, carrying out, participating with others; Passive—merely responds, remained where subject was, others determined outcome, follower).

H. Behavior of subject: Responsibility for self versus dependency.

I. Behavior of others: Treated well versus mistreated (positive/negative response from others).

Each of the three raters had received training in the Adlerian approach to ERs. The inter-rater reliability, expressed by item-to-total correlations, is displayed in Table 19.1. For each ER scale, the correlation of each rater response to the mean of the three raters is presented. As can be noted, all are quite large, except for Scale A.

TABLE 19.1 Rater Reliability

ER Scale	Rater Item-to-Total	Rater 1	Rater 2	Rater 3
		(Correlation of rater response to mean of raters)		
A	(Logic)	.59	.86	.33
B	("Should" Expectations)	.82	.86	.78
C	(Self-Confidence)	.79	.82	.88
D	(Awareness of Feelings)	.77	.83	.83
E	(Pleasantness Outcome)	.89	.91	.93
F	(Level of Curiosity)	.86	.70	.84
G	(Active-Passive Behavior)	.81	.82	.84
H	(Self Responsible	.75	.83	.86
I	(Treated Well by Others)	.85	.87	.91

Attitudes toward Personal Problems and Therapeutic Intervention. This section of the survey was divided into four questions:

1. If you were experiencing a personal problem that frequently upset you, what are the chances that you would talk it over with someone? Circle the most appropriate number. (Note: The Likert Scale for the subject was: 1—Very certain; 2—Quite probably; 3—Somewhat likely; 4—Not sure; 5—Somewhat unlikely; 6—Quite doubtful; 7—Definitely not.)
2. If you were experiencing a personal problem you knew you could not deal with by yourself and felt you definitely had to talk to someone about it, what is the likelihood you would seek out each of the following individuals (circle the most appropriate number). No expense involved for the professionals. (Note: The same Likert Scale was used for each of these individuals as was used in question 1.)

    1. Family member
    2. Close friend
    3. Minister, priest, rabbi
    4. Professional counselor
    5. Psychologist
    6. Psychiatrist

3. Listed below are broad areas in which personal problems can develop. Circle the number that best represents the chances of your seeking professional help (e.g., professional counselor or therapist) if you had an upsetting problem in that area. Assume that no expense is involved. (Note: Each of the five "lifetasks" described by Mosak [1984] and listed below was regarded by Adler as one on which everyone must take some sort of a position;

an attempt here was made to express them in "layman" terms. The Likert Scale after each of these was the same as that used for questions 1 and 2.)

1. Interpersonal (family or friends)
2. Work or school
3. Relationship to the opposite sex
4. Philosophical/existential problem
5. Coping with and/or accepting yourself

4. Assume that you have made the decision to see a counselor or therapist about an upsetting personal problem. Circle the amount of responsibility you think the counselor should take in solving the problem for you. (Note: The Likert Scale was: 1—Entire responsibility; 2—Most; 3—Somewhat more than me; 4—Share it equally; 5—Somewhat less than me; 6—Little; 7—None.)

To avoid possibly biasing the subject's answers by the sequence of requested information (e.g., the memory of the just-described ER biasing the ratings of attitudes toward personal problems and therapeutic intervention), the sequence of the halves of the survey was reversed for each half of the sample.

RESULTS

The results will be presented in five subsections. The initial four will correspond with the preceding description of the four parts of the survey that related to attitudes toward personal problems and therapeutic intervention. The fifth subsection will present the gender difference on the ER scales.

Likelihood of Talking to Someone. Only one of the nine ER scales was significantly correlated with the question related to talking a personal problem over with someone: Scale G, active versus passive; $r = -.172$ ($p = .06$). The overall mean was 2.64.

In regard to gender, there were significant mean differences for this question. The females ($M = 2.29$) were more likely to seek out someone to talk to than the males ($M = 2.91$), $t(94) = 1.83$, $p = .07$.

Likelihood of Choosing Different Helpers. Table 19.2 presents the correlation between each ER variable (for each subject, the score was the mean of the three raters' responses on the ER scale) and the subjects' responses to each of the choices of helpers. As can be noted, a number of significant correlations were found between various ER scales and the "traditional" helpers, i.e., family, friends, religious leaders; however, no significant relations were discovered for the "professional" helpers, i.e., professional counselor, psychologist, or psychiatrist.

In terms of mean rankings, however, the results were more mixed (most preferred to least): close friend (M = 2.13); family member (M = 3.25); professional counselor (M = 4.47); psychologist (M = 4.96); minister, priest, or rabbi (M = 5.04); and psychiatrist (M = 5.21).

There was only one gender difference in preference for helpers. Males (M = 4.95) were more likely to seek out a psychiatrist than females (M = 5.50), t (91) = –1.65, p = .10.

Likelihood of Seeking Help with Life Tasks. Table 19.3 indicates the correlation between each ER variable (for each subject, the score was the mean of the three raters' responses on the ER scale) and the subjects' responses to each of the tasks of life. A number of significant correlations can be found between various ER scales and four of the five tasks of life. No significance was found for the task of life of relating to the opposite sex. As noted, Scale F (internal frame of reference: level of curiosity) was significant for three of the five tasks of life.

In regard to mean rankings, the likelihood of seeking help with the five life tasks were (most likely to least): coping with and/or accepting yourself (M = 3.69); work or school (M = 3.91); interpersonal (family or friends) and relationship to opposite sex were tied (M = 4.17 for each); and philosophical/existential problem (M = 4.21). There were no gender differences in these likelihood ratings.

Degree of Responsibility Professional Helper Should Take. There were no significant correlations for the various ER variables and the degree of responsibility that the professional should take. The overall mean was 4.64. However, in regard to gender, there were significant mean differences. The females (M = 4.92) thought the professional helper should take less responsibility for the outcome than the males (M = 4.33), t (94) = –2.66, p = .009. Interestingly, no subject, male or female, indicated that the professional helper should take "entire responsibility."

Gender Differences in ER Scales. Significant gender differences were found in three of the nine ER scales. Females (M = 3.63) used logic or reason (Scale A) to a greater degree than males (M = 3.16), t (95) = –2.23, p =.03. Females (M = 3.65) used "should expectations" (e.g., a "must," "ought to," "have to") of self, others, or life (Scale B) more than

TABLE 19.2 ER Variables and Choice of Helper

ER Variables	Family Member	Close Friend	Minister, Priest, Rabbi	Professional Counselor	Psychologist	Psychiatrist
A (Logic)	.029	*.228***	*−.110*	.010	.016	.020
B (Should Expectations)	−.101	.090	−.193**	−.008	*.096*	*−.060*
C (Self-Confidence)	.029	.052	.210**	−.020	−.139	−.080
D (Awareness of Feelings)	−.100	−.090	−.124	−.039	.135	.047
E (Pleasantness Outcome)	*.288****	−.100	.269***	.014	−.042	−.019
F (Level of Curiosity)	*−.028*	.059	.203**	.110	*.029*	.071
G (Active-Passive	.052	−.152*	.146	.013	.018	−.036
H (Self-Responsible Behavior)	*.158**	−.040	.193**	*.016*	.058	.052
I (Treated Well by Others)	.097	−.119	.261***	−.051	*−.080*	−.071

*p < .10
**p < .05
***p < .01

males (M = 2.77), t (95) = −2.58, p = .01. Females (M = 4.99) had a greater awareness of feelings in self or others (Scale D) than males (M = 4.05), t (95) = 4.47, p = .0001.

DISCUSSION

One integrative pattern that tended to emerge in this exploratory study is the relatively consistent overrepresentation of the ER variables in correlation with choice of "traditional" helpers. "Traditional" helpers are defined here to mean those nonprofessional helpers or confidants who have traditionally provided nurturance and counseling, particularly before the emergence of "professional" helpers. (Traditional—family members, close friends, or religious leaders;

TABLE 19.3 ER Variables and Tasks of Life Problems

ER Variables	Interpersonal (Family or Friends)	Work or School	Opposite Sex	Philosophica l	Accepting Self
A (Logic)	–.045	–.096	–.034	–.046	–.105
B (Should Expectations)	.010	.153*	–.016	–.046	–.130
C (Self-Confidence)	.057	–.131	.055	.062	.099
D (Awareness of Feelings)	–.094	.154*	–.032	–.059	–.111
E (Pleasantness Outcome)	.086	–.187**	.004	.032	–.071
F (Level of Curiosity)	.159*	–.012	.087	.204**	.197**
G (Active-Passive Behavior)	.246***	–.021	.098	.131	.089
H (Self-Responsible Behavior)	.236***	.001	.138	.094	.105
I (Treated Well by Others)	–.002	.093	–.084	.055	.084

*p < .10
**p < .05
***p < .01

Professional—counselors, psychologists, or psychiatrists). Possibly, the material in ERs generally relates to "traditional" issues in living (e.g., relationship to family or friends, moral or religious values) and, correspondingly, the subjects intuitively chose those "traditional" helpers that would be most compatible with these issues. Or, on the other hand, perhaps the subjects were confused about, or even mistrustful of, what the "professional" helper could really do to assist them.

All of the ER variables, except "awareness of feelings," were related to at least one traditional helper. Somewhat baffling is that six of the nine ER variables were significantly related (and all of the remaining three correlated over ±.10) to choice of minister, priest, or rabbi as a helper. Somehow, the reaction of hypothetically seeking or not seeking help from a religious leader may, as discussed in the preceding paragraph, be related to the moral undertones in most ER material and, hence, in individual outlook on life.

The ER "level of curiosity" variable was significantly related to three of the five tasks of life for which the subjects would be willing to seek out help. This variable, in addition to the ER active-passive and self-responsible (behavior) variables, may be worthy of further study. Interestingly, all of the nine ER variables were significantly correlated with at least one choice of helper or task of life. These ER variables were related to choices made by subjects under the assumption of a hypothetical personal problem; an interesting study might be to investigate the stability of these same variables and helping choices when the subjects are experiencing stress (e.g., Brodt, 1985).

In regard to gender differences, the female subjects in this study certainly did not conform to the Freudian stereotypes of women as passive and somehow lacking. The females, significantly more than the males, were likely to seek out a helper, though the professional helper should take less responsibility for the outcome, had ERs involving a greater degree of (a) use of logic and reason, (b) "should" expectations, and (c) awareness of feelings of self or others. A note of caution may be in order here, however, in generalizing from the ER findings. Possibly the females were essentially more skilled in expressing the remembered ER incidents, as well as accompanying feelings, more fully or more clearly. More ER research is needed here in the area of referential activity (von Korff, 1987), i.e., the ability to link words to perceptions, images, and feelings. In terms of the overall "tone" of the ER gender difference in the investigation, however, the findings conflict somewhat with the results of Schwartz's (1984–1985) study, which used different ER measures, yet found that males reported more ERs involving positive interactions and mastery, and the females reported more ERs involving fear, anxiety, and frustration.

In regard to theoretical significance, this exploratory study found various linkages between different ER variables and attitudes toward personal problems and therapeutic intervention. These relationships are quite consistent with Adler's approach in that he viewed individuals as social beings and their problems as having social implications. Thus, the findings in this study revealed relationships between individual outlook on life, as reflected in ERs, and attitudes toward one of the most powerful and intimate social encounters, sharing personal problems with another human.

In terms of practitioner usefulness, further development of these relationships between ERs and attitudes toward personal problems and therapy might provide additional information for matching clients and professional helpers and for exploring client expectations that contribute to resistance. Imagery would seem to be a useful tool here. Furthermore, clinical attention and research could be directed toward those client attitudes, as reflected in ERs, that may work toward a person's advantage in seeking help with some of life's tasks but work to an individual's disadvantage in approaching other ones.

REFERENCES

Adcock, N. V., & Ross, M. W. (1988). Early memories, early experiences and personality. Social Behavior & Personality, 11(2), 95–100.

Altman, K., & Rule, W. R. (1980). The relationship between social interest dimensions of early recollections and selected counselor variables. Journal of Individual Psychology, 36, 227–234.

Barrett, D. (1983). Early recollections as predictors of self-disclosure and interpersonal style. Individual Psychology, 39(1), 92–98.

Bauserman, J. M., & Rule, W. R. (1988). Contextual influences on production of early recollections. Perceptual and Motor Skills, 66, 823–828.

Binder, J. L. (1980). Early memories: A technical aid to focusing in time-limited dynamic psychotherapy. Psychotherapy: Theory, Research, and Practice, 17(1), 52–62.

Brodt, A. M. (1985). The stability of early recollections. Dissertation Abstracts International, 45(7–8), 2303–B.

Bruhn, A. R. (1985). Using early memories as a projective technique: The cognitive perceptual method. Journal of Personality Assessment, 49(6), 587–597.

Chesney, S. M., Fakouri, M. E., & Hafner, J. L. (1986). The relationship between early recollections and willingness/unwillingness of alcoholics to continue treatment. Individual Psychology, 42(3), 395–403.

Farrell, R. A. (1984). Deviance importations: Early recollection and the reconstruction of self. International Journal of Social Psychiatry, 30(4), 189–199.

Himelstein, P. (1980). Early recollections: Their use in diagnosis and psychotherapy. Journal of Personality Assessment, 44(5), 554–555.

Manaster, G. J. (1982). A comparison of early recollections of counselors and clients. Individual Psychology, 38(3), 285–295.

Mosak, H. H. (1965). Predicting the relationship to the psychotherapist from early recollections. Journal of Individual Psychology, 21, 77–81.

Mosak, H. H. (1984). Adlerian psychotherapy. In R. J. Corsini (Ed.), Current Psychotherapies (3rd ed.) (pp. 56–107) Itasca, IL: F. E. Peacock.

Reichlin, R. E., & Niederehe, G. (1980). Early memories: A comprehensive bibliography. Journal of Individual Psychology, 36(2), 209–218.

Rule, W. R. (Ed.). (1984). Lifestyle counseling for adjustment to disability. Rockville, MD: Aspen Systems.

Schwartz, A. E. (1984–1985). Earliest memories: Sex differences and the meaning of experience. Imagination, Cognition & Personality, 4(1), 43–52.

von Korff, P. M. (1987). Referential activity and the therapeutic process. (Doctoral dissertation, Adelphi University, 1987). Dissertation Abstracts International, 47(12), 5069–B.

Watkins, C. E. (1985). Early recollections as a projective technique in counseling: An Adlerian view. American Mental Health Counselors Association Journal, 7(1), 32–40.

III

Career Choice

20

BIRTH ORDER AND COMMUNICATION SKILLS OF PHARMACY STUDENTS

Matthew M. Murawski, Patrick Miederhoff, and Warren R. Rule

Summary: Pharmacy educators are training graduates in a concept of practice called pharmaceutical care. The movement towards patient care requires consideration of the personal and social qualities of trainees. All individuals attracted to pharmacy may not desire involvement in patient care. This preliminary study of pharmacy students of the relationships among birth order, empathy, and assertiveness behaviors using the Interpersonal Communication Inventory showed the incidence of firstborn students in this sample was not significantly higher than in the general population but the incidence of those born second was significantly lower. Regression analysis of individual items gave significant correlations between birth order and three items on the inventory. While few conclusions can be drawn, a clear direction for further research is indicated.

This chapter, "Birth Order and Communication Skills of Pharmacy Students," from Murawski, M.M., Miederhoff, P. & Rule, W.R. *Perceptual and Motor Skills*, 1995, 80, 891–895.

Health profession educators are showing a greater concern for students' communication skills. For instance, pharmacy educators have formally committed to curricular changes that further develop the abilities of graduates to provide a new kind of pharmacy practice called pharmaceutical care (Hepler & Strand, 1989). Pharmaceutical care is considered a revolutionary philosophy of pharmacy practice that espouses, among other things, "an emotional commitment to the welfare of patients as individuals who require and deserve pharmacist's compassion, concern, and trust" (American Association of Colleges of Pharmacy, 1991, p. 14). Educating and counseling patients and interacting with other health professionals to maximize the benefits of drug therapy are expected to become primary activities of pharmacists, while the current responsibility for drug distribution will become secondary.

The movement towards a more intense involvement in patient care requires a serious reconceptualization of the curriculum and educational process, but educators in the field also need to consider the personal and social qualities of the individuals being educated. Existing research suggests that most individuals attracted to pharmacy do not have an intense interest in patient care. Several studies suggest that financial reasons figure prominently in the choice of pharmacy as a career (e.g., McCormack, 1956; Smith, 1968). Studies of personality characteristics of pharmacists indicate that pharmacy attracts individuals with a unique set of personality traits, and these traits do not seem to be influenced by the socialization process of education in pharmacy. Manasse, Kabat, and Wertheimer (1976) and Rezler, Mrtek, and Manasse (1976) reported that pharmacy is particularly attractive to students who enjoy established routine, dislike new problems, are persistent in their work habits, and are impatient with complex details but tend to be good at precise work. Miederhoff (1984) provided evidence that pharmacists tend to be introverted and low on warmth. Extensive additional research is needed to understand more fully the characteristics of individuals who are attracted to pharmacy and its various areas of practice. The focus of the present research is on the communicative skills and birth order of pharmacy students.

Over 500 studies have been completed on birth order, yet research on birth order of pharmacy students and pharmacists is rare. Also lacking are studies of pharmacists on variables related to effective communication skills, e.g., empathy and assertiveness. There is some evidence that an individual's order of birth within the family may influence career choice and characteristic style of interacting with others (Forer,

1976). For instance, Cobb and French (1966) found that firstborns were overly represented among a sample of American medical students, and Shaver, French, and Cobb (1970) indicated the same was true for Swedish medical students. Regarding empathy, Stotland concluded that laterborns tend to empathize more with people they view as similar to themselves and with whom they can interact (Stotland & Cottrell, 1962; Stotland & Dunn, 1962, 1963).

The purpose of the present study was to investigate the birth order of pharmacy students and the relationships among birth order, empathy, and assertiveness.

METHOD

The subjects in the study were 105 pharmacy students in the second professional year of training [72 (69%) women, 33 (31%) men]. The mean age of the sample was 24.1 yr. (SD =5.1). Students came from families with a mean number of 2.8 children (SD= 1.4). The instrument used to collect information on assertiveness and empathy was the Interpersonal Communication Inventory, adapted from Bienvenu (1974). This instrument, part of a teaching aid packet for developing communication skills, consists of 22 items, 11 each for Listening/Empathy and Assertiveness/Aggressiveness. No information on the instrument's reliability or validity was available. Birth order and demographic information were collected by questionnaire.

RESULTS

Expected birth-order frequencies for the mean age of the sample were used as found in The Statistical Abstract of The United States (U.S. Department of Commerce, Bureau of Census, 1984). Analysis of birth-order frequencies using the crosstabulation procedure yielded two significant findings (Table 20.1). The incidence of the firstborns in this sample was not significantly higher than in the general population ($p= .89$) but the incidence of second-borns overall was significantly lower than would be expected ($p=.01$) as was the incidence of second-borns in families of three ($p <.001$).

Mean scores were for Listening/Empathy (26.22, SD=2.39), Assertiveness/Aggressiveness (21.56, SD=2.81), and Total (45.35, SD=7.10). Scoring instructions indicate that a score below 17, the midpoint of the scale, suggests further skill development in that area may be useful. The higher the total score, the more effective interactions with others should be, with a total possible score of 66. No significant differences

TABLE 20.1 Observed and Expected Incidence of Birth Order

Family Size	Position	Observed	Expected*	p
>1	Oldest	33	32.3	.89
>1	Second	13	23.7	.01
2	Oldest	19	15.8	.18
2	Youngest	14	15.8	.68
3+	Oldest	14	18.6	.18
3+	Middle	7	34.1	<.001
3+	Youngest	15	18.6	.29

*Expected frequencies are derived from the Statistical Abstract of the United States (U.S. Department of Commerce, Bureau of Census, 1984) utilizing the birth cohort for the average age of this sample (Chi-squared analysis).

in scale total score or subscores were found by gender, age, or birth order. Analysis of the internal reliability of the Interpersonal Communication Inventory gave Cronbach alphas of .32 for total score, .28 for Listening/Empathy, and .32 for Assertiveness/Aggressiveness. This low reliability made further analysis utilizing scale scores inappropriate. Regression analysis of individual item scores with birth order indicated significant correlations between birth order and scores on three of the 22 items.

DISCUSSION

The finding of significant correlations between birth order and the scale items listed in Table 20.2 indicates that birth order does influence some aspects of communication style of these pharmacy students. Interpersonal rigidity seemed to be a unifying theme among the three items. This finding fits well with the earlier work of Manasse (1976), Rezler (1976), and Miederhoff (1984). In a profession where much emphasis is placed upon one hundred percent accuracy, such rigidity may be adaptive or the result of self-selection factors. The significant underrepresentation of second-borns is evidence of variation in birth-order categories in this group. This finding is in keeping with Stotland and Cottrell (1962), Stotland and Dunn (1962, 1963) in their conclusion that laterborns show more interactive empathy, i.e., a disproportionate number of second-borns may have "deselected" themselves from entering the field of pharmacy because its professional demands did not seem to foster this personality variable. These findings do not support the previously cited over-representation of firstborns found in the closely related field of medicine (Cobb & French, 1966; Shaver, French, and Cobb, 1970).

TABLE 20.2 Correlations of Single Items of the Interpersonal Communications Inventory with Birth Order

Item Content	Beta	p
12. Are you satisfied with the way you settle your differences with others?	−0.369	.02
17. Does it upset you a great deal when someone disagrees with you?	0.421	.01
20. Do you admit you are wrong when you know you're wrong about something?	0.452	.01

Note—Regression was performed between the numerical value of birth order (1, 2, 3, etc.) and the coding value for item response (1= no, 2 = sometimes, 3 = yes).

It seems clear, however, that some variation in birth-order frequency exists. One potential for further research is the development of birth-order data for each school of pharmacy. We have argued that some students may "deselect" themselves from pharmacy due to a perceived incompatibility with the professional image of pharmacy. If the baseline incidence of various birth orders of pharmacy students were known, changes in the birth-order frequency of student applicants might serve as an early indicator of changes in the professional image of pharmacy. Further, researchers should include other instruments to measure personality and communication characteristics. Perhaps the three significant items in this inventory could be investigated further, using other inventories measuring sensitivity, for example. Finally, to ensure adequate representation, the sample should consist of students from various schools of pharmacy in different geographic areas.

REFERENCES

American Association of Colleges of Pharmacy, Commission to Implement Change in Pharmaceutical Education. (1991) A position paper: entry level education in pharmacy: a commitment to change. Alexandria, VA, p. 14.

Bienvenu, M. J. (1974). Interpersonal Communications Inventory. San Diego, CA: University Associates.

Cobb, S., & French, J. (1966) Birth order among medical students. Journal of the American Medical Association, 195, 312–313.

Forer, L. (1976) The birth order factor. New York: David McKay.

Hepler, C. D., & Strand, L. M. (1989) Opportunities and responsibilities in pharmaceutial care. American Journal of Pharmaceutical Education, 53, 7S–15S.

Manasse, H. R., Kabat, H. F., & Wertheimer, A. I. (1976) Professional socialization of pharmacy: I. A cross-sectional analysis of personality characteristics of agents and objects of socialization. Drugs in Health Care, 3, 3–18.
McCormack, T. (1956) The druggists' dilemma: problems of a marginal occupation. American Journal of Sociology, 61, 308–315.
Miederhoff, P. (1984) Personality predictors of career satisfaction in pharmacy. Paper presented at the annual meeting of the American Association of Colleges of Pharmacy. Baltimore, MD.
Rezler, A. G., Mrtek, F. G., & Manasse, H. R. (19761 Linking career choice to personal types: a preliminary analysis of pharmacy students. American Journal of Pharmaceutical Education, 40, 121–125.
Shaver, P. R., French, J., & Cobb, S. (1970) Birth order of medical students and the occupational ambitions of their parents. International Journal of Psychology, 5, 197–207.
Smith, M. (1968) Social class background of pharmacy students. American Journal of Pharmaceutical Education, 32, 596–609.
Stotland, E., & Cottrell, N. B. (1962) Similarity of performance as influenced by interest, self-esteem, and birth order. Journal of Abnormal and Social Psychology, 64, 183–195.
Stotland, E., & Dunn, R. E. (1962) Identification, opposition, authority, self-esteem and birth order. Psychological Monographs, 76, No. 9 (Whole No. 528).
Stotland, E., & Dunn, R. E. (1963) Empathy, self-esteem, and birth order. Journal of Abnormal and Social Psychology, 66, 532–540.
U.S. Department of Commerce, Bureau of The Census. (1984) Statistical Abstract of the United States. (104th ed.) Washington, DC: Author. Accepted March 13, 1995.

21

FAMILY CONSTELLATION AND BIRTH ORDER VARIABLES RELATED TO VOCATIONAL CHOICE OF DENTISTRY

Warren R. Rule and Ann T. Comer

Summary: A relatively small amount of research has been completed on the family-group variable of birth order and the vocational-group variable of choices in the world of work. Furthermore, extremely little research has been completed utilizing the socio-psychological perspective of family constellation and birth order. A sample of 282 dentists was interviewed regarding socio-psychological birth order and related information. Relationships were found for the psychological perspectives of ordinal and socio-psychological birth order, family size, closest sibling, and changing birth-rate trends. A possible unifying theme which relates this study to other investigations of vocational choice was discussed.

A strong focus in psychology in recent years has been the individual's place of identity within the group. Two extremely important

This chapter, "Family Constellation and Birth Order Variables Related to Vocational Choice of Dentistry," from Rule, W.R. & Comer, A.T., *Psychological Reports*, 1979, 45, 883–890.

groups from a developmental perspective are the family group and the more broadly based group of vocational choices in the world of work. Researchers have been very interested in investigating possible relationships between these two groups. Yet relationships between the family group variable of birth order and the variable of choice within the vocations group have been studied by a relatively small number of investigators. In addition, the family constellation (socio-psychological) approach to birth order has been investigated even less. A review of the findings suggests a relationship may exist between "specialness" in birth order and in later vocational choice. For instance the special place within the family group of being firstborn may be related to the later choice of "special place" occupations involving prestige and achievement.

For example, firstborns were overrepresented among eminent scientists (Roe, 1953), lawyers (Very & Prull, 1970), congressmen (Zweigenhoft, 1975), and army officers (Herrell, 1972), whereas Very and Zannini (1969) found an overproportion of second borns among beauticians, a somewhat less prestigious occupation. Although there appears to be a dearth of information on the occupational focus of the present investigation, dentistry, Cobb and French (1966), for an area closely related to dentistry, found firstborns were overrepresented among a sample of American medical students, and Shaver, French, and Cobb (1970) indicated that firstborns were also overrepresented among Swedish medical students. In considering the research on birth order and vocational choice, it is difficult to make meaningful comparisons because of the different investigative approaches. For instance, many of the researchers have not incorporated into their studies such important variables as changing population trends or family size. Even fewer have focused on the important perspective of socio-psychological birth order. This study sought to investigate factors related to birth order as determined by the (traditional) ordinal method and by the possibly more accurate socio-psychological method and the influential variable in the family group of closest sibling.

In regard to the first area, birth order, the overrepresentation in the literature of firstborns, i.e., oldest and only borns, in the achievement-oriented vocations suggests that an overproportionate number of firstborns would be found among dentists as well. However, Bayer (1966) and Kohn and Schooler (1969) have indicated that last borns are as likely to go to college as first-borns, and Foyer (1976) suggests that the youngest is more likely to complete advanced education if from a four- or five-child family than from a smaller unit.

The second area of this study focused on the closest sibling. Since the sibling who is closest in age often has a great impact on one's childhood development, the phenomena of differing sibling influences related to sex and to the older-younger dimension seem worthy of investigation. For example, a study by Sutton-Smith, Roberts, and Rosenberg (1964), discussed in Sutton-Smith and Rosenberg (1970), suggests diverging developmental patterns among siblings in the family group.

METHOD

At a state dental convention, 282 dentists were interviewed at random. The interview method was felt to be superior to the usual survey method because it increases the accuracy of the responses. Moreover, it is not subject to the self-selection bias of the cooperating respondents which is reflected in the modest return rate of most surveys. An additional six dentists refused to be interviewed, thus yielding a 97.9% response rate. Insofar as sampling procedure is concerned, the sampling restrictiveness resulting from interviewing exclusively convention attendees is regarded as a delimitation; however, the nearly perfect response rate of this method of sampling appears to be a contrasting strength. All of the subjects were males. This sample comprised approximately one half of those attending the convention.

The desired information included one's childhood siblings, the siblings' age difference from the respondent, and any special circumstance which could influence birth-order calculations such as age of a sibling who died or the existence of step-siblings.

RESULTS

Traditional and Socio-Psychological Birth Order

As can be noted in Table 21.1, oldest born siblings are overrepresented at the .01 level of significance for two-child families, using the chi-squared goodness of fit technique. Yet none of the birth-order categories is overrepresented for families of three and over. In this method of analysis, the traditional categories of birth order were used; age differences and socio-psychological birth order were not considered. For instance, with this method if a subject in a two-child family had a sister as much as 15 yr. younger, he was still regarded as a firstborn, whereas his socio-psychological perspective would be that of a functional only child.

Some investigators, e.g., Mosak and Dreikurs (1973) and Shulman (1973), believe that the traditional ordinal method of regarding birth

TABLE 21.1 Observed and Expected Frequencies of Birth Order Using Traditional Ordinal Categories

Family Size	Position	Observed	Expected	χ^2
2	Oldest	61	46	9.78*
2	Youngest	31	46	
3+	Oldest	48	38.7	3.88
3+	Middle	59	69.6	
3+	Youngest	40	38.7	

*$p < .01$

order does not always consider an individual's socio-psychological perspective. Accordingly, the approach taken in Table 21.2 was to compare "true" oldest, middle, and youngest borns by excluding those of a different phenomenological perspective. All "socio-psychological onlies" were removed, i.e., those who were: (a) firstborn and six or more years older than the next sibling, or (b) later born and not having a sibling less than six years of age difference. In addition, those middle-borns were removed who were: (a) socio-psychological oldests, i.e., those having sibling(s) six or more years older and younger sibling(s) less than 6 yr. younger, or (b) socio-psychological youngests, i.e., those having sibling(s) less than 6 yr. older and younger sibling(s) 6 or more years younger. Altogether, 28 firstborns and 31 later borns were removed. The 6-yr. figure was chosen because at approximately the age of six the individual has become solidly enmeshed in a school setting; that is to say, the child has begun to broaden the range of influences received from his first social group, the family, to those of the next social group, the school.

As can be noted in Table 21.2, none of the birth order positions is significantly overrepresented for two-child families, whereas the oldest is overrepresented in families of three or more ($p = .05$). Thus, the results in Table 21.2 are directly reversed, in terms of family size, from the results in Table 21.1. This suggests that socio-psychological variations may be an influential outcome factor in birth-order categorizations and supports the effects of a grouping or constellation concept of understanding as opposed to a concept of isolation.

As can be noted in Tables 21.1 and 21.2, youngest borns are not overrepresented. Yet they are as well represented as oldest borns in three-or-more child families, using traditional categories, and in two-child families, using redefined categories by the socio-psychological method. Furthermore, in regard to Forer's assertion that the youngest is more likely to complete advanced education if from a four- or five-child family than from a smaller one, this sample provides a sharp

TABLE 21.2 Observed and Expected Frequencies of Birth Order Excluding Positions of Socio-Psychological Variation

Family Size	Position	Observed	Expected	χ^2
2	Oldest	37	30.5	2.78
2	Youngest	24	30.5	
3+	Oldest	44	31.3	7.80*
3+	Middle	45	56.7	
3+	Youngest	30	31.1	

*$p < .05$

contrast between four-child and five-child families. Further breakdown of the data indicates that the representation of the youngest-born in four-child and larger families compared with the representation in three-child and smaller families yields a non-significant χ^2 of 1.11 (df = 1). Whereas the representation of youngest-borns in five-child and larger families as compared to the representation in four-child and smaller families yields a χ^2 of 7.22 ($p = .01$, df = 1). This overrepresentation of youngest-borns in five-child and larger families is still significant ($p = .05$, $\chi^2 = 4.51$) even when analyzed using the same socio-psychological birth-order categories as were used in Table 21.2. Thus further support is given to the effects of the constellation concept of family grouping.

The important socio-psychological consideration of changing birth-rate trends in studying birth order has been discussed by several researchers, e.g., Price and Hare (1969) and Schooler (1972). If not taken into consideration, this phenomenon could contribute to inaccurate conclusions in birth-order research, particularly regarding the overrepresentation of firstborns. In the present investigation, 152 or 53.9% were firstborns (only and oldest). The highest percentage of firstborn births in the twentieth century (46.7%) occurred in 1947 (U.S. Department of Health, Education & Welfare, 1960a, 1960b). Even using this inflated post-World War II baby-boom percentage as the expected firstborn rate for the entire sample in the present investigation, a significantly greater proportion of firstborns is still indicated at the .05 level ($\chi^2 = 5.87$, df = 1).

Only-born children seem to be overrepresented in this study of dentists. In comparing the number of onlies in this investigation (43 or 15.25%) with Bayer's (1966) 10.29% found in male college students, the difference is significant at the .01 level ($\chi^2 = 6.74$, df = 1). Furthermore, using Cobb and French's (1966) 9.66% of onlies found in a sample of American medical students as the expected frequency, the difference is also significant at the .01 level ($\chi^2 = 9.12$, df = 1). It must be noted, however, that each of the above comparisons may be subject to birth-rate fluctuations. The disproportions above would, of course, be more striking if the socio-psychological onlies were combined with the onlies.

Regarding the socio-psychological onlies, defined previously, an interesting finding exists in this sample. In two-child families, the oldest-born-socio-psychological onlies are significantly more likely to become dentists ($p < .01$, $\chi^2 = 9.32$, $df = 1$) than the later-born-socio-psychological onlies. Yet there is no significant overrepresentation ($\chi^2 = .31$, $df = 1$) for families of three or more. A larger sample might have permitted a closer examination of the middle-born yet socio-psychological oldest ($n = 8$), and the middle-born yet socio-psychological youngest ($n = 5$).

Closest Sibling. The sex of the closest sibling and older-younger age dimension of the closest sibling were investigated. The results indicate that the dentists had a significantly greater number of brothers (106) as closest siblings than sisters (76). This finding was confirmed ($\chi^2 = 4.08$, $df = 1$, $p = .05$). A sibling was judged to a "closest sibling" only if this person were the closest sibling, younger or older, within an age difference of less than six years. Regarding the older-younger age dimension, a significant difference in frequencies was observed ($\chi^2 = 9.49$, $df = 3$, $p < .05$) for the four categories of closest siblings: younger brother (60), younger sister (45), older brother (43), and older sister (31).

DISCUSSION

Family size and socio-psychological birth order appear to be influential variables related to generalization about birth order and later vocational choice of dentistry: thus, the effects of constellation grouping seem to be noteworthy. The common thread of the significant relationships seems to be a function of "built-in specialness" for each of the significant birth-order socio-psychological perspectives: oldest, only, and—in contrast to findings of most other vocational studies—youngest of five or more. The eldest enjoyed specialness by being first and by perhaps creating an expectancy of recognized achievement. The only child had the special world of one who never had a pacesetter or who was never dethroned. The youngest of five or more was "the baby" and had many older siblings from whom to gain a sense of specialness. Perhaps the youngest in a family of five or more tends to behave somewhat like an achievement-oriented firstborn because, with that many other siblings, one in this position tends to form strong expectations of self and, as Mosak and Dreikurs (1973) suggest, tries to overtake the older siblings. Subsequently, dentistry may be selected because it is one of the occupations which provides an opportunity for experiencing the specialness of prestige and achievement. That dentistry was a profession held in high regard is supported by an extensive opinion survey (National Opinion Research Center, 1947) completed during the era in which many of the dentists were making vocational choices. (For this sample, approximate mean year of entry into preparation for dentistry was 1949.) This opinion survey ranked dentists as 17th of 88 in terms of occupational prestige. Thus there appears to be a parallel between an identity of specialness within the family group and in the group of world-of-work occupations, therefore lending support to the previously cited studies and, at the same time, providing additional findings.

Possibly further research can more accurately define the "specialness" characteristics of both birth order and the occupations involving prestige and achievement. Moreover, the specialness factor could be investigated for various occupations from the different point of view of socio-psychological specialness. For instance, the middle-born boy among girls enjoys a special place, as does the youngest born male who has younger sisters.

No support in this investigation was given to Sutton-Smith, Roberts, and Rosenberg's (1964) contention that in two-child families of two males, the second-born would be more likely to move toward an occupation such as dentistry. The rationale was that the second-born would be more interested in more "masculine," direct, and physical modalities of control, as exemplified, among others, by an occupation such as dentistry, whereas, the firstborn male in this same-sex family would be inclined to lean toward more indirect and symbolic modalities of control This is in view of the assumption that a tendency exists for the occurrence of opposite-sex effect with same-sex siblings. However, the possibility may exist that dentistry does appeal to those of any birth-order position who have learned to value "masculine" modalities of control as a function of competitive sibling interaction. Thus, a relevant factor of predictability may be the sex of one's (very influential) closest sibling, regardless of whether younger or older. For example, Rosenberg and Sutton-Smith (1964) found that in two-child families, boys with brothers had higher masculinity scores than boys with sisters. Consequently, this masculinity-compensation effect may in part explain the present findings that dentists had significantly more brothers as closest siblings than sisters. Additional research might investigate the relationship between chronological closeness and psychological closeness. Furthermore, the relationship could be investigated between siblings and the prestige factor of later occupational choice.

The birth-order data elicited from the respondents seem to be so concrete and time-tested in nature that this information appears unlikely to have been influenced by the biases of reflection, thus increasing the possibility that the variable of birth order, both ordinal and socio-psychological, is related to later occupational choice of dentistry.

In summary, relationships seem to exist between the family-group variable of birth order and the vocational-group variable of choices in the world of work. Additional findings were related to the psychological perspectives of family size, socio-psychological birth order, closest sibling, and changing birth-rate trends. A possible unifying theme was discussed which relates this study to other investigations of vocational choice.

REFERENCES

Bayer, A. Birth order and college attendance. Journal of Marriage and the Family, 1966, 28, 480–484.

Cobb, S., & French, J., Jr. Birth order among medical students. Journal of the American Medical Association, 1966, 195, 312–313.

Forer, L. The birth order factor. New York: David McKay, 1976.

Herrell, J. Birth order and the military: a review from an Adlerian perspective. Journal of Individual Psychology, 1972, 28, 38–44.

Kohn, M., & Schooler, C. Class, occupation and orientation. American Sociological Review, 1969, 34, 659–678.

Mosak, H., & Dreikurs, R. Adlerian psychotherapy. In R. Corsini (Ed.), Current Psychotherapies. Itasca, IL: F. E. Peacock, 1973, pp. 35–83.

National Opinion Research Center. Opinion News, 1947, 9, September 1. Price, J., & Hare, E. Birth order studies: some sources of bias. British Journal of Psychiatry, 1969, 115, 633–646.

Roe, A. The making of a scientist. New York: Dodd, Mead, 1953.

Rosenberg, B., & Sutton-Smith, B. Ordinal position and sex role identification. Genetic Psychology Monograph, 1964, 70, 297–328.

Schooler, C. Birth order effects: not here, not now! Psychological Bulletin, 1972, 78, 161–175.

Shaver, P., French, J., & Cobb, S. Birth order of medical students and the occupational ambitions of their parents. International Journal of Psychology, 1970, 5, 197–207.

Shulman, B. Contributions to Individual Psychology. Chicago, IL: Alfred Adler Institute, 1973.

Sutton-Smith, B., Roberts, J., & Rosenberg, B. Sibling association and role involvement. Merrill-Palmer Quarterly, 1964, 10, 25–28.

Sutton-Smith, B., & Rosenberg, B. The sibling. New York: Holt, Rinehart & Winston, 1970.

U.S. Department of Health, Education And Welfare. Fertility tables for birth cohorts of American women, Vital Statistics-Special Reports: I, 50. Washington, D.C.: Author, 1960a.

U.S. Department of health, education and welfare. Vital statistics of the United States: Natality: I. Washington, D.C.: Public Health Services, 1960b.
Very, P., & Prull, R. Birth order, personality development, and choice of law as a profession. Journal of Genetic Psychology, 1970, 166, 209–221.
Very, P., & Zannini, J. Relation between birth order and being a beautician. Journal of Applied Psychology, 1969, 53, 149–151.
Zweigenhoft, R. Birth order, approval-seeking and membership in Congress. Journal of Individual Psychology, 1975, 30, 205–210.

IV

Parental Behavior

22

PERSONAL ADJUSTMENT VARIABLES IN EARLY RECOLLECTIONS AND RECALLED PARENTAL STRICTNESS-PERMISSIVENESS

Warren R. Rule

Abstract

The earliest recollection along with ratings of remembered strictness-permissiveness was obtained from 118 university students. Three raters rated each early recollection on nine scales of variables related to personal adjustment. The two scales measuring behavior of self dimensions were significant as was the scale of internal frame of reference of self-confidence. Discussion was given to possibilities for further study.

Parental strictness-permissiveness has been a dimension of interest from early times to the present. In various ways, its importance has been reflected upon by most people at one time or another. From a professional perspective, researchers have attempted to study this variable

This chapter, "Personal Adjustment Variables in Early Recollections and Recalled Parental Strictness-Permissiveness," from Warren R. Rule, *Imagination, Cognition and Personality* 11(2), pp. 143–148.

using a variety of methods, ranging from observation of family dynamics on to eliciting assessments and memories of the past. Sometimes early memories have been focused for the subjects; for instance, Bruhn used directed first early memories of being punished as predictors of control stance [1]. Using memories more globally, Chandler and Willingham employed a 175-item scale of perceptions of early childhood family influence and used factor analysis to assess relationships with established lifestyles [2].

Theory, especially that of Alfred Adler [3], item scale, and research seem to indicate that the content of recalled early memory is related to the present lifestyle of the individual [4, 5]. The present study sought to investigate the relationship between personal adjustment variables in early recollections (ERs), as rated by independent raters, and self ratings of recalled parental strictness-permissiveness. The hypotheses were that each of the positive dimensions of the personal adjustment ER ratings would be related to permissiveness on the self ratings of parental strictness-permissiveness.

METHOD

Subjects

The subjects in the sample were 118 college students from a university in the middle Atlantic region. They were enrolled in sections of a required sophomore-junior level course in a school of community affairs; the variability in socio-economic background and age was considerably greater than would usually be expected in university undergraduate courses. Approximately one half were male, one half female.

Procedure

Survey. The survey requested the subject to write out a description of one's earliest recollection. Emphasis was given in the instructions to: be as specific as possible; not include a "report" (a memory of an incident that happened many times); include a memory that one is not absolutely sure occurred or regardless of how insignificant it may seen; only describe one that happened before age eight; include feelings, even mixed ones; include the names of other people there; describe the most vivid part; include what happened before and afterward along with accompanying feelings; attempt a guess at one's purpose of behavior; and state the approximate age of occurrence. For further illustration of these specifics, refer to Rule [6].

The subjects were requested to circle the number (1 = extremely strict, 7 = extremely permissive) which best reflected the childhood memory of the degree of strictness-permissiveness for each parent. In order to avoid possibly biasing the subjects' answers by the sequence of requested information (e.g., ER descriptions biasing the S-R ratings), the sequence of presentation in the survey was reversed in one half of the sample.

ER VARIABLES AND RATINGS

Each of the nine ER variables (see below) was presented to the three raters as a 1–7 Likert Scale. Each rater was asked to circle the most appropriate number ranging from "1" (no, none) to "4" (both, cannot say) on to "7" (very strong). The nine variables were selected by the investigator as among those personal characteristics which seem to be valued as measures of healthy personal adjustment in at least several of the major counseling theories (Adlerian, Person-Centered, Rational-Emotive, Behavioral, and Gestalt). The scales distinguished between the internal frame of reference of the subject (6 scales) and the behavior of the subject (2 scales) or the behavior of others (1 scale); this delineation appears to be important in ER ratings [7]. The 1–9 scales and accompanying rater definitions are as follows:

A. Internal frame of reference of subject: Use of logic or reason.

B. Internal frame of reference of subject: "Should" expectations of self, others, or life. (Note: This is an internal "rigid" message on what to do, think, or feel; expressed another way, it is an imperative, a demandingness, a "must," an "ought to," a "have to.")

C. Internal frame of reference of subject: Self-confidence vs. inferiority.

D. Internal frame of reference of subject: Awareness of feelings—self or others.

E. Internal frame of reference of subject: Pleasantness outcome.

F. Internal frame of reference of subject: Level of curiosity (eagerness or openness to learning).

G. Behavior of subject: Active vs. passive (Active = initiating, carrying out, participating with others; Passive = merely responds, remained where subject was, others determined outcome, follower).

TABLE 22.1 Rater Reliability

ER Scale	Rater Item-to-Total (Correlation of rater response to mean of raters) Rater 1	Rater 2	Rater 3
A (Logic)	.59	.56	.33
B ("Should' Expectations)	.82	.86	.78
C (Self-Confidence)	.79	.82	.88
D (Awareness of Feelings)	.77	.83	.83
E (Pleasantness Outcome)	.89	.91	.93
F (Level of Curiosity)	.86	.70	.84
G (Active-Passive Behavior)	.81	.82	.84
H (Self Responsible Behavior)	.75	.83	.86
I (Treated Well by Others)	.85	.87	.91

H. Behavior of subject: Responsibility for self vs. dependency.

I. Behavior of others: Treating well vs. mistreating (positive/negative response from others).

Each of the three raters had received training in the Adlerian approach to ERs. The inter-rater tenability, expressed by item-to-total correlations, is displayed in Table 22.1. As can be noted, all are quite large, except for Scale A.

RESULTS

Pearson correlation coefficients were calculated for each of the mean ER ratings and self ratings of parental strictness-permissiveness for mother, father, and total. The results are presented in Table 22.2.

As noted in Table 22.2, only one (Scale C) of the six "Internal frame of reference" scales was significantly related to parental strictness-permissiveness. Both (G + H) of the "Behavior of self" scales were significant, whereas the only "Behavior of others" (Scale 1) was not.

DISCUSSION

In regard to the ER internal frame of reference of the subjects, the results indicated that the more self-confident the individual, the more likely one is to judge the overall childhood rearing, especially from the mother, as permissive. Possibly this internal dimension (self-confidence), along with its correlate of parental permissiveness, somehow enables the individual to give oneself the permission to behave in a self-satisfying manner. Along this vein, and not surprisingly, both of the significant "behavior of self" scales (active and self responsible) were related to this "courage to be."

TABLE 22.2 ERS and Parental Strictness-Permissiveness

	ERM Scales	Mother	Father	Total
A	(Logic)	.126	.022	.096
B	("Should" Expectations)	.053	.101	.101
C	(Self-Confidence)	.221*	.128	.229*
D	(Awareness of Feelings)	–.165	.096	–.070
E	(Pleasantness Outcome)	.006	–.079	–.043
F	(Level of Curiosity)	.126	.100	.148
G	(Active-Passive Behavior)	.263**	.199*	.323**
H	(Self Responsible Behavior)	.193**	.119	.208*
1	(Treated Well by Others)	–.015	–.026	–.023

*p < .05
**p < .01

Gender did not appear to be a significant variable. Chi-square tests were calculated for strictness-permissiveness by mother (p = .61), father (p = .59), and total (p = .72).

Several of the scales may warrant further investigation. For instance, the lack of relationship between others treating well vs. mistreating and strictness-permissiveness seems noteworthy. A research guess might be that strictness would be related to expecting mistreatment. However, further investigation might clarify what role the issue of "fairness" plays in one's reflections on parental strategies; possibly, if the strictness is viewed as fair by the individual, its impact would not contribute to a broadened expectation of mistreatment from others. Another scale, awareness of feelings of self/others, approached significance (p = .07) as a negative correlation, i.e., the more permissive the mother, the less awareness of feelings of self/others. Thus, further research may want to explore developed intra/interpersonal sensitivities related to strictness issues. Possibly in these areas, the use of directed memories [1] might facilitate investigation. The relationship of these previously discussed variables and the dimensions of recall stability and mental states [8] would also seem to be worthy of further study.

In regard to validity and generalizability of the study, a few points are in order. The validity of this method of ER interpretation is, as noted previously, based on the Adlerian perspective. This is perhaps the major approach that focuses on the manifest content of ERs and would seem to have limited generalizability to an ER perspective, such as Freud's, which views ERs essentially as screen memories which cover up infantile sexual conflicts, murderous fantasies, or trauma. Moreover, although the sample of university students was probably older than the norm for university students, caution must be exercised in generalizing beyond this relatively homogeneous sample. Quite possibly, interesting results, as well as more balanced parental strictness-permissiveness ratings, would be obtained from a replication of this study with a sample of much older individuals, particularly parents, who have presumably "mellowed" in their memories of parental strictness-permissiveness or who have been perhaps humbled by the task of struggling to be parents themselves.

REFERENCES

1. A. R. Bruhn, Earliest Memories of Being Punished as Predictors of Control Stance, Unpublished doctoral dissertation, Duke University, Durham, North Carolina, 1976.
2. C. K. Chandler and W. R. Willingham. The Relationship between Perceived Early Childhood Family Influence and the Established Life-Style, Individual Psychology: Journal of Adlerian Theory, Research & Practice, 42:3, pp. 388–394, 1986.
3. H. L. Ansbacher and R. W. Ansbacher, The Individual Psychology of Alfred Adler, Harper, New York, 1956.
4. N. V. Adcock and M. W. Ross, Early Memories, Early Experiences and Personality, Social Behavior & Personality, 11:1, pp. 95–100, 1983.
5. B. H. Shulman and H. H. Mosak, Manual for Lifestyle Assessment, Accelerated Development Press, Muncie, Indiana, 1968.
6. W. R. Rule, Lifestyle Counseling for Adjustment to Disability, Aspen Systems, Rockville, Maryland, 1984.
7. K. Altman and W. R. Rule, The Relationship between Social Interest Dimensions in Early Recollections and Selected Counselor Variables, Journal of Individual Psychology, 36, pp. 227–234, 1980.
8. P. M. Lewinsohn and M. Rosenbaum, Recall of Parental Behavior by Acute Depressives, Remitted Depressives, and Nondepressives, Journal of Personality and Social Psychology, 52:3, pp. 611–619, 1987.

23

BIRTH ORDER AND SEX AS RELATED TO MEMORY OF PARENTAL STRICTNESS-PERMISSIVENESS

Warren R. Rule

Summary: The birth order along with ratings of remembered parental strictness-permissiveness were obtained from 116 university students. For the total sample, firstborns regarded both parents as significantly more strict than laterborns, and first-born women rated their fathers as significantly more strict than laterborn women. Discussion was given to previous investigations that were both consistent and inconsistent with these results.

The relationship between birth order and childhood experiences has been a subject of continuing interest. Some research has focused on family constellation variables, e.g., birth order, sibling ordinal position, socio-psychological birth order that relate to child-parent interaction patterns, particularly parental authority or strictness-permissiveness. For example, Shaller (1972) noted that 10-, 12-, and 14-yr.-old firstborns

This chapter, "Birth Order and Sex as Related to Memory of Parental Strictness-Permissiveness," from Rule, W.R., *Psychological Reports*, 1991, 68, 908–910.

indicated that they were subjected to more parental control than laterborns at all three ages. Corsello (1973) found that firstborn boys showed a perception of greater parental authority than second- or third-born boys. Interviews of parents in a study by Stout (1960) showed that parents were more directive with firstborns than with laterborns. With regard to acceptance of parental authority, Smith (1971) found that firstborn male adolescents accepted parental authority more fully than laterborn adolescents. Yet, findings by Bartelt (1972) indicated their firstborn adolescents did not perceive discipline as more strict than did second-borns and that adolescents were disciplined by the parent of the same sex. Caution must be exercised, however, in comparing the results of studies on family permissiveness. Possibly influential variables, such as family size, are difficult to control. Not surprisingly, differing research methods can also be influential. Thus, studies that replicate research methodology, such as this one, can be illuminating.

Using a homogeneous sample of 282 male dentists, Rule and Comer (1982) found no significant differences for birth order and memory of parental strictness-permissiveness, as measured on a Likert rating scale. In the present study, the same rating scale was used with a different sample which was also homogeneous, to replicate the prior work. The hypotheses were that firstborns, for total sample and for each sex, would rate their parents as having been more strict than the laterborns.

METHOD

The subjects were 116 college students from a public middle Atlantic university. The members of the sample were enrolled in a sophomore-junior level course in a school of community affairs. By sex they were approximately equally divided (45 men, 52 women, 19 not responding).

The subjects were requested to circle a number from 1 to 7 (1 extremely strict, 7 extremely permissive) that best reflected their childhood memory of the strictness-permissiveness of each parent. Information was requested on number of childhood siblings, the siblings' sex and age differences from the subject, and any special circumstances which could influence the birth-order assessments, such as age of a sibling who died or the existence of step-siblings.

RESULTS

t tests were calculated for first- and laterborns on their strictness-permissiveness ratings of mother, father, and total. Ratings for neither mother nor father were significant; however, for the total, the first-borns ($n = 47$, $M = 3.7$, $SD = .91$) regarded both parents as significantly more strict than the laterborns ($n = 69$, $M = 4.1$, $SD = 1.1$; $t = 2.13$, $p < .05$).

No significant differences in ratings were found between first- and later-born men. Yet, firstborn women ($n = 21$, $M = 3.2$, $SD = 1.6$) rated their fathers as significantly more strict than laterborn women ($n = 29$, $M = 4.4$, $SD = 1.4$, $t = 2.77$, $p < .01$). The difference between ratings for mother for the firstborns ($n = 21$, $M = 4.0$, $SD = 1.3$) and the later-borns ($n = 30$, $M = 3.9$, $SD = 1.2$) was virtually neglible.

DISCUSSION

The findings were generally consistent with much of the previous research in that the firstborns tended to recall greater strictness. These results, however, were not consistent with the previously noted study by Rule and Corner (1982) who gave the same survey to dentists for whom no significant differences were found. Possibly the greater homogeneity of the sample of dentists was a factor. Perhaps the presumably older age of the dentists influenced their ratings, i.e., "mellowed" their memories; also, probably more dentists than students were parents. Some support for this point is a conclusion of Robins (1985) that recall of childhood environment may be reasonably valid, but, as Masland (1987) recommended, more research is needed on what differentiates between appropriate disciplinary behaviors and those perceived as maltreatment.

That only firstborn women regarded their fathers as significantly more strict than laterborn women is somewhat intriguing. Apparently the remembered impact was distinctly different for each parent, i.e., as noted previously, the ratings for mother between first- versus laterborn women were almost identical. For a psychiatric population, Snyder, Pitts, Goodpaster, and Gustin (1984) concluded that the father was perceived as more dominant than the mother, and Benjaminsen, Jorgensen, Kragh, and Pedersen (1984) found for women that the experience of negative parental rearing factors was associated with pathological personality features whereas, in the present study, there were no significant effects for men. From a parental perspective and somewhat inconsistent with the present findings, Biber (1974) concluded that fathers maintained the same expectations for a second child as for a first child.

Possibly a fruitful direction for research lies in examining perceived appropriateness of parental strictness-permissiveness. Perhaps studies could be conducted of such issues as long-term developmental changes between first- and laterborn men and women in how each recalls parental strictness-permissiveness.

REFERENCES

Bartelt, P. W. (1972) Birth order of siblings and differences in orientation toward parents. Dissertation Abstracts International, 33, 4556–A.

Benjaminsen, S., Jorgensen, J., Kragh, H. L., & Pedersen, L. L. (1984) Memories of parental rearing practices and personality features. Acta Psychiatrica Scandinavica, 69, 426–434.

Biser, D. C. (1974) Parental attitudes and expectations towards first and second children. Unpublished doctoral dissertation, University of North Carolina, Chapel Hill.

Corsello, P. (1973) Birth order and children's perceptions of love, authority, and personality adjustment. Dissertation Abstracts International, 34, 3132–A.

Masland, D. D. (1987) An investigation of the relationship between reported parental discipline behaviors and personal, familial, demographic, social, and recalled childhood discipline experiences. Dissertation Abstracts International, 48(2–A), 343.

Robins, L. N. (1985) Early home environment and retrospective recall: a test for concordance between siblings with and without psychiatric disorders. American Journal of Orthopsychiatry, 55, 27–41.

Rule, W. R., & Comer, A. T. (1982) Childhood memory of parental authority as related to family constellation variables. Psychological Reports, 50, 1175–1178.

Shaller, J. (1972) Ordinal position and parental control. Göteborg Psychological Reports, 2, 1–7.

Smith, T. E. (1971) Birth order, sibship size, and social class as antecedents of adolescent acceptance of parent's authority. Social Forces, 50, 223–232.

Snyder, S., Pitts, W. M., Goodpaster, W. A., & Gustin, Q. L. (1984) Family structure as recalled by borderline patients. Psychopathology, 17, 90–97.

Stout, A. M. (1960) Parent behavior toward children of differing ordinal position and sibling status. Unpublished Ph.D. dissertation, University of California, Berkeley.

24

CHILDHOOD MEMORY OF PARENTAL AUTHORITY AS RELATED TO FAMILY CONSTELLATION VARIABLES

Warren R. Rule and Ann T. Comer

Summary: Several investigations of family constellation variables and parental authority have shown that firstborns demonstrate higher perception of parental authority than do later borns. This study approached early childhood perceptions from a different perspective, long-term memory. Also, an attempt was made to equalize several variables that might influence research on birth-order research and parental authority. A sample of 282 dentists was interviewed regarding childhood perceptions of parental strictness-permissiveness and family constellation variables. No relationships were found for parental strictness-permissiveness and family constellation variables. The implications of the lack of relationships were discussed.

This chapter, "Childhood Memory of Parental Authority as Related to Family Constellation Variables," from Rule, W.R. & Comer, A.T., *Psychological Reports*, 1982, 50, 1175–1178.

The relationship between family constellation and childhood development has been a subject of continuing interest. Some research has focused on family constellation variables, e.g., sibling ordinal position, socio-psychological birth order, family size, that relate to child-parent interaction patterns. One of the child-parent dimensions which has received some attention is parental authority. A number of investigators have found that firstborn children are overrepresented in factors related to parental authority. For example, Corsello (1973) found that firstborn boys demonstrated a higher perception of parental authority than second- or third-born boys. An investigation by Shaller (1972) noted that 10-, 12-, and 14-yr.-old firstborns indicated they were subjected to more parental control than later borns at all three age levels. Forer (1976) states that firstborns receive the strictest discipline. Interviews of parents in a study by Stout (1960) showed that parents were more directive with firstborns than with later borns. In regard to acceptance of parental authority, Smith (1971) found that firstborn male adolescents accepted parental authority more fully than later-born adolescents.

In the investigation of this developmental influence on firstborns, the primary source of information has been the reports of children and parents. However, a major variable related to the nature of children's reports needs to be considered, the perceptual biasing effects of firstborns' characteristics.

Regarding this biasing in investigating children's perceptions of parental authority, the assessments by firstborns may be somewhat biased by those uniquely firstborn characteristics that filter into the perceptual processes. These firstborn characteristics may not necessarily be directly related to perceptions of parental authority, yet could indirectly influence the perceptions and therefore the assessments and responses regarding parental authority in particular or authority in general. For instance, Sutton-Smith and Rosenberg (1970), in a review of much of the literature, conclude that in general firstborns are more achieving and affiliative than persons in other birth-order positions. Both characteristics might influence how parental authority is perceived, i.e., perhaps increased valuing of achievement and affiliation would correspondingly increase the regard one has for a socially respected place of achievement which, in this case, is represented by parental authority. Consequently, perhaps firstborns' overrepresentation in valuing parental authority might be a function of characteristics more influential than ordinal position in the family.

The possibility has been discussed (Alexander, 1967; Sutton-Smith & Rosenberg, 1970) that the relationships of achievement and affiliation shift with increasing age. That is to say, firstborns may shift from sensitivity to the relationship to parents (affiliation) to achievement. With young children, achievement might be the means to the end (affiliation), whereas with the passage of time affiliation might become the means to the end (achievement).

The question can be raised as to whether firstborns would still have higher perceptions of parental authority than persons in other birth-order positions, if, in the selection of respondents for the investigation, the following variables were taken into consideration: (1) the characteristics of achievement and affiliation and (2) the passage of time. Accordingly, in this investigation a sample was selected of homogeneous adults, i.e., mature in the developmental sense of the passage of time, who were recognized professionals (i.e., achievement oriented) and who were attending a state convention (i.e., a somewhat affiliated experience). Consequently the entire sample, both firstborns and later borns, would have in common at adulthood these characteristics that otherwise are overly apparent among firstborns.

METHOD

The 282 dentists were selected for interviews on a nonsystematic basis at a state dental convention. Interviews were felt to be better than the usual survey method because they increase accuracy of responses and are not subject to the self-selection bias of the cooperating respondents which is reflected in the modest return rate of most surveys. An additional six dentists refused to be interviewed, which yielded a 97.9% response rate. All of the subjects were males and comprised approximately one-half of those attending the convention.

The desired information focused on a major component of parental authority, the dimension of parental strictness-permissiveness. The respondents individually were asked identifying information and were requested to indicate the number from 1 to 7 (1 = extremely strict; 7 = extremely permissive) that best reflected the childhood memory of the degree of strictness-permissiveness for each parent. This method, chosen for its efficiency and ease of information-gathering, enabled the interviewee to look at the rating scale and to select the appropriate number. Further information included childhood siblings, the siblings' age differences from the respondent, and any special circumstances which could influence family-constellation calculations such as age of a sibling who died or the existence of step-siblings.

In analyzing the family constellation data, two procedures were used. In the first analysis, the traditional categories of birth order were used; age difference and socio-psychological birth order were not considered. For instance, with this method if a subject in a two-child family had a sibling as much as 15 yr. younger, he was still regarded as a firstborn, whereas his socio-psychological perspective would be that of a functional only child. The second method of analysis was based on a socio-psychological perspective. Accordingly, the second approach was to compare "true" oldest, middle, and youngest borns by excluding those of a different phenomenological perspective. All socio-psychological "onlies" were removed from the oldest, middle, and youngest categories, i.e., those not having a sibling within 6 years. The 6-yr. figure was chosen because at approximately the age of six the individual has become solidly enmeshed in a school setting, i.e., the child has begun to broaden the range of influences received from his first social group, the family, to those of the next social group, the school. Altogether 28 firstborns and 31 later borns were removed in this second method of analysis.

RESULTS AND DISCUSSION

For the firstborns (oldest borns and only borns) and parental strictness-permissiveness, the findings did not yield a significant relationship for either parent, using chi-squared as a test for independence. Thus, the relationship between firstborns and higher perception of parental authority, found in a number of other studies, was not supported (as measured by strictness-permissiveness) when an attempt was made to equalize the previously discussed factors. Furthermore, no relationships were found between perceptions of strictness-permissiveness and any of the birth order positions.

Several investigations (Nye, 1972; Nuttall & Nuttall, 1971) have shown that as family size increases, the degree of punishment or lack of acceptance increases. The present findings indicated no relationship between the related variables of parental strictness-permissiveness and family size.

In using memory as an information-gathering device, contrasting positions exist. One position (Gardner, 1964) states that asking questions about the past is not precise and, consequently, is somewhat unreliable as an approach. A contrasting position (Ansbacher & Ansbacher, 1956) contends that memory is selective, i.e., an individual remembers those events, impressions, feelings from the early past that are significant to the present. The approach of this investigation leaned toward the latter position. From this perspective, a further advantage in relying on adult memory is that presumably the subject's adolescent years and adult years would have developmentally provided a broad fund of comparisons (e.g., other parents and children, one's own children, etc.) which would sharpen the rating ability of the respondent. Consequently, whatever biases filtered into the ratings from this perspective would reflect a more mature developmental outlook than the influence of the biases (e.g., firstborn) which characterize a somewhat vulnerable child, who has a limited fund of comparisons from which to draw. Also, the subjects' ages indicate that a representative historical range of early childhoods existed (M = 43 yr., SD = 12.0).

An issue might be raised regarding the respondents' ability to discriminate degrees of strictness-permissiveness. In other words, the point can be raised as to whether the terms "extremely strict" and "extremely permissive" were uniformally meaningful among the respondents so that the subjects could collectively make some sort of relative assessment. Yet the distribution of the ratings tends to be encouraging in this regard: for father, M = 3.3, SD = 1.56; for mother, M = 3.4, SD = 1.28. Furthermore, a related finding tends to support the possibility that the subjects were able to make personalized discriminations that reflected differences within the sample: specialists who rated their fathers as more strict than their mothers did so with greater differences ($p < .001$) than did general practitioners ($\chi^2 = 16.4$, $df = 3$).

The lack of relationships between parental strictness-permissiveness and ordinal birth order, socio-psychological birth order, and family-size may be regarded as noteworthy. In contrast to a number of other studies which suggest overrepresentativeness of firstborns in the higher perception of parental authority, this investigation, which utilized a different perspective, found no relationships among these variables. In this study an attempt was made to equalize among the subjects the variables of achievement and affiliation and the passage of time. The lack of relationships suggests an increased likelihood of factors more influential than birth order having a bearing on the long-term perception of parental authority.

REFERENCES

Alexander, C. N. Ordinal position and sociometric status. Sociometry, 1967, 29, 41–51.

Ansbacher, H., & Ansbacher, R. (Eds.) The Individual Psychology of Alfred Adler. New York: Basic Books, 1956.

Corsello, P. Birth order and children's perceptions of love, authority, and personality adjustment. Dissertation Abstracts International, 1973, 34, 3132-A.

Forer, L. The birth order factor. New York: David McKay, 1976.
Gardner, D. Development in early childhood. (2nd ed.) New York: Harper & Row, 1964.
Nuttall, E. U., & Nutall, R. L. The effect of size of family on parent-child relationships. Proceedings of the Annual Convention of the American Psycbological Association, 1971, 6(Pt. 1), 267–268.
Nye, F. I., Carlson, J., & Garrett, G. Family size, interaction, affect, and stress. Journal of Marriage and the Family, 1972, 32, 216–226.
Shaller, J. Ordinal position and parental control. Göteborg Psychological Reports, 1972, 2(17), 1–7.
Smith, T. E. Birth order, sibship size, and social class as antecedents of adolescents' acceptance of parents' authority. Social Forces, 1971, 50, 223–232.
Stout, A. M. Parental behavior toward children of differing ordinal position and sibling status. Unpublished Ph.D. dissertation, University of California, Berkeley, 1960.
Sutton-Smith, B., & Rosenberg, B. G. The sibling. New York: Holt, Rinehart & Winston, 1970.

25

PARENTAL STRICTNESS-PERMISSIVENESS AND LONG-TERM MEMORY

Warren R. Rule and Ann T. Comer

From early in the twentieth century to the past decade, child-rearing patterns in general became more permissive (1–3) as indicated by observations, descriptive writings, child-rearing guides, shifting psychological positions, and historical variables. This study sought evidence of the pattern from the perspective of long-term memory of males from one occupation (dentistry), who had about the same educational level, and were engaged in the same voluntary activity (attending a state dental convention) at the time of sampling. A total of 282 dentists were interviewed at random. Also, six dentists refused to be interviewed. The response rate was 97.9%. This sample comprised approximately one-half of the dentists attending the convention. The respondents individually were asked for identifying information and were requested to indicate a number from 1 to 7 (1 = extremely strict,

This chapter, "Parental Strictness-Permissiveness and Long-Term Memory," from Rule, W.R. & Comer, A.T., *Perceptual and Motor Skills*, 1981, 52, 574.

7 = extremely permissive) which best reflected the childhood memory of the degree of strictness-permissiveness for each parent.

In regard to the results, the association of perceptions of strictness-permissiveness for mother and father was significant. A test for independence yielded χ^2 = of 260.62 ($p < .001$, df = 36). According to the long-term memory of these respondents, their parents took a relatively consistent position on strictness-permissiveness.

The relationship between ages of respondents and parental strictness-permissiveness supports the previously noted pattern of increasing permissiveness during the first half of the twentieth century. The strictness-permissiveness ratings were related for both mother ($p < .001$) and father ($p < .05$) to age of respondent ($\chi^2 = 65.7$, df = 30; $\chi^2 = 48.0$, df = 30). This direction may reflect change over the years as younger respondents viewed their parents as more permissive than older respondents remembered theirs.

If permissiveness in child-rearing did in fact increase over the years, the remembered consistency between parents would be expected. The possibility seems unlikely that an increase in overall permissiveness would emerge if parents did not take a relatively consistent stance during each period. Subjects' ages indicate that a representative range of early childhoods existed throughout the desired time span (M = 43, SD = 12.0).

The use of memory as an information-gathering device may have provided a somewhat balanced perspective to the ratings. The subjects' adolescent years and adult years might have developmentally contributed a broad fund of comparisons, e.g., other parents and children, one's own children, etc., which would sharpen the rating ability of the respondents. It is possible that the aging process, as opposed to historical changes, may have somewhat influenced the ratings. Perhaps a longitudinal assessment would be helpful in this. In the context of the other indicators of historical change, the present findings tend to support, from the perspective of long-term memory, a shifting pattern of parental strictness to permissiveness.

REFERENCES

1. Beekman, D. The mechanical baby: a popular history of the theory and practice of child raising. Westport, CT: Lawrence Hill, 1977.
2. Cable, M. The little darlings: a history of child rearing in America. New York: Scribner's, 1975.
3. Lomax, E., Kagan, J., & Rosenkrantz, B. Science and patterns of child care. San Francisco, CA: W. H. Freeman, 1978.

V

Personal Characteristics

26

INTELLIGENCE AND EARLIEST MEMORY

Warren R. Rule and George R. Jarrell

Summary: The relationship between intelligence and memory has been investigated mostly from the perspective of relatively short-term memory. This study focused on the relationship between intelligence and the longest-term memory, the individual's reported earliest recollection. Age of earliest memory and three measures of intelligence were obtained from 66 university students. Significant relationships were found for two of the three measures of intelligence. Possible interpretations and related findings are discussed.

The relationship between intelligence and memory has been investigated from several perspectives. For example, Magaliff (1979) found a positive relationship between intelligence and recall exercises for children. An investigation by Parham (1977) indicated that both age and intelligence have a significant effect on recall for adults. Cohen and Sandberg (1980) concluded that traditionally mental age is an important variable in predicting individual differences in short-term memory

---

This chapter, "Intelligence and Earliest Memory," from Rule, W.R. & Jarell, G.R., *Perceptual and Motor Skills*, 1983, 56, 795–798.

and vice-versa. An investigation by Kundu (1963) yielded a high positive correlation between memory and abstract intelligence, yet no relationship between memory and concrete intelligence.

From somewhat different vantage points, however, Goetze (1981) found that the IQs of children were unrelated to the performance on both the questionnaire and free-report methods of interview following a simulated crime. Haywood and Heal (1968) concluded that investigators have usually been unable to find differences in long-term retention between retardates and non-retardates of comparable mental age. Also, Klausmeier and Feldhusen (1959) found that retention in arithmetic is the same among children of low, average, and high intelligence when the task corresponded to the children's achievement level.

Taken as a whole, the findings regarding the relationships between the broad areas of intelligence and memory do not appear to be entirely consistent. The bulk of the studies seem to focus on relatively short-term memory. The present investigation concentrated on the relationship between intelligence and the longest-term memory, the individual's earliest recollection.

Both variables, intelligence and memory, might be related, in varying degrees, to problem-solving. Intelligence, at least as measured in Western civilization, largely seems to be a function of problem-solving ability. Memory, particularly early memory, as viewed by Adler (Ansbacher & Ansbacher, 1956), is a function of selective usefulness.

> The usefulness function might be regarded as a form of problem-solving. For the individual, his early memories… represent his 'Story of My Life'; a story he repeats to himself to warn him or comfort him, to keep him concentrated on his goal, and to prepare him by means of past experiences, so that he will meet the future with an already tested style of action…. Most illuminating of all is the way the individual begins his story, the earliest incident he can recall. The first memory will show his fundamental view of life, his first satisfactory crystallization of his attitude. It offers us an opportunity to see at one glance what he has taken as the starting place for his development. (Ansbacher & Ansbacher, 1956, p. 351)

In view of these possibilities, the speculation may be made that more intelligent individuals would start problem-solving for their own life adjustment at an earlier age, and, correspondingly, report earlier symbols of this problem-solving process, i.e., earlier first memories.

Specifically, this study investigated the hypothesis that an inverse relationship would exist for measures of intelligence and age of reported first memory.

METHOD

The sample of 66 university students were enrolled in testing and meas-urement classes. Each was asked to describe the earliest childhood memory and to state the approximate age at which the incident occurred. Also, the individuals were instructed to use only specific incidents or happenings, not those that occurred over and over again (e.g., "I used to…"), and to report the earliest memory regardless of how insignificant it might seem.

Three varied measures of intelligence were obtained from each of the individuals: (1) IQ on the Otis-Lennon Mental Ability Test (Otis & Lennon, 1967), which relies heavily on verbal skills and is designed to assess scholastic aptitude; (2) IQ on the Revised Beta Examination (Kellogg & Morton, 1957), which is a nonverbal test; and (3) the "G" aptitude of the General Aptitude Test Battery (U.S. Department of Labor, 1970), which is designed to measure general learning abilities and is measured by the areas of three-dimensional space, vocabulary, and arithmetic reasoning.

RESULTS AND DISCUSSION

The Pearson correlation between reported age of earliest memory and Otis-Lennon IQ was significant at the .05 level ($r = -.29$). The correlation between the Revised Beta IQs and age of earliest memory was also significant ($p < .01$, $r = -.35$). However, the relationship between GATB "G" score and age of earliest memory was not statistically significant ($r = -.13$).

These values suggest that small to moderate inverse relationships seem to exist between age of reported earliest memory and quite discrepant messages of intelligence, i.e., one relying strongly on verbal skills and the other a nonverbal test. Perhaps the lack of statistical significance for the GATB may be a function of the narrowness of the three specific areas that comprise the "G" score (three-dimensional space, vocabulary, and arithmetic reason). Apparently verbal aptitude alone is not related to reported earliest memory; the correlation with the GATB "V" (verbal) aptitude was non-significant (–.08).

Several relationships were also investigated between reported earliest memory and personal characteristics that are less cognitive in nature than intelligence. The Edwards Personal Preference Schedule (1957) was administered to explore the role of personality factors in the reporting of first memory. Relationships were calculated for the two personality variables measured by this instrument that conceivably would seem to have a bearing on process of recalling an earliest memory. However, no significant correlations were found (Achievement = –.15; Intraception = .06).

A number of possibilities can be ventured to account for the significant relationships between reported age of first memory and the two measures of intelligence. Possibly, as discussed previously, there is some linkage of problem-solving ability between age of first memory and intelligence. Or, perhaps, as more intelligent individuals move through life, their well-developed intelligence and accompanying problem-solving abilities reduce the necessity for changing core beliefs formed in childhood; therefore, the earlier memories are more likely to remain as stable orientation points. The possibility also exists that the process of being asked to recall and identify a first memory was viewed as more of a challenge by the more intelligent individuals. Consequently, these individuals may have tried harder to find the earliest memory or have even exaggerated the earliness of it. From a research perspective, the actual age of occurrence of an earliest memory is exceedingly difficult to determine primarily due to the subjective nature of remembered experiences, i.e., many early memories were highly colored by personal interpretation or were completely individual experiences that did not involve others.

Considerable variability existed for this sample even though all were university students. The mean age of reported first memory was 3.7 yr. (SD = 1.58). For the measures of intelligence: Otis-Lennon M = 113.38 (SD = 11.3); Revised Beta M = 115.24 (SD = 8.59); GATB G -Aptitude M = 119.2 (SD = 13.4). Possibly stronger relationships would be found if a sample was selected from the general population. Also, the relationship between intelligence and earliest memory could be further explored using individual, rather than group, measures of intelligence.

REFERENCES

Ansbacher, H., & Ansbacher, R. (Eds.) The Individual Psychology of Alfred Adler. New York: Basic Books, 1956.

Cohen, R., & Sandberg, T. Relation between intelligence and short-term memory. Cognitive Psychology, 1977, 9, 534–554.

Edwards, A. Edwards Personal Preference Schedule manual. New York: Psychological Corp., 1959.

Goetze, H. The effect of age and method of interview on the accuracy and completeness of eyewitness accounts (Doctoral dissertation, Hofstra University). Dissertation Abstracts International, 1981, 42(1-B), 426–427.

Haywood, H., & Heal, L. Retention of learned visual associations as a function of IQ and learning levels. American Journal of Mental Deficiency, 1968, 72(6) 828–838.

Kellogg, C., & Morton, N. Revised Beta Examination manual. New York: Psychological Corp., 1957.

Klausmeier, H., & Feldhusen, J. Retention in arithmetic among children of low, average, and high intelligence at 117 months of age. Journal of Educational Psychology, 1959, 50, 88–92.

Kundu, R. An investigation into the relationship between intelligence and memory. Journal of Psychological Researches, Madras, 1963, 7, 32–36.

Magaliff, M. The effects of verbal and imaginal mediation on long-term memory (Doctoral dissertation, Hofstra University). Dissertation Abstracts International 1979, 40(4-A), 1981.

Otis, A., & Lennon, R. Otis-Lennon Mental Ability Test, manual for administration. New York: Harcourt, Brace & World, 1967.

Parham, J. Dual coding in memory as a function of age, sex, and intelligence. (Doctoral dissertation, University of Southern California). Dissertation Abstracts International, 1977, 37(11–B), 5817.

U.S. Department of Labor. General Aptitude Test Battery manual for administration and scoring. Washington, D.C.: United States Department of Labor, 1970.

27

BIRTH ORDER AND EARLIEST MEMORY

Warren R. Rule

Summary: The purpose of this study was to determine whether differences exist between firstborns and laterborns in their longest-term memory, the reported age of earliest recollection. No significant differences were found within the sample of 64 university graduate students.

Birth-order variables have been investigated from numerous perspectives, yet very little information exists on the relationship between birth order and long-term memory. In reviews of the literature in related areas, Sutton-Smith and Rosenberg (1970) and Borer (1976) concluded that there is very little reason to assume that differences in intelligence exist between the birth-order positions; however, they also concluded that firstborns as a group are more achievement-oriented, particularly in terms of advanced accomplishments. Regarding short-term memory, Perkins (1973) found no differences between firstborn and laterborn children on Feffer's Role-taking Task, which was signifi-

This chapter, "Birth Order and Earliest Memory," from Rule, W.R., *Perceptual and Motor Skills*, 1983, 56, 601–602.

cantly correlated with auditory memory. The purpose of this investigation was to determine if differences exist between firstborn and laterborn adults in their longest-term memory, the reported age of earliest recollection.

Sixty-four university graduate students were requested to indicate birth-order position, earliest memory, and age of earliest memory. Twenty-seven were firstborn; 37 were laterborn. No significant differences were found between reported age of earliest memory for the firstborns (M = 377, SD = 1.63) and the laterborns (M = 3.70, SD = 1.54).

Measures of two personality variables, Achievement and Intraception, were obtained from the Edwards Personal Preference Schedule (1959). This was an attempt to assess possible personal characteristics of birth order that could be related to the ability to recall an earliest memory. No significant differences were found for Achievement (firstborns: M = 15.37, SD = 4.01 versus laterborns: M = 15.73, SD = 4.83) or for Intraception (firstborns: M = 19.00, SD = 3.64 versus laterborns: M = 18.32, SD = 4.54).

These achievement results are inconsistent with the formerly discussed consensus of firstborn achievement via advanced accomplishments. The achievement results are also inconsistent with results of two investigations that showed significant differences between firstborns and laterborns on the Edwards Personal Preference Schedule: Sampson (1962), who sampled undergraduate college students, and Sampson and Hancock (1967), who sampled high school students. However, Wolkon and Levinger (1965), using the same instrument with a variety of samples not selected from educational institutions, reported no significant differences. Sampling differences in levels of achievement can be related to these inconsistencies or perhaps the ipsative scoring on the Edwards Personal Preference Schedule may have affected the results of the various samples differently. Moreover, the homogeneity of the high level of achievement in the present sample of graduate students might have had a bearing on the lack of difference between firstborns and laterborns in the achievement-task of recalling one's earliest memory and the age of occurrence.

REFERENCES

Edwards, A. Edwards Personal Preference Schedule Manual. New York: Psychological Corp., 1959.

Forer, L. The Birth order factor. New York: David McKay, 1976.

Perkins, C. A study of perceptual correlates to role-taking ability with fourth through sixth grade children (Doctoral dissertation, Oregon State University, 1973). Dissertation Abstracts International, 1973, 34, 1261B–1262B.

Sampson, E. Birth order, need achievement, and conformity. Journal of Abnormal and Social Psychology, 1962, 64, 155–159.

Sampson, E., & Hancock, F. An examination of the relationship between ordinal position, personality, and conformity. Journal of Personality and Social Psychology, 1967, 5, 398–407.

Sutton-Smith, B., & Rosenberg, B. The Sibling. New York: Holt, Rinehart & Winston, 1970.

Wolkon, G., & Levinger, G. Birth order and need for achievement. Psychological Reports, 1965, 16, 73–74.

28

EARLY RECOLLECTIONS AND EXPECTED LEISURE ACTIVITIES

Warren R. Rule and Michael D. Traver

Summary: The relationship between choices of leisure and individual life-style characteristics is of considerable interest. This study focused on an abbreviated measurement of social interest in individual early recollections as related to selected expectations of choices of leisure. Based on abbreviated social interest scores in early recollections, the two most extreme groups of 14 subjects (positive-active and negative-passive) were selected from an original sample of 400 college students. The expected choices of leisure were determined by responses to the Ego Recognition Future Scale and the Adventure Future Scale of the Leisure Activities Blank. Significant differences in expected choices of leisure were found between the two extreme groups of subjects for ego recognition but not for choices related to adventure.

Individuals interested in leisure activities are intrigued by relationships between choices of leisure and unique life-style characteristics.

This chapter, "Early Recollections and Expected Leisure Activities," from Rule, W.R. & Traver, M.D., *Psychological Reports*, 1982, 51, 295–301.

Practitioners are continually seeking swift and useful techniques to clarify those relationships. For example, there has been discussion on the use of early recollections in leisure counseling (Rule & Stewart, 1977). However, there is a dearth of empirical information on the relationship between choices for leisure and early recollections. This study investigated an abbreviated measurement of social interest in early recollections as related to choices for leisure on the specific dimensions of the Leisure Activities Blank.

There are vocational and educational correlations of early recollections (Holmes & Watson, 1965; Attarian, 1973; Manaster & Perryman, 1974). Early recollections have also been used to investigate personality (Chance, 1957; Lieberman, 1957; McCarter, Schiffman, & Tomkins, 1961; Elkin, 1974; Friedberg, 1975; Eckstein, 1976). Many of the investigators of early recollections based their assumptions on Alfred Adler's writing. Adler regarded early recollections as essentially reflections of a person's outlook on life; these dimly conscious reminders orient an individual as to what to expect from self, others, and life (Ansbacher & Ansbacher, 1956). Also, Adler, who originally coined the term "life style," believed that early recollections provide insight into an individual's life style or cognitive map. His belief was that there are no "chance" memories. From the thousands of experiences which an individual has in early childhood, only those are remembered which serve as current orientation points. The early recollections function as reminders of present expectations.

This study focused on an abbreviated measurement of two important Adlerian concepts, social interest and activity. Social interest may be broadly understood to mean, according to Adler (Ansbacher & Ansbacher, 1970, p. 34), "feeling with the whole... a striving for a form of community." Investigations have been conducted on the relationship between social interest and various individual characteristics: cooperation and altruism (Crandall & Reimanis, 1976), internal-external control (Hjelle, 1977), perception (Huber & Stiggins, 1970), intelligence (Stone & Ansbacher, 1965), and counselor variables (Altman & Rule, 1980). Activity is an additional important concept for life-style understanding. Activity may be defined as the individual's tendency to initiate as opposed to observing or being initiated upon. It is conceptually related to social interest, yet is distinct from it. This dimension has been investigated in early recollections (Levy & Grigg, 1962; Tolor & Fazzone, 1966) and has been related to social interest (McCarter, Schiffman, & Tomkins, 1961; Altman & Rule, 1980).

Adler believed (Ansbacher & Ansbacher, 1956) that knowledge of an individual's social interest and level of activity can have important predictive value for the practitioner. The purpose of this investigation was to determine if significant differences exist between individuals having contrasting levels of combined social interest and activity in their early recollections and expected choices of leisure activities related to ego recognition and adventure. The rationale for this is based on the future-orientation which is involved in both early recollections and expected choices for leisure. As noted previously, early recollections reflect generalized expectations, i.e., a future orientation, of self, others, and life. Expected leisure choices, a future orientation, might also be a function of one's generalized expectations. Moreover, both early recollections and leisure activities are a function of individual choice. Early recollections are chosen at a dimly conscious level as reminders of what to expect from self, others, and life; the selection of leisure activities is also based on the assumption (Neulinger, 1981) of freedom of choice. Thus, early recollections, as reflections of one's generalized expectations, would correspondingly appear to be related to an individual's expected choices of leisure activities.

In this study, an abbreviated measure of two key dimensions, social interest and activity, was obtained from the subjects' early recollections. This abbreviated measure, consisting of the total of self-rated pleasantness and rater-rated activity, has been significantly related to a broader nine-scale measure of social interest which included an activity scale (Traver, 1978). The contrasting extremes of these combined two ratings yielded the subjects for this investigation, referred to as the positive-active and the negative-passive groups.

In investigating the leisure dimension, the Leisure Activities Blank (McKechnie, 1975) was selected, primarily because this instrument provides scales related to expected future choices for leisure. The future-orientation of expected choices, as noted previously, corresponds to the future-orientation of early recollections. The responses to the two Future Scales of Ego Recognition and Adventure were analyzed. These particular scales were selected because they were regarded as having the closest leisure parallels to the variables represented in the positive-active and negative-passive dimensions. The manual of the Leisure Activities Blank (McKechnie, 1975, p. 33) describes the Ego Recognition Future Scale as a "cluster of activities that taps a youthful and typically masculine pattern of personality functioning: adventurous, outgoing, daring, and uninhibited. The high scorer is a show-off." On the Adventure Future Scale, persons having high scores indicate "high social presence, effective intellectual functioning, alert and energetic adventure, and irresponsible, perhaps occasionally reckless, action" (p. 30).

In this investigation, early recollections, as measured by the positive-active and negative-passive extremes of abbreviated social interest, and expected choices of leisure were both regarded as being reflections of broader life-style expectations of self, others, or life. This study investigated two hypotheses regarding these relationships: those subjects with positive-active early recollections would select more activities related to ego recognition and adventure than those with negative-passive early recollections.

METHOD

Subjects

The original sample of 400 male university undergraduate students, as part of another study, volunteered to complete the revised Early Recollections Questionnaire (Rule, 1972). From this sample, two groups of 14 subjects were selected for this analysis. The procedure for selection is given below.

Ratings and Instruments

The revised Early Recollections Questionnaire has a page of instructions and elicits six early recollections with supplemental information. Each of the original subjects was requested to rate on a scale of one to seven the pleasantness of each early recollection. Raters also judged the early recollections for activity on a seven-point scale; 1 = Pleasant (positive) on the first scale and active on the second scale. The raters' scores were combined with the subjects' self-ratings and comprised the abbreviated indicator of social interest. Subsequently, the two most extreme groups of 14 subjects were chosen from this sample to participate. These constituted the positive-active and the negative-passive groups of abbreviated social interest, terms which, as noted previously, denote the total scores of pleasantness (positive-negative) and activity (active-passive). Adler believed (Ansbacher & Ansbacher, 1956) that increasing significance, when interpreting the individual's life style, should be given to correspondingly earlier memories. A criterion of selection of the positive-active group then was that each subject have at least two of the first three early recollections judged as positive-active. Similarly, two of the first three memories of the negative-passive group were to be judged as negative-passive. All subjects were paid nominal fees for completing the questionnaire and participating.

Before rating the memories of the subjects, the three raters participated in a pilot study to determine if they could (1) differentiate between active and nonactive ones and (2) consistently agree on a rating scale of nine social interest variables in memories. The active-nonactive rating procedure was an adaptation of Levy's (1965) and Lord's (1971) methods. The rating scale of nine social interest variables, evaluations of perceptions of the environment and behavior, was developed by Altman (1973), who determined that all rater-reliability correlations were significant ($p = .001$). This scale has since been utilized by Quinn (1973) and Eckstein (1976).

The subjects in the pilot study were 20 graduate volunteers who supplied three memories in response to the Early Recollections Questionnaire. The raters all had master's degrees, had completed Adlerian coursework, and were exposed to 5.5 hr. of instruction. Spearman correlations between the raters on the active-passive variable were $p1,2 = .857$, $p1,3 = .800$, and $p2,3 = .738$; all were significant ($p = .001$). For the rating scale of social interest variables, all of the raters' pairings of the nine variables were also significant ($p = .001$); the median reliability coefficients for the nine variables ranged from .56 to .77.

After having established rating reliability, the raters evaluated the original subjects on the active-passive dimension and subsequently rated each of the two extreme groups of 14 subjects on the rating scale of social interest variables. After the ratings, as expected, subjects with positive-active early recollections were rated significantly higher on the social interest scale than the subjects with negative-passive memories ($t = 6.68, p < .001$).

Regarding the leisure scales, the Ego Recognition Future Scale provides 11 choices for leisure, e.g., acting, encounter groups, football. The Adventure Future Scale has 23 choices for leisure, e.g., backpacking, sailing, skindiving. Both have small significant correlations (McKechnie, 1975) with the Sociability Scale of the California Psychological Inventory (.50 and .27, respectively) and with the Social Introversion Scale of the Minnesota Multiphasic Personality Inventory (–.37 and –.35, respectively). McKechnie (1975) cites .83 as test-retest reliability for the Ego Recognition Future Scale and .81 for the Adventure Future Scale.

For each of the "future" responses of the Leisure Activities Blank, the self-administering instructions indicated that the respondent was to mark one of three numbers: 1 = you do not expect to do it in the future; 2 = you are uncertain or don't know; 3 = you do expect to do it sometime in the future. In this investigation, only the "3's" (you do expect to do it sometime in the future) were totaled for each of the two previously discussed scales. This scoring variation was implemented to maintain theoretical consistency with the goal-directed nature of early recollections. Two of the subjects with negative-passive memories completed the scales incorrectly.

RESULTS AND DISCUSSION

The first hypothesis stated that the subjects with positive-active early recollections would select more activities related to ego recognition than those with negative-passive early recollections. As noted in Table 28.1, a t-test indicated significant difference. The first hypothesis was therefore accepted.

The second hypothesis stated that the subjects with positive-active early recollections would select more activities related to adventure than those with negative-passive early recollections. A t test indicated no significant difference, a lack of support for the second hypothesis.

The significant relationship for the first hypothesis between abbreviated social interest content in memories and future choices for leisure related to ego recognition suggests that possibly positive-active subjects may have different general goals that influence their choices. Perhaps the positive-active expectation of self, others, and life, as reflected by memories, had a bearing on the choice of opportunities for leisure that would allow the subjects to "go with the flow" of the natural currents of their life styles. Since the population variances do not appear to be equal, Satterthwaite's approximation (Dixon & Massey, 1969) to the t statistic was calculated. Again, a significant difference was found ($t = 2.30$).

Several factors may account for the lack of difference for the second hypothesis between abbreviated social interest content and selected leisure choices related to adventure. Possibly the Adventure Future Scale contains too many items which overrepresented the "active" component of the abbreviated social interest dimension. An inspection of the Adventure Future Scale items indicated that 20 of the 23 activities can seemingly be accomplished independently, i.e., without the involvement, assistance, or recognition of others. Furthermore, the fact that the subjects were volunteers, relatively young, and achievement-oriented college students, may have been biasing factors in that many of the subjects may have viewed themselves, for whatever individual reasons, as daring fellows willing to try anything and expecting to savor life's adventures.

TABLE 28.1 Leisure Data

Leisure Activities Blank	Early Recollections	*N*	*M*	*SD*	*t*
Ego Recognition	Negative-passive	12	2.00	1.15	
	Positive-active	14	3.93	2.89	2.08*
Adventure	Negative-passive	12	12.42	4.99	
	Positive-active	14	13.57	7.52	.43

* $p < .05$

Additional research could conceivably utilize ratings of early recollections of leisure-related criteria, e.g., number of playful activities, intrinsic as opposed to extrinsic rewards, process or outcome orientation. Possibly other measures of leisure could be employed, e.g., areas of current interests, similarity to those happily enjoying various activities. Perhaps other scales could be investigated, e.g., crafts, mechanics, while using corresponding criteria for early recollections. In addition, varying the heterogeneity of the sample might be interesting.

REFERENCES

Altman, K., & Rule, W. The relationship between social interest dimensions of early recollections and selected counselor variables. Journal of Individual Psychology, 1980, 36, 227–234.

Ansbacher, H. L., & Ansbacher, R. R. (Eds.) The Individual Psychology of Alfred Adler. New York: Basic Books, 1956.

Ansbacher, H. L., & Ansbacher, R. R. (Eds.) Superiority and social interest. Evanston, IL: Northwestern University Press, 1970.

Attarian, P. Early recollections: predictors of vocational preference. (Doctoral dissertation, University of Arizona, Tucson, Arizona, 1973) Dissertation Abstracts International, 1973, 34, 30.

Chance, J. Some correlates of affective tone of early recollections. Journal of Consulting Psychology, 1957, 21, 203–205.

Crandall, J., & Reimanis, G. Social interest, cooperation, and altruism. Journal of Individual Psychology, 1976, 32, 50–53.

Dixon, W. J., & Massey, H. J., Jr. Introduction to statistical analysis. (3rd ed.) New York: McGraw-Hill, 1969.

Eckstein, D. Early recollection changes after counseling: a case study. Journal of Individual Psychology, 1976, 32, 212–223.

Elkin, J. Early recollections of male homosexuals (Doctoral dissertation, U.S. Inter-national University, San Diego, California, 1974). Dissertation Abstracts International, 1974, 35, 499–500B.

Friedberg, R. Early recollections of homosexuals as indicators of their life styles. Journal of Individual Psychology, 1962, 18, 57–61.

Hjelle, L. Relationship of social interest to internal-external control and self-actualization in young women. Journal of Individual Psychology, 1977, 34, 171–174.

Holmes, D., & Watson, R. Faulty recollections and vocational choice. Journal of Consulting Psychology, 1965, 29, 486–488.

Huber, R., & Stiggins, R. Double-aspect perception and social interest. Perceptual and Motor Skills, 1970, 30, 387–392.

Levy, J. Early memories: theoretical aspects and applications. Journal of Projective Techniques and Personality Assessment, 1965, 29, 281–291.
Levy, J., & Grigg, K. Early memories. Archives of General Psychiatry, 1962, 7, 57–69.
Lieberman, M. Childhood memories as a projective technique. Journal of Projective Techniques, 1957, 21, 32–36.
Lord, M. Activity and affect in early memories of adolescent boys. Journal of Personality Assessment, 1971, 15, 448–456.
Manaster, G., & Perryman, T. Early recollections and occupational choice. Journal of Individual Psychology, 1974, 30, 232–237.
McCarter, R., Schiffman, H., & Tomkins, S. Early recollections as predictors of Tomkins-Horn Picture Arrangement Test performance. Journal of Individual Psychology, 1961, 17, 177–180.
McKechnie, G. E. Leisure Activities Blank manual. Palo Alto, CA: Consulting Psychologists Press, 1975.
Neulinger, J. To leisure: an introduction. Boston: Allyn & Bacon, 1981.
Quinn, J. Predicting recidivism and type of crime from early recollections of prison inmates. (Doctoral dissertation, Univer. of South Carolina, Columbia, 1973) Dissertation Abstracts International, 1973, 25, 197A.
Rule, W. The relationship between early recollections and selected counseling and life-style characteristics. Unpublished doctoral dissertation, University of South Carolina, Columbia, 1972.
Rule, W. R., & Stewart, M. W. Enhancing leisure counseling using an Adlerian technique. Therapeutic Recreation Journal, 1977, 11, 87–93.
Stone, P., & Ansbacher, H. Social interest and performance on the Goodenough-Harris Draw-A-Man Test. Journal of Individual Psychology, 1965, 21, 178–186.
Tolor, A., & Fazzone, R. Early memories as indicators of ego functioning. Psychological Reports, 1966, 19, 979–983.
Traver, M. The Use of Social Interest, Activity and Affect as Reflected in Earliest Recollections as Predictors of Stress in an Analogue Social Situation. Unpublished doctoral dissertation, College of William & Mary, Williamsburg, VA, 1978.

VI
Group Behavior

29

LIFE-STYLE CHARACTERISTICS: EARLY RECOLLECTIONS AND OBSERVABLE GROUP BEHAVIOR

Warren R. Rule and Donald H. McKenzie

According to Adlerian theory, the main purpose for obtaining an individual's early recollections (ERs) is to gain insight into the individual's present fundamental view of life. Adler stated that "among all psychological expressions, some of the most revealing are the individual's memories" (Ansbacher and Ansbacher, 1956: 351). In using the information contained in ERs, speculation can be made regarding attitudes, goals, and particularly relevant for this investigation, life-style characteristics. A number of research studies have indicated that a relationship exists between ERs and specific personality characteristics and psychiatric diagnoses (e.g., McCarter, 1961; Lieberman, 1957; Waldfogel, 1948; Charry, 1959; Chance, 1957; Grey, 1959; Pustel et al., 1969; Wolman, 1970).

The first area of this investigation focused on whether there is a relationship between selected life-style characteristics of an individual, as determined from ERs, and corresponding life-style characteristics of an individual that can be inferred from his observable behavior in an extended group counseling experience. The second area of investigation was concerned with whether there is a difference between levels of subject security, empathy, and genuineness in effectively perceiving life-style characteristics of group members, using the corresponding characteristics that were derived from ERs as the criteria of accuracy.

The first operational hypothesis was stated as follows: selected life-style characteristics inferred from ERs are positively correlated with corresponding life-style characteristics that are inferred from observable behavior in an extended group counseling experience.

The second operational hypothesis was as follows: as levels of (a) security, (b) empathy, and (c) genuineness increase, there should be a corresponding increase in degree of judgmental empathy (JE: effectively perceiving life-style characteristics of group members).

METHOD

Subjects

The sample of the investigation consisted of the 48 participants in a six-week summer guidance institute. The majority of the participants were full-time school counselors, several were part-time counselors, and two were full-time graduate students in guidance. Educationally, 36 had master's degrees. Thirty-three of the participants were females; 15 were males.

Procedure

On a questionnaire, each subject was asked to describe his six earliest recollections as well as any emotions or seemingly insignificant details related to each ER. Furthermore, a checklist was provided of Purcell's 15 secure-insecure characteristics and selected antonyms, 12 bipolar continuums were formed, each having 13 points. A somewhat rigorous reliability procedure was employed in which six raters rated, in addition to the 48 sets of ERs, 24 randomly selected sets of ERs from the 48 sets. Each set of the 24 was rated twice, each time by a different rater. Pearson correlation coefficients were computed for each of the 12 bipolar continuums; reliability coefficients of .70 were judged to be minimally satisfactory. Four of these continuums yielded reliability coefficients of at least .70 and were retained for further use in the investigation (see Table 29.1). The total score of the four continuums used by the ER raters comprised a subject's security score. The six ER raters yielded a rater-reliability coefficient on the overall security scores of .92, using the sum of the four continuums for both ratings of each of the 24 sets of ERs.

The composition of the four groups used in this investigation was determined by randomly assigning the 24 less-secure subjects and the 24 more-secure subjects in the following ratios: 10:2, 7:5, 5:7, and 2:10. An extended group counseling experience of 12 continuous hours was conducted for each group. Two male group leaders were used, each conducting two groups. Both group leaders had the Ph.D. degree in counseling and were experienced in group counseling. The group leaders directed the interaction primarily toward personal growth exploration and group-task exercises. The interaction provided ample opportunity for the group members to go beyond superficial levels of knowing each other. Furthermore, the groups were conducted during the second week of the six-week institute, thereby affording the participants additional opportunity in this live-in situation to become well acquainted with each other.

Immediately following each group experience, each member rated his group members on life-style characteristics inferred from observable behavior, using the bipolar continuums that were originally used by the raters of the ERs (see Table 29.1). In these ratings, the subjects were asked to rate life-style characteristics based on the ratee's internal frame of reference, i.e., the individual's attitudes and expectations toward himself, life, and social participation. The raters were also cautioned to keep in mind that outward behavior is not always a true indicator of attitudes and expectations. In addition, each member rated his group members on perceived levels of empathy and genuineness, using versions of the Carkhuff Scales of Empathic Understanding and Facilitative Genuineness. In order to attempt to control the degree to which a subject's discrimination ability of facilitative conditions might influence his ratings, a discrimination score on the Carkhuff Discrimination Index of Gross Ratings of Facilitative Interpersonal Functioning was obtained, e.g., level of functioning and experience were found to be significant sources of effect for discrimination scores by Cannon and Carkhuff (1969). The discrimination scores were obtained several days before the group experiences during a one-half day of discrimination training and usage of the Carkhuff scales.

For the first hypothesis, one variable consisted of the subject's scores on each of the four bipolar continuums of secure-insecure life-style characteristics used in the ER ratings. The second variable was calculated for each subject by obtaining the mean score of his group members' ratings on the same continuum. Partialed from the second variable were peer security and peer discrimination ability in order to remove any effects on the ratings of these two variables. Peer security for each subject was the mean value of his group members' security scores; peer discrimination ability was determined by calculating for each subject the mean value of his group members' Discrimination Indexes. The statistical procedure for this hypothesis, multiple semipartial correlation (Nunnally, 1967), can be signified as $r_1(_{2,3,4})$.

For the second hypothesis, one variable consisted of the subject's (individual security scores, empathy scores, or genuineness scores. Empathy and genuineness scores were the mean values of the group members' ratings. The second variable was the "judgmental error" score for each of the subjects, calculated by totaling the squared rating deviations from the ER scores on all of the four bipolar continuums. Zero-order Pearson correlation was used to calculate the relationship between (a) empathy and (b) genuineness and judgmental error. Peer discrimination ability was partialed out of empathy and genuineness. This procedure can be designated as $r_1(_{2,3})$.

RESULTS

The procedure of multiple semipartial correlation for the first hypothesis yielded no significant values at the .05 level; therefore, the hypothesis must be rejected (see Table 29.1). These findings do not seem to support the relationship between selected ERs characteristics and inferences from direct behavioral correlates of the same characteristics.

In the second hypothesis (as can be seen in Table 29.2) none of the correlations is significant at the .05 level. These findings are interpreted to suggest that no significant relationships exist between the stated variables.

TABLE 29.1 Correlation between Early Recollections Characteristics and Observable Characteristics

Continuum	R	t*
Unpleasantness vs. Pleasantness	–.097	–.65
Self-Inadequacy vs. Self-Sufficiency	.155	1.04
Sad, Dejected, Solemn vs. Happy, Elated, Joyful	–.081	–.54
Receiving Cruelty or Hindrance vs. Receiving Kindness or Aid	.017	.11

*t = 1.68 for $p < .05$

DISCUSSION AND CONCLUSIONS

In reference to the sample used in this investigation, it is possible that the subjects, most of whom were counseling practitioners, were unusually perceptive and sensitive in their observations. Support is given for this possibility by the closeness of the mean Discrimination Index of 0.59 for this sample to Carkhuff's (1969: 127) finding that the mean for experienced counselors is 0.6 (SD = .2). On the other hand, the subjects, particularly those with relatively insecure ERs, may have felt a self-imposed pressure to overemphasize "the helping role" that is often expected from a counselor in order to maintain professional esteem in the eyes of peers. This possible change in behavior may have influenced the observations and, hence, the ratings for both hypotheses.

In regard to the lack of relationship in the first hypothesis, the subjects were instructed to rate their group members on the members' internal frame of reference as judged from observable behavior. The possibility exists that the group members' behaviors were not always generally consistent with their fundamental attitudes as reflected in their ERs. These findings tend to support Mosak's (1958: 305, 306) contention that "the recollections describe a modus vivendi rather than a modus operandi. The characteristic outlook rather than the characteristic behavior is portrayed." He cites the example of an individual whose attitudinal frame of reference is that life is dangerous. Such a person can put this notion into practice behaviorally in a variety of ways: e.g., seeing danger where none exists and exaggerating the dangers of life with anxious or phobic behavior; compulsive behavior with the security of ritual and control as a response to potential danger, hypochondriacial behavior; becoming a strong man or dependence upon strong people in an effort to cope with potential danger. These examples of behavioral possibilities open to one generalized notion about life illustrate the difficulties of making behavioral inferences that may have contributed to a lack of significance in the first hypothesis.

Influential factors in the lack of significance in the second hypothesis are indicated by the relationship between peer discrimination ability

TABLE 29.2 Correlation between Judgmental Error and Security, Empathy, and Genuineness

Variable	Judgmental Error	t*
Security	–.171	–1.18
Empathy	.112	.76
Genuineness	.182	1.24

*t = –1.68 for p < .05

and the variables of observed unpleasantness versus pleasantness ($r = .309$; $p < .05$) and observed receiving cruelty, hindrance versus receiving kindness, did ($r = .361$; $p < .01$). These findings suggest that poorer discriminators of facilitative conditions had a tendency to inflate their ratings of these observed l.s. characteristics. The influence of these variables was partialed out of the relationships in the first hypothesis, but they were not partialed from the second hypothesis due to the nature of the question investigated.

A very interesting finding that is related to the second hypothesis is the relationship between judgmental empathy and individual discrimination ability as compared to the relationship between judgmental empathy and peer discrimination ability. The zero-order Pearson correlation between judgmental empathy and individual discrimination ability was only .085, yielding a nonsignificant t-score of .58. However, the zero-order Pearson correlation between judgmental empathy and discrimination ability was .327, yielding a t-score of 2.34 which is significant for a one-tailed t-test at the .05 level ($t = 1.68$). These findings suggest that no relationship exists between the subject's ability to accurately judge life-style characteristics in other people and the ability to discriminate facilitative conditions, whereas a relationship does appear to exist between the subject's ability to accurately judge life-style characteristics and the ability of the subjects being judged to discriminate facilitative conditions. Thus, the accuracy of an individual's judgment or life-style characteristics does not appear to be related to his being able to discriminate conditions; rather, it seems to depend on the discrimination ability of the people that he is rating. In view of the related finding that a significant relationship exists between individual discrimination ability and individual empathy ($r = -.242$, yielding a t-score of -1.69 which is significant at the .05 level), the opportunity is strengthened for speculation on the relationship between peer discrimination ability and judgmental empathy. A possible explanation for this relationship might be that individuals who were poorer in the discrimination ability of facilitative conditions and who were correspondingly not judged as accurately did not generally empathize and communicate with others and evaluate others' responses in a manner which fostered interpersonal sensitivity, self-disclosure, and personal appeal. Thus the poor discriminators possibly did not give others as much meaningful input about themselves, on which to base accurate ratings, as did the better discriminators who had a tendency to be somewhat more empathic and reinforcing.

In conclusion, the selected life-style characteristics do not seem to be directly related to inferences made from corresponding observable group behaviors. Accuracy in rating these characteristics does not appear to be related to ER security, empathy, or genuineness; however, the accuracy does seem to be related to the discrimination ability of facilitative conditions of the people who are being rated.

REFERENCES

Ansbacher, H. L. and R. R. Ansbacher [eds.] (1956) The Individual Psychology of Alfred Adler. New York: Basic Books.

Cannon, J. C. and R. R. Carkhuff (1969) "The effect of rater level of functioning and experience upon the discrimination of facilitative conditions." J. of Counseling Psychology 33: 189–194.

Carkhuff, R. R. (1969) Helping & Human Relations. New York: Holt, Rinehart & Winston.

Chance, J. E. (1957) "Some correlates of affective tone of early memories." J. of Consulting Psychology 21: 203–205.

Charry, J. B. (1959) "Childhood and teen-age memories in mentally ill and normal groups." Ph.D. dissertation, Columbia University. (unpublished)

Grey, L. (1959) "Utilization of the earliest childhood recollection in detecting maladjustment among junior college students." Ph.D. dissertation, University of Southern California. (unpublished)

Lieberman, M. G. (1957) "Childhood memories as a projective technique." J. of Projective Techniques 21: 32–36.

Mccarter, R. E. (1961) "Affective components of early recollections." Ph.D. dissertation, Princeton University. (unpublished)

Mosak, H. H. (1958) "Early recollections as a projective technique." J. of Projective Techniques 22: 302–311.

Nunnally, J. C. (1967) Psychometric Theory. New York: McGraw-Hill.

Pustel, G., M. Sternlicht, and L. Siegel (1969) "Pleasant vs. unpleasant early childhood recollections of institutionalized adolescents and adult retardates." J. of Clinical Psychology 25: 110–111.

Waldfogel, S. (1948) "The frequency and affective character of childhood memories." Psych. Monographs 62, 4: 291.

Wolman, R. N. (1970) "Early recollections and the perception of others: a study of delinquent adolescents." J. of Genetic Psychology 116: 157–163.

30

EARLY RECOLLECTIONS AS A VARIABLE IN GROUP COMPOSITION AND IN FACILITATIVE GROUP BEHAVIOR

Warren R. Rule and Donald H. McKenzie

The present investigation concentrates on a variation of the Adlerian framework for interpreting early recollections (ERs). In the Adlerian approach, an individual's ERs are viewed as being reflective of his "style of life." From the thousands of experiences to which the individual has been exposed in his early childhood, he remembers only those recollections which coincide with his current outlook on life (Ansbacher and Ansbacher, 1956). Utilizing the information contained in ERs, a person functioning in a helping capacity is often in a position to draw inferences regarding the helpee's basic attitudes and concepts of himself, life, and social participation. The usefulness of the Adlerian interpretation of ERs as a therapeutic technique has received extended clinical and research attention (e.g., Mosak, 1958, 1969; Dreikurs, 1967; Verger and Camp, 1970; Nikelly, 1971).

Carkhuff and Berenson (1967: 26) point out that "the levels at which an individual functions with others reflect the levels of his attitudes and comprehension of himself." Research exists which supports the proposition that the highly functioning counselor is characteristically a self-accepting, emotionally stable individual (e.g., Foulds, 1969a; Jansen, Robb, and Bonk, 1970; Foulds, 1969b). From a counseling perspective, it seems that ER, if found to be related to the ability to behave facilitatively toward others, would appear to be a useful variable in counselor selection and group composition. Gazda (1968) contends that research has not demonstrated ideal combinations of members for group counseling.

In terms of relating life-style outlook as determined from ERs to the facilitative dimensions, this investigation dealt with the question of whether selected secure-insecure characteristics ascribed to ERs are related to facilitative functioning within a group in the areas of (a) empathy and (b) genuineness. The second part of this investigation focused on the question of whether membership in groups consisting of systematically varied levels of ER security is related to the expressed levels of empathy and genuineness.

METHOD

The sample of the present investigation consisted of the 48 participants in a summer guidance institute. All were employed as either full- or part-time counselors, with the exception of two participants who were full-time graduate students in guidance. In regard to educational level, 36 had master's degrees. Fifteen of the participants were males, 33 were females.

Procedure

A questionnaire was employed to elicit the subjects' (Ss') ERs. The Ss were requested to describe their six earliest recollections as well as any emotions or seemingly insignificant details related to the ERs. In addition, a checklist was provided of Purcell's (1952) 15 secure-insecure characteristics, so that a subject could check however many were appropriate to a given ER. From the 15 secure-insecure characteristics and selected antonyms, 12 bipolar continuums were formed. Four continuums yielded rater-reliability coefficients of above .70 and were retained. The 13-point bipolar continuums and their respective reliabilities were:

(a) unpleasantness versus pleasantness (.93);
(b) self-inadequacy versus self-sufficiency (.71);
(c) sad, dejected, solemn versus happy, elated, or joyful (.82);
(d) receiving cruelty or hinderance versus receiving kindness or aid (.82).

The total score of the four continuums used by ER raters comprised a subject's security score. Six ER raters yielded a rater-reliability coefficient of .92 on the overall security scores.

The composition of the four groups used in this investigation was determined by randomly assigning the 24 less-secure subjects and the 24 more-secure subjects in the following ratios: 10:2, 7:5, 5:7, 2:10. An extended group-counseling experience of 12 continuous hours was conducted for each group. Two male group leaders were used, each having two groups. Both leaders had a Ph.D. degree in counseling and were experienced in group counseling. The respective group leaders met with the groups continuously and directed the interaction primarily toward personal growth exploration and group-task exercises. Immediately following each group experience, each member rated his group members on perceived levels of empathy and genuineness, using versions of the Carkhuff Scales of Empathic Understanding and Facilitative Genuineness. In order to get a measure of the degree to which a S's discrimination ability influenced his ratings of his group members on levels of empathy and genuineness, a discrimination score on the Carkhuff Discrimination Index of Gross Ratings of Facilitative Interpersonal Functioning was obtained several days before the group experience. At this time, a one-half-day orientation period was conducted for the Ss in discrimination training and usage of the Carkhuff scales. Cannon and Carkhuff (1969) found that both rater level of functioning and experience were significant sources of effect for discrimination scores.

Hypotheses

The first operational hypothesis was as follows: there is a positive correlation between degree of security, as reflected in the ratings of ERs, and levels of (a) empathy and (b) genuineness. The statistical procedure employed was semi-partial correlation. Variable one (individual security scores) consisted of the total for each subject of the four reliable bipolar-continuum values which were determined from rating ERs. Variable two (empathy or genuineness ratings) was determined for each subject by computing the mean value of a subject's group-members' ratings of him. Variable three (peer discrimination ability)

TABLE 30.1 Correlation between Facilitative Behavior and E.R. Security

Variable	E.R. Security	t*
Empathy	.036	.24
Genuineness	–.094	.63

*t = 1.68 for p < .05

TABLE 30.2 Correlation between Facilitative Behavior and Peer E.R. Security

Variable	Peer E.R. Security	t*
Empathy	–.165	–1.11
Genuineness	–.203	–1.37

*t = 1.68 for p < .05

was partialed out of variable two; peer discrimination ability was determined by calculating for each subject the mean value of his group members' discrimination indexes. The procedure can be signified as $r_1(_{2,3})$.

The second operational hypothesis was as follows: as security in group membership increases, levels of expressed (a) empathy and (b) genuineness should proportionately increase. Variable one consisted of empathy (or genuineness) scores; from variable one, the effect of peer discrimination ability (variable two) was partialed out. Variable three (peer security) consisted of calculating for each S the mean value of his group members' security scores. Individual security scores (variable four) were partialed from peer security. The procedure of semipartial correlation can be symbolically represented as $r(_{1,2})\ r(_{3,4})$.

RESULTS

For the first hypothesis, the results yielded t-scores of .24 for empathy and –.63 for genuineness (see Table 30.1). These scores are not significant; therefore, the first hypothesis was rejected.

The results for the second hypothesis yielded t-scores of –1.11 for empathy and –1.37 for genuineness, neither of which is significant (see Table 30.2). Thus, the second hypothesis was rejected.

DISCUSSION AND CONCLUSIONS

In reference to the findings of the first and second hypotheses, the fact that all of the subjects in the sample under investigation were either practicing counselors or students in counseling would seem to be advantageous in some ways for the purpose of this investigation and possibly disadvantageous in other ways. On the favorable side, the assumption could be made that counseling-oriented people would be sensitive to others and able to accurately discriminate the responses of others. There is reason to believe that this was the case for this sample in view of research cited by Carkhuff (1969: 127) which indicates that the mean discrimination index of experienced counselors is 0.6 (SD = .2) as compared to a mean of 0.59 for the sample in the present investigation. A possible disadvantage for using counselors in the sample could be the existence of a self-imposed pressure to overemphasize "the helping role" that one would expect from a counselor in order to maintain professional esteem in the eyes of peers. The summer institute setting with the accompanying emphasis on establishing close interpersonal relationships would seem particularly conducive to this expectation. During the extended group-counseling experience, it is conceivable that the less-secures might have been especially sensitive to peer expectations of professional competency and, as a result, they could have increased their efforts in facilitative communication, whereas the more-secures might have been content to have others accept them as they were.

An informal discussion was conducted with each of the two group leaders after the extended group-counseling experiences. Neither leader was aware of the nature of the investigation or of the group-member differences in ER security. Each leader described his respective group of predominately more-secures in terms suggesting confidence, independence, or confrontation, in contrast to descriptions of his group of predominately less-secures which was viewed as more accepting, having gotten along better, or more passive. The negative direction of both findings in the second hypothesis, although not statistically significant, tends to support the leaders' observations and the speculation that the groups comprised of predominately more-secures created an independent and confrontive atmosphere that was notably anxiety-producing for some. This may have inhibited the expression of facilitative responses and decreased the ratings. The effect of this possibility is supported by Rosenstiel's (1969) finding that responses of anxious individuals signify a low capacity for empathy.

Possibly a non-counselor sample not familiar with the stereotyped helping role could be used in further research. In addition, measures of empathy and genuineness might be obtained by means other than group-member ratings, such as ratings of tapes or through a one-way glass. Furthermore, an investigation might be devised which would focus on the relationship between characteristics in ERs and other facilitative conditions, e.g., respect, concreteness, immediacy, and confrontation

(Carkhuff, 1969). The condition of confrontation would appear to have particular relevance for this investigation.

The conclusion must be made in this investigation that these secure-insecure characteristics in ERs do not seem to be useful in predicting levels of empathy and genuineness, nor do they appear to be an influential facilitative factor in determining group composition.

REFERENCES

Ansbacher, H. L. and R. R. Ansbacher [eds.] (1956) The Individual Psychology of Alfred Adler. New York: Basic Books.

Cannon, J. C. and R. R. Carkhuff (1969) "The effect of rater level of functioning and experience upon the discrimination of facilitative conditions." J. of Counseling Psych. 33: 189–194.

Carkhuff, R. R. (1969) Helping and Human Relations, Vol. 1. New York: Holt, Rinehart & Winston.

Carkhuff, R. R. and B. G. Berenson (1967) Beyond Counseling and Therapy. New York: Holt, Rinehart & Winston.

Dreikurs, R. (1967) Psychodynamics, Psychotherapy and Counseling. Chicago: Alfred Adler Institute of Chicago.

Foulds, M. L. (1969a) "Postive mental health and facilitative genuineness during counseling." Personnel and Guidance J. 47: 762–766.

Foulds, M. L. (1969b) "Self-actualization and the communication of facilitative conditions during counseling." J. of Counseling Psych. 16: 132–136.

Gazda, G. M. (1968) Basic Approaches to Group Psychotherapy and Group Counseling. Springfield, Ill.: Charles C Thomas.

Jansen, D. G., G. P. Robb, and E. C. Bonk (1970) "Characteristics of high-rated and low-rated master's degree candidates in counseling and guidance." Counselor Educ. and Supervision 9: 162–170.

Mosak, H. H. (1958) "Early recollections as a projective technique." J. of Projective Techniques 22: 302–311.

Mosak, H. H. (1969) "Early recollections: evaluation of some recent research." J. of Individual Psych. 25: 56–63.

Nikelly, A. G. [ed.] (1971) Techniques for Behavior Change. Springfield, Ill.: Charles C Thomas.

Purcell, K. (1952) "Memory and psychological security." J. of Abnormal and Social Psych. 47: 443–440.

Rosenstiel, L. V. (1969) "Capacity for empathy: a function of anxiety in the production of H-responses." J. of Projective Techniques and Personality Assessment 33: 336–342.

Verger, D. M. and W. L. Camp (1970) "Early recollections: reflections of the present." J. of Counseling Psych. 17: 510–515.

VII

Social Factors

31

EARLY RECOLLECTIONS: PREDICTORS OF STRESS IN AN ANALOGUE SOCIAL SITUATION

Michael D. Traver and Warren R. Rule

Adler's approach to understanding early recollections (ERs) has been receiving increasing attention from several perspectives. There are vocational and educational correlations of early recollections, and ERs have also been used to investigate aspects of personality structure.

Adler regarded early recollections essentially as reflections of a person's outlook on life; these dimly conscious reminders orient an individual on what to expect from self, others, and life. Also, Adler believed that early recollections provide insight into an individual's lifestyle or cognitive map. His belief was that there are no so-called chance memories. From the thousands of experiences an individual has in early childhood, those remembered are the ones that serve as current orienta-tion points. The early recollections function as reminders of present expectations.

This study focuses on an abbreviated measurement of two important Adlerian concepts: social interest and activity. Social interest may be broadly understood to mean feeling with the whole of a community. Investigations have been conducted on the relationship between social interest and various individual characteristics: cooperation and altruism, internal/external control, perception, intelligence, and several counselor variables. Activity is an additionally important concept for lifestyle understanding. Activity may be defined as the individual's tendency to initiate as opposed to observing or being initiated upon. It is conceptually related to social interest yet distinct from it.

In this study, an abbreviated measure of these two dimensions, social interest and activity, was obtained from the subjects' early recollections. The contrasting extremes for these combined two ratings, consisting of the total of self-rated pleasantness and rater-rated activity, yielded the subjects for this investigation, referred to as the positive-active and the negative-passive groups.

The purpose of this investigation was twofold—to assess in ERs the relationship of this abbreviated measure (1) to the broader dimension of social interest and (2) to individual reactions in phases of an experimentally stressful situation. In this stressful situation, stress was produced by placing responsibility on male subjects to impress favorably a female confederate in the presence of another male who supposedly was rating the performance. The expectation was that individuals having memories that were predominantly both unpleasant and passive would be more prone to experience stress and have more difficulty in stress reduction than would individuals having memories that were predominantly both pleasant and active.

METHOD

Subjects

The original sample of 400 male university undergraduate students volunteered to complete the revised Early Recollections questionnaire (Rule, 1972). Subsequently, from this sample two groups of 15 subjects were selected for this analysis. The procedure for selection is given below.

Ratings and Instruments

The revised Early Recollections questionnaire contains a page of instructions and elicits six early recollections with supplemental information. Each of the original subjects was requested to rate, on a scale of 1 to 7, the pleasantness of each early recollection. Raters also judged the early recollections for activity on a 7-point scale; 1 = pleasant (positive) on the first scale and active on the second scale. The raters' scores were combined with the subjects' self-ratings and comprised the abbreviated indicator of social interest. Subsequently, the two most extreme groups of 15 subjects were chosen from this sample to participate. These constituted the positive-active and the negative-passive groups of abbreviated social interest; these are terms that, as noted previously, denote the total scores of pleasantness (positive-negative) and activity (active-passive). Adler believed that when interpreting the individual's lifestyle, increasing significance should be given to correspondingly earlier memories.

A criterion of selection of the positive-active group, then, was that each subject have at least two of the first three early recollections judged as positive-active. Similarly, two of the first three memories of the negative-passive group were to be judged as negative-passive. All subjects were paid nominal fees for completing the questionnaire and participating.

Before rating the memories of the subjects, the three raters participated in a pilot study to determine (I) if they could differentiate between active and non-active subjects and (2) if they could consistently agree on a rating scale of nine social interest variables in memories.

The subjects in the pilot study were 20 graduate volunteers who supplied three memories in response to the Early Recollections questionnaire. The raters all had master's degrees, had completed Adlerian coursework, and were exposed to 5.5 hours of instruction. Spearman correlations between the raters on the active-passive variable were $p_{1,2} = .857$, $p_{1,3} = .800$, and $P_{2,3} = .738$; all were significant ($p = .001$). For the rating scale of social interest variables, all of the raters' pairings of the nine variables were also significant ($p = .001$); the median reliability coefficients for the nine variables ranged from .56 to .77. After establishing rating reliability, the raters evaluated the original subjects on the active-passive dimension and subsequently rated each of the two extreme groups of 15 subjects on the rating scale of social interest variables.

Two measures of stress were employed in this investigation—the State-Trait Anxiety Inventory and heart rate. Spielberger's State-Trait Anxiety Inventory includes an A-State Scale, which may vary with intensity or fluctuate with time, and an A-Trait, which is viewed as a relatively stable emotional characteristic. Only the A-State Scale was employed. Reliability and validity of this scale have been confirmed.

The second measure of stress and heart rate was recorded by a Physiograph Six, manufactured by the E & M Instrument Co., Inc. Heart rate was picked up by a Photoelectric Pulse Pick-up made by Narco Bio-System, Inc., and recorded on graph paper. All instrumentation was located in a room adjacent to the laboratory, visible by way of a one-way mirror. A number of investigations demonstrated that heart rate is responsive to social interactions.

PROCEDURE

With relevant aspects of procedure confirmed by a pilot study, each subject was seated in a recliner chair and the pulse pick-up attached to his left index finger. He was told that the experimenter had to "calibrate" the instruments and that he should relax. After 10 minutes, the subject was told that the purpose of the task was to determine one's social skills, as compared with others, in favorably impressing a female who was shortly to enter the room. Furthermore, an explanation was given for both the presence of a male rater and for a video camera; the camera was to record verbal and facial expressions that would be rated by a panel of instructors. The female confederate was limited to a moderately positive approach to all subjects, while letting the burden of conversation fall on the subject. Communication on her part was limited to answering questions in concise, quick responses limited to 5 seconds or less; if silence persisted for more than 20 seconds, she was to initiate a topic. The interaction was maintained for 3 minutes; at the end of this period the confederates were excused by the experimenter. Prior to leaving, the subject was asked to complete an A-State Anxiety Scale.

Data were premeasurements and postmeasurements on the A-State Anxiety Scale, while base, stress, and postmeasurements were collected for heart rate. Both ERs and pretest A-State data were collected about two weeks prior to the experiment. Heart rate was collected continuously and pretest or baseline activity recorded during the last 10 seconds of the 10-minute calibrating period. During the stress period, heart-beats were counted at the beginning of each 30-second interval throughout the interaction period for a total of seven measurements. Posttest for heart rate was assessed during the last 10 seconds of the interaction phase.

RESULTS

The first hypothesis, stating that subjects with active-positive ERs will rate significantly higher on the social interest ER Scale than will subjects with passive-negative ERs was confirmed. A t-test indicated a significant difference between the active-positive and passive-negative groups; a value of 6.97 ($p < .001$) was found for cumulative scores on the first three memories and a value of 3.47 ($p < .001$) for the second three memories. The t value for the global score of all the memories was 6.68 ($p < .001$).

Also supported was the second hypothesis, which suggested that there would be no difference in state anxiety in the pre-experimental phase (as measured by the A-State Anxiety Scale) between subjects with active-positive ERs and subjects with passive-negative ones. A t-test showed no significant difference.

The third hypothesis, stating that there would be no difference in baseline (resting phase) heart rate between active-positive and passive-negative groups, also was confirmed. A t-test indicated no significant difference between groups in resting phase heart rate.

The fourth hypothesis, indicating that during the analogue social situation the active-positive subjects would show a significantly greater mean decrease in a rate over time (180 sec.) than would passive-negative subjects, was rejected. When one-way analysis of covariance controlling for resting heart rate (with mean heart rate as the dependent variable) was performed between the active-positive and passive-negative groups, no significant differences were found.

Also rejected was the fifth hypothesis—that subjects with active-positive ERs would have significantly lower scores at the conclusion of the social analogue situation (as measured by the A-State Anxiety Scale) than would subjects with passive-negative ones. Analysis of covariance, covarying for the pre-stress anxiety rating determined by responses on the A-State Anxiety Scale, showed no significant differences between groups on postexperimental anxiety scores.

Finally, the sixth hypothesis, proposing that subjects with active-positive ERs would record significantly lower heart rates at the conclusion of the analogue social situation than would subjects with passive-negative ERs also was rejected. Analysis of covariance controlling for the resting heart rate showed no significant difference between groups as to mean heart rate at the conclusion of the experimental condition.

DISCUSSION

The first hypothesis successfully predicted that subjects with active-positive ERs would rate higher on the Social Interest Scale than would the subjects with passive-negative ones. Thus, for research purposes, the variables of activity—as rated by raters—and pleasantness—as rated by the subjects themselves—appear to yield a quick, concise measure that corresponds highly with the global social interest score.

The second and third hypotheses successfully predicted no significant differences between active-positive and passive-negative groups as to resting heart rate and preexperimental state anxiety. If the experimental social situation was a valid indicator of stress, the data partially support Adler's assertion that lifestyle may be more readily observed under periods of stress but difficult to detect when the style of life is functioning well.

The data did not support the fourth, fifth, and sixth hypotheses, which predicted differences between the investigated groups in their reactions to a socially stressful situation. It may be possible that in the attempt to classify subjects on relatively specific dimensions, the fullness of individual creativity, which Adler emphasized, was not considered. In practice, Adlerians holistically consider other types of childhood information in addition to ERs when attempting to obtain an understanding of an individual lifestyle. Further, some of the subjects may have creatively developed patterns of, compensatory behavior that, paradoxically, would appear to be inconsistent with the outlook reflected by the ERs. For example, a subject with passive-negative memories may still be very sensitive to rejection yet have learned to reduce this negative intensity by reacting very quickly in an assertive manner to a threatening situation. Thus, the real or imagined success of the assertiveness correspondingly lowers the heart rate; yet this behavior pattern is not potent enough over the long run to alter the person's outlook of vulnerability in this area.

The subjects were volunteers and, by virtue of their college status, had a history of high achievement. These self-selection factors may have confounded the results in such an achievement-focused experiment. Moreover, some of the active-positive subjects may have been taken aback at the limited reinforcement of the female confederate, thus generating more stress as a result of this unexpected occurrence. On the other hand, some of the passive-negative subjects may have not become unduly alarmed in reaction to the limited reinforcement, since, for them, business was proceeding as usual.

Regarding ER ratings, a system might be developed that would allow for individual ER inconsistencies. Different criteria could be used in the ratings, such as security or even anxiety. Perhaps physiological correlates of anxiety in ERs could be investigated in an analogue situation.

In summary, activity and pleasantness, as rated in ERs, appeared to reflect a global social interest score. As expected, active-positive and passive-negative groups did not differ prior to the experimental situation. However, the scores of these extreme groups on this particular activity and affect continuum did not predict stress as experienced in a social analogue situation.

REFERENCE

Rule, W. (1972). The Relationships Between Early Recollections and Selected Lifestyle Characteristics. Unpublished doctoral dissertation, University of South Carolina, Columbia.

32

THE RELATIONSHIP BETWEEN SOCIAL INTEREST DIMENSIONS OF EARLY RECOLLECTIONS AND SELECTED COUNSELOR VARIABLES

Kathryn E. Altman and Warren R. Rule

A review of the psychological literature indicates that early recollections have been of great interest for many years. The approach taken by Adlerians is that perception and memory are both related to the individual's frame of reference or attitudinal set. The early recollections of a person are seen as reflecting the person's perceptual framework within which life's experiences are interpreted.

The present investigation focused on interpreting early recollections in order to identify selected dynamics of an individual's personality. Adler (1931, p. 73) wrote that of all psychic expressions, some of the most revealing were the individual's memories. Researchers from both

This chapter, "The Relationship between Social Interest Dimensions of Early Recollections and Selected Counselor Variables," from Kathryn E. Altman and Warren R. Rule, *Journal of Individual Psychology* 36:2, pp. 227–234.

Adlerian and non-Adlerian frames of reference have found that early recollections have important personality correlates (e.g., Chance, 1957; Charry, 1959; Grey, 1959; Lieberman, 1957; McCarter, 1957; Mosak, 1969; Pustel, Sternlicht, & Siegel, 1969; Tolar & Fazzone, 1966; Waldfogel, 1948; Wolman, 1970).

The purpose of this study was to investigate the relationship of social interest characteristics in early recollections to the counselor variable of empathy as well as to counselor birth order and sex. Several investigations related to these factors have been performed. Rule (1972), using Purcell's (1952) 15 secure-insecure characteristics for evaluating early recollections, found no significant relationship between early recollections and group ratings of empathy. In reference to the relationship between empathy and birth order, Stotland and Dunn (1962) found later borns identify more with other people than do first or only borns. Stotland and Dunn (1963) demonstrated that later born children empathize more than do first or only children; however, a replication (Stotland & Walsh, 1963) did not produce the same results. Regarding the relationship between empathy and sex of subject, O'Hem and Arbuckle (1964) found no significant differences between the sexes and sensitivity; Taylor (1972) discovered no significance in counselors' level of empathic understanding on the basis of the sex of the counselor or client.

METHOD

Phase 1

The first phase of the investigation entailed an interrater reliability study which was conducted to determine if raters could rate early recollections reliably. The earliest recollection of 40 graduate students enrolled in graduate guidance courses were rated independently by six raters. The six raters were each experienced in analyzing early recollections within the Adlerian framework. The early recollections were rated using The Early Recollections Rating Scale of Social Interest Characteristics. This instrument contained nine 7-point continua selected, in consultation with experts in Adlerian psychology, as possibly having value in determining the degree of social interest inherent in early recollections. Each rater was paired with each of the other raters, and Pearson Product Moment correlations were obtained for each variable. Continua 1–4 were rated according to the behavior exhibited in the early recollection (also included is the media correlation of each variable): Gregarious vs. withdrawal (.56); activity vs. passivity (.69); benevolence, kindness, vs. agression, hostility (.65); befriended, treated well vs. mistreated (.79). Continua 5–9 were rated according to the perception of the environment: friendly, nurturing vs. threatening, frustrating (.77); acceptance vs. rejection (.69); self-confidence vs. inferiority (.64); cheerful vs. depressing (.76); independence vs. dependence (.56). Each of the reliability coefficients was significant at the $p < .001$. All were retained and comprised the basis of Phase 2 of the investigation.

Phase 2

Subjects. The subjects were 48 participants in a 6-week guidance institute held at the University of South Carolina, selected from nine southeastern states. All but three were employed as either full- or part-time counselors. Thirty-eight held master's degrees, and the remainder had some graduate study. The mean age was 34.1 years. Males comprised 22 of the participants while 26 were females.

Procedures. An Early Recollections Questionnaire (Rule, 1972) was used to obtain six early recollections from each subject. The six raters used in Phase I served as raters of the early recollections, using the Early Recollections Rating Scale of Social Interest Characteristics. Based on random assignment, each rater rated six early recollections of eight subjects. Each rater was asked to check on the rating scale a value of 1 to 7, inclusive, on each of the nine continua for each early recollection. The Social Interest score for each of the nine continua for each subject was the mean of six scores for that continuum. The Global Social Interest Score was the total of nine means.

The subjects were administered ten communication index excerpts (Carkhuff, 1969) with audio tape excerpts during the first week of the institute. The communications index score was obtained by ratings on the Ratings of Facilitative Interpersonal Functioning Scale (Carkhuff, 1969). The ratings were made by three judges who rated each excerpt. The judges were all experienced in the rating of communication index scores. The mean for all ten excerpts was calculated, and in turn the mean of the three judges was then calculated. To determine if the judges rated reliably, a Pearson Product Moment correlation was obtained. The correlation between Judge 1 and Judge 2 was 0.9253, between Judge 1 and Judge 3 was 0.8927, and between Judge 2 and Judge 3 was 0.9568.

To determine birth order, a Family Constellation questionnaire was distributed to each subject. For the analysis of this investigation such factors as age distance between the subject and siblings or sex of the nearest sibling were not controlled because of the relatively limited number of subjects. There were 27 (15 males, 12 females) who were classified as first borns; later borns accounted for the remaining 21 (7 males, 14 females).

RESULTS

First Hypothesis

The first hypothesis was stated as a positive relationship between selected social interest dimensions ascribed to early recollections and empathy. The statistical procedure used was correlation. Variables 5-13 (see Table 32.1) consisted of the mean score of the nine social interest dimensions. Variable 14 (empathy) was determined for each subject by computing the mean value of the three sets of ratings on empathy.

To be significant at the .05 level, a value of .29 was required. An examination of Table 32.1 reveals that five of the social interest scores correlate significantly with empathy: benevolence vs. aggression; befriended vs. mistreated; friendly vs. threatening; acceptance vs. rejection; and cheerful vs. depressing.

In an added process, a stepwise regression was performed in eight steps with empathy as the dependent variable to determine the most effective and efficient way of predicting empathy using the social interest scores (see Table 32.2).

The correlation does not improve substantially after Step 3. Therefore a regression equation formula was written which included the first three variables. To predict empathy (X′14) the following regression equation could be used:

$$X'14 = 1.265 + 0.172x_7 + 0.256x_9 - 0.214x_{11} .$$

Second Hypothesis

The second hypothesis stated that there is a positive correlation between the global social interest score and empathy. Table 32.1 indicates a correlation of .306 ($p < .05$) supporting the hypothesis.

Third Hypothesis

The third hypothesis suggested a positive relationship between the social interest variables and birth order. Table 32.1 reveals no significant correlations. This hypothesis was not supported.

TABLE 32.1 Correlation Matrix for Empathy, Social Interest, and Other Related Variables

	1	2	3	4	5	6	7	8	9	10	11	12	13	14	15
	Birth Order	Sex	Race	Rater No.	Greg.	Act.	Ben.	Be-Mend.	Friend.	Accept.	Self-Con.	Cheer: hi	Independence	Empathy	Global
1	1.000	0.175	–0.118	0.024	–0.194	–0.158	0.011	–0.066	–0.273	–0.015	–0.280	–0.249	–0.021	0.161	–0.185
2		1.000	–0.237	0.098	0.382*	–0.042	0.189	0.202	0.112	0.082	0.088	0.101	–0.139	0.396*	0.149
3			1.000	–0.104	–0.368*	–0.157	–0.034*	–0.404*	–0.198	–0.298*	–0.186	–0.261	–0.128	–0.361*	–0.331*
4				1.000	0.235	0.196	0.186	0.110	0.089	0.161	–0.026	0.068	–0.126	0.021	0.120
5					1.000	0.505*	0.413*	0.615*	0.633*	0.492*	0.625*	0.578*	0.400*	0.277	0.767*
6						1.000	0.037	0.224	0.278	0.213	0.430*	0.3920	0.574*	–0.100	0.523*
7							1.000	0.767*	0.533*	0.688*	0.390*	0.570*	0.068*	0.373*	0.605*
8								1.000	0.818*	0.872*	0.7070	0.790*	0.186	0.360*	0.871*
9									1.000	0.860*	0.831*	0.873*	0.244	0.388*	0.909*
10										1.000	0.696*	0.835*	0.168	0.369*	0.848*
11											1.000	0.775*	0.488*	0.180	0.886*
12												1.000	0.290*	0.300*	0.894*
13													1.000	0.018	0.448*
14														1.000	0.308*
15															1.000

* Significant beyond the .05 level of confidence.

TABLE 32.2 Stepwise Regression of Social Interest Variables

1	7 -	Benevolence vs. aggression	0.3726**
2	9 -	Friendly vs. threatening	0.4232*
3	11 -	Self-confidence vs. inferiority	0.4702*
4	6 -	Activity vs. passivity	0.4848*
5	5 -	Gregarious vs. withdrawal	0.5073*
6	13 -	Independence vs. dependence	0.5194*
7	10 -	Acceptance vs. rejection	0.5218*
8	8 -	Treated well vs. mistreated	0.5229

* Significant at the .05 level.
**Significant at the .01 level.

Fourth Hypothesis

The fourth hypothesis, that the social interest variables are positively correlated for female subjects, is supported for only one of the variables: gregarious vs. withdrawal.

Both sex (female) and race (Caucasian) were found to be correlated with empathy, although these relationships were not hypothesized. An additional multiple stepwise regression was performed to include those variables in addition to the three social interest variables used in the regression equation discussed with the first hypothesis. The stepwise regression using five variables was as follows: sex (0.39509); friendly vs. threatening (0.51232); self-confidence vs. inferiority (0.554111); race (0.59687); benevolence vs. aggression (0.60243).

To predict empathy (X′14), using the first four steps, the following regression equation (Sex: 1 = male, 2 = female; Race: 1 = Caucasian, 2 = Negro) could be used in future research: $X'14 = 1.765 + .296(S) + .285x_9 - .231x_{11} - .224(R)$.

Fifth Hypothesis

The fifth hypothesis stated that there is a positive correlation between empathy and birth order. This hypothesis was not supported.

Discussion

In reference to the first and second hypotheses, this investigation supported one aspect of Adler's definition of social interest: "To see with the eyes of another, to hear with the ears of another, to feel with the heart of another" (Ansbacher & Ansbacher, 1956, p. 135). Since empathy is defined in a similar fashion, it is not surprising that the two were found to be related. In regard to counselor training, exploration of early recollections of beginning students might reveal that certain prescriptive experiences for persons with a lower probability of success in empathic counseling might be helpful in overcoming biased self-perceptions which interfere with their effective functioning.

In reference to the relationship between (a) sex and the social interest characteristic of gregarious vs. withdrawal; and between (b) sex and empathy, it may have been possible that the instruments used were biased in favor of the women. Similarly, the instruments may have been culturally biased in view of the significant relationship between empathy and race; the stimulus situations given may have been situations which were not as relevant to Blacks who grew up in the South.

From a theoretical perspective, a well-rounded understanding of an individual's social interest probably cannot be gleaned from early recollections alone. A more valid picture would be apt to emerge when considering other life-style information as well, e.g., description of self and siblings, parental influences, family atmosphere, etc. As Mosak (1958, p. 305) has indicated, "The recollections describe a modus vivendi rather than a modus operandi." From an operational perspective, Adler often pointed out that one can never be certain of a person's social interest unless it is tested by stressful problems to solve (Dreikurs & Mosak, 1966). Perhaps future research could compare the responses to this early recollections scale with existing social interest scales (e.g., Crandall, 1975) that are not constructed from early recollections.

REFERENCES

Adler, A. What life should mean to you. New York: Capricorn Books, 1931.

Ansbacher, H. L., & Ansbacher, R. R. (Eds.) The individual psychology of Alfred Adler. New York: Basic Books, 1956.

Carkhuff, R. R. Helping and human relations (Vol. 2). New York: Holt, Rinehart & Winston, 1969.

Chance, J. E. Some correlates of affective tone of early memories. Journal of Consulting Psychology, 1957, 21, 203–205.

Charry, J. B. Childhood and teen-age memories in mentally ill and normal groups. Unpublished doctoral dissertation, Columbia University, 1959.

Crandall, J. E. A scale for social interest. Journal of Individual Psychology, 1975, 31, 187–195.

Dreikurs, R., & Mosak, H. H. The tasks of life I. Adler's three tasks. Individual Psychologist, 1966, 4(1), 18–22.

Grey, L. Utilization of the earliest childhood recollection in detecting maladjustment among junior college students. Unpublished doctoral dissertation, University of Southern California, 1959.

Lieberman, M. G. Childhood memories as a projective technique. Journal of Projective Techniques, 1957, 21, 32–36.

McCarter, R. E. Affective components of early recollections. Unpublished doctoral dissertation. Princeton University, 1957.

Mosak, H. H. Early recollections as a projective technique. Journal of Projective Techniques, 1958, 22(3), 302–311.
Mosak, H. H. Early recollections: Evaluation of recent research. Journal of Individual Psychology, 1969, 25, 56–63.
O'Hern, J. S., & Arbuckle, D. S. Sensitivity: A measurable concept. Personnel and Guidance Journal, 1964, 42, 572–576.
Purcell, K. Memory and psychological security. Journal of Abnormal and Social Psychology, 1952, 47, 433–440.
Pustel, G., Sternlicht, M., & Siegel, L. Pleasant vs. unpleasant early childhood recollections of institutionalized adolescents and adult retardates. Journal of Clinical Psychology, 1969, 25, 110–111.
Rule, W. R. The relationship between early recollections and selected counseling and life-style characteristics. Unpublished doctoral dissertation, University of South Carolina, 1972.
Stotland, E., & Dunn, R. E. Identification, "oppositeness," authoritarianism, self-esteem and birth order. Psychological Monographs, 1962, 76(9, Whole No. 528).
Stotland, E., & Dunn, R. E. Empathy, self-esteem and birth order. Journal of Abnormal and Social Psychology, 1963, 66, 532–540.
Stotland, E., & Walsh, J. A. Birth order and an experimental study of empathy. Journal of Abnormal and Social Psychology, 1963, 66, 610–614.
Taylor, C. E., JR. Counselor's level of empathic understanding as a function of counselor sex and client sex. Unpublished doctoral dissertation, University of South Carolina, 1972.
Tolar, A., & Fazzone, R. A. Early memories as indicators of ego functioning. Psychological Reports, 1966, 19, 979–983.
Waldfogel, S. The frequency and affective character of childhood memories. Psychological Monographs, 1948, 62(4, Whole No. 291).
Wolman, R. N. Early recollections and the perception of others: A study of delinquent adolescents. Journal of Genetic Psychology, 1970, 116, 157–163.

Conclusion

33

ADLER'S APPROACH: PRESENT CONTRIBUTIONS AND FUTURE IMPLICATIONS

Malachy Bishop

The purpose of this brief concluding chapter is to discuss the present status and the future implications of Adlerian theory and related research activity. Rather than a comprehensive overview of Adler's theory, which the content of this text has already achieved, or of the range of research currently associated with the Adlerian approach, this chapter will reflect on the current status of Adler's approach and suggest the need for and benefits of continued attention to and evaluation of Adler's theory.

PRESENT CONTRIBUTIONS OF THEORY

In the analysis of the scope of Adler's impact on psychology, counseling, and psychotherapy, a paradox has frequently been noted. On the one hand, in terms of both general principles and, to a lesser extent, specific techniques, Adler's ideas permeate modern psychology. Indeed, Adler's influence is so prevalent in modern psychological thought and practice that, as Adler and Deutsch (1959) suggested with regard to mental health practitioners, "the proper question is not whether one is an Adlerian, but how much of an Adlerian one is" (p. xv). On the other hand, although Adler's insights continue to implicitly imbue and inform the theoretical base of each subsequent generation of theoreticians and practitioners, "few may know his name, and even fewer seem to realize how close their systems are to his" (Mosak & Maniacci, 1999, p. 170). The curious absence of recognition of Adler's important, if not central role in guiding 20th century understanding of psychological processes, relative to such theoreticians as Freud and Rogers, suggests that Ellenberger's well-known observation concerning the difficulty in finding "another author from which so much has been borrowed from all sides without acknowledgment" (1970, p. 645) continues to ring true.

Every year thousands of students are introduced to Alfred Adler's approach to counseling and psychology, with most making this acquaintance through an introductory textbook in a course in undergraduate counseling, psychology, or related mental health courses. Frequently Adler's approach is presented immediately on the heels of Freud's psychoanalysis and its more recent extensions. I imagine that, as was the case for me, many are impressed with Adler's optimistic and encouraging view of humanity, particularly when presented in immediate contrast with Freud's determinism and rather more pessimistic perspective. In the typical process, Adler's theory is then followed by an increasing number of recently established behavioral and humanistic theories.

Frequently, therefore, perhaps as a function of its place in history, Adler's theory is conceived of as an interesting contrast to Freud's, and a forerunner of the humanistic perspective, or third wave of psychology, which has in the last half-century gained increasing popular and professional acceptance and utility. Few may understand, however, Adler's direct and personal influence on, as Ansbacher (1990, p. 45) described them, "the three co-founders of humanistic psychology," Abraham Maslow, Rollo May, and Carl Rogers; or the less direct, but perhaps no less profound influence of Adler on later theorists. For example, both Frankl and Ellis have explicitly noted the influence of Adler's ideas upon the development of their own theories.

This discussion is not meant to suggest, of course, that Adler's ideas live on only, or even primarily, within the context of subsequent personality theories. Rather, they live and thrive, as did Adler himself, in the active discourse and vibrant exchanges of Adlerian psychologists and other practitioners. Mosak (2005) reports that Adlerian training institutes currently offer certificates in several U.S. and Canadian cities;

individual courses and programs of study are offered at numerous universities. The *Journal of Individual Psychology* regularly offers the latest in Adlerian research and discourse, and the Adlerian professional society, the North American Society of Adlerian Psychology, continues its over-50-year existence.

However, compared with what may be described as the general impact of Adler's humanistic views, some of the specific components of Adlerian psychology, those unique to Adler and specific to his comprehensive view of personality and psychotherapy, such as the concept of the lifestyle, social interest, birth order, and early recollections, have been less generally accepted or integrated.

Many students engaged in the process of their introduction to psychological or counseling theory collect and assimilate into what will eventually become an "eclectic" personal theory, a number of uniquely Adlerian techniques. Other students may see practical value in incorporating in their work selected components of the broader theory, such as the concept of the lifestyle, and disregard others, such as social interest, as esoteric and impractical.

The currently prevalent and generally utilized approach to psychological education, albeit perhaps somewhat hasty and piecemeal, is undoubtedly the natural result of the combination of current educational organizational structure and an ever-growing set of professional requirements. However, this approach frequently restricts students' abilities to spend sufficient time to develop a comprehensive understanding of any one theory (possibly contributing to the current trend toward eclecticism).

Although, from this perspective, proponents of any single theory are likely to say that their own approaches, in particular, merit more time, I will take this opportunity to argue only for Adler's, and say that the richness and depth of this comprehensive set of ideas about individuals, humanity, and psychotherapy cannot possibly be explored in the course of a chapter or a lecture or two. Mosak and Maniacci (1999) have suggested that clinical psychology continues to move closer to the position adopted by individual psychologists, and that, for this reason among others, a good understanding of Adler's approach is helpful. Further, because Adler's ideas have informed the development of many subsequent theories, an understanding of Adlerian psychology provides a useful framework for understanding other theories.

Adler's approach is, by design, both comprehensive and comprehensible. It is a psychology of use, with, particularly for those who are willing to explore it in depth, tremendous capacity for both increased understanding of people and their problems, and practical utility. In the course of the present text and the career-long efforts of the first author, Adler's ideas have been effectively explicated and their practical utility in the increasing range of practice settings and situations explored. An important next step, for those being introduced to Adler's approach, is to explore directly the writings of Adler himself. There can be no question that Freud was a gifted and prolific writer, and an important contributor to 20th century thinking. However, the professional requirements of the title aside, and based solely on his deterministic view of human nature and the esoteric and complex nature of his writing, one may read the collected works of Freud and still not be a psychoanalyst. Conversely, Adler's ideas about human nature, which are more closely aligned with currently accepted views, and his compelling and approachable style of writing lead me to believe that one who reads Adler cannot help but become an Adlerian.

CURRENT RESEARCH WITH ADLER'S THEORY

As suggested above, despite the general acceptance and integration into psychological theory and clinical practice of Adler's broad views of humanity, in the course of the last century many specific and integral components of Adlerian psychology have to some extent been neglected, excluded, or at least received less explicit consideration in the development of psychological and personality theory. Examples of those contributions that may be considered uniquely Adlerian have been the focus of many of the chapters in the present text, and include the concept of the lifestyle, social interest, birth order, and early recollections. Although attention to these specific constructs has, to some extent, seemingly been restricted to or existed primarily within Adlerian circles and literature, an examination of the general psychology literature over the last two decades suggests that exploration of the tenets of individual psychology is perhaps more active than ever. For example, a cursory search (looking specifically at terms within article titles) within the major psychological literature databases suggests that well over 1000 articles focusing on early recollections, social interest, and, most prevalent, birth order, have been published since 1985. Certainly a more extensive review would unearth many more.

In the present text the projective clinical technique of asking an individual to relate his or her earliest recollections was frequently discussed. This important key to understanding the individual's view of his or her life and role in the world was described by Rudolf Dreikurs (1973) as "probably Adler's greatest single contribution to psychology"

(p. 25). As a uniquely Adlerian clinical technique, however, it is certainly, and unfortunately, among the least frequently incorporated in practice by general (non-Adlerian) mental health practitioners. However, as Clark (2004, p. 105) recently suggested, "since Adler introduced early recollections as a projective technique, the procedure has been a focus of a vast number of investigations" and recently was the focus of a special issue of the *Journal of Individual Psychology* (vol. 60, no. 2, 2004).

Perhaps in the future, Adlerians will refine therapeutic strategies for evaluating and reorienting the extremely powerful conclusions made during adolescence. This potent developmental period has been somewhat de-emphasized by Adlerians, with their theoretical focus on the early formative years of the lifestyle. However, more facilitative techniques and teaching tools need to be formulated along the lines of one developed by Walton (1998), an international consultant and pioneer in Adlerian approaches to adolescence. His therapeutic strategy, portrayed in a practical teaching video (Walton, 1996), employs autobiographical memory, particularly of the early adolescent years, as related to belief system and parenting style.

Research associated with birth order, which among Adler's theoretical tenets has probably received the most popular acceptance in the general population, has examined the relationships between birth order and intellectual abilities, academic achievement (e.g., Bohmer & Sitton, 1993; Cherian, 1990; Marjoribanks, 1997; Sputa & Paulson, 1995; Zajonc & Mullally, 1997), occupational choice and status (e.g., Bohmer & Sitton, 1993; Kessler, 1991; Marjoribanks, 1997; Somit, Arwine, & Peterson, 1994), and economic resources and family intellectual environment (Travis & Kohli, 1995).

Over time, birth order research has produced inconsistent conclusions, resulting in an active and ongoing debate in the professional literature. Based on a comprehensive review of more than 1000 studies between 1946 and 1980, in which Ernst and Angst (1983) investigated the presence of a relationship between birth order and a variety of outcomes, these authors concluded that the lack of a theoretical basis in birth order research was problematic, and suggested a moratorium on birth order research until this had been rectified. Other researchers (e.g., Guastello & Guastello, 2002) have formed similar conclusions. However, in numerous other examinations support for the birth order construct has been established. Recently, Sulloway (2002), based on his examination of 50 years of research articles on the relationships between birth order and personality characteristics, offered the following conclusions:

> Overall, the birth-order literature from 1940 to the end of 1999 shows significant trends for all five dimensions of the Five Factor Model of personality, although the trend for Neuroticism is somewhat weaker than for the other four personality dimensions. Compared with later-borns, first-borns tend to be more conscientious, extraverted (in the sense of being assertive), and neurotic, whereas later-borns, compared with first-borns, tend to be more agreeable, open to experience, and extraverted (in the sense of being sociable and fun-loving). Discrepancies in tallies reached by different investigators and caused by different methods of analysis, or because of a failure to examine the original literature, should not be confused with the more important issue of whether statistically significant trends emerge when tallies of independent outcomes are subjected to hypothesis testing using formal statistical methods. When one conducts five separate meta-analyses on the available birth-order data—one for each dimension of the Five Factor Model of personality—significant and robust trends emerge by any generally accepted method of analysis.

In the history of research with Adler's theory, there have been times when the style he used in presenting his theory has clashed with, or at least failed to accommodate, currently accepted methods and processes of scientific inquiry. That is, Adler "intentionally set out to make his system accessible," and "based his system upon philosophy, not science" (Mosak & Maniacci, 1999, p. 163). In accordance with his goal of making his ideas comprehensible and useable by all, he frequently discussed his concepts in molar, or even simplistic terms (Ford & Urban, 1963). A consequence of this approach is that researchers have at times struggled to operationalize such broad philosophical concepts as social interest.

Throughout the course of the past century, Adler's ideas about human nature have consistently been developed and extended and specified for application in new contexts. The process of attempting to operationalize and define his sometimes broad theoretical constructs has frequently resulted in contrasting opinions and ideas about, in effect, what he really meant. As a result, research on Adler's approach has been neither universally supportive nor consistent. Significant questions and important challenges have frequently been raised, and continued research is certainly necessary. However, for the most part Adler's overall theory and its separate components have stood the test of time. Indeed, in the current sociopolitical climate, some, like social interest, may be said to have become more relevant and more important than ever.

Finally, it is worth revisiting the idea suggested by Rule in the present text, and by other Adlerians elsewhere, that dividing Adler's comprehensive theory into parts in order to study the whole can somehow ruin the essence of what is being studied. However, in both the context of the present mental health environment of managed care, consumerism, and accountability, and the broader context of increasing scientific scrutiny, such an argument faces increased barriers. It is likely, therefore, that critical evaluation shall continue, and further, it is unlikely that Adler would have minded.

Adler's life was, in many ways, a study in courage. He repeatedly showed the willingness to openly examine his own beliefs and those of others, and the courage to, as a result of such examination, modify or adapt both his personal beliefs and his public theory. It seems likely therefore that he would enthusiastically welcome active exploration of his theory and its ongoing development.

REFERENCES

Adler, K. A., & Deutsch, D. (Eds.) (1959). Essays in Individual Psychology. New York: Grove Press.

Ansbacher, H. L. (1990). Alfred Adler's influence on the three leading cofounders of humanistic psychology. Journal of Humanistic Psychology, 30(4), 45–54.

Bohmer, P., & Sitton, S. (1993). The influence or birth order and family size on notable American women's selection of careers. Psychological Record, 43, 375–380.

Cherian, V. I. (1990). Birth order and academic achievement of children in Transkei. Psychological Reports, 66, 19–24.

Clark, A. J. (2004). Early recollections. Journal of Individual Psychology, 60(2), 105–106.

Dreikurs, R. (1973). The private logic. In H.H. Mosak (Ed.), Alfred Adler: His Influence on Psychology Today (pp. 19–32). Park Ridge, NJ: Noyes Press.

Ernst, C., & Angst, J. (1983). Birth Order. Berlin: Springer-Verlag.

Ford, D. H., & Urban, H. B. (1963). Systems of Psychotherapy. New York: Wiley.

Guastello, S. J., & Guastello, D. D. (2002). Birth category effects on the Gordon Personal Profile Variables. Journal of Articles in Support of the Null Hypothesis. 1(1), 1–7.

Kessler, Daniel. (1991). Birth order, family size, and achievement: Family structure and wage determination, Journal of Labor Economics, 9(4), 413–426.

Marjoribanks, K. (1997). Ordinal position, family environment, and status attainment among Australian young adults. The Journal of Social Psychology, 137, 398–399.

Marjoribanks, K. (1991). The sibling resource dilution theory: An analysis. The Journal of Psychology, 125, 337–346.

Mosak, H. H. (2005). Adlerian Psychotherapy. In R.J. Corsini and D. Wedding (Eds.), Current Psychotherapies (pp. 52–95). Itasca, IL: F.E. Peacock Publishers.
Mosak, H., & Maniacci, M. (1999). A Primer of Adlerian Psychology: The Analytic Behavioural—Cognitive Psychology of Alfred Adler. Philadelphia, PA: Brunner/Mazel.
Somit, A., Arwine, A., & Peterson, S. A. (1994). Birth and British prime ministers: A second look. Political Studies, 42, 120–127.
Sputa, C. L., & Paulson, S. E. (1995). Birth order and family size: Influences on adolescents` achievement and related parenting behaviors. Psychological Reports, 76, 43–51.
Sulloway, F. J. (2002). Technical report on a vote-counting meta-analysis of the birth-order literature (1940–1999). Retrieved January, 5, 2004 from http://www.sulloway.org/metaanalysis.html.
Travis, R., & Kohli, V. (1995). The birth order factor: Ordinal position, social strata, and educational achievement. The Journal of Social Psychology, 135, 499–507.
Walton, F. X. (Producer & Director). (1996). The use of most memorable observations in counseling and parent consultation [Video]. (Available from Adlerian Child Care Books, P.O. Box 210206, Columbia, SC 29211.)
Walton, F. X. (1998). Use of the most memorable observation as a technique for understanding choice of parenting style. Journal of Individual Psychology, 54(4), 489–494.
Zajonc, R. B., & Mullally, P. R. (1997). Birth order: Reconciling conflicting effects. American Psychologist, 2(7), 685–699.

INDEX

A

Achievement orientation, 11, 194, 256, 260–261, 278–279, 293–294; *see also* Self-actualization (S/A)
Ackerman, J. M., 191, 199
Adjustment to disability
  Adlerian approach, 11–12, 127, 128–130
  contemporary approaches to, 131–133
  and early recollections, 121–122, 123–124, 125
  and family constellation, 121, 124–125
  and frame of reference, 11–12, 119–120
  and leisure satisfaction, 165, 171
  in lifestyle interpretation phase, 20–22
  in lifestyle investigation phase, 19–20
  overview, 10–12
  in relationship phase, 15–19
  in reorientation phase, 22–29
Adler, Alfred
  background, 5–8
  early concepts, 8–9, 128–129
  influence on modern psychology, 341–347
  on memory, 307
  and nature of man, 122
  on self-actualization, 211
Adolescent counseling, 97–103, 107–108
Adventure Future Scale *(Leisure Activities Blank)*, 297, 299–302
Alternating rhythm principle, 171
Altman, K., 301
Angels/devils metaphor, 45–52
Animism, 5–6
Ansbacher, H. L., 118
Ansbacher, R. R., 118
Appell, M. L., 84
Artistic approach to helping, 12–13
Assertiveness training in offender rehab, 157
Attending process, 16–17
Avocational counseling
  action phase, 172–175, 186
  analysis and self exploration, 169–172, 184–186
  assessment tools, 166–169
  in correctional rehab, 158
  and early recollections, 181–184
  exploratory phase, 165–166
  overview, 163–164, 179–180
Avocational Title Card Sort (Overs and Page), 168
Awareness; *see also* Self-awareness
  disability and lifestyle, 127
  of frame of reference, 16–19, 34, 84, 139, 147

B

Bach, C. R., 230, 233
Bandler, R., 24
Bartelt, P. W., 274

Bayer, A., 256
Beecher, M., 49
Beecher, W., 49
Behavioral counseling, 28–29, 76, 157
Behavior modification strategies, 155–158, 173–174, 186
Belonging, desire for, 33, 56, 97, 118, 121, 138–139
Berenson, B. G., 316
Binder, J. L., 238
Birth order, influence of
  and career choice, 249–253, 255–262
  from child's viewpoint, 98
  and early recollections, 293–294
  overview, 345–346
  and parenting, 98, 142, 151–152, 273–276, 277–281
  and personality, 345–346
Body image theory, 127–128
Bolles, R. N., 164, 171
Bolton, B., 10–11, 128, 131, 133
Britton, S., 132–133
Bruhn, A. R., 268

C

Campbell, D. P., 167
Campbell, Joseph, 217, 219
Cannon, J. C., 309
Career choice, 249–253, 255–262
Carkhuff, Robert R., 16, 17, 60, 76, 147, 309, 316
Carkhuff Discrimination Index of Gross Ratings of Facilitative Interpersonal Functioning, 309, 311
Carkhuff Scales of Empathic Understanding and Facilitative Genuineness (Carkhuff), 309
Carson, R. C., 86
Cartoons as therapeutic tools, 192
Cause-and-effect approach, limitations of, 118
Cautela, J. R., 168
Chance, J., 193
Chandler, C. K., 268
Change, strategies for, in offender rehab, 155–158
Change-producing processes, 46–47
Characteristic attitudinal position, 119
Childhood memories, *see* Early recollections
Children, counseling of, 100–103, 105–111
Children: The Challenge (Dreikurs and Soltz), 102
Clairborne R., 221
Clark, A. J., 345
Client-counselor compatibility, 86
Client resistance, 45–52
Cobb, S., 250–251, 256
Cognitive map, 21, 47–48, 151; *see also* Goals
Cohen, R., 287
Cohn, N. K., 132
Comer, A. T., 274
Communication skills and birth order, 249–253
Compton, D., 164–165, 173
Concept of self in S/A, 210–212, 219–220
Constructive Leisure Activity Survey, 168
Consumerism and lifestyle, 4
"Context" psychology, 118
Correctional rehabilitation
  group counseling, 144–158
  and nature of man, 138–144
  and negativism, 55–62
  overview, 137–138
  strategies for change, 155–158
Corsello, P., 274, 278
Counseling processes; *see also* Avocational counseling
  for adolescents, 97–103
  behavioral, 28–29, 76, 157
  for children, 100–103, 105–111
  Gestalt counseling, 29, 157
  group counseling, 30–32, 100, 102, 144–158, 191–196
  lifestyle interpretation phase, 20–22, 97, 151–153
  lifestyle investigation phase, 19–20, 97, 122–127, 141–143, 149–151
  relationship phase, 15–19, 97, 147–149
  reorientation phase, 22–29, 97, 153–158
  school psychology/counseling, 95–103, 105–111
Counselor-client compatibility, 86
Crime and lifestyle, 143–144; *see also* Correctional rehabilitation
Cull, John G., 148, 157

D

Dangers, perceived, 35–36, 119–120, 311–312
Defensive patterns, 35–36, 119–120
DeMarco, Barbara, 184
Determinism, soft vs. hard, 117–118
Deutsch, D., 341
Devils/angels metaphor, 45–52

Dinkmeyer, D., 25–26, 148
Disability; *see also* Adjustment to disability
 body image theory, 127–128
 and lifestyle awareness, 127
 and nature of man, 116–117, 122
 negative attitudes toward, 128
 and personality, 130–131
 and resistance to help, 34–35
 self-esteem and, 33–34
 semantics issues, 9–10
 social context for, 118
 social role theory, 127–128
Disciplinary approaches, 107
Distress vs. stress, 90
Dreikurs, R.
 on Alder's early concepts, 128–130
 counseling of children, 102
 on early recollection, 344–345
 on heredity, 117
 lifestyle questionnaire, 56, 98–99, 123, 142–143, 201
 on resistance to help, 34
 on selective memory, 141
 on tasks of life/social living, 19
Dunham, C. S., 9–10
Dunham, J. R., 9–10
Dyer, Wayne W., 31, 148–149, 191

E

Early recollections
 and adjustment to disability, 121–122, 123–124, 125
 and attitudes toward intervention, 237–246
 and birth order, 293–294
 in children/adolescents, 96–97, 108–109
 and choice of leisure activities, 297–303
 collection technique study, 229–234
 and correctional rehab, 140, 142
 and counselor sensitivity, 307–313
 and group behavior, 307–313, 315–320
 and intelligence, 287–290
 interpreting, overview, 65–68
 and leisure counseling, 181–184
 overview, 98, 344–345
 and recalled parental permissiveness, 267–272
 and selectivity of memory, 20, 56–58
 as social stress predictor, 323–328
Early Recollections Questionnaire (Rule), 300–301, 333
Early Recollections Rating Scale of Social Interest Characteristics, 332–333
Eddy, J., 164–165
Edington, C. R., 173
Edwards, P. B., 168, 170
Edwards Personal Preference Schedule, 289–290, 294
Ego Recognition Future Scale, 297–301, 299
Eisenberg, M., 33, 132, 165
Ellenberger, H., 8, 340
Ellis, Albert, 8, 28, 79, 158, 191, 199
Elusive goals, 37, 75–81
Emotions
 as barriers, 36–37
 as energizers of goals, 120
 and impulsive behavior, 157
 and insight vs. outsight in group setting, 32, 34, 153
 in RET, 28
 in self-actualization, 213, 220–221
Empathy vs. sympathy, 17
Encouragement in counseling process, 25–26
English, R. W., 127
Evil vs. good metaphors, 45–52
Exaggeration as therapeutic tool, 192–196
Experiential learned behavior, 114–118, 141, 143–144
Extrinsic motivation, 170

F

Facilitative-response framework and negativism, 55–62
Falek, A., 132–133
Family constellation
 and adjustment to disability, 121, 124–125
 and adolescent counseling, 98–99, 107–108
 and career choice, 255–262
 and correctional rehab, 142
 and recalled parental permissiveness, 277–281
 and selective memory, 56–58
Family counseling for children, 100–103
Fay, A., 89, 168
Feffer's Role-taking Task, 293
Feldhusen, J., 288
Ferenczi, S., 230
Ford, D. H., 7, 46
Forer, L., 256, 278
Forgus, R., 47

Frame of reference
in adjustment to disability, 11–12, 119–120
in early recollection studies, 238–239, 269–270
increasing of subject's awareness, 16–19
of individuals in group counseling, 145
in practitioner awareness, 34, 84, 139, 147
French, J., 250–251, 256
Freud, Sigmund, 65, 233, 344

G

GATB (General Aptitude Test Battery), 289
Gazda, G. M., 316
Geller, M. H., 86
Gender issues, 237–246, 273–276
General systems theory, 6–7
Gerler, W., 86
Gestalt counseling, 29, 157
Goals
ambiguity of, 50–51
in children, 100–101, 121–122
elusive, 37, 75–81
goal-change framework, 22–28, 119–120, 123–158
goal-directed movement, 50–51, 215–218
goal-directedness and behavior, 139–140
interpretation of, 20–22
mutual exclusion of, 49–50
of reorientation phase of counseling, 22–23
in self-actualization, 212–214, 220
self-awareness of, 23–24, 96–97
and self-exploration, 16
of therapist vs. subject, 46
Goetze, H., 288
Goldenson, R. M., 9
Good vs. evil metaphors, 45–52
Goudsmit, S., 221
Grinder, J., 24
Grotz, G., 217
Group behavior studies, 307–313, 315–320
Group counseling
humor as a therapeutic tool in, 191–196
lifestyle approach to, 30–32
in offender rehabilitation, 144–158
in school counseling, 100, 102
Gunther, M., 132

H

Hancock, F., 297
Handicap, *see* Disability
Hansen, J. C., 167
Hanson, C. J., 173
Happiness
externalizing responsibility for, 58, 152
and humor as counseling tool, 25
preoccupation with, 79
as related to S/A, 218
and self-actualization, 218
Hard vs. soft determinism, 117, 127–128
Hardy, Richard E., 148, 157
Hare, A. Paul, 145
Haywood, H., 288
Heal, L., 288
Hedvig, E. B., 230
Heine, R. W., 86
Heredity and behavior, 117
Holism, 6
Holland, J. L., 168
Homework as therapy tool, 23, 29, 59, 78, 89, 145
Horizontal vs. vertical movement, 216–218
"A House Divided" (Lincoln), 77, 90–91
Howe, L. W., 168
Hubert, E., 167
Humanistic psychology movement, 7
Human nature, 95–97, 116–117, 122, 138–144
Humor in Adlerian therapy, 25, 158, 191–196, 199–203
Hyperactivity in children, 106–111

I

I Can if I Want To (Lazarus and Fay), 89
Ideal social self, 69–73, 96–97, 120–122
Idiographic laws, 20, 125, 126, 143, 180
Impulsive behavior, 156–157
Individual psychology approach, overview, 8
Inferiority differentiation, 129–130
Information sharing process, 18–19
Insight vs. outsight in group setting, 32, 34, 153
Intellectualism vs. emotionalism as resistance maneuver, 36
Interpersonal Communication Inventory, 249
Interpretation phase of counseling, 20–22, 97, 151–153
Interview techniques
in investigation phase, 19–20, 97, 122–127, 141–143, 149–151

in leisure counseling, 168–169
lifestyle questionnaire, 56, 98–99, 123, 142–143, 201
Intrinsic motivation, 170
Investigation phase of counseling, 19–20, 97, 122–127, 141–143, 149–151

J

Jackson, D. A., 199
Jastrow, R., 223–224

K

Kadis, A. L., 192, 199
Karoly, P., 174
Kastenbaum, R., 168
Kirschenbaum, H., 168
Kir-Stimon, W., 33–34
Kivel, C., 48
Klausmeier, H., 288
Kohn, M., 256
Kopp, R. R., 48
Krasner, L., 215
Kubler-Ross, E., 131
Kuder, G. F., 168
Kuder Preference Record–Vocational (Kruder), 168
Kundu, R., 287–288

L

"Law of movement," 56
Lazarus, A., 89, 168
Leisure; *see also* Avocational counseling
and adjustment to disability, 165, 171
barriers to enjoyment, 173–174
as behavior/self-management tool, 173–174, 186
and early recollections, 297–303
as stress management tool, 174–175
Leisure Activities Blank (LAB), 167, 297–298, 299
Leisure Interest Inventory, 167
Leval, P. N., 219–220
Levinger, G., 297
Lewinsohn, P. M., 168
Lifestyle
and behavior causation, 114–118
and crime, 143–144
deficits in, 34, 60–62
definitions, 4–5, 55–56, 96–97, 116, 139
exaggeration of as therapy, 192–196
questionnaire, 56, 98–99, 123, 142–143, 201
themes, 71–72, 99, 126, 140
Lifestyle assessment/approach, *see* Counseling processes
Lifestyle convictions framework, 22
Lincoln, Abraham, 77, 90–91
Lister, J., 84
Lombardi, D. N., 123

M

Magaliff, M., 287
Maniacci, M., 343
Maslow, Abraham, 342
Masquerade as self-awareness tool, 32, 192–196
Masters, J. C., 174
May, Rollo, 342
McDowell, Chester F., 158, 165–166, 168
McKechnie, G., 167
Mechanistic approach to counseling, 5–6
Medeiros, D. C., 212
Medical model of adjustment, 10
Memories, *see* Early recollections
Mendelsohn, G. A., 86
Merleau-Ponty, M., 12, 223
Metaphor, use of, 45–52
Michener, James A., 217–218
Misbehavior and goals in children, 100–103
Modeling methods, 28–29, 31, 148–149, 202
Mosak, B., 99
Mosak, H. H.
on acceptance of patient, 34
on early recollections, 311
and incompatible goals, 81
on lifestyle conclusions and behavior, 119–120
lifestyle interpretation frameworks, 21–22
lifestyle themes/typology, 71–72, 99, 126, 140
on self-esteem of disabled, 33
on self-responsibility for emotions, 36
on static assessment, 213
on temper, 60
Movement, goal-directed, 50–51, 215–218
Munoz, R. F., 168

N

Nature of man, 95–97, 116–117, 122, 138–144
Negativism, 34–36, 55–62
Neulinger, J., 170
Neuro-linguistic programming, 29
Nonmothetic laws, 20, 125, 126, 143, 180
Nonverbal vs. verbal behavior, 17
North American Society of Adlerian Psychology, 343

O

Objective vs. subjective helping perspective, 12–13
O'Connell, Walter E.
 on Adler, 8
 on goals vs. emotions, 32, 153
 on humor, 158, 191–192, 199–200
 on reframing, 81
O'Conor, Elizabeth, 184
Offender rehabilitation, *see* Correctional rehabilitation
Organ inferiority, 8, 129
Otis-Lennon IQ, 289
Outsight vs. insight in group setting, 32, 34, 153
Overs, Robert P., 168, 184

P

Page, C. M., 168
Parenting; *see also* Family constellation
 birth order issues, 98, 142, 151–152
 participation in school counseling, 101–103, 105–111
 recalled permissiveness studies, 267–272, 273–276, 277–281, 283–284
Parham, J., 287
Passons, W., 84–85
Peer involvement in counseling approaches, 110–111
Perceived danger, 35–36, 119–120, 311–312
Perceived freedom and leisure, 170
Perfection as goal, 79, 173
Perkins, C. A., 293
Perls, F., 29
Permissiveness, parental, 267–272, 273–276, 277–281, 283–284
Personal disability model, 10–11
Personality; *see also* Self-actualization (S/A)
 and birth order, 345–346
 and career choices, 250, 252–253
 and counseling group selection, 146
 and counselor-client compatibility, 86
 and disability, 127, 130–131
 and early recollections, 181, 289, 331–337
 flaws of testing methods, 219
 and practitioner self-awareness, 84, 115–116
 and uncoordinated goals, 80
Personalizing process, 17–18
Personal Orientation Inventory (Shostrom), 214
Phares, J., 193
A Pleasant Events Schedule, 168
Positive contingency control, 174
Positive striving model of adjustment, 10
Powers, R., 100–101
Process vs. achievement in adjustment, 11
Progress as goal, 79
Psychological "territory," 121
Purcell, K., 230

Q

Quay, H., 230
Questionnaires
 Early Recollections Questionnaire, 300–301, 333
 lifestyle, 56, 98–99, 123, 142–143, 201

R

Rational emotive therapy (RET), 8, 28, 157
Reality therapy, 29
Recognition reflex, 21
Reframing process, 24, 45–52, 70
Rehabilitation, correctional, *see* Correctional rehabilitation
Reinforcement Survey Schedule (Cautela and Kastenbaum), 168
Relationships; *see also* Family constellation; Parenting
 in group counseling, 30–32, 147–149
 as phase of lifestyle counseling, 15–19, 29, 97, 147–149
Reorientation process, 22–29, 32, 97, 153–158
Resistance to help, 34–36, 45–52, 157
Responding process, 17, 60

RET (rational emotive therapy), 8, 28, 157
Richardson, F., 37, 79, 89
Rilke, Rainer Maria, 46
Rimm, D. C., 174
Roessler, R., 10–11, 128, 131, 133
Rogers, Carl, 342
Rokeach, M., 231
Rokeach Dogmatism Scale (Rokeach), 231
Role playing, 157
Rosenberg, B., 261, 278
Rotter, J., 193
Rotter's Internal-External Control Scale (Rotter, Chance and Phares), 193
Rule, Warren R., 26–28, 158, 274
Rychlak, J. F., 25, 129

S

Sampson, E., 294
Sandberg, T., 287
Schafer, W., 89, 90
Schleien, S., 167
Schooler, C., 256
School psychology/counseling, 95–103, 105–111
Secure-insecure characteristics and group dynamics, 315–320
Selective memory, 20, 56–58, 97, 123, 141; *see also* Early recollections
Self-actualization (S/A); *see also* Achievement orientation
  and concept of self, 210–212, 219–220
  as goal, 79
  limitations in modern methods, 218–224
  overview, 209–210
  as process vs. outcome, 212–215
  successful goodness concept, 215–218
  time frame in, 210, 213–214, 221
Self-awareness; *see also* Early recollections; Investigation phase of counseling
  and goals, 23–24, 77–81, 96–97, 124
  in group counseling, 32, 149–151, 192–196
  and humor-based therapy, 192–193, 202
  of practitioner, 83–91, 115–116, 146–147
Self-Directed Search, 168
Self-encouragement, 88
Self-esteem, safeguards to, 48, 81, 87, 140
Self-exploration, 16–19, 69–73
Selye, H., 89, 90, 175
Semantics issues
  barriers to practitioner/client understanding, 21
  connotations of self-actualization, 215
  disability vs. handicap, 9–10
Shaller, J., 273–274, 278
Shared interpretation approach, 70–73
Shaver, P. R., 251, 256
Shelton, J. L., 191, 199
Shoben, E. J., Jr., 84, 85, 91
Shontz, F. C.
  on disability, 10–11
  disability and personality, 130–131
  on generalizing illness, 133
  historical review of health practices, 5–6
  holistic healthcare principles, 18
  on self-image theories, 128
Shostrum, E. L., 214
Shulman, B. H., 35, 36, 47, 116, 117, 192
Sibling order, *see* Birth order
Siller, J. R., 133
Simon, S. B., 168
Smith, T. E., 274, 278
Social life; *see also* Group counseling
  Adlerian context, 22, 118, 138–139
  early recollections as social stress predictor, 323–328
  ideal social self, 69–73, 96–97, 120–122
  social role theory, 127–128
  tasks of life/social living, 19, 51, 140–141, 150
Soft vs. hard determinism, 117, 127–128
Soltz, V., 102
Stability-maintaining processes, 46–48
Stewart, Morris W., 158
Stout, A. M., 274, 278
Stress
  comfort zone for, 175
  vs. distress, 90
  early recollection relevance study, 323–328
  and lifestyle expression, 19, 67–68, 87
  management of, 29, 89–91, 174–175
  and resistance, 35–36
  and uncoordinated goals, 80
Strictness, parental, 267–272, 273–276, 277–281, 283–284
Strong-Campbell Interest Inventory (Campbell and Hansen), 167–168
Stubbins, J., 12
Subjective exploration, 16–19
Subjective mental framework, 5, 119, 139

Subjective vs. objective helping perspective, 12–13
Successful goodness concept of S/A, 215–218
Sullivan, H. S., 32
Sulloway, F. J., 345–346
Survival model of adjustment, 10
Sutton-Smith, B., 261, 278
Sweeney, Thomas J., 30, 147–148
Sympathy vs. empathy, 17
Symptoms as psychological safeguards, 36–37, 48–49
Systems concepts, individual, 7

T

Tasks of life/social living, 19, 51, 140–141, 150
Tate, G. A., 214
Teachers, role in counseling, 105–106, 109–111
Temper and negativity, 60–62
"Territory," psychological, 121
Tharp, R., 77
Therapeutic context, 229–234
Thomas, Lewis, 12
Thompson, D. D., 132
Time frame in self-actualization, 210, 213–214, 221
Training opportunities in Adlerian approach, 342–343
Transactional analysis, 29, 157
Trieschmann, R., 37, 165

U

Ullmann, L. P., 215
Uncoordinated goals, 37, 80–81
Unfocused goals, 37, 77–78
Unrealistic goals, 37, 78–80
Urban, H. B., 7, 46

V

Verbal vs. nonverbal behavior, 17
Vertical vs. horizontal movement, 216–218
Very, P., 256
Von Bertalanffy, L., 6–7, 175
Vriend, John, 31, 148–149

W

Walton, F. X., 100–101, 345
Watson, D., 77
Wehman, P., 167
Welch, I. D., 214
Willingham, W. R, 268
Wilson, W., 180
Winick, C., 192, 199
Wolkon, G., 297
Woolfolk, R., 37, 79, 89
Wright, B. A., 131
Wright, G. N., 9

Y

Youngren, M. A., 168

Z

Zannini, J., 256
Zeiss, A. M., 168

For Product Safety Concerns and Information please contact our EU representative GPSR@taylorandfrancis.com
Taylor & Francis Verlag GmbH, Kaufingerstraße 24, 80331 München, Germany

www.ingramcontent.com/pod-product-compliance
Ingram Content Group UK Ltd.
Pitfield, Milton Keynes, MK11 3LW, UK
UKHW022115190926
475702UK00013B/1449

* 9 7 8 0 4 1 5 8 6 1 2 2 9 *